Muhammad ʿAbduh

Muhammad ʿAbduh

Modern Islam and the Culture of Ambiguity

Oliver Scharbrodt

I.B.TAURIS
LONDON • NEW YORK • OXFORD • NEW DELHI • SYDNEY

I.B. TAURIS
Bloomsbury Publishing Plc
50 Bedford Square, London, WC1B 3DP, UK
1385 Broadway, New York, NY 10018, USA
29 Earlsfort Terrace, Dublin 2, Ireland

BLOOMSBURY, I.B. TAURIS and the I.B. Tauris logo are
trademarks of Bloomsbury Publishing Plc

First published in Great Britain 2022

Series design by Adriana Brioso
Cover image © *The Press and Poetry of Modern Persia* by
Edward G Browne, Cambridge, 1914

A catalogue record for this book is available from the British Library.

A catalog record for this book is available from the Library of Congress.

ISBN: HB: 978-1-8386-0730-2
ePDF: 978-1-8386-0733-3
eBook: 978-1-8386-0732-6

Typeset by Newgen KnowledgeWorks Pvt. Ltd., Chennai, India

To find out more about our authors and books visit www.bloomsbury.com
and sign up for our newsletters.

To Yafa

A person with knowledge is not a stranger anywhere

– Quoted by Ibn Qutayba

Contents

List of Figures viii

Preface ix

Note on Transliteration xi

1 Introduction 1

2 Early formation: 'Abduh's mystical turn 35

3 The making of a Muslim activist and intellectual 67

4 Exile: From Paris to Beirut 105

5 Return to Egypt: A new approach 143

6 'Abduh and the discourse of Islamic Reform 175

7 Conclusion: 'Abduh's contested legacy 213

Bibliography 239

Index 255

Figures

1 Sayyid Jamal al-Din al-Afghani 42
2 Muhammad 'Abduh in London, 1884 109
3 Muhammad 'Abduh in Tunis, 1903 150
4 Muhammad Rashid Rida in Egypt, 1909 195

Preface

'I am wondering what new you will have to say about Shaykh Muhammad 'Abduh.' This remark by an eminent professor of Islamic Studies at a prestigious British university made twenty years ago when I undertook my PhD implies that we know everything about this nineteenth-century Muslim reformer that there is to know. 'Muhammad 'Abduh (1849–1905) is probably the most researched figure in modern Islamic thought'[1] – yet, most studies focus on the intellectual output produced towards the end of his life and neglect his earlier works. These earlier outputs, however, illustrate his complex engagement with a diverse range of Islamic intellectual traditions and provide important nuances and different perspectives of his reformist work. This book broadens our understanding of 'Abduh's intellectual work by embedding him in Islam's culture of ambiguity.[2] By doing so, this book addresses the question why his intellectual legacy appears contradictory, inconsistent and ambiguous. Undertaking an intellectual genealogy of his ideas also steers away from a common approach in scholarship which measures the success of modern Muslim reformers by the extent to which their ideas are shaped, influenced and aligned to paradigms of Western modernity. This book moves away from such an approach and thereby engages with recent contributions in Islamic Studies which highlight the intellectual culture of ambiguity prevalent throughout Islamic history. This culture of ambiguity provides the vantage point of 'Abduh's reformist endeavours and invites us to unlearn certain preconceptions around 'orthodoxy' and 'heterodoxy' in Islam or the apparent distinction between religion and 'the secular'. Thereby, the book makes a wider contribution to how to approach the intellectual history of modern Islam and its genealogy in pre-modern Islamic thought.

The cover image of this book showing 'Abduh with some of his Iranian associates during his exile in Beirut illustrates his complex embeddedness in a variety of contexts and his very diverse interlocutors. In many book publications, 'Abduh's associates are cut out of the image and only 'Abduh in his late thirties is depicted. I find this erasure of 'Abduh's Iranian associates from the photograph quite symptomatic for ignoring the diversity of his interlocutors and for the reductionist reception of his ideas. In the photograph, 'Abduh is flanked on his right by Muhammad Baqir Bawanati, an Iranian resident in Beirut with whom he collaborated in various publications. Bawanati was the Persian teacher of renowned Cambridge Orientalist Edward G. Browne and experimented in his poetry with a synthesis between Islam and Christianity, he called 'Islamo-Christianity'. To 'Abduh's left sits Hajj Husayn Pirzadeh Na'ini, an itinerant Iranian Sufi master who was in Beirut at that time. Behind them, Bawanati's children and one of his students are depicted. This rarely used photograph illustrates the complex personal, religious and intellectual entanglements 'Abduh entertained throughout his life and this book discusses.

I would like to thank Lester Crook who many, many moons ago approached me in the first place to write this book on Muhammad 'Abduh. I have to thank in particular Sophie Rudland of I.B. Tauris for her immense patience and Yasmin Garcha for her assistance in putting the book together. The two anonymous reviewers provided very constructive suggestions which helped in refining the book's argument. Research for this book started more than twenty years ago, when I was a PhD student at SOAS, and numerous people have guided and inspired research for this book. Needless to say, all the mistakes contained in the book are my own. My wife, Yafa Shanneik, has been a critical companion of this book during its composition pushing me to explore the implications of my argument further. I dedicate this book to her.

Lund, March 2022

Notes

1 Florian Zemmin, 'Book Review: Ammeke Kateman: *Muḥammad 'Abduh and His Interlocutors: Conceptualizing Religion in a Globalizing World*', *Die Welt des Islams*, 61(1) (2021): 127.

2 Thomas Bauer, *Die Kultur der Ambiguität: Eine andere Geschichte des Islams* (Berlin: Verlag der Weltreligionen, 2011). For a recently published English translation, see Thomas Bauer, *A Culture of Ambiguity: An Alternative History of Islam* (New York: Columbia University Press, 2021).

Note on Transliteration

I follow the transliteration system of the *International Journal of Middle East Studies* (*IJMES*), because it is the most commonly used across disciplines. In line with the *IJMES* guidelines I do not transcribe names of people and places and use their official or most commonly used spelling. I have transcribed titles of books and other content originally produced in Arabic and Persian. All transcribed Arabic and Persian words are italicized except if they have become standard in English, such as Qur'an, hadith, Salafi, jihad, fatwa or shari'a.

1

Introduction

Al-G͟hazālī is the most difficult author, if not an outright impossible one, to understand in any coherent manner.[1]

Fazlur Rahman (1919–1988) expresses his frustration about how the famed Sunni scholar Abu Hamid al-Ghazali (1058–1111) approaches the issue of prophecy in Islam. On the one hand, al-Ghazali establishes the view on the role and characteristics of prophets from the perspective of, what Rahman calls, 'orthodox Islam'.[2] At the same time, his discussion 'is almost word for word borrowed from Avicenna'.[3] How is this possible? Al-Ghazali's works demarcate Sunni theology from philosophy and define most beliefs of philosophers like Ibn Sina (980–1037) as constituting disbelief (*kufr*). Why would he then use his philosophical approach to define the 'orthodox' Islamic understanding of prophecy? Rahman does not have a clear answer to this question. He suggests the need to establish a clear chronology of al-Ghazali's writings distinguishing between philosophical and post-philosophical phases. Another option for him is to query al-Ghazali's authorship; perhaps some philosophical works attributed to him were not really authored by him. However, Rahman doubts that either of these two approaches will be helpful. The third and most plausible possibility for Rahman is that he addressed different audiences: his philosophical works were meant for an inner 'esoteric' circle of scholars, versed like him in theology, philosophy and Sufism. His 'public' works denounce philosophy in categorical terms and were meant to discourage its study, as most Muslims would not be able to stomach it. Philosophy would confuse them and shatter their beliefs. However, then the question arises which of these works represent al-Ghazali's actual beliefs – surely his esoteric ones as his other works were just meant for popular consumption?[4]

Similar issues and debates have emerged in the reception of the prominent modern Muslim scholar and activist Muhammad 'Abduh (1849–1905). This book is about him and provides a new intellectual biography of the Egyptian reformer. ʿAbduh's complex and varied intellectual legacy has confused both his followers and academics, along the lines of Rahman when he tries to find consistency in al-Ghazali's thought. Albert Hourani in his seminal book on the *nahḍa*, the revival of Arab thought, literature and culture in the nineteenth century, points at ʿAbduh's 'eclecticism' which includes 'a tendency to evade difficult questions'[5] and 'to blur intellectual distinctions'.[6] ʿAbduh tries to combine different and often contradictory intellectual traditions and does not take clear sides which results, for Hourani, in inconsistencies, contradictions and ambiguities.[7] To resolve the apparently contradictory nature of ʿAbduh's intellectual legacy, Muslim scholars and academic researchers have resorted to similar strategies that have been used to reconcile inconsistencies and ambiguities in al-Ghazali's thought:[8] they can be explained by radical shifts and turns in ʿAbduh's biography or by questioning the attribution of certain works to him.

How to approach the complex intellectual legacy of a modern Muslim thinker like ʿAbduh who has been characterized as a beacon of Sunni orthodoxy and 'a free thinker' and 'a sceptic'[9] at the same time? The book explains the apparent contradictions, inconsistencies and ambiguities in his thought by situating him in the capaciousness of Islamic intellectual history. In order to achieve this, the restrictive reception of ʿAbduh's life and thought in academic scholarship needs to be challenged in the first place. His Syrian disciple Muhammad Rashid Rida (1865–1935) has played a central role in shaping the posterior image of ʿAbduh. A native of Tripoli in Lebanon, Rida moved to Cairo in 1898 and became ʿAbduh's student. They both began to publish a journal together in 1899, *al-Manār* (The Lighthouse), and Rida edited and published his teacher's works and produced the most comprehensive biography of him.[10] Rida presents ʿAbduh's approach to Islamic reform as an act of restoring pristine Islam. According to him, ʿAbduh followed the model of 'the pious ancestors' (*al-salaf al-ṣāliḥ*), the first three generations that lived after the death of the Prophet Muhammad.[11] Early twentieth-century Orientalist scholars began to identify both ʿAbduh and Rida as representatives of a modern Islamic reform movement, they called Salafism – a designation that proved highly influential.[12] As they were engaged in a modern reform of Islam, the epithet 'modernist' was attached to it. Modernist Salafism seeks to retrieve authentic Islam from its primary sources and to restore its original purity before doctrinal deviations entered its fold. Such a reconstituted and essentialized Islam, for modernist Salafis, would prove that it is a rational, scientific and progressive religion.[13] ʿAbduh, however, never self-ascribed the label Salafi to his reformist work and never identified himself with a reform movement called Salafism. It was his disciple Rida who associated him with the pious ancestors and defined his project as aiming to restore the Islam of the first three Muslim generations.[14]

This book argues that 'Abduh's spiritual and intellectual formation in Sufism and in its esoteric and philosophical elements demonstrates an intellectual orientation much broader than what a Salafi restoration of primeval Islam would suggest. While other scholarship has questioned 'Abduh's simplistic alignment with Salafism, this book further argues that his early immersion in Sufism and different strands of Islamic philosophy shaped his intellectual outlook throughout his life and also defined his approach in communicating his ideas to different audiences. As such, the book demonstrates how Islamic mysticism and practical philosophy are crucial in directing 'Abduh's trajectory of Islamic reform: they provided both the impetus for reform and a roadmap for adapting to the different expectations of actors and constituencies he had to engage with throughout his life. Using different epistemic approaches and discursive genres, 'Abduh sought to reach out to different constituencies but also left a legacy full of contradictions, inconsistencies and ambiguities.

Despite 'Abduh's significance and influence, no comprehensive biography has been published on him in English for almost ninety years.[15] While research on him has been ongoing and new insights produced, one of the reasons for the lack of a comprehensive scholarly engagement with his life and thought is that a particular portrayal of 'Abduh has been taken for granted and alternative readings which are informed by his understudied intellectual outputs produced at earlier stages of his life were not really explored. Early scholarship on 'Abduh was produced in the mid-twentieth century after Rida had published his biography in 1931 and a complete edition of the extensive Qur'an commentary he produced together with 'Abduh, *Tafsīr al-Manār* (The Lighthouse Commentary), became available in 1947. This scholarship, despite its enormous benefits in initiating academic research on 'Abduh, suffered from two problems. First, it remained too faithful to Rida's Salafi portrayal of his teacher and also failed to sufficiently distinguish between 'Abduh and Rida. This scholarship approaches both figures as intellectual twins who espouse the same ideas.[16] Charles C. Adams's book, sofar the only comprehensive biography in English, published two years after Rida's book adheres to the latter's reading of his life and focusses primarily on 'Abduh's later writings, in particular his influential theological work, *Risālat al-Tawḥīd* (Treatise on Divine Unity), which he presents as 'his mature work of theology'.[17] Similar approaches are visible in works discussing 'Abduh's and Rida's Qur'an commentary[18] and their legal and political theories.[19] In both instances, both 'Abduh and Rida are presented as following the same school of thought not considering sufficiently how Rida diverted from the teachings of his Egyptian mentor.

The second issue is the assumption of a clear delineation between 'orthodoxy' and 'heterodoxy' in Islam – a legacy of Orientalist scholarship. Legalistic and scripturalist Sunnism is represented as 'orthodox' Islam while Sufism, Islamic philosophy and other esoteric traditions constitute 'heterodoxy' and are therefore not sufficiently Islamic. Rida was eager to align 'Abduh with the first understanding of Islamic orthodoxy and either suppressed or re-interpreted ideas and writings that would suggest he deviated therefrom.[20] This image received its first challenge when Iraj Afshar and Asghar Mahdavi unearthed material on 'Abduh's teacher Jamal al-Din al-Afghani (1838–1897) in the National Archives of Iran. The publication of this material in 1963 proved Afghani's Iranian roots and illustrated his complex religious orientations, in particular his attraction to mystical and esoteric schools of thought in Twelver Shia Islam. The publication of this material initiated the production of scholarly works on Afghani, informed by these newly discovered sources providing a more complex reading of him.[21] Elie Kedourie used this material to investigate the relationship between Afghani and 'Abduh by discussing their correspondence.[22] The language and approach that come to the fore in their letters show for Kedourie that ultimately they were atheist free thinkers who only used Islam for their anti-imperialist activities. Kedourie also argues that both are modern representatives of traditions of 'Islamic heterodoxy'[23] – namely Sufism and esoteric philosophy. As 'heterodox' intellectuals they did not really believe in Islam. Kedourie's assessment is based, like other scholarship at this time, on problematic Orientalist demarcations of orthodoxy and heterodoxy in Islam.

The most substantial challenge to Rida's depiction of 'Abduh and its uncritical adoption in subsequent academic scholarship has come from the Tunisian scholar Mohamed Haddad, a student of Mohammed Arkoun (1928–2010). As Haddad writes in French and Arabic, his works have not had such an impact on academic writing on 'Abduh in English. More recent articles and encyclopaedia entries regularly cite his French articles[24] – not his substantial Arabic monograph[25] – but do not utilize them fully to revise Rida's account of 'Abduh.[26] Haddad questions Rida's authority in writing a biography of 'Abduh and reveals his editorial strategies when publishing the works of 'Abduh which omit material that questions his adherence to Sunni notions of orthodoxy or arrange it in a manner to minimize the significance of such passages. Haddad's work provides a crucial inspiration for this book. However, Haddad is not entirely free of imposing his own intellectual agenda on 'Abduh either. By pointing at the influence of a wide range of Islamic intellectual traditions on 'Abduh, Haddad seeks to present him as a secular thinker more than a religious scholar who was liberal in his political orientation and made arguments in support of the secular separation of religion and politics. Thereby, Haddad follows the modern dichotomy between religion and the secular and seeks to align him with the latter. 'Abduh was for him more 'modern intellectual' than 'religious scholar'.[27]

My own previous work on 'Abduh follows Haddad in questioning Rida's portrayal of 'Abduh and explains the apparent contradictions in his thought biographically.[28] While 'Abduh was shaped by mystical philosophy in his early years under Afghani's tutelage and collaborated with him to counter European imperialism, he undertook a complete political and intellectual U-turn accepting European colonial presence as a reality and aligning himself with mainstream Sunni traditions of law and theology. This portrayal is also too linear and teleological and does not question his association with Salafism. My previous work is still based on the implicit assumption that there is an inherent contradiction between mystical philosophy and 'orthodox' Islam which – as it becomes manifest in 'Abduh's life – needs to be explained away by pointing at significant biographical shifts and turns to make sense of the apparent inconsistencies in his religious and intellectual orientations.

Mid-twentieth-century scholarship on modern Islam measures figures like 'Abduh in light of standards of Western modernity. The success of Islamic reform movements is determined by how much they embrace modern ideas with a presumption that one cannot be completely faithful to the Islamic tradition and embrace Western modernity in its entirety. Therefore, any intellectual reform of Islam will always be somehow lacking, inconclusive and caught between these two forces.[29] This scholarship also posits the notion of a gradual decline of Islamic cultural and intellectual life from the classical period, receiving a low-point in the eighteenth century before the modern revival began in the nineteenth century. More recent scholarship has questioned this depiction by pointing at the strong intellectual culture of pre-modern Muslim societies and Islam's own tradition of renewal (*tajdīd*) and reform (*iṣlāḥ*) that have become manifest throughout Islamic history.[30] Samira Haj's work is such an attempt to indigenize 'Abduh's reformist work by placing it in Islamic traditions of reform.[31] For her, 'Abduh was not a liberal in the European sense and rejected the secularizing drive of the colonial state which aims at minimizing the influence of Islam in personal morality, social life and politics. Embedding 'Abduh's reformist work in Islamic concepts of reform is important, but aligning him simplistically with concepts of renewal which implies a restoration of 'orthodoxy' falls short of understanding the variety of Islamic intellectual traditions he engaged with and reduces the understanding of his approach to a particular restrictive trajectory.

The most recent trend in academic scholarship on 'Abduh seeks to avoid turning him and other Muslim reformers into passive recipients of Western modernity who inefficiently sought to incorporate modern ideas in the Islamic tradition or align them with pre-defined notions of orthodoxy and heterodoxy in Islam. Examining his later theological and apologetic works in particular, this scholarship places 'Abduh in an 'emerging global public sphere'[32] and 'Islamic modernism' more generally in a 'global intellectual landscape'[33] which framed discourses around religion across the world.[34] These discourses were shaped by post-Enlightenment Protestant paradigms which consider religion as an individual interiorized experience, emphasize ethics over law and separate religion from the secular.[35] 'Abduh in his later theological and apologetic writings engages with these Protestant notions of religion and re-reads them in Islamic terms, seeking to demarcate in particular Islam's essential theological features from Christianity. The particular benefit of this approach is that it contextualizes 'Abduh as an active actor in globalizing discourses of the late nineteenth century and points at the cosmopolitan intellectual environment and various networks he engaged with within and outside of the Muslim world. This recent scholarly trend moves away from notions of imitative deficiency attributed to Muslim reformers in mid-twentieth-century scholarship by illustrating the complex global intellectual entanglements of figures like 'Abduh and focussing on their appropriation of modern paradigms and their translation into and projection onto Islam.

Yet, this scholarship still favours 'Abduh's later writings over his earlier ones and does not fully encapsulate the wide range of Islamic traditions he incorporated in his thought. These scholars also tend to be disinterested in identifying the Islamic roots of 'Abduh's ideas and still exhibit an implicit responsive approach by investigating how paradigms of Western modernity have been indigenized.[36] While rightly pointing at the impact of such global discourses on religion on figures like 'Abduh, these works do not sufficiently problematize their underlying Protestant assumptions that emphasize belief over praxis, theology over law, inner experience over external performativity and separate 'the religious' from 'the secular'. These assumptions have shaped approaches to religions in Religious Studies and defined what makes something 'religious' as opposed to being 'secular'.[37] Applied to Muslim contexts, such approaches over-theologize Islam.[38] For this reason, 'Abduh's later theological works have received more attention than his earlier mystical, philosophical and socio-political writings, as they are better aligned to a Religious Studies agenda that primarily engages with theological discourses in modern Islam. Equally, his later writings are better aligned with the emergent global discourse of religious modernism which 'Abduh as key figure in the articulation of 'Islamic modernism' was part of. 'Abduh's *Risālat al-Tawḥīd*, despite being 'surprisingly brief, and still more, even popular in form',[39] is seen as his *magnum opus*, as it essentializes Islamic doctrines and gives them a modernist spin. 'Abduh's early political and social writings were from this perspective not 'Islamic' enough, lacked the essentializing tendencies of religious modernism and appeared too 'secular' to be considered in academic scholarship. They contain too little theology. According to this trend in scholarship, his early mystical and philosophical works were equally not 'orthodox' enough and could therefore be ignored.

Despite this criticism of existing scholarship on 'Abduh, these previous works have informed and enriched this book, as evident in its copious references to their important contributions. This book seeks to present a more comprehensive and complex discussion of his intellectual legacy which does not reduce it to theological works produced at the end of his life. This is done in four steps. First, this book directs the attention to 'Abduh's creative and eclectic engagement with the plurality of Islamic intellectual traditions which other more recent contributions have identified as a significant research gap but not further investigated.[40] Secondly, more emphasis is laid on 'Abduh's earliest mystical, philosophical, theological and political writings. In studies on him, they are usually just mentioned *en passant* for reasons outlined above. Rather than dismissing them as early intellectual formations without any further relevance, this study engages more with them and illustrates that they are crucial to understand 'Abduh's further intellectual development and approach to Islamic reform. Engaging with his earliest writings reveals the innovations in his thought and allows for a much more nuanced reading of his oeuvre.[41] Thirdly, the book reveals important continuities of certain concepts and tropes from his earlier to his later writings. Rather than suggesting a complete re-appraisal of his earlier mystical and philosophical interests, his most prominent theological works and his Qur'an commentary re-articulate similar ideas in an idiom that appears more aligned with Sunni notions of orthodoxy. 'Abduh engages with a variety of intellectual traditions which he synthesizes in order to show that in cultural and intellectual terms Islam can find its place in the modern world. Finally, the book does not search for intellectual consistency. What Rahman and other researchers have failed to achieve when studying al-Ghazali, this book does not attempt to do when it comes to 'Abduh. The book tries neither to explain contradictions away by identifying important turns in his biography nor to question his authorship of certain books. Both options – though popular – are too convenient. The book argues instead that 'Abduh was socialized in an intellectual culture of ambiguity that was comfortable with contradictions and inconsistencies and developed particular strategies to cope with them. These strategies proved particularly fruitful when it came to translating modern intellectual paradigms into the Islamic tradition or identifying discursive convergences between them.

In order to arrive at a more comprehensive understanding of 'Abduh in his fullness, with all the contradictions, inconsistencies and ambiguities that mark his intellectual output, he needs to be embedded in the capaciousness of Islamic thought. This not only requires taking his earlier mystical and philosophical works more seriously in tracing the contours of his reformist work. More importantly, it is necessary to unlearn certain dichotomies which implicitly shape the study of Islam. While categories of 'orthodox' and 'heterodox' have been discarded in contemporary scholarship for the most part, Islamic Studies still suffers from the tendency to centre articulations of Islamic religiosity that are scripturalist, legalist and doctrinal (exegesis, law, theology) and to de-centre others that are experiential, esoteric, mystical and rationalistic (Sufism, philosophy). As the former are based on the scriptural sources of Islam – Qur'an and the Prophetic tradition (*sunna*) – they appear more 'Islamic', while the latter incorporate pre-Islamic philosophical traditions of Greece, the Middle East and India and hence seem 'less Islamic'.[42] Furthermore and in connection with this tendency, the religion–secular divide, foundational to modern conceptualizations of religion, prioritizes scriptural sources, creeds and normative practices as the loci of religion while philosophical and political discourses and cultural productions are secular in nature and therefore not religious.[43] By discussing how 'Abduh is shaped by the capaciousness of Islamic thought, the book not only seeks to make a contribution to understanding this important nineteenth-century Muslim reformer. More than that, the book suggests a pathway to study modern Islam that avoids categorizations that implicitly inherit notions of orthodoxy and heterodoxy and the dichotomy between religion and the secular. The book therefore engages with recent scholarship arguing for a fuller appreciation of the complexity of Islamic intellectual history.

Islam as a culture of ambiguity

Two recent contributions suggest an intellectual climate of ambiguity as central to understanding Islamic intellectual history. Thomas Bauer's *Die Kultur der Ambiguität: Eine andere Geschichte des Islams* (The Culture of Ambiguity: An Alternative History of Islam)[44] is the first intervention to make this point. As an academic publication in German which only very recently has been translated into English[45] it has not received much attention in Islamic Studies in English. A more impactful contribution within English-speaking academia has been the posthumously published book *What Is Islam?: The Importance of Being* Islamic by the late Shahab Ahmed.[46] The approach and propositions of both books are quite similar, though their authors' agendas differ as do some of their conclusions. Bauer's main premise is that pre-modern Muslim societies and their intellectual life exhibited a strong tolerance towards ambiguity and accepted conflicting claims to truth. This cultural ambiguity became manifest in language, literature and other textual or verbal discourses but also in acts of daily life and of religious worship.

Bauer discusses different areas of Islamic intellectual and cultural life where this tolerance towards ambiguity was evident. A plurality of Islamic discourses was accepted and efforts were made to reconcile conflicting worldviews without vindicating one at the expenses of the other. Al-Ghazali is a particular prominent example of this synthesizing tendency of Islamic thought seeking to embed certain aspects of philosophy and Sufism within Sunni theology and jurisprudence. Islamic jurisprudence traditionally accommodated different legal principles and sources of law and considered a variety of legal interpretations as equally valid. Islamic discourses on politics were not just based on conceptualizations in theology and jurisprudence. Political discourses were much more informed by panegyric poetry and treatises on successful statecraft, so-called mirrors for princes. These two latter genres of political discourse incorporated pre-Islamic literary and political traditions and co-existed with theological and jurisprudential reflections on governance, sovereignty and legitimacy in Islam without always agreeing with them. Pre-modern Islamic exegesis conceived the Qur'an as deliberately revealed by God as an ambiguous text. Hence, exegetical praxis was always an exercise in probability and never arrived at complete certainty. The mystical poetry of Sufis deliberately played with semantic ambiguity. Finally, the tolerant and inclusive ethos of Muslim societies was evident in their material culture: architecture, art and aesthetic conventions more generally incorporated with pride the heritage of non-Muslim cultures.[47]

The aim of Bauer's book is to open the eye of historians of Islam to the significant tolerance towards ambiguity as a particular cultural achievement of pre-modern Islamic intellectual life. This tolerance marks the capaciousness of Islamic thought and allowed the co-existence of conflicting views: one could live with contradictions, inconsistencies and ambiguities. In addition, the cultural and intellectual sources of Islamic thought and Muslim societies were not solely the Qur'an and the *sunna* of the Prophet but non-Islamic sources in philosophy, ethics, politics and literature that preceded Islam. Equally, Bauer points out that the genres of Islamic discourses were not just theology and jurisprudence but Islam was also discussed, represented and theorized in philosophy, poetry, literature and material culture. Religious and non-religious elements were thereby blended in Muslim societies, made possible by their tolerance towards ambiguity. Bauer seeks to avoid, what he calls, the Islamization of Islam ('*Islamisierung des Islams*'): an approach that reduces the Muslim world to acts and discourses of piety that marginalizes non-Islamic elements as deviations.[48]

Ahmed's book makes a similar intervention. He approaches Islam as '*a human and historical phenomenon of exploration, … of ambiguity and ambivalence, … of relativism, and … of internal contradiction*'.[49] Rather than compartmentalizing different discourses as Sufi, philosophical, juristic, theological and thereby as contradictory to one another and mutually exclusive, Islam is expressed in its discursive diversity. What appears contradictory, inconsistent or ambiguous is implicated in a discursive process that seeks to define what it means to be Islamic. Ahmed conceives Islam as '*hermeneutical engagement*'[50] and introduces a triad of *pre-text*, *text* and *con-text* to describe this engagement. The act of divine revelation is the starting point which is not just restricted to the revealed text of the Qur'an but includes any 'act of disclosure or communication or revelation'[51] of the divine to humanity which can assume different forms. This constitutes the 'text' around which meaning is created. The pre-text denotes the cosmological and epistemological presuppositions which define the nature of the text and the approach to interpreting it. Islamic philosophers uphold the primary of reason (*ʿaql*) and understand the act of divine self-disclosure as an intellectual process. For Sufis, divine revelation is constant and manifest in a cosmic spiritual experience of oneness with God. For Islamic jurists the text – in their case specifically the Qur'an and the Prophetic traditions (*aḥādīth*) – is a source to deduce laws, for theologians a repository to establish creedal propositions. Ahmed defines the con-text not just as the specific historical and social contingencies that shape hermeneutical engagements in Islam but as '*lexicon of means and meanings of Islam* that has been historically generated and recorded up to any given moment: it is the full *historical vocabulary of Islam* at any given moment'.[52] Con-text is the accumulated discursive traditions and their hermeneutical tools that different Muslim actors in their engagement with Islam resort to in order to define what it means to be Islamic.

The nexus between pre-text, text and con-text explains the different and often contradictory meanings that have been constructed in Islam which are not solely depended on historical contingencies. Islamic intellectual traditions have developed different strategies to make contradictions coherent and meaningful. For Ahmed, Muslims developed an epistemological hierarchy that distinguishes between different registers of truth. There are higher and lower levels of truth; the latter are for the common people while access to and understanding of the former requires sufficient philosophical sophistication, esoteric initiation or theological erudition. Intellectual elitism allowed for the co-existence of different truth regimes. Related to this hierarchization of truth, private and public modes of meaning-making were established. Different discursive, social and physical spaces existed to allow Muslim actors to pursue their various hermeneutical engagements with Islam. This spatio-social segregation of discourses provided space for their co-existence: a Muslim actor would attend a Sufi convent to engage in Sufi rituals and would express their experiences in mystical love poetry in Persian. They would attend a *madrasa* to study jurisprudence and write scholarly treatises in Arabic.[53]

The disciplinary and discursive boundaries between these different approaches were mostly blurred. They were often physically located next to one another, if not housed under the same roof, and a Muslim scholar would not attend either the Sufi convent or the *madrasa* but both respecting at the same time the conventions and parameters that demarcate the different spaces and modes of Islamic meaning-making. The ideal was the erudite scholar (*adīb*) whose education perfected both intellect and character. They possessed such a mastery of language that they could yield intellectual discourses that simultaneously appeal to different registers of truth, various audiences and their presuppositions and intellectual abilities and create multi-faceted layers of meaning.[54] Such an approach required the skilful use of language, as Bauer observes as well.[55]

Bauer and Ahmed seek to alert readers to the capaciousness of pre-modern Islamic thought and culture. While Bauer introduces a model to investigate Islamic history, Ahmed's agenda is more ambitious as he seeks to reconceptualize how Islamic and Religious Studies approach Islam as a human and historical phenomenon. The differences in their conclusions are perhaps best illustrated by the question whether a wine goblet can be called Islamic. For Bauer, the answer is clear: talking about an Islamic wine goblet makes as much sense as talking about Christian adultery.[56] Ahmed disagrees. A wine goblet can be called Islamic because Muslims have always drunk wine since the beginning of Islam. In addition, he refers to the prevalence and long history of wine drinking in Muslim societies, as a collective act expressed in poetry, literature and material culture, that makes it Islamic.[57] Bauer still follows a distinction between religion and the secular.[58] For him referring to a wine goblet as a piece of Islamic metalwork in a museum is an example of Islamizing secular aspects of the social life in Islamic history. Ahmed, however, rejects this religious-secular dichotomy as potentially reducing what is Islamic to a set of restrictive normative practices.[59] However, Ahmed's suggestion is not unproblematic either. To approach '*whatever* Muslims say or do as a potential site or locus for expression and articulation of *being Muslim*'[60] reduces Muslim actors to their Muslimness and ignores the intersectionality and different layers of their identities. Muslims are not only and not always Muslims and do not engage in meaning-making by solely referring to Islam or their Muslimness.

Where Bauer and Ahmed agree on is in their conclusion that modern Islam has lost its tolerance towards ambiguity and its cultural and intellectual capaciousness. The colonial moment and the military conquest, political subjugation and economic exploitation of most parts of the Muslim world in the nineteenth century instilled a sense of cultural inferiority among Muslim political and intellectual elites and facilitated a discourse of decline. Islamic intellectual history was revisited by Muslim reformers and elements identified responsible for the decline of Islam. Sufism was marked out as anti-modern, irrational and superstitious. Its pervasive role in pre-modern Muslim societies was to be blamed for their decline. Philosophy was deemed to be outside the fold of Islam. A true restoration of Islam can only be achieved by radically cleansing it from non-Islamic elements. Nineteenth-century global discourses on religion with their Protestant biases favoured theology and encouraged intellectual reform activities that over-theologized Islam and encouraged a retreat to essentializing dogmatism. The formation of modern nation-states led to the codification of Islamic law. Islamic jurisprudence which once was a discursive tradition at ease with different methods and interpretations was distilled into positive state law which diminished its flexibility and variety to an unrecognizable degree. The rise of Islamism with its totalitarian approach to Islam as being both religion and state (*dīn wa-dawla*) and the global spread of Salafism with its emphasis on rigorous piety, legalism and scripturalism destroyed the tolerance towards ambiguity that marked pre-modern Muslim intellectual, social and cultural life.[61]

The conclusions Bauer and Ahmed draw about the particular trajectories of modern Islam are certainly true – when presented in such broad and generalized terms. However, a closer look at modern Islamic movements, scholars and intellectuals will equally reveal contradictions, inconsistencies and ambiguities. Both target political Islam as being responsible for the end of cultural and intellectual ambiguity. Yet, a closer look at prominent Islamist ideologues, for example, will reveal that they were not short of ambiguities either. The leader of the 1979 Islamic Revolution in Iran, Ayatollah Khomeini (1902–1989) was trained in and taught mystical philosophy.[62] His politicized reading of Twelver Shia Islam, which serves as the ideological foundation of the Islamic Republic of Iran, owes more to Platonic ideas of politics than to Islamic jurisprudence. Sayyid Qutb (1906–1966), often portrayed as intellectual precursor of contemporary jihadist movements,[63] was a litterateur. His Qur'an commentary is a highly personal and eloquent encounter with the text and a popular reading outside of Islamist circles.[64] The trajectories of modern Islamic thought are no less flexible, accommodative and elastic than its pre-modern variants, as any in-depth investigation into the intellectual life of prominent figures will reveal.

This book seeks to do so by investigating the complex and diverse sources of 'Abduh's reformist oeuvre and the different epistemic registers and discursive genres he employed to communicate his ideas to different audiences. That 'Abduh was conscious about the need to adapt his discourse to the expectations of different audiences is evident when he compares the communicative strategies he and his teacher Jamal al-Din al-Afghani employed:

> Sayyid Jamal al-Din taught philosophy (*ḥikma*) to those who followed it and those who did not. It was specific to him that he would direct his speeches to those he wanted to even if they were not his supporters. I envied him because of this, because the condition of a meeting and the timing influenced me. My soul would not be inclined to talk unless I found it opportune. It is the same with my writing.[65]

'Abduh seems to praise his teacher's ability to address an audience directly and communicate his points regardless of whether it was receptive to his ideas or not. 'Abduh presents himself as always hesitant, searching for the right occasion to present his ideas. What appears to be a compliment could also be read as a rebuke: Afghani threw his opinions on his interlocutors disregarding whether he might antagonize them with his views. ʿAbduh, however, was better in aligning his discourse to the expectations of his respective audience and in framing an issue in speech and writing so that his addressees would be more receptive. Rida, otherwise sceptical of Sufism, attributes ʿAbduh's ability to master the culture of ambiguity to his Sufi background. Writing about his teacher's involvement in Sufism, Rida admits that

> he considered it necessary to conceal (*wujūb al-kitmān*) everything one has obtained from the fruits of Sufism. He adapted to the qualities and conditions of the people he associated with. It was like this: among philosophers, he was a philosopher; among jurisprudents, he was a jurisprudent; among literati, he was a litterateur; among historians, he was a historian; among officials and judges, he was the most capable official and the most just judge. He talked with each group and each individual according to how he viewed their capacity (*istiʿdād*), while holding onto truthfulness and independent mindedness.[66]

His complex literary oeuvre equally illustrates how he mastered the intellectual parameters and linguistic conventions of different scholarly genres and knew how to address different audiences in line with their abilities and expectations: he wrote Sufi treatises for fellow mystics, provided a philosophical commentary on Islamic theology to rehabilitate philosophy in the eyes of theologians, was active as a journalistic writer throughout his life, issued fatwas as grand mufti of Egypt that implemented the legal prescriptions the Hanafi school of law, produced catechisms that confirmed Sunni notions of orthodoxy for young Muslim students and gave public lectures on the Qur'an to encourage lay Muslims to engage with their sacred scripture.

Modes and agents of reform in Islam

Bauer and Ahmed alert readers to different epistemological registers of meaning-making and Islamic discourses, suggesting the capaciousness and elasticity of pre-modern Islamic intellectual life. ʿAbduh, steeped in this tradition, sought to retrieve this richness in order to reform the understanding of Islam among his contemporaries who were unable or unwilling to respond to the challenge that modernity in its colonial form posed to the Muslim world. Which modes of reform are most suitable to understand ʿAbduh's approach? The afore-mentioned al-Ghazali suggests one possible pathway:

> Subsequently I consulted on that matter a number of those skilled in discerning hearts and visions and they were of one mind in advising me to abandon my seclusion and to emerge from my religious retirement. In addition to that, certain godly men had many recurrent dreams attesting that this move of mine would be a source of good and a right procedure, and that it had been decreed by God – Praised be He! – for the beginning of this century. For God – Praised be He! – has indeed promised to revivify His religion at the beginning of each century.[67]

Describing the reasons for his return to scholarly activities after years of retirement, al-Ghazali admits his apprehensions of resuming a path which he has abandoned in the past. After his disillusionment with the life of a religious scholar, he withdrew from his teaching position in Baghdad and lived the life of a wandering dervish before founding a Sufi convent near his hometown Nishapur. As a response to the perceived moral laxity of the people, the demise of the scholarly class and political turmoil, al-Ghazali decided to shun this world and pursue the lifestyle of a mystic. However, the grand vizier ordered al-Ghazali to return to Nishapur and to continue teaching, an order which he initially ignored but later made him realize that the proper response to the corruption of religion caused by the moral decline of his co-religionists is not abandoning the world but guiding them to the truth. After discussing his reluctance with fellow Sufis, al-Ghazali's conviction grew that he was destined by God to restore Islam in his time. Al-Ghazali paraphrases in this statement a hadith which appears in the canonical collection of Abu Dawud: 'Verily, God, the Exalted, sends to this community at the beginning of each century someone who renews its religion (*man yujaddidu lahā dīnahā*).' As his re-conversion to a religious scholar occurred at the beginning of the fifth century after the *hijra*, al-Ghazali must have felt that he was the one God has chosen as the renewer (*mujaddid*) of Islam in his time.[68]

Unlike other epithets and titles, the term *mujaddid* has not played a prominent role in discussions of religious authority in the Islamic tradition. The title has been applied to eminent Sunni scholars – such as al-Ghazali – praised for their restoration of genuine Islam as embodied in the Qur'an and the *sunna* of the Prophet. The *mujaddid* was understood to be the restorer of pristine Islam against its adulteration by alien innovations (*bida'*). The identification of renewal with the restoration of Islam in its original form upholds the primary importance of the Qur'an and the *sunna* as the repositories of the perfect model of Islam. Hence, the *mujaddid* advocates a stricter and more rigorous application of the authoritative sources of Islam and thereby targets practices of popular religiosity which have no foundations in these sources and the adoption of non-Islamic ideas, in theology and philosophy in particular, which delude the purity of Islamic doctrines. The *mujaddid* argues for an independent interpretation of the primary sources of Islam (*ijtihād*) ignoring the legal and exegetical tradition preceding him and its imitation (*taqlīd*) by other scholars.[69] The *mujaddid* thereby becomes the epitome of restoring Sunni notions of orthodoxy, reinstating Islam in its alleged purity.

Rida is eager to align his teacher 'Abduh with this particular Sunni reading of the centennial renewal of Islam and attaches the label *mujaddid* to both 'Abduh and Afghani, considering them to be 'amongst the greatest manifestations'[70] of religious renewal in Islam. To counter the objection that with Afghani and 'Abduh there were two simultaneous renewers – a notion that is not evident in the text of the hadith – Rida refers to later Muslim commentators like Jalal al-Din al-Suyuti (1445–1505). According to their understanding, renewal does not necessarily occur in the whole of Islam by one major figure, but there are usually several reformers who work in different fields. Some renewers labour on the reform of religious scholarship, while other reformers have a political or military mission.[71] In a similar vein, Afghani focused on 'reform and renewal through politics',[72] while 'Abduh prioritized 'reform and renewal through teaching and education'.[73] Yet, Rida's alignment of 'Abduh and his teacher Afghani with different types of Islamic renewal conceals more than it reveals. It creates an artificial distinction between political and intellectual activism and seeks to downplay 'Abduh's involvement in politics. Their identification with the centennial *mujaddid* as restorer of genuine Islam seeks to obscure their intellectual immersion in mystical and philosophical traditions of Islam – traditions which Rida viewed as heterodox. A better understanding of their reformist approaches is achieved when considering another model of reform and renewal in Islam.

Such a different model is based on charismatic forms of authority and renewal and mystical philosophy. This model is not oriented towards the past but assumes the continuity of divine guidance with its notion of sainthood (*wilāya*) which found its most pervasive expression within Sufism. The most influential exposition of Sufi sainthood has been provided by Ibn 'Arabi (1165–1240), the prominent Andalusian Sufi scholar, who was one of the first major theorists of Sufi philosophy which proved highly influential. In his *Fuṣūṣ al- Ḥikam* (Bezels of Wisdom), Ibn 'Arabi describes a vision in which he saw all the prophets and all the saints walking behind them in the footsteps of the prophets (*'alā aqdām al-anbiyā'*). This vision illustrates how the saints adopt the charisma of the prophets and by walking in their footsteps assume a quasi-prophetic role.[74]

Sufism developed a hierarchical understanding of sainthood with Sufis acquiring different degree of *wilāya* depending on their mystical status and spiritual perfection. On top of the hierarchy of saints stands the Perfect Man (*al-insān al-kāmil*) or pole (*quṭb*) to whom Hakim al-Tirmidhi (d. 912) and Ibn 'Arabi also refer to as the seal of saints (*khātim al-awliyā'*). The saint who has achieved this highest stage of sainthood truly assumes a quasi-prophetic role. As the most superior spiritual successor of the Prophet Muhammad, he becomes like the prophets in the past the ultimate isthmus, connecting humanity with God.[75]

The Sufi model of charismatic authority around sainthood provides a means for the continuous divine guidance of Muslims and the further development of Islam rather than just looking back onto the past and seeking the restoration of some sense of pristine Islam based on a restrictive reading of its scriptural sources. This Sufi model of a charismatic rejuvenation of Islam, that is directed by God, is more flexible, irenic and accommodative to change and innovation. The charismatic Sufi reformers appears to stand in contradiction to the *tajdīd* model of Sunni reform by the scholarly restorer of the *sunna* of the Prophet. However, there are many examples illustrating the fluidity of boundaries between these two approaches. This is evident in al-Ghazali's attraction to both philosophy and Sufism which has confused Rahman but is also manifest in other Sufi figures in pre-modern Islam.[76]

Despite Rida's efforts to present Afghani as an 'orthodox' Sunni reformer, he embodies more ambiguous modes of Islamic renewal which combine charismatic authority, mystical philosophy and esoteric secrecy. 'Abduh as Afghani's student and protégé would be introduced into the mystical and esoteric traditions of Twelver Shiism from which Afghani originated – traditions that would shape the further trajectories of his reformist work. Coming from a family of religious scholars in Iran, Afghani pursued a traditional religious education initially in Iran before continuing in Najaf, Iraq, which hosts the most important seminarian institutions of Shii learning (*ḥawza*). In the course of his studies of traditional scholarship, Afghani appeared to have experienced a spiritual crisis similar to al-Ghazali's:

> From the world of comfort and happiness I fell into the realm of misery and arrogance and spent my days studying various branches of knowledge – formal, exceptional and otherwise. From my studies – with the exception of study breaks – I did not reap any benefits. I spent my short life with futile and pointless matters. I had no clue about the beginning of the world nor any impression of its end … I fell into the sea of despair and began to search for 'The one who knows himself knows his Lord'. The service of superficial scholars who are

> uninformed about the spiritual world (*'ālam-i ma'nawī*) I rejected and placed much effort and exigency into research and investigation for my confusion not to increase and not to yield any further doubt. When I reached the conclusion of my reflection, I saw that each sect in the doctrines to which it lends its credence is limited … The scholar is enslaved in his knowledge, the sage content with his philosophy, the intellectual immersed in his talk, the fool happy with his actions, the worshipper attached to his acts of worship, the ascetic intoxicated by his asceticism and the ruler (*sulṭān*) in his palace accustomed to his kingdom – whether it is affluent or poor. Everyone had given his heart and their steps follow it. I saw that this world was only an unreal mirage and appearance. Its power was precarious and its sufferings unlimited, hiding a venom in every delight, and an anger in every benefit. Thus, I was inevitably led to remove myself from the tumults and to break all my ties of attachment. With support of those close to God I was lifted out of the world of darkness and reached the world of the spirit, became placid by the power of the light and chose to follow the Prophet and his Companions.[77]

Frustrated with the traditionalism of the religious scholars under whom he studied, Afghani developed a keen interest in philosophical and esoteric traditions of Islam. He turned in particular to the Shaykhi School which was established by Ahmad al-Ahsa'i (1753–1826). Al-Ahsa'i found followers among religious scholars both in Iran and Iraq and became the founder of a separate school in Twelver Shiism in the nineteenth century. Al-Ahsa'i stands in the tradition of Ibn 'Arabi's mystical philosophy and a particular school of Shii mystical philosophy, known as theosophy (*ḥikmat-i ilāhī*) as developed by the prominent Shii philosopher of Safavid Iran Mulla Sadra (1572–1640).[78] What attracted Afghani to the doctrines of the Shaykhi School was their 'combination of philosophy, mystical ideas, and religious innovation'.[79] Al-Asha'i attempted to synthesize the different religious and intellectual strands of the Islamic tradition into a holistic system which combines rationalist Peripatetic philosophy, Sufism, Shii theology and jurisprudence. The orientation of the Shaykhi School towards charismatic authority appealed to Afghani as well. The Perfect Shia (*al-shī'a al-kāmil*), based on the Sufi notion of the Perfect Man, becomes a single divinely guided religious leader who acts as a quasi-prophetic renewer of Islam.[80] The particular effort of the Shaykhi School to synthesize the various intellectual traditions of Shii Islam into a new religious system that incorporates their variety provided Afghani with a discursive approach to harmonize different knowledge traditions and to overcome their apparent contradictions.

The attraction of the Shaykhi School lied not only in its universalism but also in its intellectual dynamism. Like Ismailism and other esoteric Shii groups, al-Ahsa'i tends to elevate the Shii Imams over the Prophet Muhammad, as they fulfil an important function in relation to the prophetic revelation. Whereas the prophetic revelation brought exoteric knowledge, namely the theological foundations of religion as well as religious laws, the task of the Imams is to disclose the inner, esoteric meaning behind revelation – its spiritual core. The latter task is implicitly superior to the former, because Shii esoteric traditions prioritize the inner meaning (*bāṭin*) of revelation over its outer form (*ẓāhir*). The elevation of the Imams whose interpretations are equally if not more important than prophetic revelations implies the constant renewal and expansion of revelation, as its esoteric contents is discovered continuously. For Kazim Rashti (1793–1843), the successor of al-Ahsa'i as leader of the Shaykhi School, the exoteric revelation matures in the process of its esoteric interpretation by the Imams in accordance with the growing maturity of humanity.[81] Sayyid Kazim adopts Mulla Sadra's dynamic understanding of creation. For Mulla Sadra, everything is moving to the status of perfection and only God as the perfect creator does not change.[82] For Rashti, divine legislation must respond to the needs of people in a particular time. Therefore, several revelations were sent to humanity in accordance with the growing intellectual capacity of humanity. The Islamic revelation is final but still evolving. Rashti compares the initial Qur'anic revelation with a child which has to grow and whose nutrition has to change in their evolution.[83] The Perfect Shia is the charismatic agent guiding the gradual maturation of the Islamic revelation.

Afghani's initial intellectual formation was shaped by a combination of Sufism and Islamic philosophy, as expounded by the Shaykhi school, and assumed an evolutionary development of Islam as central to its reform rather than a restoration of its primordial state as the Sunni *tajdīd* model of change suggests. His attraction to such ideas brought him the rebuke of religious scholars in Iraq who considered his interest in mystical and esoteric philosophy as unfitting for a young aspiring scholar. Their opposition also made him aware of being circumspect when sharing his religious views with different audiences. By presenting himself as a Sunni Muslim from Afghanistan, he concealed his actual Iranian Shii background and practised *taqiyya* (pious dissimulation) which denotes in Shiism to permissibility and at times obligation of Shii Muslims to conceal their religious identity to avoid persecution. Pious dissimulation became generally part of esoteric traditions in Islam to hide convictions that might contradict prevalent notions of orthodoxy or to communicate ideas in accordance with the capacity of a particular audience. Within mystical and esoteric traditions of Islam, pious dissimulation was a coping mechanism which dealt with contradictions and deliberately employed discourses of ambiguity.[84]

Ambiguity in Muslim (auto-)biographical writing: some notes on sources

Dissimulation, concealment and ambiguity also characterize the various biographical sources on the life of Muhammad 'Abduh. Discussing the representation of religious scholars in biographical works, Dale F. Eickelmann makes a useful distinction between 'individual' and 'person'. The 'individual' denotes the self-reflective human being with their desires, inner thoughts, hopes and beliefs, while 'person' describes the social status attributed to the individual comprising the expectations, roles and the overall significance that society credits to the individual. Following these social expectations, a traditional biographical account of a Muslim scholar would contain information on their formal education, the age when they memorized the entire Qur'an, the names of their teachers and the books they studied as well as their own contributions in the field of religious scholarship. Everything outside the scope of what would define a religious scholar, like other political or commercial activities, would usually be ignored.[85]

More importantly, biographies lack speculations on the inner thoughts and motives of the individual described. An esoteric tendency within traditional biographies has been noted. Very often, biographers practise their own type of *taqiyya*, concealing the true feelings and beliefs of the portrayed figure. When the religious and political context in which the author is writing might prove unfavourable for such feelings and beliefs and their revelation might harm the reputation of a person, they remain undisclosed.[86] The person is not seen as evolving over time and changing their identity in response to events in their life. Traditional biographies rather attribute 'fixed qualities'[87] to the individual without any interest or awareness of possible developments in their personality. The individual is presented as having had for their entire life all the qualities that conform to the social expectations regarding the role they fulfilled in society. Stressing the social person and their conformity with their role in society provides one of the main motivations for writing a biography. There is a certain apologetic drive behind biographical writing. Biographies serve the purpose of showing the merits and achievements of the portrayed figure, be they a scholar, saint or political leader, and to create an inspirational image of them for the targeted audience, a source of guidance and emulation for those wishing to follow in their footsteps.[88]

Another important feature to bear in mind in dealing with Muslim biographical works is what has been called the tradition of imitative writing in Middle Eastern historiographies. Studies of medieval Persian chronicles have shown how later authors reproduced an earlier model text and used it as a standard narrative for their own rendering of the chronicle. Imitating the works of precursor chroniclers acknowledges and preserves their works and also expresses the commitment of later authors to conventions of historical and biographical writings which had been established earlier.[89] However, the imitation of earlier works does not merely imply their complete *verbatim* reproduction. While earlier narratives are accepted as a template, very often changes to the original text are added and certain information is omitted. The alteration of the model text is often motivated by the concerns and agendas of the later author and their target audience.[90] For example, changes in early Safavid chronicles were an important instrument to provide legitimacy for the dynasty. The Sunni origin of the Safavid Sufi order had to be reinterpreted and its founders to be presented as Twelver Shiis, because the Sunni origin of the order and the later Shii commitment of the dynasty contradicted each other.[91]

The biographical sources used for the reconstruction of ʿAbduh's life – although all written in the twentieth century – include the aforementioned characteristics of Middle Eastern historiographical and biographical writing. ʿAbduh never produced an autobiography himself and only wrote memoirs around a particular episode in his life: the ʿUrabi Revolution of 1881–2 which led to the British occupation of Egypt.[92] Shortly before ʿAbduh's death Rida asked him a few questions about his family origins and educational background. These autobiographical remarks by ʿAbduh are the only information available on his life by himself and can be found in a series of articles Rida published in his journal *al-Manār* in 1905 shortly after ʿAbduh's death.[93] These articles provide the first comprehensive survey of ʿAbduh's life and include useful information that Rida omitted in his later biography, such as his involvement in Freemasonry. These articles also constitute the foundation of Rida's voluminous biography of his teacher *Taʾrīkh al-Ustādh al-Imām al-Shaykh Muḥammad ʿAbduh* (The History of Muhammad ʿAbduh) which consists of three volumes. The first volume contains the actual biography – expanded from the first biographical articles published in *al-Manār*. A selection of books, articles and letters penned by ʿAbduh can be found in the second volume, while the third volume contains a selection of newspaper articles, poems and eulogies on ʿAbduh.[94]

Rida's biography is certainly the most important, valuable and comprehensive source for gaining information on the life of ʿAbduh. It is not just a history of ʿAbduh but constitutes a set of 'histories' as it comprises a selection of memoirs and accounts of his associates and disciples, including detailed commentaries by Rida himself. However, Rida's work has to be treated with caution, as he imposes his own particular reading on his teacher.[95] In the introduction, Rida contends to be the closest of ʿAbduh's disciples who promised his teacher to write a biography after his death.[96] Their close relationship constitutes Rida's claim to intellectual succession as the heir of his teacher. Although his claim has been disputed,[97] he managed to position himself as the almost undisputed authority on the life and teachings of ʿAbduh. The rather short period of time ʿAbduh and Rida had worked together is used as evidence against a close relationship between them. Rida moved to Cairo in 1898, just seven years before the death of his teacher. When ʿAbduh died, Rida was not invited as member of a committee of ʿAbduh's former associates and disciples whose task was to collect ʿAbduh's writings for publication and to compile a biography.[98] It was only because of political circumstances and the death of most of ʿAbduh's associates that Rida could fill a lacuna thereby created.[99] That the first volume of Rida's biography was published in 1931, after the publication of the second and third volumes, indicates that Rida could only assume the position where he could write a complete biography after the death of most other disciples and friends of ʿAbduh.[100]

Before the publication of Rida's book no one had written a biography of ʿAbduh. The 1940s suddenly witnessed an increased interest in him in Egypt. From the ascendancy to power of King Faruq (1920–1965) in Egypt in 1936, renewed efforts were undertaken to reform and modernize al-Azhar in Cairo, the most prestigious and oldest educational institution of Sunni religious scholarship. These reforms needed to find a precursor in the past for their justification, and this figure was found in ʿAbduh. Hence biographies were written by followers of ʿAbduh which lay particular stress on his attempts to introduce changes in this institution during his own lifetime. Three biographies written in this time were born out of the need to use ʿAbduh's prestige in support of reforms at al-Azhar. ʿAbd al-Munʿim Hamada penned the second comprehensive biography on ʿAbduh[101] and also follows Rida's objective in buttressing his commitment to a Sunni revival and using him as a precursor of the Salafi movement. ʿUthman Amin's and Mustafa ʿAbd al-Raziq's biographies are not as complete as those of Rida and Hamada and focus on ʿAbduh's endeavour to reform al-Azhar particularly.[102] That 'Abd al-Raziq published his biography when he became rector of al-Azhar in 1945 shows how he used 'Abduh's fame for his own agenda.[103] All three biographies accept Rida's *Ta'rīkh* as a model text and often reproduce Rida's narrative *verbatim*, adding their own observations and interpretations.

Other important sources of information on the life of 'Abduh are the memoirs of his friend Wilfrid Scawen Blunt (1840–1922) and of the British consul-governor in Egypt Earl of Cromer (1841–1917).[104] Unlike 'Abduh's Egyptian biographers, Blunt and Cromer, two British diplomats of different kinds, belonged to the same age group as 'Abduh and claimed to have had a good rapport with him. The Arabophile Blunt was a champion of the independence of Egypt and other Middle Eastern countries from foreign occupation. Cromer stands politically at the other end of the spectrum from Blunt as supporter of British colonial interests in the Middle East and as governor of Egypt but, like Blunt, he entertained a good relationship with 'Abduh. Being disinterested in buttressing 'Abduh's adherence to Sunni Islam as religious reformer, Blunt and Cromer provide good insights into 'Abduh's political activities and difficult relationship with the political and religious establishment in Egypt which his later biographers either neglected or obscured.

The most comprehensive collection of 'Abduh's works has been undertaken by the Egyptian scholar Muhammad 'Imara (1931–2020) which includes his writings and other material such as letters and journalistic pieces.[105] 'Imara excluded, however, 'Abduh's earliest works like, his mystical treatise *Risālat al-Wāridāt* (Treatise on Mystical Inspirations)[106] and his philosophical commentary on a medieval Islamic catechism, *Sharḥ al-'Aqā'id al-'Aḍudiyya* (Commentary on the Catechism of 'Adud al-Din al-Iji).[107] For 'Imara, both works were not authored by him but by his teacher Afghani. 'Imara provides two main reasons why 'Abduh could not have penned both works but just acted as a scribe taking notes of Afghani's teaching sessions. The *Risālat al-Wāridāt*, unlike 'Abduh's other writings at that time, is not written in rhyme prose (*saj'*). In addition, this mystical treatise as well as the more extensive theological commentary exhibit a thorough understanding of different and complex theological and philosophical debates in Islam. For a young Azhari student like 'Abduh who had just been taught for four years by Afghani, it would have been impossible to produce works of such insight and complexity, as 'Imara suggests.[108] 'Imara's ideological approach in framing biographies has been noted elsewhere which weakens his stylistic and intellectual arguments against 'Abduh's authorship.[109] According to Haddad, he follows Rida by excluding works attributed to 'Abduh that compromise his apparent adherence to Sunni notions of orthodoxy.[110] For 'Imara, both works contradict in many theological respects his later *Risālat al-Tawḥīd*. For him, these contradictions can only be resolved by questioning ʿAbduh's authorship.[111]

Questions around ʿAbduh's authorship of these early works are legitimate for a number of reasons, however.[112] It was not uncommon for Afghani to instruct his disciples and associates to publish his own material under their names. In Cairo, ʿAbduh became one of 'his two scribes (*kātibayhī*)'[113] and published articles containing Afghani's ideas which he further redacted. As ʿAbduh assumed the role of Afghani's mouthpiece in his early journalistic articles, it is not unlikely that he also acted as his scribe for his mystical, philosophical and theological teaching sessions. The Iranian editor of Afghani's complete works, Hadi Khosroshahi (1938–2020), points to a letter Afghani's other Egyptian scribe, Ibrahim al-Laqqani, sent to him in 1874 returning a copy of the *Risālat al-Wāridāt* 'to its author'.[114] This provides sufficient evidence for Khosroshahi that Afghani was the author of this work to include it in his collection of his writings. Further evidence for Afghani's and not ʿAbduh's authorship of the theological commentary on the *Sharḥ al-ʿAqāʾid al-ʿAḍudiyya* are the inclusion of Persian words which ʿAbduh would not have known and never used in his other writings.[115]

It is certainly true that ʿAbduh took notes of Afghani's teaching sessions and redacted his writings. In this sense, both early works are records of them. To argue these writings do not contain ʿAbduh's original ideas or even his own theological points of view is however misleading. These books contain mystical, philosophical and theological views that were central to his intellectual formation and steered him towards Islamic reform. They were part of his convictions in that period of life. The attempt to exclude these works from his oeuvre illustrates how the image of ʿAbduh as a Salafi reformer who adhered to Sunni notions of orthodoxy has become widely accepted to an extent that his immersion in Sufism and Islamic philosophy had to be explained away as it contradicts this image. Such a restrictive reading of ʿAbduh ignores Islam's culture of ambiguity with its different epistemic registers and discursive genres in which a scholar like ʿAbduh as his pre-modern forebearers manoeuvred comfortably without concern for intellectual consistency and for conformity to narrow definitions of orthodoxy. ʿAbduh agreed to these works being attributed to him throughout his life. He requested Rida to publish the *Risālat al-Wāridāt* in 1904 and claimed authorship for this work when this was done. Equally, the theological commentary was published under his name posthumously. This gives evidence that he wanted to be associated with these works and with the ideas they expounded – very much to Rida's consternation.[116] That ʿAbduh provided instructions and made arrangements for their publications also suggests that he felt they were still relevant to his own intellectual work. A scholar who wanted his intellectual legacy to be steered away from the mystical and philosophical approaches that characterize these works would not have deliberately sought their publications. As the further discussion in the book indicates, concepts and tropes that are visible in these early works also re-emerge and are re-articulated in his theological and apologetic writings later in his life.

Chapter outline

The different chapters of the book follow the chronology of Muhammad 'Abduh's biography. Each chapter contextualizes his activities and writings in the different periods of his life and provides a detailed discussion of key literary outputs. Chapter 2 covers his initial intellectual formation from his encounter with traditional modes of instruction at the mosque school in Tanta and later at al-Azhar in Cairo. He found in Sufism a refuge and later aligned himself with Afghani who gave his mystical leanings philosophical depth. This chapter also includes a detailed discussion of his two earliest writings, the mystical treatise *Risālat al-Wāridāt* (Treatise on Mystical Inspirations) and the philosophical commentary on the *Sharḥ al-'Aqā'id al-'Aḍudiyya* (Commentary on the Catechism of 'Adud al-Din al-Iji). 'Abduh's foray into public life of Egypt in the 1870s is discussed in Chapter 3. He became part of a new cosmopolitan intelligentsia in Egypt that contributed to the nascent Egypt press and discussed modern notions of civilization, progress, nationalism and constitutionalism in their circles and their journalistic pieces. 'Abduh became a key figure in Egypt shaping discourses as editor-in-chief of the governmental *al-Waqā'i' al-Miṣriyya* (The Egyptian Events). He also observed the increasing colonial intrusion of European powers and supported the 'Urabi Revolution of 1881 that challenged both autocratic rule in Egypt and foreign dependency. After the failure of the revolution and the British occupation of the country in 1882, 'Abduh was forced into exile.

His activities in exile in Paris and Beirut are covered in Chapter 4. He joined his teacher Afghani in Paris and published with him the anti-British journal *al-'Urwa al-Wuthqā* (The Firmest Bond) in 1884. Despite its short life, the journal was highly influential in reconceptualizing Islam as an anti-imperialist ideology and setting the contours of Pan-Islamism. 'Abduh moved to Beirut in 1885 and became involved in various educational activities and engaged with a variety of scholars and intellectual of a diverse range of religious and sectarian backgrounds. In 1888, 'Abduh was allowed to return in Egypt. Chapter 5 illustrates how 'Abduh re-entered Egyptian public life and assumed various influential roles as member of the consultative assembly and of the administrative council implementing reforms at al-Azhar and finally as grand mufti of Egypt. 'Abduh used these various public political, religious and educational roles to present a new type of activist scholar who engages with the practical needs of modern Muslim societies and supports state-led efforts to institutionalize Islamic public life.

Chapter 6 includes a discussion of key works 'Abduh produced in the final fifteen years of his life: his *Risālat al-Tawḥīd*, his apologetic journalistic pieces and his Qur'an commentaries *Tafsīr al-Manār*, which he published together with Rida, and his little known *Tafsīr Juz' 'Amma*. These works have been usually used to point at 'Abduh's Salafi approach or to present him as an Islamic modernist who sought to harmonize Sunni theology with modernity. However, their detailed discussion will illustrate how he synthesizes very different intellectual traditions to embed Islam doctrinally in the modern world and to prove to their readers that one can be modern and Muslim at the same time – not because of a simplistic identification of modern concepts within the Islamic tradition but because of the inherent capaciousness of Islamic thought. The conclusion then discusses 'Abduh's contested legacy. His disciples had to deal with the contradictions, inconsistencies and ambiguities of his intellectual legacy. In an age where such ambiguities were less tolerated, they decided to resolve them by disambiguating his ideas and taking them into their own directions.

* * *

This book does not intend to attach a label to 'Abduh – new or old – but argues that describing him as a Salafi, even in conjunction with the epithet 'modernist', evokes too restrictive associations. It suggests a strict scripturalism and an effort to restore an essentialized Islam as it was practised by the first generations of Muslims. It is based on the assumption that 'Abduh believed that pristine Islam – contained in its scriptural sources and embodied by early Islam – is somehow in harmony with the values that shaped the modern world in the nineteenth century. Calling 'Abduh an Islamic modernist equally falls short. The modernist label purports that either he was merely a passive recipient of modern ideas which he sought to integrate into an Islamic worldview or he translated modern intellectual paradigms into an essentialized understanding of Islam. However, 'Abduh was a more complex thinker. This book does not deny the novelty of the cultural, intellectual, social and political challenges 'Abduh and his generation of Muslim reformers faced which required creative and innovate approaches to indigenize modern intellectual paradigms into Islam. He knew, however, that indigenizing modernity in Muslim societies cannot be achieved by scripturalism or nostalgia for the past. To create an alternative modernity that was Islamic, the rich and diverse spectrum of pre-modern intellectual heritage of Islam had to be mobilized and synthesized. This was an intellectual tradition that had developed strategies to manage contradictions, to cope with inconsistencies and to live with ambiguities and therefore allowed for a selective appropriation and re-interpretation of its heritage and its multi-faceted articulation in different idioms, depending who one seeks to address. By rediscovering these traditions and combining them successfully, – 'Abduh suggests – Muslims would be intellectually and culturally equipped to find their place in the modern world. His efforts to achieve this synthesis contain their own contradictions, inconsistencies and ambiguities, as this book equally illustrates.

Notes

1 Fazlur Rahman, *Prophecy in Islam: Philosophy and Orthodoxy* (London: George Allen & Unwin, 1958), 94.

2 Ibid., 98.

3 Ibid.

4 Ibid., 95.

5 Albert Hourani, *Arabic Thought in the Liberal Age: 1798–1939* (Cambridge: Cambridge University Press, 1983), 142.

6 Ibid., 143. See also Nasr Hamid Abu Zayd, 'The Dilemma of the Literary Approach to the Qur'an', *Alif: Journal of Comparative Poetics*, 23 (2003): 39–40.

7 Hourani, *Arabic Thought*, 144–5.

8 Ahmad S. Dallal, 'Review: Ghazali and the Perils of Interpretation', *Journal of the American Oriental Society*, 122(4) (2002): 773–4.

9 Elie Kedourie, *Afghani and 'Abduh: An Essay on Religious Unbelief and Political Activism in Modern Islam* (London: Frank Cass, 1966), 14.

10 Muhammad Rashid Rida, *Ta'rīkh al-Ustādh al-Imām al-Shaykh Muḥammad 'Abduh*, 3 vols (Cairo: al-Manar, 1924–31).

11 'The best people are those of my generation, then those who come after them, then those who come after them.'

12 The French Orientalist Louis Massignon was probably the first to coin the term 'Salafiyya' and included 'Abduh as one of its main representatives. See Henri

Lauzière, *The Making of Salafism: Islamic Reform in the Twentieth Century* (New York: Columbia University Press, 2016), 37–9.

13 Ibid., 4–6. See also Wlliam E. Shepard, 'Islam and Ideology: Towards a Typology', *International Journal of Middle East Studies*, 19 (1987): 311–14.

14 Lauzière, *The Making of Salafism*, 37–9.

15 Charles C. Adams, *Islam and Modernism in Egypt: A Study of the Modern Reform Movement Inaugurated by Muhammad 'Abduh* (London: Oxford University Press, 1933). Sedgwick produced a very brief introduction to 'Abduh's life useful for non-specialist readers. See Mark Sedgwick, *Muhammad Abduh* (Oxford: Oneworld, 2010).

16 Ignaz Golziher conflated both 'Abduh and Rida and gave their reform movement the designation 'cultural Wahhabism'. See Ignaz Goldziher, *Schools of Koranic Commentators* (Wiesbaden: Otto Harrassowitz, 2006), 204.

17 Adams, *Islam and Modernism*, 111.

18 Jacques Jomier, *Le Commentaire Coranique du Manâr: tendances modernes de l'exégèse en Egypte* (Paris: Maisonneuve, 1954).

19 Malcolm H. Kerr, *Islamic Reform: The Legal and Political Theories of Muhammad 'Abduh and Rashid Rida* (Berkeley: University of California Press, 1966); Y. Seferta, 'The Concept of Religious Authority According to Muhammad 'Abduh and Rashid Ridha', *Islamic Quarterly*, 30 (1986): 159–64.

20 Mohamed Haddad, 'Les Oeuvres de 'Abduh: histoire d'une manipulation', *Revue de l'Institut des Belles Lettres Arabes*, 180 (1997): 197–222.

21 Homa Pakdaman, *Djamal-El-Din Assad Abadi dit Afghani* (Paris: Maisonneuve, 1969); Nikki R. Keddie, *Sayyid Jamāl ad-Dīn 'al-Afghānī': A Political Biography* (Berkeley: University of California Press, 1972).

22 These letters have been reprinted in 'Ali Shalash, *Silsilat al-A'māl al-Majhūla Muḥammad 'Abduh* (London: Riad al-Rayyes, 1987), 43–55.

23 Kedourie, *Afghani and 'Abduh*, 66–9.

24 Mohamed Haddad, 'Les Oeuvres de 'Abduh'; Mohamed Haddad, "Abduh et ses lecteurs: pour in histoire critique de "lectures" de Muhammad 'Abduh', *Arabica*, 45 (1998): 22–49; Mohamed Haddad, 'Relire Muhammad Abduh (à propos de l'article "M. Abduh" dans l'Encyclopédie de l'Islam)', *Revue de l'Institut des Belles Lettres Arabes*, 185 (2000): 61–84.

25 Mohamed Haddad, *Muḥammad 'Abduh: Qarā'a Jadīda fī Khiṭāb al-Iṣlāḥ al-Dīnī* (Beirut: Dar al-Tali'a li-l-Taba'a wa-l-Nashr, 2003).

26 Anke von Kügelgen, "Abduh, Muḥammad', in *Encyclopaedia of Islam, THREE*, ed. Kate Fleet, Gudrun Krämer, Denis Matringe, John Nawas and Everett Rowson, http://dx.doi.org/10.1163/1573-3912_ei3_COM_0103.

27 Sedgwick, *Abduh*, 124.

28 Oliver Scharbrodt, *Islam and the Baha'i Faith: A Comparative Study of Muhammad 'Abduh and 'Abdul-Baha' 'Abbas* (London: Routledge, 2008).

29 Samira Haj, *Reconfiguring Islamic Tradition: Reform, Rationality, and Modernity* (Stanford: Stanford University Press, 2009), 1–6. For more detailed discussion, see Armando Salvatore, 'Tradition and Modernity within Islamic Civilisation and the West', in *Islam and Modernity: Key Issues and Debates*, ed. Muhammad Khalid Masud, Armando Salvatore and Martin van Bruinessen (Edinburgh: Edinburgh University Press, 2009), 36–53; Muhammad Khalid Masud and Armando Salvatore, 'Western Scholars of Islam on the Issue of Modernity', in *Islam and Modernity: Key Issues and Debates*, ed. Muhammad Khalid Masud, Armando Salvatore and Martin van Bruinessen (Edinburgh: Edinburgh University Press, 2009), 36–53.

30 Ahmad S. Dallal, *Islam without Europe: Traditions of Reform in Eighteenth Century Islamic Thought* (Chapel Hill: University of North Caroline Press, 2018).

31 Haj, *Reconfiguring Islamic Tradition*, 7–9.

32 Johann Buessow, 'Re-imagining Islam in the Period of the First Modern Globalization: Muhammad 'Abduh and His *Theology of Unity*', in *A Global Middle East: Mobility, Materiality and Culture in the Modern Age, 1880*–1940, ed. Liat Kozma, Cyrus Schayegh and Avner Wishnitzer (London: I.B. Tauris, 2015), 303.

33 Monica M. Ringer, *Islamic Modernism and the Re-enchantment of the Sacred in the Age of History* (Edinburgh: Edinburgh University Press, 2020), 29.

34 Dietrich Jung, 'Islamic Reform and the Global Public Sphere: Muhammad Abduh and Islamic Modernity', in *The Middle East and Globalization: Encounters and Horizons*, ed. Stephan Stetter (New York: Palgrave Macmillan, 2012), 153–69; Ammeke Kateman, *Muḥammad 'Abduh and His Interlocutors: Conceptualizing Religion in a Globalizing World* (Leiden: Brill, 2019); Joachim Langner, 'Religion in Motion and the Essence of Islam: Manifestations of the Global in Muhammad 'Abduh's Response to Farah Antūn', in *A Global Middle East: Mobility, Materiality and Culture in the Modern Age, 1880*–1940, ed. Liat Kozma, Cyrus Schayegh and Avner Wishnitzer (London: I.B. Tauris, 2015), 356–63; Dyala Hamzah, 'Pensée d'Abduh à l'âge utiliaire: l'intérêt general entre maṣlaḥa et manfa'a', in *Modernités islamiques: Actes du colloque organisé à Alep à l'occasion du centenaire de la disparition de l'imam Muḥammad 'Abduh, 9–10 novembre 2005*, ed. Maher Al-Charif and Sabrina Mervin (Damascus: IFPO, 2006).

35 Buessow, 'Re-imagining Islam', 303; Dietrich Jung, *Orientalists, Islamists and the Global Public Sphere: A Genealogy of the Modern Essentialist Image of Islam* (Sheffield: Equinox, 2011).

36 Buessow, 'Re-imagining Islam', 274. Ringer also acknowledges that scholarship needs to engage more with the diversity of Islamic traditions modern Muslim reformers considered. See Ringer, *Islamic Modernism*, 176–7.

37 Shahab Ahmed, *What Is Islam?: The Importance of Being Islamic* (Princeton: Princeton University Press, 2016), 176–97.

38 Thomas Bauer, *Die Kultur der Ambiguität: Eine andere Geschichte des Islams* (Berlin: Verlag der Weltreligionen, 2011), 376–405.
39 Adams, *Islamic and Modernism*, 112.
40 Kateman, *Muḥammad ʿAbduh and His Interlocutors*, 244, and for more general remarks on the engagement of Muslim reformers with their own tradition Ringer, *Islamic Modernism*, 176–7.
41 Haddad, *Qarāʾa Jadīda*, 15.
42 Ahmed, *What Is Islam?*, 117–29.
43 Ibid., 176–211.
44 Bauer, *Kultur der Ambiguität.*
45 Thomas Bauer, *A Culture of Ambiguity: An Alternative History of Islam* (New York: Columbia University Press, 2021).
46 Ahmed, *What Is Islam?*
47 Bauer, *Kultur der Ambiguität*, 41–53.
48 Ibid., 192–223.
49 Ahmed, *What Is Islam?*, 303 [emphasis in the original].
50 Ibid., 345 [emphasis in the original].
51 Ibid., 346.
52 Ibid., 357 [emphasis in the original].
53 Ibid., 367–86.
54 Ibid., 379–81.
55 Bauer, *Kultur der Ambiguität*, 249.
56 Ibid., 194; Ahmed, *What Is Islam?*, n. 6, 409–10.
57 Ahmed, *What Is Islam?*, 57–71.
58 For Ahmed's critique of this binary, see ibid., 197–211.
59 Bauer equally suggests that divide between the religious and the secular is not relevant to Islam historically. See Bauer, *Kultur der Ambiguität*, 199–203.
60 Ahmed, *What Is Islam?*, 538 [emphasis in the original].
61 Bauer, *Kultur der Ambiguität*, 385–405; Ahmed, *What Is Islam?*, 514–37.
62 Alexander Knysh, '*Irfan* Revisited: Khomeini and the Legacy of Islamic Mystical Philosophy', *Middle East Journal*, 46(4) (1992): 631–53; Lloyd Ridgeon, 'Hidden Khomeini: Mysticism and Poetry', in *A Critical Introduction to Khomeini*, ed. Arshin Adib-Moghaddam (Cambridge: Cambridge University Press, 2014), 193–210.
63 John Calvert, *Sayyid Qutb and the Origins of Radical Islamism* (London: Hurst, 2010).
64 Adnan A. Musallam, 'Prelude to Islamic Commitment: Sayyid Quṭb's Literary and Spiritual Orientation, 1932–1938', *The Muslim World*, 80 (1990): 176–89.
65 Muhammad Rashid Rida, 'Mulakhkhaṣ Sīrat al-Ustādh al-Imām', *al-Manār*, 8 (1905): 390; Adams, *Islamic and Modernism*, 114.
66 Rida, *Taʾrīkh al-Ustādh al-Imām al-Shaykh Muḥammad ʿAbduh*, vol. 1 (Cairo: al-Manar, 1931), 126.

67 Al-Ghazali, *Freedom and Fulfilment: An Annotated Translation of Al-Ghazali's al-Munqidh min al-dalal and Other Relevant Works of al-Ghazali by Richard Joseph McCarthy* (Boston: Twayne, 1980), 106–7.

68 Hava Lazarus-Yafeh, 'Tajdid al-Din: A Reconsideration of Its Meaning, Roots, and Influence in Islam', in *Studies in Islamic and Judaic Traditions: Papers Presented at the Institute for Islamic-Judaic Studies*, ed. William. M. Brunner and Stephen David Ricks (Atlanta: Scholars Press, 1986), 103; Ella Landau-Tasseron, 'The "Cyclical Reform": A Study of the *Mujaddid* Tradition', *Studia Islamica*, 70 (1989): 86.

69 John O. Voll, "Renewal and Reform in Islamic History: *Tajdid* and *Islah*', in *Voices of Resurgent Islam*, ed. John L. Esposito (New York: Oxford University Press, 1983), 32–47.

70 Rida, *Ta'rīkh*, vol. 1, 974.

71 Ibid.

72 Ibid.

73 Ibid.

74 Michel Chodkiewicz, *Seal of the Saints: Prophethood and Sainthood in the Doctrine of Ibn 'Arabi* (Cambridge: The Islamic Texts Society, 1993), 74–88.

75 Ibid., 147–73; Bernd Radtke, and John O'Kane, *The Concept of Sainthood in Early Islamic Mysticism: Two Works by Al-Ḥakīm Al-Tirmidhī* (London: Curzon, 1996), 101–11.

76 A prominent example is the South Asian Naqshbandi Sufi scholar Ahmad Sirhindi (1564–1624) who combined the claim to be the renewer of Islam in its second millennium (*mujaddid-i alf-i thānī*) with access to quasi-prophetic revelations. See Yohanan Friedmann *Shaykh Aḥmad Sirhindī: An Outline of His Thought and a Study of His Image in the Eyes of Posterity*, 2nd edn (New Delhi: Oxford University Press, 2001).

77 Afghani wrote down this personal note in Herat, Afghanistan, in 1866. See Iraj Afshar and Asghar Mahdawi, eds, *Majmū'a-yi Asnād wa-Madārik Chāp Nashuda Dar Barā-yi Sayyid Jamāl al-Dīn Mashhūr Ba Afghānī* (Tehran: University of Tehran, 1963), folio 1, images 1, 2 and 4. See also Keddie, *'al-Afghānī'*, 38. I would like to thank Mostafa Movahedifar for his assistance in transcribing the handwritten Persian note.

78 Henri Corbin, *En Islam iranien: Aspects spirituels et philosophiques*, vol. 4 (Paris: Gallimard, 1973), 205–6. For an overview of possible sources of Shaykh Ahmad's thought see Armin Eschraghi, *Frühe Šaiḫī- und Bābī Theologie: Die Darlegung des Beweises für Muhammads besonderes Prophetentum* (Ar-Risāla fī Iṯbāt an-Nubūwa al-Ḫāssa) (Leiden: Brill, 2004), 13–19. For a discussion of Shaykh Ahmad's attitude towards Sufism see Juan R. I. Cole, 'Individualism and the Spiritual Path in Shaykh Ahmad al-Ahsa'i', *Occasional Papers in Shaykhi, Babi and Baha'i Studies*, 1 (1997). http://www.h-net.org/~bahai/bhpapers/ahsaind.htm (accessed 6 May 2021).

79 Keddie, *'al-Afghānī'*, 38
80 Pakdaman, *Afghani*, 357–61; Keddie, *'al-Afghānī'*, 406; Mangol Bayat, *Mysticism and Dissent: Socioreligious Thought in Qajar Iran* (Syracuse: Syracuse University Press, 1999), 145.
81 Eschraghi, *Šaiẖī- und Bābī Theologie*, 77–9.
82 Fazlur Rahman, *The Philosophy of Mulla Sadra* (Albany: State University of New York Press, 1975), 94–108. For a discussion of Shaykh Ahmad's cosmologies, see Juan R. I. Cole, 'The World as a Text: Cosmologies of Shaykh Ahmad al-Ahsa'i', *Studia Islamica*, 80 (1994): 1–23; Eschraghi, *Šaiẖī- und Bābī Theologie*, 56–9.
83 Bayat, *Mysticism and Dissent*, 52–4.
84 Nikki R. Keddie, 'Symbol and Sincerity in Islam', *Studia Islamica*, 19 (1963): 46–63.
85 Dale F. Eickelman, 'Traditional Islamic Learning and Ideas of the Person in the Twentieth Century', in *Middle Eastern Lives: The Practice of Biography and Self-Narrative*, ed. Martin Kramer (Syracuse: Syracuse University Press, 1991), 39–40. On the tendency to downplay individuality in biographical dictionaries, see Dwight F. Reynolds, ed., *Interpreting the Self: Autobiography in the Arabic Literary Tradition* (Berkeley: University of California Press, 2001), 40–3.
86 Marilyn R. Waldman, *Toward a Theory of Historical Narrative: A Case Study in Perso-Islamicate Historiography* (Columbus: Ohio State University Press, 1980), 10–12.
87 Eickelman, 'Traditional Islamic Learning', 41.
88 Bernard Lewis, 'First-Person Narrative in the Middle East', in *Middle Eastern Lives: The Practice of Biography and Self-Narrative*, ed. Martin Kramer (Syracuse: Syracuse University Press, 1991), 34; Reynolds, *Interpreting the Self*, 38–40.
89 Waldman, *Historical Narrative*, 15.
90 Reynolds, *Interpreting the Self*, 242.
91 Sholeh A. Quinn, *Historical Writing during the Reign of Shah 'Abbas: Ideology, Imitation, and Legitimacy in Safavid Chronicles* (Salt Lake City: University of Utah Press, 2000), 141–2.
92 Tahir Tanahi, ed., *Mudhakkirāt al-Imām Muḥammad 'Abduh* (Cairo: Dar al-Hilal, n.d.).
93 Muhammad Rashid Rida, 'Mulakhkhaṣ Sīrat al-Ustādh al-Imām', *al-Manār*, 8 (1905), part 10: 379–400; part 11: 401–16; part 12: 453–65; part 13: 487–95; part 14: 534–52; part 15: 597–9.
94 Rida, *Ta'rīkh*, vol. 1–3.
95 Tannahi, *Mudhakkirāt 'Abduh*, 6–7.
96 Rida, *Ta'rīkh*, vol. 1, 1–2.
97 See Kedourie, *Afghani and 'Abduh*, 6; Shalash, *Silsilat al-A'māl 'Abduh*, 7–14; Haddad, 'Les oeuvre de 'Abduh', 197–222; Haddad, ''Abduh et ses lecteurs', 22–49.

98 Rida acknowledges the assistance of 'Abduh's lifelong associates in compiling the biography in order to increase its reliability and authenticity. See Rida, *Ta'rīkh*, vol. 1, 2.

99 According to Rida, he published the biography rather late, as he felt its publication would only be opportune after the British had ended their colonial rule over Egypt. See ibid., 4.

100 Haddad, "Abduh et ses lecteurs', 24–9.

101 'Abd al-Mun'im Hamada, *al-Ustādh al-Imām Muḥammad 'Abduh* (Cairo: al-Maktaba al-Tijariyya, 1945).

102 'Uthman Amin, *Muḥammad 'Abduh* (Cairo: Dar Ajya' al-Kutub al-'Arabiyya, 1944).

103 Haddad, "Abduh et ses lecteurs', 41.

104 Wilfrid S. Blunt, *Secret History of the English Occupation of Egypt: Being a Personal Narrative of Events*, 2nd edn (London: Fisher Unwin, 1907); Evelyn Baring, Earl of Cromer, *Modern Egypt*, vols 1–2 (London: Macmillan, 1908).

105 Muhammad 'Imara, ed., *al-A'māl al-Kāmila li-l-Imām Muḥammad 'Abduh*, 5 vols (Beirut: Dar al-Shuruq, 1972–3).

106 Muhammad 'Abduh, *Risālat al-Wāridāt: fī Naẓariyyāt al-Mutakallimīn wa-l-Ṣūfiyya fī-l-Falsafa al-Ilāhiyya*, 2nd edn (Cairo: al-Manar, 1925).

107 Sulayman Dunya, ed., *al-Shaykh Muḥammad 'Abduh bayna-l-Falāsifa wa-l-Kalāmiyīn*, vols 1–2 (Cairo: 'Isa al-Babi al-Halabi, 1958).

108 Muhammad 'Imara, 'al-Muqaddima', in *al-Ta'līqāt 'alā Sharḥ al-'Aqā'id al-'Aḍudiyya*, Jamal al-Din al-Afghani and Muhammad 'Abduh (Cairo: Maktabat al-Shuruq al-Duwwaliyya, 2002), 15–23.

109 Rudi Matthee, 'Jamal al-Din al-Afghani and the Egyptian National Debate', *International Journal of Middle East Studies* 21, no. 2 (1989): 156–9.

110 Haddad, *Qarā'a Jadīda*, 68–9.

111 'Imara, 'al-Muqaddima', 16.

112 Rotraud Wielandt, 'Main Trends of Islamic Theological Thought from the Late Nineteenth Century to Present Times', in *The Oxford Handbook of Islamic Theology*, ed. Sabine Schmidtke (Oxford: Oxford University Press, 2016), 716–19.

113 Salim 'Anhuri, *Siḥr Hārūt* (Damascus: al-Matba'a al-Hanafiyya, 1885), 180.

114 Hadi Khosroshahi, 'al-Muqaddima', in *al-A'māl al-Kāmila li-Jamāl al-Dīn al-Afghānī*, vol. 2, ed. Hadi Khosroshahi (Tehran: al-Majma' al-'Alami li-l-Taqrib bayna-l-Madhahib al-Islamiyya, 2000), 9.

115 'Imara, 'al-Muqaddima', 28–30.

116 Rida added to the second edition of the treatise a Sunni catechism penned by 'Abduh and changed its title to suggest that 'Abduh merely presented views of mystical philosophy without adopting them. See Haddad, *Qarā'a Jadīda*, 68.

2

Early formation: ʿAbduh's mystical turn

Introduction

A common motif in Muslim autobiographical writing revolves around crisis and resolution.[1] The young scholar or adept experiences a spiritual crisis being dissatisfied with the state of knowledge transmitted to him or his spiritual constitution and is close to abandoning the scholarly or spiritual path he hoped to follow. However, the accidental encounter with a charismatic figure or a key text responds to the young adept's yearning for an alternative vision of knowledge or religiosity and guides the initially disillusioned disciple to an approach which constitutes his later fame and reputation. Sufism often holds a prominent place in solving the young scholar's intellectual and spiritual crisis. Al-Ghazali and his autobiographical *Al-Munqidh min al-Ḍalāl* (The Deliverer from Error)[2] is the paradigmatic example of this convention of Muslim biographical writing which is also evident in an autobiographical fragment of ʿAbduh's teacher Afghani who experienced a similar crisis, being frustrated with the traditionalism of religious scholars he studied with. Afghani turned to mystical philosophy, as articulated in the texts of the Shaykhi School that attracted him because of their philosophical foundation and intellectual dynamism.[3]

Given the prevalence of this motif of crisis and resolution, it is not surprising to find it in ʿAbduh's own autobiographical vignettes in which he equally articulates his frustration with his initial scholarly training. However, his exposure to Sufism and its reformist tendencies in particular which had become prominent in his time positioned him critically towards religious traditionalism and allowed him to articulate his opposition to an imitative approach towards the scholarly traditions of Islam. The second more crucial step in ʿAbduh's intellectual formation was his encounter with Afghani who remained a central figure in the first half of his life. He gave ʿAbduh's reformist Sufi inclinations more philosophical depth and, as a trained Shii scholar himself, introduced him to intellectual traditions of Islam that had been marginalized in mainstream Sunni thought.

The mystical, philosophical and theological instructions by Afghani that encouraged an intellectual engagement with European thought laid the foundation of 'Abduh's reformist intellectual oeuvre. By providing a discussion of the first two scholarly works by 'Abduh – his mystical *Risālat al-Wāridāt* (Treatise on Mystical Inspirations) and his theological-cum-philosophical commentary on a medieval catechism, *Sharḥ al-'Aqā'id al-'Aḍudiyya* (Commentary on the Catechism of 'Adud al-Din al-Iji) – this chapter redresses a tendency in academic scholarship that overlooks 'Abduh's early mystical and philosophical writings. This disregard reflects a wider tendency in Islamic Studies to consider philosophy and Sufism as entertaining a precarious relationship to Islamic 'orthodoxy'. As articulations of Islamic religiosity, deemed marginal or deviant, they are positioned at the periphery of what mainstream Islam is.[4] Such presuppositions have also shaped scholarly approaches to 'Abduh's intellectual output by questioning his authorship of these works or representing his Sufi immersion as an adolescent phase in his life which was superseded by his later more prominent mature works in which he rediscovered orthodoxy.[5] This chapter argues on the contrary that his early works contain an engagement with central philosophical and theological themes and their intellectual sources which shaped 'Abduh's intellectual trajectory throughout his life. These themes and sources are crucial to understanding his reformist approach to Islam and his efforts to articulate an Islamic response to debates around modernity, progress and development in his later writings.[6]

The reluctant scholar

Muhammad 'Abduh was born into a peasant family from Lower Egypt in 1849. He was probably born near Tanta[7] but he grew up in the village of Mahallat Nasr in the Buhayra region which is located in the north-western part of Lower Egypt, after his father had settled there. His father had to adopt an itinerant lifestyle from the age of fourteen when 'Abduh's grandfather had to leave his village after being discredited to the local authorities for having given refuge to a number of men who have fled from another village, probably escaping the forced labour regime (*corvée*). The Egyptian ruler at that time, Muhammad 'Ali (1769–1849) initiated significant agricultural reforms which also included conscripting farmers for infrastructural projects or the army.[8] It was not uncommon for farmers to escape conscription by moving from one village to another.[9] 'Abduh's father was of Turcoman origin while his mother's family claimed descent from the second caliph 'Umar ibn al-Khattab – a genealogy 'Abduh himself was doubtful about.[10]

Despite his humble background, his father managed to do well in the village, could afford to have more than one wife and arranged for the private instruction of his children at home. Therefore, 'Abduh was exposed rather late to the local *maktab* at the age of ten. His parents became aware of their son's talent, as he began to memorize the Qur'an at that age, and, in 1862, sent him to the mosque school in Tanta to study the recitation of the Qur'an under the auspices of one of his maternal uncles.[11] Due to his parents' support, 'Abduh was able to seize the opportunity for the gifted sons of rural Egypt to leave their social background and use a religious education as means for further social mobility.

After two years of studying the Qur'an in Tanta, he began attending lectures on grammar and Islamic law. At this stage, 'Abduh encountered for the first time the inefficiency of traditional teaching methods. His description of the learning environment at the *madrasa* is quite similar to experiences of many of contemporaries who encountered a similar educational culture.[12] Students were confronted with grammatical and legal treatises and dubious technical terms while the teachers did not take into account their students' intellectual capacity and refused to answer any questions. The only requirement for passing exams consisted in memorizing textbooks without any intrinsic understanding of their contents. 'Abduh, who was incapable of understanding the texts and subjects dealt with in the lectures and lacked anybody who could assist him in comprehending them, considered himself to be incompetent to pursue such studies and withdrew from them:

> I did not understand anything because of the deficient teaching methods. The teachers confronted us with grammatical and legal technical terms which we did not understand. They were not concerned with explaining their meanings to those who did not know them. Therefore, resignation reached me. I fled the lessons and disappeared for three months.[13]

His father forced him to return to Tanta and to continue his studies. However, 'Abduh fled again and retreated to a nearby village where Shaykh Darwish al-Khadir, his paternal great-uncle, approached 'Abduh. Because of his bad eyesight, he asked him to read some of the letters Sayyid Muhammad ibn Hamza al-Madani (1780–1847) wrote to his son, the shaykh of the Shadhili Sufi order (*ṭarīqa*), Muhammad Zafir al-Madani (d. 1904):[14]

> I rejected his request with vigour and cursed reading books. Whoever occupies himself with it, I shun with great distaste. When he put the book in my hand, I threw it away. But the shaykh smiled and showed the kindest forbearance. He did not cease insisting until I took the book and read some lines from it. Then, he immediately explained the meaning of what I just read in clear words which defeated my initial rejection. They conquered and entered my soul.[15]

For several days, 'Abduh studied the letters with Shaykh Darwish and discussed with him terms and subjects he did not understand. These letters were concerned with the spiritual development of the soul, its moral education, its purification and detachment from the superficialities of this world and introduced 'Abduh to Sufism:

> On the seventh day, I asked the shaykh: 'What is your *ṭarīqa*?' He replied: 'Islam is my *ṭarīqa*.' I asked: 'But are not all these people Muslims?' He said: 'If they were Muslims, you would not see them contending over trivial matters and would not hear them swearing by God while they are lying with or without a reason.' These words were like fire which burned away all that I held dear of the baggage from the past.[16]

According to 'Abduh, the words of his uncle made him aware of the captivity of Muslims in religious traditionalism and offered Sufism as an alternative mode of Islamic religiosity which transcends the limitations of traditional Islamic scholarship.[17]

Sufism was central to both rural and urban religious life in nineteenth-century Egypt as it was in other parts of the Muslim world. 'Abduh was, however, exposed to reformist Sufi tendencies. They had reached Egypt in the early nineteenth century having their origins in North African Sufi orders like the Sanusiyya and Tijaniyya,[18] in particular through the teachings of reformist Sufis like the Moroccan mystic Ahmad ibn Idris (1760–1837).[19] As a student of Muhammad al-Madani and follower of the Shadhili order, Shaykh Darwish would have been linked to Idris as one of his students was al-Madani.[20] Idris rejected any false adherence to past authorities (*taqlīd*) and claimed direct prophetic illuminations of the saint from the Prophet Muhammad. For these Sufis, *ijtihād* was not merely the individual effort of a scholar to arrive at a legal ruling but the prerogative of the Sufi shaykh based on his access to prophetic inspiration.[21]

For Ahmad ibn Idris, Islamic spirituality should revolve solely around the figure of the Prophet Muhammad. Rather than following human authority like a Sufi shaykh or religious scholar, Muslims only owe obedience to the Prophet. Therefore, Ahmad ibn Idris rejected the affiliation to a particular Sufi order (*ṭarīqa*) or the emulation of the legal rulings of a specific legal school (*madhhab*) and promulgated the return to the Qur'an and to the *sunna* of the Prophet as the only true *ṭarīqa* and only valid *madhhab* Muslims should follow. He used the term *ṭarīqa muḥammadiyya* (Path of Muhammad)[22] to designate his Pan-Islamic Sufism and his call for the restoration of the *sunna* of the Prophet. Exoterically it implied a revival of hadith studies, which had occurred throughout the entire Muslim world in the eighteenth century,[23] esoterically the need to constantly visualize the Prophet in order to receive visions and inspirations from him.[24] Rather than basing his authority as a Sufi shaykh on the spiritual genealogy (*silsila*) of a specific order, Ahmad ibn Idris claimed to have been directly initiated by the Prophet himself, as so many other great Sufi shaykhs in the past.[25]

'Abduh's encounter with ideas of early nineteenth-century Sufi reform movements through his uncle Shaykh Darwish managed to resolve his disillusionment with traditional religious scholarship. His depiction of Shaykh Darwish exhibits many features of Sufi reformism. Shaykh Darwish had some preliminary training in different branches of Islamic scholarship and had memorized among other works the *Muwaṭṭaʿ* by Malik ibn Anas (711–795),[26] one of the earliest hadith collections whose study was particularly stressed by contemporaneous Sufis and hadith scholars.[27] Despite his association with the Shadhiliyya Order, he did not insist on his affiliation to it but rather revealed a pan-Islamic Sufism, echoing Idris' *ṭarīqa muḥammadiyya*. Shaykh Darwish urged him to read the Qur'an as both a devotional and a scholarly exercise and to grasp its meaning gradually. Hence, Shaykh Darwish is not depicted as a conservative representative of Sufism, but as one who upheld the importance of mystical experience, stressed an ethical and spiritual reading of Islam but at the same time was open to new intellectual pursuits and intended to overcome the constraints of tradition: 'he is shown to be a pivotal figure in leading the young 'Abduh to a truer understanding of Islam as a progressive and reasonable religion compatible with modern sciences and modern technologies.'[28] Despite their hostility towards traditional Islam and its representatives, Sufi reformers like Ahmad ibn Idris did not attempt to rehabilitate the role of reason in the Islamic tradition.[29] Hence, to what extent Shaykh Darwish instilled in the young 'Abduh a more rational understanding of Islam cannot be ascertained. 'Abduh's emphasis on the rationality of Islam goes more likely back to his later studies of Islamic philosophy under Afghani.

Nevertheless, his exposure to the thought of contemporary Sufi reformers provided the young ʿAbduh with an expression of Islamic religiosity which transcends the traditionalism of the religious establishment and is oriented towards the charismatic authority of the Sufi shaykh. It allowed him to attach himself to a reform movement with a critical stance towards religious traditionalism. For their opponents, consisting of mainstream Sufis and Muslim scholars (*ʿulamāʾ*), followers of the *ṭarīqa muḥammadiyya* movement were seen as heretics who deviated from the established consensus of the Muslim community by rejecting recognized Sufi orders and the canonical schools of law. Sufi reformers acknowledged their conflict with the religious environment in which they lived, since as religious reformers they critiqued the way their contemporaries understood, practised and taught Islam.[30]

In 1866, ʿAbduh moved from Tanta to Cairo to continue his studies at al-Azhar, one of the most prestigious and prominent institutions of Islamic learning in the Sunni world. At al-Azhar, he continued to experience the same frustrations with the repetitive modes of instruction and the limitations of the traditionalist curriculum. However, the continuous support of his uncle who encouraged him to undertake spiritual exercises such AS fasting and reciting Sufi litanies (*dhikr*) allowed ʿAbduh to find a retreat from the repetitive teaching methods he encountered at al-Azhar and, given his own rural background, to adapt to the rapidity of urban life in Cairo. ʿAbduh also taught Sufism and the spiritual exercises he had adopted from his uncle to some of his peers in Cairo.[31]

Shaykh Darwish also encouraged him to study subjects outside the standard curriculum such as logic (*manṭiq*), arithmetic (*ḥisāb*) and geometry (*handasa*).[32] For this reason, ʿAbduh tried to identify teachers who could provide tuition in these subjects and associated himself with those interested in literature, logic and philosophy in particular. He was though not always entirely satisfied with the quality of instruction these teachers could provide – though there were a few exceptions such Shaykh Hasan Tawil under whom he studied logic and philosophy.[33] ʿAbduh had to encounter the hostility and opposition of the more traditionalist teachers at al-Azhar who frowned upon such subjects and discouraged their study.[34] The distinction between traditional knowledge (*ʿilm naqlī*) and Islamic jurisprudence (*fiqh*) over rational knowledge (*ʿilm ʿaqlī*) prioritized the former and considered logic and linguistics only as instruments in understanding scripture and building valid legal arguments. Shaykh Darwish whom he continued to visit in his village during teaching breaks encouraged him to ignore such reprimands and to broaden his intellectual interests, because 'there is no type of knowledge detested in the presence of God and no type of ignorance praised in His presence'.[35]

As a student at al-Azhar, 'Abduh must have gained a reputation among his peers for being independent-minded and pursuing scholarly interests outside of the mainstream. He also began teaching a group of students certain works that were not necessarily part of the standard curriculum, using the *Isagoge* to teach logic or the theological commentary *Sharḥ al-'Aqā'id al-Nasfiyya* (Commentary on the Catechism of al-Nasafi) by Sa'd Taftazani (1322–1390). The inclusion of such textbooks in theology was rejected by some senior teachers at al-Azhar. His interest in logic and philosophy and his unconventional intellectual interests led to the suspicion that he had become a follower of the rationalist Mu'tazila school of theology in favour of the Sunni mainstream Ash'ari school. An anecdote about a confrontation with the conservative Shaykh 'Ilish (1802–1882) exemplifies these suspicions:

Shaykh 'Ilish:	'It has come to my notice that you prefer the Mu'tazila school over the Ash'ari school.'
'Abduh:	'If I had given up imitating (*taqlīd*) the Ash'ari school, how could I then imitate the Mu'tazila school? Thus, I have given up imitating any school altogether and only follow evidence (*dalīl*).'
Shaykh 'Ilish:	'A trustworthy person has told me that.'
'Abduh:	'Let the person come forward to testify that he may– here in front of us – distinguish between both schools and let us know which I prefer.'
Shaykh 'Ilish:	'Does someone like you even understand the *Sharḥ al-'Aqā'id* [*al-Nasfiyya*]?'
'Abduh:	'The book is here and I am here. Ask me whatever you want.'[36]

While such anecdotes might be stylized and presented in view of 'Abduh's later reputation as Islamic reformer who does not blindly follow tradition, they still suggest that the young 'Abduh was a kind of renegade in the conservative environment of al-Azhar which could not sufficiently satisfy his intellectual needs. Yet, teaching Taftazani's commentary alone would not have sufficed to accuse 'Abduh of Mu'tazila tendency. Taftazani and the author of the book he wrote his commentary about, 'Umar al-Nasifi (d. 1142), were affiliated with the more rationalist Maturidi school of theology and were not Mu'tazilis. Perhaps, the issue was more that 'Abduh was prepared to use more demanding treatises and commentaries when teaching advanced students, as suggested also by Shaykh 'Ilish final question.

The sage from the East

It needed someone like Jamal al-Din al-Afghani (Figure 1) to give 'Abduh's intellectual and spiritual pursuits a new direction. Afghani, nicknamed the

Figure 1. Sayyid Jamal al-Din al-Afghani.

sage from the East (*ḥakīm al-sharq*), combined personal charisma with a fresh intellectual approach which neither Shaykh Darwish nor the *'ulamā'* at al-Azhar could have provided. Afghani had arrived in Cairo in 1871, after having met 'Abduh already in 1869 when he stopped in Cairo on his way to Istanbul.[37] Invited by the reform-oriented Egyptian notable and politician Mustafa Riyad Pasha (1835/6–1911) to Cairo, Afghani started giving lessons at al-Azhar but stopped teaching given the opposition of conservative scholars at the institution.[38] Living in the Khan al-Khalili bazaar adjacent to the al-Azhar mosque, Afghani offered instead private lessons at night, 'a forum for scholars and literati',[39] which not only attracted al-Azhar students like 'Abduh but also government officials and notables eager to meet a Muslim activist and intellectual who antagonized the representatives of traditionalism. The meetings had a rather secretive nature in order to avoid the hostility and opposition of conservative *'ulamā'*.[40] These gatherings provided 'Abduh with a milieu which was in stark contrast to the conventional manner of instruction at al-Azhar and attracted a mind like his.

Rida accredits the dissemination of classical Islamic philosophy, whose traditions had been kept alive in the Persianate intellectual world but marginalized in the Arab world, to Afghani by attracting young students, intellectuals and journalists to his study sessions and through his publishing activities. Rida describes how Afghani's philosophy contained a mix of classical Islamic and contemporary European philosophy and Sufism. Rida also notes Afghani's attraction to Islamic esotericism, using the within Sunni circles rather derogatory term *bāṭiniyya*.[41] Among the philosophical works studied were Ibn Sina's *Kitāb al-Ishārāt wa-l-Tanbīhāt* and his *al-Hidāya*. The strong mystico-philosophical orientation and the influence of Iranian Theosophy are evident in the inclusion of the *Risālat al-Zawrā'* by Jalal al-Din al-Dawani (1426–1502),[42] the *Kitāb al-Ishrāq* by Shihab al-Din Suhrawardi (1153–91) and the *Ḥikmat al-'Ayn* by al-Katibi al-Qazwini (d. 1276).[43] Afghani used *al-Talwīḥ ilā Kashf Ḥaqā'iq al-Tanqīḥ* by Sa'd al-Din Taftazani (1322–1390)[44] to teach the principles of Islamic jurisprudence (*uṣūl al-fiqh*), and his Maturidi theological work *Sharḥ al-'Aqā'id al-Nasfiyya* which 'Abduh taught at al-Azhar as well.[45] Afghani also taught logic, using the standard textbook of Shii seminaries, *Sharḥ al-Shamsiyya* by Qutb al-Din Razi (1236–1311)[46] and also included the *Isagoge* to which 'Abduh referred when teaching logic among al-Azhar students.[47] Works on astronomy and geography by Mahmud ibn Muhammad al-Jaghmini (d. around 1344)[48] and Nasir al-Din Tusi (1201–1274)[49] were also included.[50] As 'Abduh would later teach the *Muqaddima* by Ibn Khaldun and classical *ādāb*-literature such as Ibn Miskawayh's (932–1030) *Tahdhīb al-Akhlāq*, they might have also been part of Afghani's instructions.[51]

The philosophical material included in the teaching sessions includes traditions which Ahmed terms as 'the Sufi-philosophical amalgam'[52] to denote the combination of three branches of classical Islamic philosophy: 'the Aristotelianism of Ibn Sīnā, the Neoplatonism of Suhrawardī, and the monism of Ibn 'Arabī'.[53] Scholars like Dawani, Suhrawardi and Qazwini synthesized these three types of Islamic philosophy and exercised immense influence on the School of Isfahan, the precursor of the nineteenth-century Shaykhi School.[54] The works included in the teaching session were part of traditional theological and philosophical training in the wider Persianate world and feature prominently in the curricula of Shii seminaries,[55] reflecting Afghani's early education in this context. In terms of their theological leanings, authors such as Dawani or Taftazani represent the more rationalistic Maturidi school of Islamic theology.[56] In addition to this mystico-philosophical corpus of Islamic literature, Afghani acquainted his followers with examples of contemporary European writings such as *L'histoire générale de la civilisation en Europe* by the French liberal statesman and social philosopher François Guizot (1787–1874), an evolutionary, progressive history of European societies, which had been translated into Arabic in 1878.[57] The study sessions also included debates of current political issues in Egypt and the wider Muslim world and provided a more liberal environment in which lively debates and discussions could occur.[58]

When 'Abduh met Afghani the first time, he was twenty years old, a young mystic searching for a charismatic guide and alternative modes of learning and religiosity. Afghani was able to respond to the young mystic's expectations and both entered the relationship between a Sufi novice and his master (*murīd-murshid*) which lasted for at least fifteen years and is documented in 'Abduh's first writings and in his letters to Afghani. Afghani embodied for his admirers like 'Abduh a religious charisma as represented in the quasi-prophetic status of the Sufi saint. Furthermore, his attachment to esoteric and philosophical traditions in Iranian Shiism endowed Afghani with a kind of knowledge that enabled him to connect with 'Abduh intellectually and spiritually. 'Abduh encountered many basic principles of Sufi thought as part of his introduction to Islamic mysticism such as emanation theology and the belief in a hierarchy of saints with the Perfect Man on top. These fundamental doctrines shaped Sufism in Egypt both in its traditional and reformist forms and were shared with the esoteric traditions of Iranian Shiism.[59] Aware of 'Abduh's mystical inclinations, Afghani enriched his mysticism with the heritage of Islamic philosophy and thereby drew him to a more rationalized interpretation of Islam.[60]

The close emotional attachment between Afghani and 'Abduh which clearly resembles the relationship between a Sufi shaykh and his adept is indicated in the foreword of his mystical treatise *Risālat al-Wāridāt* (Treatise on Mystical Inspirations)[61] and in letters 'Abduh wrote to his mentor during his later exile in Beirut. In the introduction to his first treatise, 'Abduh mentions his doubts and disorientation when he first discovered his interest in philosophy. His environment at al-Azhar considered the study of philosophy to be prohibited (*ḥarām*). 'Abduh remained in this state of confusion torn between his desire to study marginalized subjects and their rejection by the religious mainstream until 'the sun of truths rose (*ishraqat shams al-ḥaqā'iq*) so that the most subtle particularities became clear to us. With the arrival of the perfect sage and the established truth – our teacher Sayyid Jamal al-Din al-Afghani – the fruits of knowledge did not cease'.[62]

The language 'Abduh employs to describe Afghani's impact on him is couched in a Sufi framework and alludes to the symbolism of Ishraqi philosophy. Afghani's identification with the sun of truth which has risen to enlighten 'Abduh mirrors the light symbolism of the Ishraqi philosophy of Suhrawardi who uses it in his cosmology and emanation theology.[63] The contents of Afghani's instructions are characterized as mystical inspirations (*wāridāt*) and revelations (*tajalliyyāt*). These two terms frequently occur in Sufi literature. The term *tajalliyyāt* is used in the context of emanation theologies as Suhrawardi and Ibn 'Arabi developed them. *Tajalliyyāt* denote the process of divine creation when the divine attributes become manifest in the different cosmological realms.[64] The personified embodiment of the creative manifestation of divine attributes is the Perfect Man represented in this world by the prophets and the saints who are the perfect mirrors of all divine attributes to creation. As the divine attributes manifest themselves in creation through them, they connect creation with the divine as personifications of the *axis mundi* (*quṭb*). 'Abduh's use of a terminology which has its origin in mystical and esoteric emanation theologies to describe the role of Afghani suggests that he considers him to be the Perfect Man.

'Abduh's letters written to Afghani give clearer evidence of this suggestion. These letters written in 1883 in Beirut bear witness to 'Abduh's strong attachment to Afghani and employ terms usually used in a Sufi context to praise a shaykh. In the first letter 'Abduh addresses Afghani as 'my greatest master (*mawlāyi al-aʿẓam*)'[65] and pays tribute to his insight into his disciples' souls and the guidance he offers to them:

> You know what is in my soul, as you know what is in yours. You have made us with your hands, invested our matter with its perfect shapes (*ṣuwarahā al-kamāliyya*) and created us in the best form (*fī aḥsan taqwīm*). Through you have we known ourselves, through you have we known you, through you have known the whole universe. Your knowledge of us is, as it will not be hidden from you, a necessary knowledge. It is the knowledge you have of yourself, your confidence in your power and will; from you have we originated and to you, to you do we return (*wa-ilayka ilayka al-mā'b*).[66]

This passage suggests the quasi-prophetic status of the shaykh, a status which is almost elevated to that of the divine creator. Afghani is portrayed as omniscient at least in regard to the inner feelings and thoughts of his disciples and as their fashioner in a spiritual and intellectual sense. One is reminded of Qur'anic passages which introduce God's creative power and omniscience such as: 'We have created humans in the best form (*fī aḥsan taqwīm*).'[67] The parallel ʿAbduh draws between Afghani as his personal fashioner and God as the creator of the world as stated in the Qur'anic verses is thereby obvious:

> He created the heavens and the earth for a true purpose; He formed you and formed you well (*wa-ṣawarakum fa-aḥsan ṣuwarakum*): you will all return to Him (*wa-ilayhī al-maṣīr*). He knows what is in the heavens and earth; He knows what you conceal and what you reveal. God knows very well the secrets of every heart.[68]

Other expressions used in the letter also hint at the quasi-prophetic charisma of Afghani. ʿAbduh reports on the situation of his companions who have accompanied him to his exile and writes how 'their states have been changed after what has been sent down through you (*baʿd nuzūl ma nuzila bika*).'[69] In this instance, ʿAbduh employs a technical term of Islamic theology to describe the divine revelation which was sent down from heaven to Muhammad and the other prophets before him: 'We sent (*anzalnā*) Our Messengers with clear signs, the Scripture and the Balance, so that people could uphold justice.'[70] Another expression usually associated with the Prophet Muhammad is *sunna* (custom/practice). The *sunna* of the Prophet describes the totality of the deeds, habits and sayings of Muhammad which Muslims should emulate and abide by. In a similar manner, the Sufi disciple follows the *sunna* of his shaykh, because he owes obedience to him and regards him as a spiritual role model.

In his letter, 'Abduh reassures Afghani of his loyalty and obedience: 'We are following your customs and your practice (*naḥnu sālikūn fī sunanika wa-'alā sunnatika*).'[71]

The following section illustrates again the use of Sufi imagery and terminology and 'Abduh's identification of Afghani with the Perfect Man:

> As far as I am concerned, you have three spirits (*arwāḥ*). Were one of them released into the world completely, it would petrify into a perfect man (*insān kāmil*). Your visible likeness is manifest in my imaginative faculty and commands over my combined senses. With me is the picture of nobility, the image of wisdom, and the temple of perfection. To it I refer all my perceptions, and in it are annihilated (*funiyat*) all my visual impressions ... Your photograph which in the shrine of my prayers (*fī qiblat ṣalātī*) I set up as a guardian over all my actions and as a ruler over all my conditions. I never did an action or spoke a word, never aimed at some objective or abandoned it, until the perfection of your spirits – which are three – coincided with my actions.[72]

'Abduh recalls Afghani's face so as to receive inspiration from him. As part of his devotional practices, he placed Afghani's photograph in his prayer niche. It was common among Sufis to visualize a picture of their shaykh while performing *dhikr*. Later in his life, 'Abduh alludes to the quasi-prophetic status his mentor held for him. Although not a prophet himself, Afghani comes closest to what constitutes one:

> If I said that what God gave him from the power of intellect, the width of reason and the means of sight is the maximum of what he has conferred to non-prophets (*li-ghayr al-anbiyā'*), I would not be exaggerating.[73]

The language and imagery 'Abduh employs to describe the spiritual status of his teacher Afghani and his relationship to him shows how much he was immersed in Sufism and how his Sufi involvement finds a particular articulation in his attraction to Afghani. While such a portrayal might appear problematic from the perspective of narrow notions of Sunni orthodoxy, such appellations are quite common in Sufi definitions of charismatic authority. However, Afghani was not a traditional Sufi shaykh. He did not formally belong to a particular Sufi order and did not initiate 'Abduh into a particular order. Rather, he used 'Abduh's attraction to Sufism to introduce him to mystical philosophy with the aim of steering him to a more activist understanding of Islam.

Treatise on Mystical Inspirations

The literary manifestation of Afghani's instruction in mystical philosophy is ʿAbduh's first treatise, *Risālat al-Wāridāt*, written in 1874 and first published in 1904. While the treatise contains a summary of Afghani's teachings, the ideas articulated in the treatise not only reflect ʿAbduh's immersion into mystical philosophy in that state of his life but were also the crucial intellectual foundation shaping his future reformist work and overall intellectual outlook. That ʿAbduh instructed his student Rida to publish the treatise later in his life suggests that he intended to be identified as its author and to popularize its ideas among a wider educated Muslim readership, as it provides an accessible summary and introduction to mystical philosophy. ʿAbduh also wrote another Sufi treatise, discussing the controversial notion of *waḥdat al-wujūd* (unity of being), which is usually understood as signifying existential monism. This work has been lost, however.[74] In the *Risālat al-Wāridāt*, ʿAbduh also alludes to *waḥdat al-wujūd*, without mentioning the term explicitly. He thereby left the text ambiguous: a reader sufficiently versed in Sufi thought will immediately recognize how the concept informs his discussion, while ʿAbduh does not name the controversial concept as such. The treatise combines elements of Avicennan philosophy, Suhrawardi's Illuminationism and Sufi theology. It deals with the philosophical proofs of God's existence and His nature, presents a Sufi cosmology and develops a rationalistic understanding of prophecy. ʿAbduh also refers to several major controversies between theologians and philosophers, namely the question of the extent of divine knowledge, whether it includes both universals and particulars, the meaning of resurrection, whether it is physical, spiritual or both, and the dispute around free will and predestination.

ʿAbduh discusses three major philosophical proofs of God's existence which had been articulated for the first time in this form by Ibn Sina and include 'the metaphysical proof from necessity',[75] 'the proof from causality'[76] and the ontological proof of God's existence. Thereby, ʿAbduh merely recounts Ibn Sina's formulations, based on Afghani's discussion of these proofs during his private study sessions. However, Ibn Sina's philosophical theology contains elements which are difficult to reconcile with Sunni theology of the Ashʿari School. ʿAbduh himself does not dissociate himself from these elements but agrees with them. For instance, ʿAbduh rejects the theologians' assumption that there is an inherent gap between God and His creation, that God as the embodiment of perfection is necessarily transcendent from creation (*tanzīh*). On the contrary, he expounds the notion of *waḥdat al-wujūd*:

> They [the theologians] claim that this is the transcendence of His presence (*hādhā tanzīh li-haḍratihī*). But we believe: there is no existence (*wujūd*) apart from His existence and no attribute apart from His attribute. He is existent and anything else is non-existent … Do not fall into the delusion that this is the belief in incarnation (*ḥulūl*). Incarnation rather occurs between two beings when one of the two becomes the other. But we believe: there is no existence apart from His existence.[77]

'Abduh's implicit reference to the doctrine of *waḥdat al-wujūd* sets his understanding of the relationship between God and His creation in line with the theories developed in the mystical philosophies of Ibn Sina, Suhrawardi and Ibn 'Arabi. The assertion that 'there is no existence apart from His existence' does not imply that God's essence itself becomes manifest within creation. Rather than supporting that notion of God incarnating in the world, 'Abduh asserts that creation results from the emanation of divine attributes from His essence. This emanation theology, as developed in mystical philosophy and theosophy, contradicts the theologians' understanding of *creatio ex nihilo* and presents the view that God and His creation are co-existent and co-eternal.

'Abduh's adherence to the emanation theology of Islamic mystical philosophy becomes more apparent in his cosmology. Summarising cosmological conceptions of previous mystical philosophers, 'Abduh introduces a hierarchical structure of creation with different cosmic ranks (*marātib*) and degrees (*darajāt*).[78] The hierarchization of the physical world into the ranks of plants, animals and human beings indicates the Neoplatonic origin of the emanation theology 'Abduh describes and adopts from earlier Sufi philosophers. However, Abduh's presentation lacks the complexity of similar cosmological systems as developed by Ibn Sina or Suhrawardi. At the top of the cosmic hierarchy stands the Necessary Existent Being (*wājib al-wujūd*) or 'the truth of truths (*ḥaqīqat al- ḥaqā'iq*)'[79] and at the bottom, the physical world (*nāsūt*/*al-'ālam al-hayūlānī al-ṭabī'ī*). Between these two are several cosmic ranks inhabited by angelic beings, some of which are referred to as Universal Souls.[80]

The technical terms 'Abduh takes from his predecessors to describe the process of creation via emanation are *tajallī* and *tanazzul*. While *tajallī* is very often translated as emanation, it also contains the meaning of revelation. With the term *tanazzul*, literally meaning descent, the connection between creation and revelation is more evident. Related to one of the technical terms for revelation, namely *tanzīl*, *tanazzul* not only denotes the descent of various divine emanations as part of creation but also its connotations with revelation. Creation via emanation means the revelation of divine attributes within the different cosmic ranks to varying degrees. The lower one moves on the cosmic hierarchy, the fewer divine attributes become manifest, implying consequently a lesser degree of perfection in the lower cosmic ranks. 'Abduh uses a modern technical analogy to define the process of emanation: 'The people talk about the electric flow (*al-sayyāl al-kahrabā'ī*) in the world which only becomes apparent in its effects.'[81] Similarly, divine emanation is 'the spiritual flow in the world'.[82]

At first glance, 'Abduh's cosmology appears to be merely a sketched summary of the much more sophisticated cosmological systems which have been developed among mystical philosophers. However, that 'Abduh adhered to such a cosmology has wider intellectual implications for his religious thought. Implicit in this scheme of emanation theology is the constant movement of creation both upwards and downwards. Creation is the descent of divine attributes and their manifestation to lessening degrees in the different cosmic levels. This does not occur at any single moment in time but is a permanent process necessary to maintain the cosmic hierarchy. The assertion that 'the world would never stop moving in this movement'[83] is implicit in this emanationist scheme of creation and has been articulated most explicitly by Mulla Sadra and his concept of substantial movement (*ḥaraka jawhariyya*). As everything in the world has a natural inclination towards perfection, evolution is inherent in creation.[84] This notion of progress and evolution is also reiterated by 'Abduh: 'The world is in progress according to its development within existence.'[85] Transposed to the societal level, such an evolutionary and progressive understanding of human history and the development of human societies was also expounded in Guizot's historiography which Afghani taught his students in Cairo. Finding Islamic antecedents for such ideas in mystical philosophy facilitated their appropriation within the emerging terms of Islamic reformist discourse. Such a *weltanschauung* contains a hidden impetus for socio-political action, as it counters the fatalistic acceptance of a corrupt world and encourages a more active stance to alter the state of society.[86]

'Abduh's exposition of the nature of prophecy is also closer to that of mystical philosophers than to mainstream Sunni prophetology. His reference to the Prophet Muhammad as 'the divine sage (*al-ḥakīm al-ilāhī*)'[87] already suggests that he adheres to a more inclusivist understanding of religious and intellectual authority which does not attribute to the various divine prophets and messengers an exceptional status as sole recipients of divine revelations but defines them as outstanding mystically inspired and intellectually gifted individuals. In Abduh's cosmology, the Gabrielian Soul, one of the four Universal Souls, is responsible for bestowing knowledge onto creation in general. The distribution of knowledge depends on the ontological status of beings within creation, being therefore different and varied:

> Regarding the Gabrielian cosmic rank (*al-martaba al-jibrā'iliyya*), as education (*ta'līm*) of the universals and particulars stems from it, so stems from it the external education (*al-ta'līm al-ẓāhirī*), as it has occurred with some of the holy ones (*al-qiddisīn*) like the prophets.[88]

Hence, the bestowal of knowledge is a constant process in creation from which certain individuals in the human world benefit more than others. Individuals who have achieved a certain degree of sanctity (such as saints and prophets) receive more than ordinary human beings. Gabriel, as the conveyor of divine revelations, features prominently in descriptions of Muhammad's prophetic experiences. However, when Muhammad describes how 'he came and saw him [Gabriel] filling the whole horizon',[89] then 'this is only a metaphor (*ramz*)',[90] describing how Muhammad received knowledge from the Gabrielian Soul as part of the divine emanations.

The description of revelation as a process of illumination by the Gabrielian Soul has its origins in Ibn Sina's notion of prophecy, as does his understanding of the qualities of a prophet. 'Abduh, following Ibn Sina, defines a prophet as an individual who has attained all human perfections, someone who is 'the Perfect Man (*al-rajul al-kāmil*)'.[91] In Ibn Sina's understanding of prophecy, the term denotes how all the prophets have acquired perfection within the human world, be it intellectually, spiritually or morally. It is this distinctive status they have achieved that enables them to receive direct illuminations from the Gabrielian Soul, unlike other human beings whose illuminations are minimal in comparison.[92] 'Abduh expounds an understanding of prophecy that is identical to Ibn Sina's in terms of the constituent qualities of a prophet but also in terms of their role and function. In the same way as God provides sustenance for human bodies, so does he take care of 'the education of their intellects and the refinement of their souls'.[93] Therefore, God sends individuals 'endowed with a sanctified soul, purified from all forms of negligence, revealing to it the secrets and truths that will lead to the attainment of wisdom (*ḥikma*) out of their innate disposition (*fiṭra*)'.[94] These prophetic figures are the main teachers of humanity who provide it with all the knowledge it requires – knowledge they have attained by their own innate ability. The distinction between a prophet as the chosen divine messenger and an enlightened philosopher-sage is thereby blurred, as in Ibn Sina's prophetology.

The treatise appears to be the work of traditional mystical philosophy, summarizing various philosophical and theological controversies and offering a Sufi resolution to many of these. Given 'Abduh's later career as a political activist and intellectual, and his reputation as a Muslim reformer, this treatise has greater significance. The mystical and philosophical lessons which he learned from Afghani and articulated in this treatise prepared the way for the critical re-examination of the Islamic tradition. Efforts to reconcile and synthesize various intellectual strands within the Islamic tradition have always been part of Iranian Sufism or its philosophical expression in the theosophical School of Isfahan and Iranian traditions of mystical philosophy. Afghani, intellectually stemming from these traditions, led 'Abduh to a different understanding of Islam. This Islam was not scripturalist and legalist and embroiled in traditionalism, but open to criticism, the questioning of religious authority and of traditional modes of knowledge, an Islam that was open to change, development and progress. This reading of Islam appeared to be more akin to modern ideas since it was influenced by intellectual traditions that aimed to reconcile philosophy and mysticism.[95] Such a reading is also more indebted to the capaciousness of pre-modern Islamic intellectual discourses and their culture of ambiguity.

Commentary on the *Sharḥ al-'Aqā'id al-'Aḍudiyya*

Similar theological concerns informed by approaches of mystical philosophy are evident in 'Abduh's second book, written in early 1876, a commentary on the *Sharḥ al-'Aqā'id al-'Aḍudiyya* by Jalal al-Din al-Dawani (1426–1502), an Iranian rationalist and philosophically minded theologian with Maturidi leanings.[96] Dawani's commented on a brief theological catechism of 'Adud al-Din al-Iji (1281–1356) who was a Shafi'i jurist and Ash'ari theologian from Azerbaijan.[97] Both works were popular in the curriculum of *madrasas* given their accessible and concise introductions to Ash'ari theology. The structure of 'Abduh's commentary is quite traditional: at the centre of each page is al-Iji's text with Dawani's commentary (*sharḥ*) on the margins and 'Abduh's glosses (*ta'līqāt*) added further onto the margins.

The choice of this text for 'Abduh's first foray into Islamic theological discourse contains different layers of ambiguity: al-Iji's catechism is apologetic including a strong anti-Shii tone and vindicating the Ash'ari school of theology as the sole expression of Islamic orthodoxy. Dawani reaffirms the apologetic tone of the original catechism in his commentary, although his religious orientation remains ambiguous. Dawani produced works in which he exhibited Shii tendencies, praised members of the family of the Prophet (*ahl al-bayt*) and disavowed the first three caliphs which suggests that he practised *taqiyya* when defending Ashʿari theology in his commentary.[98] By choosing this commentary, ʿAbduh engaged with a key text used for instructing students in Ashʿari theology, and added glosses to a commentary by an author whose sectarian identity remains ambiguous. ʿAbduh's own glosses undo the apologetic intentions of the original catechism and its explicit Ashʿari orientation. Rather than further justifying the sole orthodoxy of the Ashʿari school, ʿAbduh promotes an irenic attitude towards sectarian differences in Islam.

Similar to the *Risālat al-Wāridāt*, ʿAbduh's commentary on the *Sharḥ al-ʿAqāʾid al-ʿAḍudiyya* contains and summarizes the lessons given by Afghani on Dawani's work. The commentary engages with mystical philosophy and adopts a theological discourse either to propose mystical philosophical solutions to theological controversies, as does the *Risālat al-Wāridāt*, or to reconcile Sunni theology of Ashʿari provenience with views developed within Islamic philosophy. The commentary can be read as a response to al-Ghazali's influential critique of Islamic philosophy, *Tahāfut al-Falāsifa* (The Incoherence of the Philosophers). For al-Ghazali, there are three reasons why Islamic philosophy is heretical: philosophers believe in the eternity of the world, deny God's knowledge of the particulars and question the reality of the physical resurrection on the Day of Judgement.[99] By adopting the discursive ductus of Islamic theology and engaging critically with Ashʿari theology, ʿAbduh hopes to rehabilitate Islamic philosophy. The *Risālat al-Wāridāt* uses Sufi imagery and terminology to do so, and his theological commentary espouses similar ideas,[100] including the notion of *waḥdat al-wujūd*.[101]

The irenic tone of ʿAbduh's commentary is set in the very first discussion of the treatise, an interpretation of the prominent hadith attributed to the Prophet Muhammad in which he foresees the division of his community in different sects: 'My community (*ummatī*) will divide in 73 sects, all of which will enter hellfire except one: those who follow me and my Companions.' While for Dawani following al-Iji, it is clear that the followers of 'the saved sect' (*al-firqa al-nājiyya*) are those who follow the Ashʿari theological school,[102] ʿAbduh offers a more complex answer. The criterion provided in the hadith to determine the saved sect, to follow the Prophet and his Companions, is rather vague and allows various sects to claim for themselves to be the one that escapes hellfire. The condition to be saved requires the sect to follow the Qurʾan and the *sunna* of the Prophet. All sects refer to these sources in order to justify their particular beliefs.

For instance, the philosophers believe in the pre-existence and eternity of the world and use Qur'anic verses and hadith reports to legitimize their worldview. In contrast, Sufis follow the notion of *waḥdat al-wujūd*, the unity of all being, justifying their belief with references to the Qur'an and traditions attributed to the Prophet and his Companions. Both, philosophers and Sufis, use scriptural and rational evidence to portray themselves as followers of the Prophet and his Companions.[103]

The divisions within different theological schools are equally justified with references to relevant scriptural and rational evidence. The Mu'tazila school maintains that God is obliged to punish the sinner, while Sunnis emphasize divine omnipotence: it is God alone who decides who will be punished or rewarded. The Mu'tazila school believes in human free will, while Sunnis uphold divine predestination. All these contradictory positions are supported by relevant scriptural evidence. Among all the Prophet's companions, Shiis give preference to 'Ali citing the hadith of *ghadīr khumm*, while Sunnis cite the hadith stating that 'after the Prophet, the sun shone never on a person who was more preferred than Abu Bakr'.[104]

While these contradictory beliefs constitute the *raison d'être* of these different sects and groups, they also use their distinctive features to claim that they are the mentioned saved sect. 'Abduh offers the following solution to these divisions:

> All these sects are saved, in the sense that they all conform to the teachings of the Prophet and his Companions and the foundational principles known to us: divinity (*alūhiyya*), prophethood (*nubuwwa*) and resurrection (*ma'ād*). All those teachings on which they disagree cannot be considered certain knowledge (*'ilm al-yaqīn*).[105]

'Abduh thereby emphasizes the common denominators of legitimate Islamic discourse: doctrinally, it is based on monotheism, prophecy and resurrection, scripturally it refers to the Qur'an and the traditions of the Prophet Muhammad and his Companions, and methodically it combines both scriptural and rational arguments to legitimize a particular theological interpretation. Theological differences only occur on details (*tafāṣīl*):[106] whether divine attributes are part of His essence or not, whether the world is eternally existent or not or whether good and evil can be rationally grasped without revelation or not.[107]

'Abduh's particular objective of these discussions is less to define what constitutes Islamic orthodoxy but rather to overcome the narrow mind-set that has been created in Islamic intellectual history by the followers of different schools and sects to prove that their beliefs constitute orthodoxy, that they are 'the saved sect'. 'Abduh criticizes this intolerant attitude which not only heightened inner-Islamic divisions but also resulted in infighting within particular theological schools where 'the perpetrator [with a different opinion] is an unbeliever (*kāfir*) or corrupter (*fāsiq*), even if he is from his party (*ḥizbihī*)'.[108] However, an irenic attitude based on shared foundational principles will overcome partisanship (*taḥazzub*) and achieve reconciliation (*ṣulḥ*).[109]

The tolerant attitude introduced in the beginning of the commentary also determines 'Abduh's approach to a number of theological questions discussed in his work such as the nature of divine attributes, human actions and their relationship to divine predestination, the question of seeing God on the Day of Judgement, the Word of God and the Qur'an and the question of bodily resurrection. Very often, the viewpoints of different schools are presented without supporting a particular party or particular theological and philosophical positions. In particular Islamic philosophers, for example, are defended against the charge of constituting heresy or disbelief (*kufr*) by pointing at semantic differences that do not sufficiently prove a substantial theological disagreement.[110] However, 'Abduh tends to favour a more rationalist approach towards certain theological issues without, however, fully embracing the standpoints of the rationalist Mu'tazila school. The prominence of theological works by Maturidi schools in Afghani's teaching sessions might explain why 'Abduh adopted a middle position between the Ash'ari school and the Mu'tazila school. However, it seems that he takes issue of the tendency of both schools to discredit the followers of the other as heretics and disbelievers – a mindset his work intends to overcome.[111]

On three particular issues, 'Abduh's preference for a more rationalist approach that challenges the Ash'ari interpretation is evident: the question of whether moral categories are rational, whether the Qur'an is created and whether on the Day of Judgement a bodily resurrection occurs. Juxtaposing the respective viewpoints of the Ash'ari school, on the one hand, and the Mu'tazila and Maturidi schools, on the other, 'Abduh rejects the notion that good and evil, or using the more aesthetic terms beauty (*ḥusn*) and repugnance (*qubḥ*), are solely determined and known to humanity by divine revelation. The injunction of commanding good and forbidding evil (*al-amr bi-l-ma'rūf wa-l-nahī 'an al-munkar*) is only reasonable on two accounts: that humans possess mechanism to determine good and evil, 'by conjecture, by proof or something else',[112] and that human actions are not entirely predestined by God but the result of free will. The more rationalist orientation of 'Abduh becomes quite visible here, as human reasoning is given priority in establishing morality and revelation is not even directly mentioned but only referred to as 'something else'.

'Abduh engages with the prominent theological controversy in early Islam whether the Qur'an as the Word of God is eternal and uncreated (a position upheld by the Ash'ari school) or created in time (as maintained by the Mu'tazila school). 'Abduh's positions holds a middle-ground between the two schools and avoids addressing the crucial question of the nature of the Qur'an itself.[113] Beginning with less controversial terrain, 'Abduh defines 'the Word of God in Itself (*kalām allāh al-nafsī*)'[114] as part of His divine essence as pre-existent (*qadīm*) and eternal (*azalī*). 'Abduh distinguishes the Word of God in Itself from the recited Word of God (*kalām lafẓī*), for instance, when reading the Qur'an, which as 'uttered speech is created (*ḥadīth makhlūq*)'.[115] By differentiating between the Word of God in Itself and the recited Word of God, 'Abduh suggests that the theological controversy is based on a semantic misunderstanding[116] and appears to aim for a reconciliation by concluding that both sides are right based on the aspect of the Word of God they focus on:

> However, on this issue, there is agreement between us and all parties: the Qur'an or the Word [of God] only mean the words, as they are recited by human tongues and written down on their folios (*maṣāḥif*). There is an agreement that they are contingent (*ḥudūth*). What we receive in the texts is, however, uncreated (*ghayr makhlūq*). It also comes forth without having a creator.[117]

For the sake of achieving consensus, 'Abduh avoids addressing the question whether the Qur'an itself is created or eternal by pointing out the theologically obvious: the Word of God as such is eternal and the words of the Qur'an, in the moment they are uttered by a reciter, are created. This conclusion reflects the irenic tone of the commentary which is further reiterated in the conclusion of the chapter on the Qur'an in which 'Abduh emphasizes the moral message of the Qur'an as more important than minor theological differences around its nature.[118]

For Dawani in his commentary, the philosophers' belief in the eternity of the world and their rejection of bodily resurrection on the Day of Judgement constitutes unbelief (*kufr*) and therefore moves them outside of the fold of Islam which mirrors one of al-Ghazali's key charges against Islamic philosophers.[119] The issue of resurrection is crucial in the argument of the commentary as belief in it as one of the *sine qua non* of being a Muslim, according to 'Abduh. He defends the philosophers' stance on the question of resurrection by stating they do not reject the resurrection *per se* but approach this issue and how it will occur differently. Summarizing Ibn Sina's argument, 'Abduh attempts to explain the rationale of his rejection of a bodily resurrection: it is impossible that a thing that has ceased to exist can come back into existence. However, this premise does not preclude resurrection to occur. For the philosophers, resurrection rather means that humans move from one form of existence to another one without ceasing existence completely. 'Abduh seems to align with the philosophers when he characterizes the Qur'anic descriptions of bodily resurrections and the sensual pleasures (or pains) humans await in the afterlife as targeting the general populace (*'awwām*) to encourage them to follow divine revelation.[120] For someone holding a different understanding of resurrection beyond its literal meaning, 'to judge him as being an unbeliever (*ḥukm takfīrihī*) is not justified'.[121] Understandings and approaches differ, and 'only God knows the truth of the matter best'.[122]

'Abduh's commentary sets the stage for his later reformist work and is therefore a crucial testimony of his intellectual formation. For this reason, Haddad considers it 'among Muhammad 'Abduh's most important religious books'[123] providing a record of his philosophical and theological orientations which would shape the direction of his subsequent intellectual pursuits. The commentary adopts the tone and discourse of Islamic theology while opening it up for rationalistic strands of Islamic intellectual history, whether doctrinal aspects of the Mu'tazila and Maturidi schools of theology or Islamic philosophy, both in its Peripatetic and mystical manifestations. While the blind emulation (*taqlīd*) and dogmatism of the Ash'ari school are his particular target, 'Abduh equally critiques any articulation of Islamic religiosity that defines orthodoxy at the expense of other articulations by declaring them heretical or outside of the fold of Islam. In his rejection of blind emulation, 'Abduh highlights that scholars like Abu al-Hasan al-Ash'ari (874–936) confirmed that following past authorities does not lead to certain knowledge and can lead to disbelief if past authorities are unquestionably accepted.[124] Rather, 'revelation and reason (*al-shar' wa-l-'aql*)'[125] lead to the truth together, and specific doctrinal positions need to develop based on both sources 'with utmost research (*taḥarrī*) and independent reasoning (*ijtihād*)'.[126] Hence, 'Abduh seeks to bring theological doctrines and debates from the realm of blind imitation (*taqlīd*) to the realm of independent reasoning (*ijtihād*). Adherence to such doctrines is not externally enforced by social conformity or imitated as part of a scholarly tradition but results from rationally accepting and internalizing them as part of one's own intellectual effort.[127]

Conclusion

Abduh's encounter with Sufism – first its reformist branch through his paternal great-uncle – was given philosophical substance through Afghani's intellectual and spiritual mentorship who introduced him to traditions of Islamic thought that were not necessarily accessible to Egyptian religious students in a Sunni environment at that time. The relationship between 'Abduh and Afghani was more than one between a teacher and his student. The charismatic aura Afghani must have possessed is evident in the letters 'Abduh addressed to him and also attested by others.[128] The Sufi-style *murīd-murshid* relationship, between a Sufi master and his disciple, that both formed with one another explains the quasi-prophetic and quasi-divine status Afghani held for 'Abduh. While the language 'Abduh uses to describe his mentor appears problematic from the perspective of anti-Sufi stances in Sunni Islam, they were quite common within Sufism. The close relationship between them also had bearings on the authorship of the books 'Abduh wrote under Afghani's tutelage. Efforts have been made to dissociate 'Abduh from these works by attributing authorship solely to Afghani.[129] However, such an understanding overlooks the close intellectual bond between 'Abduh and Afghani: his two early works were summaries of Afghani's mystical, philosophical and theological teaching sessions which 'Abduh published to illustrate how he had appropriated and internalized these views which proved to be crucial for his early intellectual formation and would exert continuous influence on his later reformist work. Despite their potentially controversial nature, 'Abduh prepared the publication of both works and wanted to be identified as their author at the end of his life.

Later biographers, like Rida in his edition of the correspondence between 'Abduh and Afghani and also later editors of 'Abduh's works like 'Imara, have omitted passages in 'Abduh's letters which give expression to a personal veneration and a type of image worship which contemporary Salafis would label idolatry (*shirk*) but was quite common among Sufis. Kedourie and Shalash in their translations and editions of the letters point out the selective approach and textual manipulations of 'Abduh's works by later recipients.[130] However, reading these letters as sign of their disbelief in religion, heterodoxy or heresy disregards that the language and imagery they use are rooted in Sufism. Kedourie uses a particular statement by 'Abduh as evidence that his and Afghani's adherence to Islam was insincere and just an instrument to win support for their political activities among the broader Muslim masses. 'Abduh wrote to Afghani that 'the head of religion can only be cut by the sword of religion'.[131] While Kedourie understands this statement as a clear articulation of their complete disregard of Islam and their opportunistic use of it, 'Abduh articulates here his disillusionment with the traditionalist orientation of Muslim authorities which can only be challenged by using the actual capaciousness of Islamic traditions to counter restrictive interpretations and to broaden its discursive parameters.[132] In reality, 'Islam – in its essence – is a religion of philosophy (*ḥikma*), reason (*'aql*) and civilization (*madaniyya*)'[133] and as such not an obstacle to progress and development. A restrictive understanding of traditionalist Muslim authorities and their followers exclude intellectual traditions of mystical philosophy and reduce Islam to narrow sectarian and doctrinal perspectives.

The aim of Afghani's teaching sessions and of 'Abduh's publications stemming therefrom was to create a sensitivity to the doctrinal unity of Islam and to synthesize its different intellectual traditions. However, their approach was not to reduce Islam to essential features shared by all Muslims but to overcome the heightened sense of sectarian differences and to rehabilitate philosophy, both in its mystical and Peripatetic forms, against attacks by Sunni theologians. The strategies the two early works by 'Abduh employ are quite similar. His *Risālat al-Wāridāt* suggests a Sufi resolution of sectarian and doctrinal differences by evoking the notion of *waḥdat al-wujūd* – without explicitly mentioning this controversial concept. There is only one existence, God, and all creation is just a manifestation of divine attributes and inherently united and connected. Differences of opinion and their diversity are the result of limited human perception that cannot fathom the essential unity of creation with God. 'Abduh's theological commentary makes a similar argument by emphasising the core theological doctrines of Islam shared by all Muslims and dismissing theological and philosophical disagreements as secondary and the result of semantic variations or different intellectual objectives and foci. Referring to a controversy in early Islamic theology, 'Abduh suggests that the Qur'an is both eternal and created, depending how one looks at it. Finally, 'Abduh rehabilitates Islamic philosophy to espouse an Islam with strong rational foundations: one's commitment to Islam should derive from rationally understandable theological convictions rather than being based on inherited beliefs that are just emulated.

Afghani's relationship to 'Abduh resembled the rapport between a Sufi master and his disciple. However, Afghani used his position not to initiate him into a particular Sufi order but to steer him towards political activism, as the next chapter illustrates. His philosophical and mystical instructions equally intended to open 'Abduh to more activist and progressive readings of Islam. The distinction between different cosmic ranks and the presentation of a Sufi spiritual hierarchy in the *Risālat al-Wāridāt* introduces a gradualist sense of individual spiritual development that needs to go through different stages. In his political writings, 'Abduh presents a similar gradualism and translates it into an evolutionary scheme of the development of societies that equally need to proceed through different stages as part of their civilizational progress.

Notes

1 Elizabeth Sirriyeh, *Sufis and Anti-Sufis: The Defence, Rethinking and Rejection of Sufism in the Modern World* (Richmond: Curzon, 1999), 90. Adams was probably the first who noted the parallels between 'Abduh's description of his intellectual and spiritual crisis and its resolution offered by Sufism with similar accounts of other famous mystics in the Islamic tradition like al-Ghazali. See Charles C. Adams, *Islam and Modernism in Egypt: A Study of the Modern Reform Movement Inaugurated by Muhammad 'Abduh* (London: Oxford University Press, 1933), 25–6, n. 2.

2 al-Ghazali, *Freedom and Fulfilment: An Annotated Translation of Al-Ghazali's al-Munqidh min al-dalal and Other Relevant Works of al-Ghazali by Richard Joseph McCarthy* (Boston: Twayne, 1980).

3 Nikki R. Keddie, *Sayyid Jamāl ad-Dīn 'al-Afghānī': A Political Biography* (Berkeley: University of California Press, 1972), 38; Mangol Bayat, *Mysticism and Dissent: Socioreligious Thought in Qajar Iran* (Syracuse: Syracuse University Press, 1999), 144–5.

4 Ahmed Shahab, *What Is Islam?: The Importance of Being Islamic* (Princeton: Princeton University Press, 2016), 10–31.

5 On Rida's own involvement in Sufism and his changing attitudes, see Albert Hourani, 'Sufism and Modern Islam: Rashid Rida', in *The Emergence of the Modern Middle East*, ed. Albert Hourani (Berkley: University of California Press, 1981), 90–102.

6 Mohamed Haddad, *Muḥammad 'Abduh: Qarā'a Jadīda fī Khiṭāb al-Iṣlāḥ al-Dīnī* (Beirut: Dar al-Tali'a li-l-Tabi'a wa-l-Nashr, 2003), 15–20.

7 Richard Gottheil, 'Mohammed 'Abdu, Late Mufit of Egypt', *Journal of the American Oriental Society*, 28 (1907): 190.

8 Muhammad Rashid Rida, *Ta'rīkh al-Ustādh al-Imām al-Shaykh Muḥammad 'Abduh*, vol. 1 (Cairo: al-Manar, 1931), 14–15.

9 Mark Sedgwick, *Muhammad Abduh* (Oxford: Oneworld, 2010), 1.

10 Rida, *Ta'rīkh*, vol. 1, 16.

11 Ibid., 20.

12 Benjamin C. Fortna, 'Education and Autobiography at the End of the Ottoman Empire', *Die Welt des Islams*, 41 (2001): 1–31.

13 Muhammad Rashid Rida, 'Mulakhkhaṣ Sīrat al-Ustādh al-Imām', *al-Manār*, 8 (1905): 381.
14 Mark Sedgwick, *Saints and Sons: The Making and Remaking of the Rashidi Ahmadi Sufi Order, 1799–2000* (Leiden: Brill, 2005), 21, 90.
15 Rida, 'Mulakhkhaṣ', 383.
16 Ibid., 384–5.
17 Ahmad Amin, *Zu'amā' al-Iṣlāḥ fī-l-'Aṣr al-Ḥadīth* (Cairo: Maktabat al-Nahda al-Misriyya, 1948), 284.
18 Nicola A. Ziadeh, *The Sanusiyah: A Study of a Revivalist Movement in Islam* (Leiden: Brill, 1958); Jamil M. Abun-Nasr, *The Tijaniyya: A Sufi Order in the Modern World* (Oxford: Oxford University Press, 1965). Fazlur Rahman developed the term 'Neo-Sufism' for these Sufi reformist movements. See Fazlur Rahman, *Islam*, 2nd edn (Chicago: University of Chicago Press, 1979), 209–11. For a critique of the term 'Neo-Sufism', see Seán R. O'Fahey and Radtke Bernd, 'Neo-Sufism Reconsidered', *Der Islam*, 70 (1993): 52–87.
19 Seán R. O'Fahey, *Enigmatic Saint: Ahmad Ibn Idris and the Idrisi Tradition* (London: Hurst, 1990).
20 Gilbert Delanoue, *Moralistes et politiques musulmans dans l'Egypte de XIXe siècle (1798–1882)* (Cairo: Institut Français de l'Achéologie Orientale du Caire, 1982), 248; Sedgwick, *Saints and Sons*, 90.
21 Reinhard Schulze, *Islamischer Internationalismus im 20. Jahrhundert: Untersuchungen zur Geschichte der islamischen Weltliga* (Leiden: Brill, 1990), 25–6, 35–6. Delanoue connects the Sufi stress on *ijtihād* as expressed by Ahmad ibn Idris during his stay in Egypt in 1800 with 'Abduh's later criticism of the religious establishment. See Delanoue, *Moralistes et politiques musulmans*, 210–11. Although the renewed stress on *ijtihād* is usually associated with these Sufi reformers, *ijtihād* forms part of traditional Sufi epistemology and understanding of jurisprudence. Ibn 'Arabi rejected *taqlīd* of the prevalent legal schools and based his *ijtihād* on direct prophetic illuminations. For his approach towards jurisprudence see Michel Chodkiewicz, *Un océan sans rivage: Ibn Arabî, le Livre et la Loi* (Paris: Éditions du Seuil, 1992), 76–80; Eric Winkel, 'Ibn 'Arabi's *Fiqh*: Three Cases from the *Futuhat*', *Journal of the Muhyiddin Ibn 'Arabi Society*, 13 (1993): 54–74.
22 The term was originally created by Ahmad al-Wasiti (1258–1311), a Sufi disciple of Ibn Taymiyya. See Sedgwick, *Saints and Sons*, 26–31.
23 John O. Voll, 'Muhammad Hayya al-Sindi and Muhammad ibn 'Abd al-Wahhab: An Analysis of an Intellectual Group in Eighteenth-Century Madina', *Bulletin of the School of Oriental and African Studies*, 38 (1975): 32–9; John O. Voll, "Hadith Scholars and Tariqahs: An Ulama Group in the 18th Century Haramayn and Their Impact on the Islamic World', *Journal of Asian and African Studies*, 15 (1980): 264–73.

24 Valerie J. Hoffman, 'Annihilation in the Messenger of God: The Development of a Sufi Practice', *International Journal of Middle East Studies*, 31 (1999): 351–69.

25 Sedgwick, *Saints and Sons*, 44–6.

26 Rida, *Ta'rīkh*, vol. 1, 21.

27 Sedgwick, *Saints and Sons*, 38–9. On the importance of this early legal compendium for the eighteenth-century South Asian Muslim reformer Shah Wali Allah (1703–1762), see Ahmad S. Dallal, *Islam without Europe: Traditions of Reform in Eighteenth Century Islamic Thought* (Chapel Hill: University of North Carolina Press, 2018), 249–53.

28 Sirriyeh, *Sufis and Anti-Sufis*, 90.

29 Sedgwick, *Saints and Sons*, 37.

30 Mark Sedgwick, 'Sects in the Islamic World', *Nova Religio*, 3 (2000): 216–18.

31 Rida, *Ta'rīkh*, vol. 1, 130

32 Ibid., 24.

33 Ibid., 25; Ahmad, *Zu'amā' al-Iṣlāḥ*, 290–1.

34 Rida, *Ta'rīkh*, vol. 1, 24–5.

35 Ibid.

36 Rida, *Ta'rīkh*, vol. 1, 134.

37 Sedgwick, *Abduh*, 9.

38 Salim 'Anhuri, *Siḥr Hārūt* (Damascus: al-Matba'a al-Hanafiyya, 1885), 178–9.

39 Ibid., 179.

40 Rida, *Ta'rīkh*, vol. 1, 31–7.

41 Ibid., 79–80.

42 Seyyed Hossein Nasr and Mehdi Aminrazavi, eds, *An Anthology of Philosophy in Persia, Volume 4: From the School of Illumination to Philosophical Mysticism* (London: I.B. Tauris, 2012), 93–120, 121–35.

43 On al-Katib al-Qazwini, see Henry Corbin, *History of Islamic Philosophy* (London: Routledge, 2014), 265–6.

44 On Taftazani, see ibid., 271–2.

45 Rida, *Ta'rīkh* vol. 1, 133.

46 On Qutb al-Din al-Razi, see Corbin, *Islamic Philosophy*, 266–7.

47 Rida, *Ta'rīkh*, vol. 1, 133.

48 On Jaghmini, see Sally P. Ragep, 'Jaghmini', in *The Biographical Encyclopedia of Astronomers*, ed. Thomas Hockey et al. (New York: Springer, 2007), 584–5.

49 On al-Tusi, see Corbin, *Islamic Philosophy*, 319–24.

50 Rida, *Ta'rīkh*, vol. 1, 26.

51 See ibid., 135–6. On Afghani's personal library in Cairo, see also Albert A. Kudsi-Zadeh, 'Islamic Reform in Egypt: Some Observations on the Role of Afghānī', *The Muslim World*, 61(1) (1971): 1–12.

52 Ahmed, *What Is Islam?*, 31.

53 John Walbridge, *God and Logic in Islam: The Caliphate of Reason* (Cambridge: Cambridge University Press, 2010), 95; Sayyid Hossein Nasr, *Three Muslim Sages: Avicenna, Suhrawardī, Ibn 'Arabī* (Cambridge, MA: Harvard University Press, 1964), 7.

54 Corbin, *Islamic Philosophy*, 329–31.

55 Sabrina Mervin, 'The Clerics of Jabal 'Amil and the Reform of Religious Teaching in Najaf since the Beginning of the 20th Century', in *The Twelver Shia in Modern Times: Religious Culture and Political History*, ed. Rainer Brunner and Werner Ende (Leiden: Brill, 2001), 79–86; Moojan Momen, *An Introduction to Shi'i Islam: The History and Doctrines of Twelver Shi'ism* (New Haven: Yale University Press, 1985), 207.

56 Thomas Hildebrandt, 'Waren Ǧamāl ad-Dīn al-Afghānī und Muḥammad 'Abduh Neo-Mu'taziliten?', *Die Welt des Islams*, 42(2) (2002): 215.

57 See Rida, *Ta'rīkh*, vol. 1, 133. On Guizot, see Sedgwick, *Abduh*, 16–17. On Guizot's influence on Afghani, see Margret Kohn, 'Afghānī on Empire, Islam, and Civilization', *Political Theory*, 37(3) (2009): 412–16.

58 Rida, *Ta'rīkh*, vol. 1, 26–7.

59 Valerie J. Hoffman, *Sufism, Mystics, and Saints in Modern Egypt* (Columbia: University of South Carolina Press, 1995), 50–68. On the vitality of theosophical ideas in Sufism of nineteenth-century Ottoman Syria, see Itzhak Weismann, *Taste of Modernity: Sufism, Salafiyya and Arabism in Late Ottoman Damascus* (Leiden: Brill, 2001), 141–92.

60 Rida, *Ta'rīkh*, vol. 1, 25–7; Rida, 'Mulakhkhaṣ', 388–90; 'Uthman Amin, *Muḥammad 'Abduh* (Cairo: Dar Ajya' al-Kutub al-'Arabiyya, 1944), 23–7; Mustafa 'Abd al-Raziq, *Muḥammad 'Abduh* (Cairo: Dar al-Ma'arif, 1946), 51; Keddie, *al-Afghānī*, 81–92; Elie Kedourie, *Afghani and 'Abduh: An Essay on Religious Unbelief and Political Activism in Modern Islam* (London: Frank Cass, 1966), 1–12.

61 For a comprehensive discussion of this treatise, see Oliver Scharbrodt, 'The Salafiyya and Sufism: Muḥammad 'Abduh and His *Risālat al-Wāridāt* (*Treatise on Mystical Inspiration*)', *Bulletin of the School Oriental and African Studies*, 70 (2007): 89–115; Martino M. Moreno, 'La Mistica di Muhammad 'Abduh', *Oriente Moderno*, 60 (1980): 403–35.

62 Muhammad 'Abduh, *Risālat al-Wāridāt: fī Naẓariyyāt al-Mutakallimīn wa-l-Ṣūfiyya fi-l-Falsafa al-Ilāhiyya*, 2nd edn (Cairo: al-Manar, 1925), 2.

63 Henri Corbin, *En Islam iranien: Aspects spirituels et philosophiques*, vol. 2 (Paris: Gallimard, 1971), 81–140.

64 For the similarities and differences between Suhrawardi's and Ibn 'Arabi's emanation theologies, see Ian R. Netton, *Allāh Transcendent: Studies in the Structure and Semiotics of Islamic Philosophy, Theology and Cosmology* (Richmond: Curzon, 1989), 256–320.

65 'Ali Shalash, *Silsilat al-A'māl al-Majhūla Muḥammad 'Abduh* (London: Riad al-Rayyes, 1987), 47.
66 Ibid., 47. For an English translation, see Kedourie, *Afghani and 'Abduh*, 66.
67 Qur'an 95:4.
68 Qur'an 64:3–4.
69 Shalash, *Silsila*, 48.
70 Qur'an 57:25.
71 Shalash, *Silsila*, 50.
72 Ibid., 47. For an English translation see Kedourie, *Afghani and 'Abduh*, 67.
73 Rida, *Ta'rīkh*, vol. 1, 34.
74 Rida, 'Mulakhkhaṣ', 482.
75 Netton, *Allāh Transcendent*, 172.
76 Ibid., 173.
77 'Abduh, *Wāridāt*, 6.
78 'Abduh, *Wāridāt*, 14.
79 Ibid.
80 Ibid.
81 'Abduh, *Wāridāt*, 15.
82 Ibid.
83 Ibid., 16.
84 Fazlur Rahman, *The Philosophy of Mulla Sadra* (Albany: State University of New York Press, 1975), 94–108.
85 'Abduh, *Wāridāt*, 16.
86 Bayat, *Mysticism and Dissent*, 54–8; see also Abduh's *al-Ahrām* article which is critical of fatalism, published in Muhammad Rashid Rida, *Ta'rīkh al-Ustādh al-Imām al-Shaykh Muḥammad 'Abduh*, vol. 2 (Cairo, 1924), 12–13.
87 'Abduh, *Wāridāt*, 14.
88 Ibid., 15.
89 Ibid.
90 Ibid.
91 Ibid., 18.
92 Nasr, *Three Muslim Sages*, 42–3.
93 'Abduh, *Wāridāt*, 17.
94 Ibid.
95 Nikki R. Keddie, 'Islamic Philosophy and Islamic Modernism: The Case of Jamāl ad-Dīn al-Afghānī', *Iran*, 6 (1968): 55.
96 Hildebrandt, 'Neo-Mu'taziliten?', 216; Andrew J. Newman, 'Davānī, Jalāl-al-Dīn Moḥammad', *Encyclopaedia Iranica*, 7, fasc. 2, 132–3.
97 Josef van Ess, 'Ażod-al-Dīn Ījī', *Encyclopaedia Iranica*, 3, fasc. 3, 269–71.
98 Newman, 'Davānī'.

99 Ovamir Anjum, *Politics, Law, and Community in Islamic Thought: The Taymiyyan Moment* (Cambridge: Cambridge University Press, 2012), 151.

100 Sulayman Dunya, ed., *al-Shaykh Muḥammad 'Abduh bayna-l-Falāsifa wa-l-Kalāmiyīn*, vol. 1 (Cairo: 'Isa al-Babi al-Halabi, 1958), 61; Hildebrandt, 'Neo-Mu'taziliten?', 216–17.

101 Jamal al-Din al-Afghani and Muhammad 'Abduh, *al-Ta'līqāt 'alā Sharḥ al-'Aqā'id al-'Aḍudiyya* (Cairo: Maktabat al-Shuruq al-Duwwaliyya, 2002), 350.

102 Ibid., 41.

103 Ibid., 157.

104 Ibid., 159.

105 Ibid., 160.

106 Ibid., 161.

107 Ibid., 160–1.

108 Ibid., 163.

109 Ibid., 162.

110 Ibid., 332.

111 'Abduh's irenic approach reflects the criticism of eighteenth-century reformers of the strict adherence to one's legal school (*tamadhdhub*) and declaring Muslims following different schools of thought unbelievers. See Dallal, *Islam without Europe*, 56–7.

112 al-Afghani and 'Abduh, *al-Ta'līqāt*, 476.

113 A similar view is presented in 'Abduh's *Risālat al-Tawḥīd*; Hildebrandt, 'Neo-Mu'taziliten?', 252–6.

114 al-Afghani and 'Abduh, *al-Ta'līqāt*, 490.

115 Ibid.

116 Ibid.

117 Ibid., 491.

118 Ibid., 492.

119 Ibid., 121.

120 Ibid., 502.

121 Ibid.

122 Ibid.

123 Haddad, *Qarā'a Jadīda*, 69.

124 al-Afghani and 'Abduh, *al-Ta'līqāt*, 164.

125 Ibid.

126 Ibid.

127 Haddad, *Qarā'a Jadīda*, 36–7.

128 On Afghani's messianic allure, see Homa Pakdaman, *Djamal-El-Din Assad Abadi dit Afghani* (Paris: Maisonneuve, 1969), 90.

129 Hadi Khosroshahi, 'al-Muqaddima', in *al-A'māl al-Kāmila li-Jamāl al-Dīn al-Afghānī*, ed. Hadi Khosroshahi, vol. 2 (Tehran: al-Majma' al-'Alami li-l-Taqrib

bayna-l-Madhahib al-Islamiyya, 2000), 9; Wielandt, Rotraud, 'Main Trends of Islamic Theological Thought from the Late Nineteenth Century to Present Times', in *The Oxford Handbook of Islamic Theology*, ed. Sabine Schmidtke (Oxford: Oxford University Press, 2016), 716–19.

130 Kedourie, *Afghani and 'Abduh*, 66–9; Shalash, *Silsila*, 9–14.

131 Shalash, *Silsila*, 53.

132 According to Shalash, 'Abduh uses the expression 'the sword of religion' in reference to the Qur'an that needs to be used to challenge current religious and political leaders in the Muslim world and their understanding of Islam. See Shalash, *Silsila*, 45.

133 Mustafa 'Abd al-Raziq, 'Dhikrā Rīnān fī-l-Jāmi'a al-Miṣriyya', *al-Manār*, 24 (1923): 303–17. Mustafa 'Abd al-Raziq defends in this lecture Afghani and 'Abduh against allegations of heresy and argues that they made a distinction between 'the Islam of the Qur'an (*islām al-qur'ān*)' which encourages acquiring knowledge and furthering civilizational progress and the common understanding of traditional Muslim authorities and those who follow them, which is responsible for the cultural and intellectual stagnation of the Muslim world.

3

The making of a Muslim activist and intellectual

Introduction

> If a philosopher wears rough clothes, lengthens his rosary and attends the mosque, he is a mystic (*ṣūfī*). If he sits in the Matatia coffee-house and smokes the hubble-bubble, then he is a philosopher only.[1]

These remarks attributed to Jamal al-Din al-Afghani articulate the change in Muhammad 'Abduh's intellectual outlook. Before his encounter with Afghani, 'Abduh was an austere ascetic. Afghani not only gave his mysticism a philosophical foundation but also changed the orientation of his activities steering his protégé to socio-political activism and journalistic writing. The change of life-style is expressed in the places 'Abduh increasingly frequented. In coffee-houses, scholars, poets and intellectuals met to listen to musical and poetical performances. In the nineteenth century, they became places where the latest political developments were discussed and political ideas exchanged, meeting points for intellectuals and dissidents.[2] Although the statement attributed to Afghani suggests consecutive stages in the 'Abduh's development, in fact, he engaged in these discourses simultaneously. Under Afghani's tutelage, he wrote his mystical treatise and philosophical-cum-theological commentary while smoking the hubble-bubble in the Matatia coffee house and discussing and writing about politics and society. Being socialized in an intellectual culture of ambiguity, 'Abduh did not consider the concurrent engagement in different discourses as contradictory.

This chapter covers 'Abduh's foray into the public life of Egypt on the eve of the British occupation of the country in 1882. Afghani encouraged 'Abduh and his other Egyptian disciples to engage with modern ideas and reformist thought that began to be circulated in the Middle East at that time and also effected intellectual debates and public discourses in Egypt. The first step was to immerse them in rationalist and philosophical traditions of Islamic thought in order to equip them with the ability to formulate Islamic responses to these debates and to avoid imitating blindly European ideas, habits and mannerisms that characterized the new modern elites that emerged in the Middle East at that time. Their pro-European outlook smoothed the way for the intrusion of European colonial powers, Afghani suggested.

Reformist thought and discourses around civilizational progress and development, constitutional and parliamentary forms of government dominated the public sphere in Egypt as in other parts of the Middle East. In Egypt, Rifa'a al-Tahtawi (1801–1873) who had studied at al-Azhar was one of the first Egyptian authors discussing modern ideas in his writings. In 1826, he accompanied one of the first educational missions of young Egyptians to study in Paris.[3] After he had returned in 1831, he established and headed the School of Languages (or School of Translators) in 1835 to make European scientific and philosophical works accessible in Arabic.[4] Observing the political culture in France, al-Tahtawi was also one of the first advocates of curbing political despotism and of increasing the political accountability of rulers as essential preconditions for civilizational progress.[5] 'Abduh became an active participant in these debates from the mid-1870s onwards and joined a new group of the cosmopolitan Egyptian intelligentsia whose discourse was utilitarian and proto-nationalist and who extolled Egyptian patriotism, the development of modern education and political reforms. 'Abduh developed his own distinct voice in these debates which this chapter discusses. His approach was framed by the limits Egypt's autocratic system imposed on him as a journalist, his sense of intellectual elitism and a discursive ambiguity that alluded to certain implications of ideas that others spelled out more explicitly.

The period this chapter covers is also marked by the increasing colonial intrusion of Europe into Egyptian affairs culminating in the British occupation of Egypt in 1882. The 'Urabi Revolution (1881–2) (*thawrat al-'urābī*)[6] was the first major challenge to the absolute authority of Egypt's ruler and sought to resist European colonial encroachment by initiating constitutional and parliamentary reforms to strengthen the political sovereignty of Egypt. 'Abduh's role in the 'Urabi Revolution will be discussed by investigating the evolution of his political ideas in the course of its events.

Egypt under the Muhammad 'Ali dynasty

When 'Abduh was born, Egypt had just witnessed the end of the reign of Muhammad 'Ali (1769–1849) who had ruled the country from 1805 until 1848. Born in today's

Greece into a family of Albanian descent, Muhammad ʿAli was a commander in the Ottoman army who played a leading role in ending the French occupation of Egypt (1798–1801) and managed to seize military control of the Ottoman province. In 1805, he was appointed governor (*walī*) under Ottoman suzerainty and later managed to secure Egypt's quasi-autonomous status within the Ottoman Empire and the hereditary rule of his own dynasty which would rule the country until the Free Officer's coup under Gamal Abdel-Nasser (1918–1970) in 1952. Under Muhammad ʿAli, Egypt remained nominally a vassal state of the Ottoman Empire which included tributary payments to the High Porte in Istanbul and military assistance if needed and required every governor being officially appointed by the Ottoman sultan, even though the position remained within his family. Muhammad ʿAli undertook a rapid modernization programme, initiating bureaucratic and military reforms and centralizing the economy by confiscating all agricultural land and placing industrial and commercial activities under state control.[7]

Following the Ottoman model, Muhammad ʿAli's reforms sought to strengthen and modernize the military and to introduce a more efficient state bureaucracy to increase tax revenues. Muhammad ʿAli started sending young Egyptians on educational missions to Europe and introduced a dual educational system. While the traditional religious educational institutions such as al-Azhar remained untouched, he formed a network of state schools to train the military and to provide technical, scientific, medical and administrative schooling for a new generation of indigenous engineers, doctors, teachers and state officials whose educational formation followed European models.[8] The new cultural elite that emerged out of educational missions to Europe and as graduates of new state schools 'had a significant impact in reorienting Egyptian culture from the Ottoman empire with its Islamic heritage to a more European, mostly French, model'.[9]

These modernization policies continued under Muhammad ʿAli's successors many of whom were French-educated such as his son Saʿid (1822–1863) and his grandson Ismaʿil (1830–1895). In particular during the reign of the latter from 1863 onwards, Egypt experienced a Europeanization of its cultural and intellectual life. Ismaʿil managed to secure recognition for the title of viceroy (khedive) of the Ottoman sultan in 1867. He was known for his particular 'penchant for pageantry'[10] and sought to enhance the urban culture of Cairo. In 1869, he opened the Cairo Opera House, the first on the African continent and in the Arab world, established another theatre nearby and became an important patron of a variety of cultural activities.[11] The modernization of the military and bureaucracy, significant infrastructure development projects, the foundation of state schools that followed European models and the patronage for European-style cultural activities in Cairo were funded by the expansion of cotton production and other agricultural commodities and their export over which the state initially possessed a monopoly. Cotton export experienced a peak during the American Civil War (1861–5) leading to a brief surge in state revenues.[12]

However, the costs of development and infrastructure projects and declining revenues from agricultural commodities caused a major debt crisis in the 1870s, further aggravated by the immense construction costs of the Suez Canal which was opened in 1869. As state debts to European banks increased, the government was forced to declare bankruptcy in 1876 which had severe consequences for the fiscal and political sovereignty of Egypt and ultimately led to the British occupation in 1882. A significant proportion of the state budget was allocated for the payment of European creditors. An increasing number of commercial concessions were given to Europeans disadvantaging local Egyptian producers and traders. The introduction of a mixed-court system in Egypt in 1875 gave European traders and landowners access to their own jurisdiction in courts that operated primarily on European law and were staffed by Egyptian and European judges who often adjudicated in favour of European defendants and claimants. Egypt's integration into global trade, which these policies and legal changes increased, perpetuated the country's dependency on European fiscal, economic and political support. As a consequence of the debt crisis, the system of dual control was implemented in 1876 in which important state policies were determined by the British and French governments. From 1878, the Egyptian government included a British finance minister and a French labour minister who possessed a de facto veto on all fiscal decisions made at the cabinet table. By 1882, over one thousand Europeans worked in the Egyptian state bureaucracy, constituting 2 per cent of senior officials but consuming 16 per cent of the salaries allocated for state officials.[13] While Egypt, in particular the major cities of Cairo and Alexandria, had become more cosmopolitan in their cultural lives and with the presence of over 90,000 foreigners in the country, the modernization of the previous decades came with a huge political and economic cost which the Egyptian state could not bear by the mid-1870s.[14]

'Abduh on modern civilization

'Abduh moved to Cairo in 1866 during Isma'il's reign and observed these socio-cultural transformations in Egypt. He completed his traditional religious education at al-Azhar and passed the final examination in 1877.[15] Despite being often at odds with the conservative religious establishment at al-Azhar, he also began teaching there, instructing students in logic and Sunni-Ash'ari theology.[16] In 1878, 'Abduh became involved in the new state school system teaching Arabic language at the Dar al-Lisan al-Khadawiyya (Khedivial School of Languages) and history at the Dar al-'Ulum, a teachers' training college.[17] He was thereby able to witness the educational bifurcation within Egypt between traditional Islamic and modern state-led educational institutions resulting in the emergence of a new intellectual and cultural elite that was European in its orientation and increasingly disinterested in Islamic intellectual traditions. On the other side stood an al-Azhar trained religious establishment that failed to engage with modern ideas. Afghani's tutelage enabled 'Abduh to critique the scholastic traditionalism of the religious class while initiating the formulation of an indigenous response to the tropes of reform, development and modernization. Teaching rationalistic and mystical philosophy, Afghani encouraged 'Abduh to recuperate elements of the Islamic intellectual heritage that have been forgotten and to identify resonances with modern European thought to which he introduced 'Abduh and his other Egyptian students as well. At the same time, Afghani was aware of the entrapments of European imperialism whose *modus operandi* under the British he had directly experienced in India and whose first inklings were observable in Egypt.

'Abduh, in one of his first journalistic pieces of 1877, connects his own engagement with the rationalistic streams of Islamic thought, whether in philosophy or theology, with the need to acquire modern sciences. Expertise in rationalist Islamic thought is needed to acquire the intellectual skills to base knowledge claims on 'proofs (*barāhin*)' and 'clear rational evidences (*al-adilla al-'aqliyya al-qaṭ'iyya*)'.[18] In addition, reviving these Islamic rationalist traditions paves the way for adopting 'the useful new sciences'[19] that have come from Europe. Rather than defending any sense of religious, cultural or intellectual authenticity against European influences, 'Abduh argues that the cultural and intellectual exchange between Egypt and Europe needs to intensify for the development and modernization of the country. Acquiring such sciences is essential for 'the protection of our nation (*millatinā*), our state (*dawlatinā*) and our religion (*dīninā*)'.[20] The very 'integrity of Islam (*bayḍat al-islām*)'[21] is at stake, appealing in particular to the conservative religious establishment of al-Azhar that refuses to engage with modern thought. Yet, unlike many of his European-educated Egyptian contemporaries who had lost interest in the Islamic intellectual heritage,

ʿAbduh seeks to embed the engagement with modern European sciences with an equally important foundation in rationalist Islamic thought.

This conflation of modern thought with antecedents in the Islamic tradition is also visible in his reception of European discourses around civilizational progress. While teaching at Dar Al-ʿUlum, ʿAbduh used the *Muqaddima* by the prominent North African historian Ibn Khaldun (1332–1406) as textbook for his history lessons.[22] Ibn Khaldun's historiography seeks to explain historical developments and the environmental, political, social, cultural and economic factors that cause 'the differences between peoples (*umam*), places and eras regarding their conduct, manners, customs, creeds, doctrines and other conditions (*aḥwāl*)'.[23] A particular interest for him lies in the rise and fall of a dynasty (*dawla*). Like human beings, dynasties have a lifespan rising, reaching their peak and eventually declining to be replaced by another dynasty. An important element deciding the political success of a ruling dynasty is for Ibn Khaldun the concept of *ʿaṣabiyya*. Originating from a sense of tribal solidarity among nomads (*badū*), Ibn Khaldun uses this term to designate any form of social solidarity or cohesion that binds people together into a community and can be based on kinship, locality or religion. Strong social bonds within a community are central to achieve and sustain power (*mulk*), and its weakening results in losing one's grip to power and in the disintegration of a dynasty to be replaced by another one with a stronger sense of *ʿaṣabiyya*.[24] Ibn Khaldun's 'theory of history is neither cyclical nor evolutionary, but wave-like: the rise and decline of dynasties repeats itself again and again, driven by the same basic forces'.[25]

ʿAṣabiyya is the driving force behind obtaining power (*mulk*) and forming dynastic rule (*dawla*) in a process that occurs within two basic social modes of human civilization (*ʿumrān*): rural-pastoral society (*badāwa*) and urban-sedentary society (*ḥaḍāra*). While social mores in cities are more refined, sophisticated, complex and, in this sense, more civilized, Ibn Khaldun attributes a stronger sense of *ʿaṣabiyya* to tribal nomads who dwell outside of cities. Urban centres are the natural seats of power, but the more refined urban life-style with its distractions and luxuries undermines *ʿaṣabiyya* and initiates the decline of a ruling dynasty. Pastoral nomads are unruly, and their strong tribal solidarity propels them to seek power and to replace a declining dynasty, dwelling in the city, by forming their own dynasty. The dichotomy between *badāwa* and *ḥaḍāra* helps to explain the rise of the Arab-Muslim empire, when Islam gave Arab tribes a new sense of *ʿaṣabiyya* that allowed them to conquer their neighbouring empires, or the Mongol conquest of the Middle East whose aftermath Ibn Khaldun directly witnessed.[26] It equally reflects his immediate geographical origin in North Africa where nomadic tribes conquered cities and established themselves as rulers, forming various dynasties that followed one after the other.

Ibn Khaldun's discourse 'on the rise of states (*duwwal*) and their downfall, on matters of civilization (*'umrān*) and on its principles within its nation (*ummatihī*)'[27] informed 'Abduh's views but gained a particular evolutionary reading. Civilization (*tamaddun* or *madaniyya*) became one of the keywords marking the government policies under Khedive Isma'il and shaped wider reformist discourses and intellectual debates in Egypt and in the Ottoman Empire at that time.[28] Civilization was considered as stemming from Europe and associated with modernizing reforms, progress and Enlightenment thought by government officials who went on educational missions to Europe or graduated from the newly founded state schools.[29] 'Abduh in his early journalistic writings also uses civilization (*tamaddun*) in this sense.[30] He praises the Khedive Isma'il for his efforts to expand modern education across the country, extending invitations to foreigners to teach in newly established state schools and his support of publishing literature and newspapers following the example of European rulers in the past 'who had risen in the dissemination of civilization (*nashr al-tamaddun*) in their domains'.[31] Furthermore, the successful implementation of such reform initiatives requires increasing relations between Egypt and 'the civilised nations (*al-umam al-mutamadduna*)',[32] namely European countries.

Ibn Khaldun introduces the distinction between nomadic Bedouins (*badū*) and sedentary city-dwellers (*madanī*; from *madīna*, meaning city) and uses the term *tamaddun* to denote the urbanization of nomadic tribes – the process of their sedentarization in urban settlements when they have achieved power and form more complex structures of socio-political organization.[33] Before Ibn Khaldun, Persianate Islamic philosophers like Nasir al-Din Tusi (1201–1274) equally link the term *tamaddun* to urbanization but point out that it denotes 'not the residence of the inhabitants of a city but a particular social organization (*jam'iyyatī*) among the inhabitants of a city. This is what the philosophers mean when they say "human beings are civic (*madanī*) by nature", meaning they possess the natural need to form a social organisation which is called civilisation (*tamaddun*)'.[34] For Tusi, *tamaddun* not just means the geographical formation of cities but equally entails the formation of a socio-political entity, a polity, based on law, order and political leadership structures. 'Abduh and his contemporaries adopted the term *tamaddun* or developed the neologism *madaniyya* from *madanī*, meaning urbanized or civic, but read them in evolutionary terms, echoing nineteenth-century notions of civilizational progress and development. For them, Ibn Khaldun's dichotomy between nomadic culture and urban culture and Tusi's understanding of the characteristics which distinguish a polity as a complex socio-political formation from more primitive forms signify different stages in civilizational progress. They thereby followed theories that were promulgated by European thinkers such as the French writer and statesman François Guizot. His book provides an evolutionary account of the development of European history which became available in Arabic translation in 1878 and was part of Afghani's private instructions in history and politics.[35] Afghani also encouraged 'Abduh to write a positive review of the book.[36]

For Guizot, the roots of European civilization lie in the ability of both the social structure and municipal order of the Roman Empire and the moral vision espoused by Christianity to tame the unruly urge for freedom characteristic of Europe's 'barbarians'[37] before the Middle Ages. The politico-legal legacy of the Roman Empire and Christianity in a sense civilized their barbaric habits and attitudes and formed European civilization.[38] In 'Abduh's reading, Guizot's distinction between unruly barbaric Europe and the political and moral order of Rome and Christianity resonates with Ibn Khaldun's distinction between *badāwa* and *ḥaḍāra* – but only to certain extent. While for Ibn Khaldun both social modes stand in perpetual tension with one another leading to the rise and fall of dynasties throughout history, 'Abduh places these social modes in an evolutionary sequence: from more primitive social formations around tribes (*qabā'il*) to more complex societies around nations (*umam*) and peoples (*shu'ūb*) which require more sophisticated structures of authority and leadership to transcend the anarchic structure of tribal societies determined by sheer force.[39] Polities emerged based on law (*qānūn*) and order (*niẓām*)[40] which provide security and stability and a socio-political environment that brings 'the advantages of sedentary civilization (*maḥāsin al-ḥaḍāra*)'.[41] In 'Abduh's combined reading of Guizot and Ibn Khaldun *tamaddun* shifts its meaning from sedentism to civilizational progress. While Guizot refers to the civilizational force of Christianity in early medieval Europe, 'Abduh adopts the discursive ductus of pre-modern Islamic practical philosophy which in its conceptualizations of how societies are formed and law and order maintained does not engage with Islamic scriptural sources but primarily refers to Aristotelian conceptions of politics.

'Abduh and Egypt's new cosmopolitan intelligentsia

As part of the modernizing activities under the reign of Khedive Isma'il and his aim to enhance the country's cultural and intellectual life following European models, Egypt witnessed the emergence of the Egyptian press in the mid-1870s. Syrian Christians who had escaped stricter censorship laws in the Ottoman Empire thereby played a central role. Isma'il deliberately encouraged their settlement in Egypt to foster his image as a patron of cultural life and to present himself as more liberal than his Ottoman overlord.[42] The Syrian-Christian Taqla brothers established the newspaper *al-Ahrām* (The Pyramids) in 1875, for example. Afghani played an important role in providing his students and his circle of reformist intellectuals with platforms for journalistic activities. The Syrian-Christian playwrights Adib Ishaq (1856–1885) and Salim al-Naqqash (d. 1884) moved to Egypt in 1875 after hearing of the particular interest of Khedive Isma'il in patronizing theatre productions. Both became part of the study circles held by Afghani who also helped them to gain a license to publish newspapers. Afghani's contacts to the Egyptian notable and later prime minister Riyad Pasha who sponsored his stay in Egypt paved the way for Ishaq and al-Naqqash to obtain their newspaper licenses.[43] Ishaq's newspaper *Miṣr* (Egypt) in particular became one of the most popular and influential newspapers and 'spread the ideas advanced by al-Afghānī'.[44] The Egyptian-Jewish writer Ya'qub Sanu' (1839–1912) held cultural salons to discuss literary, social and historical issues since 1874 which were also attended by Afghani and his disciples. Sanu' was one of the first Arab authors using colloquial Arabic both in his plays and his journalistic work such as in articles and cartoons in his satirical magazine *Abū Naẓẓāra Zarqā'* (The Man with Blue Spectacles) which he established in 1877, following Afghani's encouragement.[45] All these individuals were part of the new cosmopolitan intelligentsia in Egypt that had a significant presence of minority groups, such as Christians and Jews, and included young reformist students and scholars from al-Azhar like 'Abduh and graduates from state schools who worked in the military or bureaucracy. Afghani introduced his own group of students to the cultural activities of these intellectuals and writers and particularly encouraged them to engage in journalism.[46]

The nascent Egyptian press that emerged in the mid-1870s primarily targeted the literate educated elite. However, the public reading of newspapers in coffee-houses and the increased literacy because of the expansion of state schools contributed to the rise of an Egyptian public sphere whose published discourses were significantly shaped by Afghani and his associates. The Russo-Turkish War of 1877–8, for example, was widely covered by Egyptian newspapers, informed its readers about events in an unprecedented manner and created an awareness of the vulnerability of the Ottoman Empire after it had lost the war.[47] Following Afghani's encouragement, 'Abduh also ventured into journalism which provided him with a new avenue for articulating and spreading the reformist ideas Afghani taught him.[48] He applauded the establishment of the newspaper *al-Ahrām* and became one of its first contributors.[49] For him, the newly established newspapers and journals are 'a great hope for the progress of nations and the arrangement of the affairs of states'.[50] In line with his positive view of the modernization policies in Egypt, 'Abduh describes newspapers as means for civilizational progress by providing information on the causes of development and the reasons why certain nations have become successful and powerful. Equally, however, newspapers should be true mirrors for princes assessing the strengths and weaknesses of their policies, showing when they enacted justice but also revealing their oppressive acts. A newspaper editor is compared to 'a preacher (*khaṭīb*) who climbs the pulpit of the world, holds in his hand Israfil's trumpet[51] and calls out what is despicable and what is exalted'.[52]

In a similar sense, 'Abduh combined the roles of preacher and journalist and moved between different discourses as religious scholar and public intellectual with ease to address different audiences simultaneously.[53] The conflation of both roles in his publication activities did not occur consecutively but concurrently, as he published articles in Egyptian newspapers at the same time when he was engaged in scholarly writing. His work on the mystical *Risālat al-Wāridāt* or theological commentary on the *Sharḥ al-'Aqā'id al-'Aḍudiyya* gives evidence of his ability to move with ease between different literary genres and writing styles. It also indicates that there was no contradiction between his mystical and philosophical inclinations and his publishing activities. As stated by himself in one of his early journalistic pieces,[54] 'Abduh considers his exposure to Islamic philosophy as a prerequisite for his critical positioning towards traditional Islam and for his ability to formulate an Islamic response to reformist discourses that had entered Egypt at that time. Both activities were inspired and supported by Afghani and express 'Abduh's engagement with political and social reforms, as they were discussed in Egypt and other parts of the Ottoman Empire.[55]

Political debates and activism: Constitutionalism and Freemasonry

One central theme of these debates revolved around constitutional and parliamentary forms of government as they just emerged in Europe. Khedive Isma'il established a Council of Deputies (*majlis al-nawwāb*) in 1866 whose members were wealthy landowners and urban merchants. It primarily had a consultative role without any real legislative authority or oversight over the government. The first Ottoman constitutional era (1876–8) had repercussions on similar debates in Egypt and across the Middle East. Reform-oriented bureaucrats and reformist intellectuals, known as Young Ottomans, succeeded in implementing the first constitution which limited the powers of the Ottoman sultan and also included provisions for the election of a Council of Deputies.[56] In 1878, the first Ottoman constitution was abolished and the ruling Sultan ʿAbdül-Hamid II (1842–1918) restored absolutist rule. The repercussions of events in the Ottoman Empire also featured in the Egyptian press with Afghani's students and associates playing a central role in debating the feasibility of similar reforms in Egypt. One of the strongest advocates for emulating the Ottoman constitutional experiment was Adib Ishaq.[57] In an article published in his newspaper *Miṣr* during the Russo-Turkish War of 1877–8, he distinguishes between autocratic (*mustabidd*) and consultative (*shūrāwī*) forms of government characterizing the latter as more advanced and well established 'among all civilised states (*al-duwwal al-mutamaddina*)' such as France or Britain.[58] Similarly, the Ottoman Empire and Egypt have reached a similar degree of development so that 'both have made their governments consultative'.[59] Echoing renewed calls for placing more power into the Council of Deputies, Ishaq and his friend al-Naqqash supported a consultative order (*niẓām shūrī*) in an article published in 1879.[60]

Ishaq's and al-Naqqash's enthusiasm for a constitutional government in that period reflected similar views of Young Ottoman reformers, like Namık Kemal (1840–1888), who led early calls for implementing constitutional reforms, as means to strengthen the Ottoman state against external and internal enemies.[61] Afghani, however, appeared less enthusiastic. Writing in *Miṣr* in 1879, he does not disagree with the benefits of a constitutional government but considers 'an Easterner' not being ready for it because of the long historical experience of sustained despotism, the spread of superstitious beliefs and lacking expertise in modern sciences. The best option is 'the learned and skilful government (*al-ḥukūma al-mutanaṭṭisa*)',[62] led by an enlightened despot who advances education and the dissemination of knowledge, develops the economy and establishes an efficient and just bureaucracy based on the rule of law. Afghani's more sceptical tone towards constitutional reforms contradicts the more supportive voice of his disciples Ishaq and al-Naqqash. Quite often he would instruct his students to disseminate ideas while he himself would not expose his more radical ideas openly or publish under pseudonyms.[63] In this sense, Ishaq might have been tasked to circulate more revolutionary political ideas with which Afghani was unwilling to be associated with publicly.[64] Afghani himself was under the patronage of Riyad Pasha who supported the khedive's modernization programme but equally rejected constitutional reforms and consultative forms of government. Being on the payroll of an Egyptian notable[65] who favoured an approach Afghani defined as enlightened despotism explains his public support for this model.

In reality, Afghani was not a stranger to revolutionary activism and became more embroiled in Egyptian politics and efforts to depose Khedive Ismaʿil in 1879. Freemasonry and various Masonic lodges that had formed in Egypt at that time were important platforms for the political mobilization against Ismaʿil. Egypt was the first country of the Arab world in which Freemasonry set foot. Initially Italians played an important role in setting up Masonic lodges in Alexandria in 1830.[66] Other lodges following different national traditions (Scottish, French and English in particular) emerged in the following decades in both Alexandria, which was the initial centre of Masonic activities, and Cairo. While initially established by foreigners in Egypt, some of these lodges began to open membership for Egyptians, probably from around 1860.[67] Efforts were also made to establish specifically Egyptian lodges or to create umbrella bodies such as the Grand Orient of Egypt to unite various lodges across the country in 1874. By 1878, around fifty-six lodges existed, twenty-nine of which were open to both Europeans residing in Egypt and local Egyptians and Syrians.[68] These mixed Masonic lodges provided social spaces for European expatriates and locals to intermingle outside other more formal settings.[69] While these lodges officially refrained from political activities – an attitude also important to secure their approval by government authorities – they became instruments for political mobilization.[70]

Afghani sought membership in one of the Masonic lodges in 1875 and had attended meetings of a number of lodges by 1876 with different national affiliations. His entry into Freemasonry, according to Ishaq, was motivated by his desire to identify a new platform for political activism, being particularly concerned about the increasing European dependency of Egypt and the inability of Khedive Ismaʿil to counter it.[71] He became a leading member of the English Star of the East lodge which included among its members representatives of the Egyptian elite such as Ismaʿil's son and crown prince Tawfiq (1852–1892), influential notables and state bureaucrats, members of the Council of Deputies and army officers. Afghani brought his disciples and associates into this Masonic lodge, such as ʿAbduh, Ishaq, al-Naqqash, Sanuʿ and also the later important Egyptian statesman Saʿd Zaghlul (1859–1927)[72] and was elected as president of this lodge in 1878. Through the Masonic Lodge, Afghani established contacts with the crown prince Tawfiq and, at least from Spring 1879 onwards, hoped to install him as new khedive replacing his father. Tawfiq presented himself towards Afghani with a more liberal orientation promising the implementation of constitutional reforms that Afghani's disciples advocated.[73] Afghani lobbied French authorities in Egypt to assist him in deposing Isma'il[74] and also had plans to assassinate him which 'Abduh approved.[75] However, his instrumentalization of Freemasonry as a political tool for opposing the Khedive Isma'il met resistance from other members. Some rejected Afghani's activism from within the Masonic lodge misusing its network for political purposes and fearing government repression. Afghani was expelled as a consequence but established his own lodge afterwards.[76]

Afghani's involvement in Freemasonry allowed him to establish a rapport with Tawfiq and gave his leadership ambitions further momentum but Afghani's biographers quite likely exaggerate his actual role in Isma'il's downfall in 1879 which was caused by a number of other factors.[77] Isma'il, seeing his actual power eroded under the Franco-British dual control regime, saw an opportunity to re-assert his power when dismissed Egyptian army officers brought their grievances to the government that was unwilling to concede and arrested the complaining officers. Isma'il also responded to rising calls among some members of the Council of Deputies to end European fiscal control. Most members were wealthy landowners and merchants who feared higher taxation because of Egypt's debt commitments or suffered from European trade concessions that disadvantaged local traders. In April 1879, Isma'il dismissed the government and appointed a new one without any European ministers. However, his intervention initiated his demise: both France and Britain stepped in and persuaded the Ottoman sultan to dismiss Isma'il as viceroy and to appoint his son Tawfiq as his successor in June 1879. His ascension was initially greeted with enthusiasm by Afghani's associates. In an article published in July 1879, 'Abduh is full of praise of the new khedive, his initial ministerial appointments and legislative initiatives, indicating how 'our country has entered a new age'.[78] For 'Abduh, there is no doubt that with all the measures implemented so far Egypt will eventually achieve 'its complete national independence'.[79]

Although Tawfiq introduced some reforms that seem to confirm the liberal hopes among his supporters, he still accepted foreign influence on Egyptian politics and French and British control over its fiscal policy – reinstating the dual control regime. Disillusioned by Tawfiq's collaboration with the French and the British, Afghani began to influence public opinion against him and argued in his speeches that opposition to a ruler is permissible when he cooperates with the enemies of his own people. Due to his public agitation against the khedive, Afghani was arrested and expelled from Egypt and his disciple 'Abduh exiled to his home village in lower Egypt in September 1879.[80]

One eve of the revolution: 'Abduh as journal editor

Abduh's inner exile did not last for very long, as Riyad who became Egyptian prime minister in 1879 following the ascension of Tawfiq decided to invite him back to Cairo. Riyad was sceptical towards radical changes and sought a gradual implementation of reforms,[81] a top-down approach as adopted by Ottoman bureaucrats and emulated by Muhammad 'Ali and Khedive Isma'il earlier. Riyad curbed the activities of political groups and exiled their leaders, strengthened censorship laws and closed down a number of newspapers, such as those published by Ishaq and al-Naqqash.[82] At the same time, Riyad wanted to improve the official journal *al-Waqā'i' al-Miṣriyya* (The Egyptian Events) which was established by Muhammad 'Ali in 1828 to publish governmental policies. Riyad intended to change the nature of this journal from merely announcing decrees of the khedive and governmental departments to a forum in which political, social, cultural and religious ideas are discussed and the modernization policies of the government are communicated to the educated elite of the country. After having read 'Abduh's articles in *al-Ahrām* and following the recommendation of some young fellow Azharis, Riyad invited him to become co-editor and later editor-in-chief of the journal.[83]

Following his return from exile and appointment as editor, 'Abduh was in a position to observe developments in Egyptian politics that would lead to the 'Urabi Revolution (*thawrat al-'urābī*) and the British occupation of Egypt in 1882. As editor of the official journal, 'Abduh was allowed some editorial freedom and had his own journalistic space to comment on educational, social, economic and political issues outside of the official announcements from various state departments the journal published. For instance, he condemned certain popular Sufi rituals[84] and engaged in one article with the question of polygamy and its social harm advocating a preference for monogamous marriages as implicitly encouraged by the Qur'an.[85] He also penned a number of articles on various political issues which give insights into the development of his political ideas on the eve and during the 'Urabi Revolution. These articles constitute 'Abduh's earliest political writings which reflect and resonate with ideas discussed by Afghani and other intellectuals a few years earlier and are therefore the best avenue to understand his political ideas at this stage of his life and the manner in which he articulated these ideas within the restored autocracy of Khedive Tawfiq.

In his first year as editor of the official journal from his appointment in October 1880 to the start of the 'Urabi Revolution in September 1881, 'Abduh supported the top-down modernizing reforms and provided journalistic justification for the approach Riyad embodied. In line with this commitment, a number of his articles present respecting and implementing 'the rule of law (*ḥukm al-qānūn*)'[86] as a central source for a country's prosperity:

> The law (*al-qānūn*) is the secret of life and the pillar of the happiness of nations (*sa'ādat al-umam*). Power does not yield any real fruits unless it is supported by following the divine law (*al-shar'*) and the general law (*al-qānūn*) obeying of which intellectuals have established as necessity.[87]

'Abduh rebukes 'the mistake of intellectuals'[88] who seek to adopt European socio-political models of state and governance without Egyptian society being ready for them. These intellectuals treat Egypt like a European country and seek to impose principles and laws that lack the necessary social basis to be effectively implemented. 'Abduh gives as a positive example the democratic governance of the United States with basic freedoms being guaranteed by law and regular elections being held to ensure the peaceful transfer of power. However, such a political system would not work in a country like Afghanistan which has not reached the degree of civilizational development that would make the US political system feasible. Bringing a country like Afghanistan to the level of development of the United States would take centuries (*qurūn*).[89] Using Afghanistan as a comparative example is a veiled reference of Egypt which is not yet ready for democratic political systems as they exist in Europe and North America in 'Abduh's view.[90]

'Abduh's rejection of premature socio-political reforms provides intellectual support to the reformist agenda of the prime minister Riyad who was sceptical of radical changes and preferred a gradual approach to the modernization of Egyptian state and society, ultimately led by the khedive and his government. Equally, for 'Abduh different legal systems and the socio-political orders they establish are ultimately rooted 'in the difference within the conditions of nations (*bi-ikhtilāf aḥwāl al-umam*)'.[91] 'Abduh adopts here Ibn Khaldun's terminology but provides it with an evolutionary reading. Egyptian society as a whole does not yet possess the moral and intellectual capacity (*isti'dād*) to successfully implement democratic reforms certain intellectuals demand.[92] Law as the source of the socio-political order reflects the moral and intellectual capacity of a particular society which equally informs the legislative process: 'The laws of every nation emerge in relation to its degree of cognition (*'irfān*), and the laws differ based on how nations differ in ignorance (*jahāla*) and knowledge (*'ilm*).'[93] It is quite clear from these expositions that 'Abduh does not reject the introduction of European-style socio-political reforms because of inherent cultural differences between European societies and Arab-Muslim societies. On the contrary, he finds the achievements of European and North American political culture worthy of emulation but suggests that Egyptian society as a whole is not sufficiently prepared to implement such a political culture, its legal basis and institutional manifestations at this stage.[94] Establishing such a political culture, based on the rule of law and a commitment to the common good, needs to be developed gradually by raising educational levels, encouraging social activism and developing people's political consciousness.[95]

In these articles, 'Abduh assumes the role of a modern public intellectual using the printing press as vehicle to disseminate his ideas. At the same time, this modern public role is informed by the traditional mandate of an Islamic philosopher who imparts moral guidance to society or at least tries to turn attention to the right moral conduct. The intellectual elitism of classical traditions of Islamic philosophy are also visible in his articles: 'Abduh assigns to the elite of country – using the Qur'anic designation 'those firm in knowledge (*al-rāsikhūn fī-l-'ilm*)'[96] – with the particular mandate to guide society towards civilization (*tamaddun*) and to develop solutions for its economic, social and political problems.[97] These articles appeal to the universality of reason which needs to guide the ethical conduct of individuals and society and impart on both the virtues to achieve welfare and prosperity. Breaking the law – whether state or religious – is not reprimanded by referring to the punishments such violations might carry. The rule of law is justified on utilitarian grounds: understanding the rationales for specific laws and following them unites society and yields prosperity. 'Those civilised countries'[98] in Europe are still role-models Egypt should seek rapprochement with, as its laws are derived from the same universal reason Islamic philosophers appealed to in the past. These common roots in a universal rationality allow the cultural cross-fertilization between Europe and the Arab-Muslim world. Universal reason is the root for 'the real unity of humanity', but abandoning rationally anchored morality has undermined this unity: 'Its [humanity's] sound innate disposition (*fiṭratuhū al-salīma*) has turned to manners that do not have any relation to its sacred and honourable essence.'[99]

This emphasis on the primacy of ethical development and its rational foundation resonates with an approach to ethics espoused by the genre of ethical literature during the 'Abbasid period. This literature engages with ethics and manners, known as *ādāb*, and focusses on the development of individual morality. Ethicists like Ibn Miskawayh (d. 1030) sought to balance the needs of the soul with those of the body to achieve moral perfection and connected individual welfare and the acquisition of virtues with the objective to make society as a whole more virtuous and prosperous.[100] Ibn Misakawayh articulates how his views are informed by Aristotle – though he does not agree in every respect with the Greek philosopher when it comes to establishing the conditions for human happiness. 'Abduh was well aware of his works such as *Tahdhīb al-Akhlāq* (The Refinement of Manners), which he taught in Dar al-'Ulum. This need for society and its individual members to seek self-improvement in intellectual and moral terms to advance society and achieve civilizational progress is presented as part of the unchangeable laws of history which are evident if one studies the rise and fall of different nations and communities.[101] Echoing again Ibn Khaldun but reading him in light of social evolutionary thought of the nineteenth century, the political decline of a state is preceded by the intellectual and moral decay within society. To regain political power, social cohesion needs to be strengthened, a renewed sense of *'aṣabiyya*. The primary means to achieve this is by the proper implementation of the law, the collective internalization of its spirit and the creation of a virtuous society. Such a society overcomes differences and conflict and establishes 'unity and concord'.[102]

As a political commentator, 'Abduh is not concerned with ensuring that all aspects of individual and social life are governed by Islam but more interested in raising the ethical consciousness of individuals to direct their efforts to the general welfare of society.[103] The discourse in these articles is utilitarian and lacks any significant engagement with Islamic sources of authority and theories of governance. His primary concern is the implementation of state law (*qānūn*) with not much attention paid to the relevance of Islamic law (shari'a) and its role in determining an Islamic socio-political order. The Arabic term *qānūn* denotes the discretionary legal authority of the ruler and was used in relation to 'laws primarily based on reason and custom'[104] made by the ruler. In 'Abduh's reading, it includes the legislative authority of the khedive and his government and is the legal foundation of 'the civil order for a nation (*al-niẓām al-madanī li-umma*)'.[105] *Qānūn* is distinct from Islamic law (shari'a) which is formulated by the legal scholars (*fuqahā'*). Both types of law (*qānūn* and *shar'*) complement each other and are necessary for state and society to function, as ʿAbduh alludes to as well.[106] However, his primary concern is the development of a legal order that advances Egypt's civilizational progress – a task given to and exercised by the khedive and his government.

The existence of laws alone is not sufficient: to be effective, the spirit behind them needs to be internalized by increasing the moral and intellectual capacity of members of society through an expansion of education. This need to instil within society a concern for common welfare and prosperity is also articulated on proto-nationalist terms in two articles ʿAbduh wrote about patriotism (*waṭaniyya*). His interest in this term also resonated with contemporaneous intellectual discourses in Syria that equated being civilized (*mutamaddin*) with love for one's country (*waṭan*).[107] Members of society with the appropriate intellectual insights and moral constitution will seek prosperity for the entire country (*waṭan*) rather than pursuing the limited interests of their own social group, community or class: 'Patriotism (*al-waṭaniyya*) is nothing else but pure love for one's country (*al-maḥabba li-l-waṭan*) which raises the effort with complete exertion to embrace what brings progress and salvation.'[108]

In these articles during the first year of his tenure as editor of the official journal *al-Waqāʾiʿ al-Miṣriyya*, ʿAbduh seems to endorse the autocratic leadership re-asserted by the new Khedive Tawfiq and enforced by his prime minister Riyad. The law, as issued by the ruling authority, needs to be implemented and followed. The focus of government policies needs to be on developing education to prepare society for further socio-political reforms. ʿAbduh criticizes Europeanized intellectuals for their superficial emulation of European culture and their unrealistic demands for radical change – in contrast to the more measured approach of Riyad. Yet, a closer reading of these articles suggests various instances of semantic ambiguity that allow for their different reading without challenging the existing political order under whose constraints he had to operate as a public intellectual writing for an official state journal. ʿAbduh defends the political authority of the khedive and his government, but equally criticizes forms of despotism that have marked Egypt's more recent history. Perhaps in reference to the despotic and ruthless leadership style of Muhammad ʿAli and his excessive use of forced state labour (*corvée*) for development projects during his reign, ʿAbduh points at the antipathy people developed towards their rulers who exploited them and exercised their authority based on their whims and fancies. This experience had a detrimental effect on the political consciousness of the people, as their political oppression undermined their intellectual freedom: 'With such outer and inner enslavement (*al-istirqāq al-ẓāhirī wa-l-bāṭinī*) will power was annihilated, freedom of choice died and the light of thought was entirely blown out.'[109]

The law whose virtues and benefits 'Abduh extolls equally delimits the power of the ruler for his own benefit and for that of his subjects. By overcoming his own inclination to cling to absolute power, the ruler needs to implement the law for the sake of his subjects' prosperity.[110] The legislative process of 'setting laws (*waḍ' al-qawānīn*)'[111] involves different actors and needs to follow certain conditions. It involves religious scholars (*'ulamā'*) and political leaders (*siyāsiyūn*) who need to consider the customs and traditions of their society and the intellectual and moral development of its people to ensure that laws are understood, followed and reap the benefits they seek to achieve:

> The conditions of the nations themselves are the true legislator (*al-mushri' al-ḥaqīqī*) and the wise and competent guide. The ruling power follows the power of its subjects, as the former does not take any steps unless the latter can follow them.[112]

'Abduh describes the dynamics of the legislative process in carefully crafted wording. It is not the ruler who actually possesses legislative sovereignty but the conditions of society that determine the laws and policies a ruler can effectively implement. While 'Abduh affirms in the following sentence the rightful legislative authority of the ruler, his phrasing implicitly subverts the power dynamics by making the success of legislation dependent on the social conditions among his subjects. This can be read as a veiled reference to more constitutional forms of government Ottoman and Egyptian reformers have advocated that bestow legislative authority to representatives of the people, as they are aware of the social conditions – knowledge of which is needed to effectively legislate. Such a conclusion is justified by the example 'Abduh cites afterwards: he describes the transition of France 'from absolute to constitutional (*muqayyida*) monarchy and then to free republic (*al-jumhūriyya al-ḥurra*)'.[113] This transformation was not solely achieved by measures implemented by the ruling elite at the political level but made possible because of the intellectual and social transformation of French society as a whole. With statements such as these, 'Abduh does not openly challenge the existing political order but reminds of its initial promises and of the need to aspire to a change of a political culture that restricts the absolute authority of the ruler and includes elements of political participation for the benefit of the country. The 'Urabi Revolution which began in September 1881 radically changed the political context and provided 'Abduh with an opportunity to articulate these political views more openly.

'Abduh and the 'Urabi Revolution (1881–2): From supportive observer to active participant

In September 1881, the Egyptian army officer Ahmad 'Urabi headed a military demonstration to the 'Abdin place, the seat of the khedive, and demanded the dismissal of Riyad's government and the full reinstatement of Chamber of Deputies following new elections. This event is usually seen as marking the beginning of the 'Urabi Revolution which began as an initiative to address grievances of Egyptian army officers and turned into a revolutionary movement challenging both the position of the khedive and European control over Egypt. Despite the semi-autonomous status of Egypt within the Ottoman Empire, the state bureaucracy and the officers' corps of the Egyptian army were dominated by Circassians, a Turkish-speaking elite, brought in from different parts of the empire by Muhammad 'Ali to ensure that he could rely on a body of loyal bureaucrats, courtiers and army officers without any social ties to the local Egyptian population. While many Circassians intermarried into Egyptian families and assimilated into Egyptian society and Arabic had replaced Turkish as the official language of the administration, Circassian dominance was particularly pronounced in the Egyptian army where Turkish was still used and the positions of senior officer were not available to native Egyptians.[114]

Ahmad 'Urabi was a colonel in the Egyptian army – the most senior position an Egyptian could hold. 'Urabi led the first confrontation between Egyptian army officers and the government in January 1881 when he and his colleagues demanded the dismissal of the Circassian minister of war for blocking the further promotion of Egyptian officers. 'Urabi and the other officers were arrested but rescued by their own battalions forcing Prime Minister Riyad and Khedive Tawfiq to pardon them. The arrest, rescue and pardon initiated the politicization of 'Urabi and other army officers. From February to September 1881, 'Urabi frequented the political and intellectual circles of reformist intellectuals and notables, meeting 'Abduh and members of the Chamber of Deputies who identified both the unchecked authority of the khedive and increasing foreign dependency as problems they considered the government unable to address. 'Urabi and notables who sought to expand the power of the Chamber of Deputies presented themselves as champions of the people seeking to curb the despotism of the Khedive Tawfiq and his government and to address the severe economic challenges foreign dependency had brought.[115]

The military demonstration at the 'Abdin Palace in September 1881 forced Tawfiq to dismiss Riyad's government, to promise the election of a new Chamber of Deputies and to increase the size of the Egyptian army. The 'Abdin demonstration turned 'Urabi and the Egyptian army into the central player of Egyptian politics. The newly elected Chamber of Deputies which convened in December 1881 was constituted according to the law of 1866 which ensured the dominance of wealthy landowners and merchants. Equally, the new parliament did not initially call for expanding its powers but was unequivocal in rejecting the dual control regime, posing thereby a challenge to the influence and power of France and Britain over Egyptian politics. The insistence of both countries in maintaining dual control regime illustrated how the power of the khedive increasingly depended on European support.

'Abduh initially disagreed with the dismissal of Riyad Pasha, his erstwhile patron, but retained his position of editor of *al-Waqā'i' al-Miṣriyya* and used his position to provide cautious support for the demands and changes made by 'Urabi and his supporters within the parliament and the new government while at the same time countering the notion that the 'Abdin demonstration and its fallout mark a revolutionary change in Egyptian politics. In the first months of the 'Urabi Revolution, 'Abduh positions himself as a voice of moderation supporting the measures implemented by the new government while affirming the political authority of the khedive.[116] In a series of articles on 'the political life' published in November 1881, 'Abduh oscillates between affirming enlightened despotism to achieve progress and development, on the one hand, and advocating freedom (*ḥurriyya*) and political rights (*al-ḥuqūq al-siyāsiyya*),[117] on the other. 'Abduh embeds the discussion of these two poles within an evolutionary scheme of the development of human social and political consciousness which evolves in three consecutive phases: the first, most primitive, phase is that of 'innate disposition (*fiṭra*) which is the natural existence (*al-wujūd al-ṭabī'ī*)'[118] and followed by the second phase, 'the phase of society (*al-ijtimā'*) which is the state of civilization (*al-madaniyya*)'.[119] Providing an evolutionary reading of Ibn Khaldun's and Nasir al-Din Tusi's political philosophy, 'Abduh outlines the progression from a natural, unruly form of human life to the formation of societies which as part of more complex social interaction and division of labour leads to the creation of civilization. The third phase is that of politics (*siyāsa*).[120]

For 'Abduh, the particular challenge of the current historical moment lies in the transition Egypt experiences from the second to the third phase which will result in the complete political maturation of Egyptian society. However, Egypt has not yet arrived there and requires the guidance of an enlightened ruler, 'a wise leader',[121] who needs to lead the country into political maturity: his leadership does not denote a restoration of despotism but is an essential means in the evolutionary development of political consciousness that will lead to freedom and independence. ʿAbduh praises the Khedive Tawfiq for his awareness of the political aspirations of his subjects and his support for the establishment of literary societies, publishing houses and newspapers to expand publications and the scope of freedom of expression.[122] Despite ʿAbduh's reverence to the khedive and affirmation of the authority of his government, the ultimate destination of his tripartite evolutionary scheme is clear: the creation of a society able to embrace political freedoms and to determine its own fate.

ʿAbduh articulates this most explicitly when he distinguishes two meanings of the term country (*waṭan*). Its initial meaning refers to a place of residence in which one lives. However, the term equally carries a political meaning as 'the place in which a person possesses political rights and obligations'.[123] The second meaning is more important as it elevates one's country from a place where one happens to live in to a place to which one can develop patriotic feelings. Such patriotism cannot evolve 'in the state of oppression (*al-istibdād*)', as 'there is no country (*waṭan*) without freedom (*ḥurriyya*)'.[124] For this reason, Egyptians can only develop a patriotic connection to their country and strive for its welfare if they see in their country more than the source of their material wealth but a political entity that defines their rights and obligations. National unity therefore requires the introduction of more political freedoms.

ʿAbduh penned a series of articles at the time when the newly elected Chamber of Deputies convened in December 1881 which provide unequivocal support for a government based on consultation (*shūrā*), aligning himself with the discourses of Young Ottoman reformers and arguments made a few years earlier by his two Syrian associates Ishaq and al-Naqqash. In his discussion of the necessity of consultation, ʿAbduh illustrates his ability to approach a topic from different discursive angles to meet the diverse expectations of his audiences. When arguing for the necessity of *shūrā*, he refers to Islamic sources, political necessities and the utilitarian considerations of practical philosophy. The new constitutional momentum created by the ʿUrabi Revolution also allowed ʿAbduh to articulate his support for parliamentary forms of governance more explicitly in contrast to his earlier circumspect intimations.

In one article, ʿAbduh refers to Islamic scriptural sources and history to dismisses the notion that despotism is a desirable mode of governance. ʿAbduh argues that throughout Islamic history the ruler's 'executive authority'[125] was limited by Islamic law (shariʿa). Islamic legal provisions circumscribe the ruler's power and also minimize his potential misuse of power. Equally, the community (*umma*) is bound to follow the shari'a and possesses the collective mandate of commanding good and prohibiting evil (*al-amr bi-l-ma'rūf wa-l-nahī 'an al-munkar*). This communal role holds those in power accountable and exercises control over the extent of their power. 'Abduh provides a detailed discussion of Qur'an 3:159 'And consult with them in matters ...', the verse the Young Ottoman Namık Kemal had used to justify the need to establish a consultative government in the Ottoman Empire.[126] Consultation is the institutional manifestation of the mandate of Islamic community (*umma*) to guide the ruler on the right path. The form it can take is not specified and varies dependent on historical circumstances but as a fundamental principle of governance, 'consultation is religiously obligated (*wājib shar'ī*)'[127] and not 'the imitation of foreigners (*taqlīd al-ajānib*)'.[128]

In two other articles on consultation 'Abduh moves away from an Islamic discourse and uses political, proto-nationalist and utilitarian arguments in support of it. Cautious not to undermine the political power of the khedive, he commends him for his generous agreement to more consultative forms of government – an obvious political euphemism as the khedive was pressured by army officers around 'Urabi to give into their demands. Yet, for 'Abduh, the time has arrived for 'our Egyptian country'[129] to implement these democratic reforms. As both the people (*umma*) and the government (*ḥukūma*) support a consultative form of government, its establishment becomes a political necessity.[130] 'Abduh's third and final piece on consultation returns to his particular concern with the formulation and implementation of state law (*qānūn*). His earlier intimations that legislation needs to conform to the capacity and needs of the population are now clearly spelled out by connecting the legislative process with consultation: 'The most noble laws and the most powerful in their benefits are those that stem from the general opinion of the people (*ra'ī al-umma al-'āmm*), I mean, that are based on the principles of consultation (*shūrā*).'[131] Praising the election of new Chamber of Deputies, for 'Abduh recent events illustrate that the Egyptian people have reached the capacity (*isti'dād*) to implement a consultative form of government, that their minds exhibit 'the spirit of unity' and are guided by 'love for reform'.[132]

Further developments occurring in 1882 would turn 'Abduh from a supportive observer of events to an active participant. 'Urabi's role in the change of government was recognized by the new prime minister Muhamad Sharif Pasha (1826–1887) who made him undersecretary of war in January 1882. The revolutionary development gained further momentum in February

1882 when a new government was appointed under the leadership of Mahmud Sami al-Barudi (1839–1904) giving ʿUrabi a more prominent role as minister of war. A new Basic Law was approved on 7 February 1882, providing the Chamber of Deputies with legislative authority over bills submitted by the government, oversight of state officials (including Europeans) and control over half of the state's budget. Khedive Tawfiq became increasingly worried about the restrictions of his power and adopted a more confrontational stance to ʿUrabi and his followers, the new government and the Chamber of Deputies. France and Britain further emboldened the khedive to seek a final confrontation with ʿUrabi and his supporters within the government and the Chamber of Deputies until events in May 1882 further escalated the situation and led to direct foreign intervention.[133]

ʿAbduh's articles, published between February and May 1882, illustrate his difficult role as editor of the official state journal, being ultimately responsible to the government and the khedive, and his support for the constitutional reforms that were enacted in this period. He applauds the introduction of the new Basic Law and the establishment of 'a constitutional government (*ḥukūma qānūniyya*)'[134] but equally emphasizes the ultimate political authority of the khedive under whose auspices these changes were implemented. In one of his final articles in April 1882, before the events further escalated, ʿAbduh emphasizes the need of unity (*ittiḥād*).[135] Aware of the growing rift between ʿUrabi and his supporters in the government and the Khedive Tawfiq, ʿAbduh appeals to all involved parties to act as members of a united national body solely eyeing the general welfare of the country rather than working against one another. While this can be a read as an appeal to all involved parties to deescalate their actions and avoid further confrontations, ʿAbduh appeals in particular to the Khedive Tawfiq to pursue 'the good of our country'.[136]

In his role as editor of an official state journal, ʿAbduh sought to provide support for different involved parties, backing the political changes implemented by ʿUrabi and his followers while affirming the ultimate authority of the Khedive Tawfiq. However, the ultimatum issued by France and Britain on 25 May 1882, demanding the entire government to resign and to send ʿUrabi into exile further strengthened ʿAbduh's alignment with the revolutionaries. Afghani's strong opposition towards European imperialism also shaped his own political activism and determined his course of action when the choice was between the European-backed khedive and ʿUrabi who sought to avert the foreign occupation of Egypt. While Tawfiq was unable to gain full control of the army and had to keep ʿUrabi as minister of war, ʿUrabi could equally not secure sufficient support for deposing the khedive. Ensuing riots between Egyptians and foreigners in Alexandria in June 1882, provided sufficient pretext for British naval forces to attack the city in July. For ʿAbduh, supporters of the khedive deliberately instigated these riots in order to invite the British intervention against ʿUrabi.[137] While Khedive Tawfiq initially called for resistance, he welcomed the British intervention in reality as an opportunity to re-assert his authority and to dispose of ʿUrabi. His calls for a ceasefire were ignored by ʿUrabi whose supporters made preparations to resist the British forces entering Egypt. ʿAbduh was now centrally involved in organizing the opposition to the khedive. With the collapse of the government, ʿUrabi involved in war preparations and Tawfiq siding with the British, a provisional council (*majlis ʿurfī*) was formed which called the congregation of a general assembly (*jamʿiyya ʿumūmiyya*) in Cairo. ʿAbduh acted as the secretary of its meetings in July which denounced Tawfiq as traitor and called for jihad against the British.[138] Despite these public declarations of support for ʿUrabi, many members of the Chamber of Deputies sided with Tawfiq or retreated to their country estates. The Circassian elite and most Egyptian landowners equally supported Tawfiq.[139]

On 13 September 1882, British forces finally defeated ʿUrabi forcing him and his supporters to surrender. He together with his associates, including ʿAbduh, were imprisoned and tried.[140] ʿAbduh was convicted to three years of exile. While in prison, ʿAbduh wrote a letter to his associate Saʿd Zaghlul. The tone of the letter is gloomy and full of regret of the turn of events that resulted in the British occupation of Egypt which he sought to prevent. At the same time, ʿAbduh does not show any remorse about his own actions and their motivations:

> Shall I regret that I headed towards good deeds? Shall I regret that I proceeded towards noble deeds? Shall I regret that I showed courage in defending those that are dear to me? Shall I regret that I displayed pride and zeal so that no harm or humiliation would occur to those close to me? Do I need to lay claim to the hardship I had to endure for the love for my country, while the people only hated it? No! By God, this will not happen.[141]

ʿAbduh and the ʿUrabi Revolution: An assessment

Much of the assessment of ʿAbduh's attitude towards the ʿUrabi Revolution and his involvement is shaped by the account provided by his disciple Muhammad Rashid Rida, as so much of posterior perceptions of his early political activism.

Rida argues that 'Abduh fundamentally disagreed with 'Urabi and his allies and considered these army officers as ignorant and incapable of thoroughly reforming and modernizing Egypt.[142] More contemporaneous observers, however, state 'Abduh's immediate support for the 'Urabi Revolution and his central role. The British diplomat and friend of 'Abduh, Wilfrid Scawen Blunt who supported the revolution calls him 'the intellectual head of a political revolution'.[143] Both Blunt and 'Abduh co-authored the 'programme of the National Party of Egypt'[144] in December 1881, which the former then sent to the British prime minister William Gladstone (1809–1898) to alleviate concerns about the rise of 'Urabi.[145] The later British consul-general in Egypt Lord Cromer (1841–1917) who met 'Abduh in the 1890s suggests that 'he was one of the leading spirits of the Arábi ['Urabi] movement'.[146] Ridwan Fahmi, who was involved in translating the correspondence between the 'Urabi revolutionaries and the High Porte into Turkish, describes 'Abduh as 'the Aristotle of their philosophy',[147] referring to his articles in the official journal *al-Waqā'i' al-Miṣriyya*. More cautiously, 'Uthman Amin refers to the articles which 'Abduh wrote as laying the intellectual groundwork for the 'Urabi Revolution and concludes that 'he was one of its causes'.[148]

What did 'Abduh himself say about 'Urabi and his involvement in the 'Urabi Revolution? In the 1890s, 'Abduh produced his own account of the 'Urabi Revolution in a work commissioned by the then ruler of Egypt Khedive 'Abbas Hilmi II (1874–1944), Tawifq's son. 'Urabi is presented as a tragic and naive figure whose demise was the result of the betrayal he suffered from various sides such as notables and segments of the army who initially pledged loyalty to him. 'Abduh doubts, however, 'Urabi's full commitment to the constitutional process and his complete understanding of its implications. 'Urabi hoped that a proper parliament would strengthen his position towards the khedive and legitimize decisions made by him and army officers as a legislature empowered by the military which acts based on a popular support.[149]

'Abduh recounts a meeting he had with 'Urabi in August 1881, a month before the start of the revolution with the demonstration at the 'Abdin palace. While 'Abduh pleaded for a gradual approach, raising the people's political consciousness via education to prepare them for the political freedoms a constitutional government would provide, 'Urabi favoured the immediate establishment of a strong parliament and a constitutional government. For 'Abduh, a parliament (*majlis shūrī*) established on the authority of the army would be illegitimate (*ghayr mashrū'*) and 'built on foundations that are non-Islamic (*ghayr shar'ī*)'.[150] Such a course of actions would ultimately lead to the foreign occupation of Egypt. 'Abduh's account of his discussion with 'Urabi was written with the benefit of historical hindsight. Hence, the warnings and misgiving of 'Urabi's intentions need to be qualified to a certain extent, in particular 'Abduh's warning of foreign occupation. However, the gradualist approach 'Abduh suggests in response to the demand for immediate democratic reforms was in line with his political writings at that time.

A more reliable source which provides 'Abduh's immediate assessment of the 'Urabi Revolution is a letter he wrote in February 1883, a few months after he had arrived in Beirut, to Alexander Broadley (1847–1916). Broadley acted as defence lawyer for 'Urabi in the trial following the British conquest of Egypt and was sympathetic to the aims of his revolution.[151] In the letter, 'Abduh criticizes the continuous dominance of the Turkish-Circassian elite in Egypt as oppressive, rejects foreign domination of any kind and wishes 'that my country will be free and independent and its ruler guided by the respect for law (*qānūn*) and not by his [the khedive's] whims and fancies'.[152] In defining his relationship to the different parties of the 'Urabi Revolution, 'Abduh suggests that the objectives were agreed by all participants: to end despotism and foreign rule and establish a free and just government. However, there were differences on the means to achieve these objectives. Some proceeded cautiously and within the existing political structures while others wanted to achieve change in a very short time. 'Abduh positions himself between both groups supporting change at an accelerated space if it is driven by Egyptians themselves. However, when some actors in the revolution had become reckless, 'I was on the side of those who were prudent (*al-hukamā'*) and abandoned the one ['Urabi] and his cause who took unnecessary risks'.[153]

'Abduh did not agree with everything 'Urabi did and was ultimately devastated by the consequences of the 'Urabi Revolution: the British occupation of Egypt. He was sceptical of 'Urabi, being a military man claiming to be a champion for the Egyptian people when he met him before the start of the revolution.[154] However, after the 'Abdin demonstration and the constitutional changes it initiated, 'Abduh provided support through his journalistic activities, actively participated in some key events and sided with 'Urabi when British occupying forces entered Egypt. In his later reflections on his role in the 'Urabi Revolution, 'Abduh presents the agreement between the revolutionaries and the government and the khedive to implement constitutional reform as the turning point which led him to support 'Urabi[155] – despite his initial scepticism towards the outcome of the revolution led by Egyptian army officers.[156] With 'Urabi and his revolution, reforms were implemented that Afghani and 'Abduh had advocated with their political activities and journalistic writings and which had inspired the various political groups and intellectuals that formed the proto-nationalist movement in Egypt. 'Abduh saw the revolution as the fruit of Afghani's endeavours in particular, the result of the revival (*nahḍa*) Afghani initiated in Egypt at that time.[157] The events prior and during the 'Urabi Revolution also illustrate 'Abduh's cautious evolution as a political writer and activist: under the protection of the autocratic Prime Minister Riyad Pasha and employed for the official state journal, 'Abduh never challenged the existing political order and only implicitly called for political reforms. With the constitutional momentum of the 'Urabi Revolution, he provided further intellectual support for a stronger parliament and the new constitution while still affirming the ultimate authority of the khedive and his government. Only when Tawfiq collaborated with the British, he – along with other scholars, notables and intellectuals – not only sided with 'Urabi but actively opposed the khedive.

Conclusion

This chapter covered a crucial phase in the evolution of 'Abduh's intellectual life in his career where his exposure to mystical and rationalistic strands of Islamic thought is directed into journalistic writing and political activism. Afghani's instructions in elements of Islamic political philosophy inform the socio-political articles written by 'Abduh in that time. The fusion of different Islamic intellectual traditions that characterized Afghani's teaching sessions was utilized to promote an indigenous response to emergent discourses around modern civilization, development and progress and the social, cultural, educational and political reforms that need to accompany them. 'Abduh's journalistic writings appear to show little concern for ensuring that the reformist debates are thoroughly anchored in the scriptural foundations of Islam and that implemented legal and political reforms are in conformity with Islamic law. Utilitarian, ethical and proto-nationalist arguments hold primacy in his journalistic writings. However, ignoring the need for Islamic legitimacy based on the Qur'an, the *sunna*, Islamic theology or jurisprudence does not mean that he proposed a secular approach disinterested in redefining Islamic socio-political teachings in light of these modern challenges. Rather, he intended to mobilize the broadest range of Islamic intellectual traditions to illustrate the confluence between Islamic and modern European discourses on progress, civilization and politics.

The sources ʿAbduh used were figures like the ʿAbbasid moral philosopher Ibn Miskawayh or the historian and social philosopher Ibn Khaldun. In his political discourse, ʿAbduh engaged with pre-modern works of practical philosophy – and not relevant works of Islamic jurisprudence – because 'it is under the conceptual canopy of *akhlāq*-ethics that Muslims have tended historically most to discuss political theory – that is, the subject of how Muslims should govern their collective affairs in a polity'.[158] Pre-modern discourses on the welfare of state and society occurred in works of practical philosophy or the 'mirrors for princes' genre on successful statecraft. Therefore, ʿAbduh refers to these genres in his political journalism. In response to emergent discourses around modern reforms in the Middle East, the appeal of these genres of Islamic literature to universal reason or universal laws of history appeared more congruent with evolutionary notions of human development, rationalistic foundations of morality and a nascent scientific worldview. ʿAbduh intended to find antecedents for modern discourses within Islamic intellectual traditions to empower the new cultural elite and to counter their blind imitation of European norms, values and attitudes – seen as preface to a complete European colonial intrusion about which Afghani was particularly concerned. Thereby, ʿAbduh and other reformist intellectuals developed a new modern vocabulary based on terms they encountered in the sources of Islamic thought they engaged with. Dynasty (*dawla*) assumed the meaning of state which can rise and fall depending on the degree of its development.[159] A community or a people (*umma*) were identified with the European concept of nation, the collective body that forms the state.[160] Ibn Khaldun's understanding of urban sedentization (*tamaddun*) like the neologism *madaniyya* denotes civilizational progress and the development of more complex forms of political organization. One's place of birth or residence (*waṭan*) is turned into one's homeland or country. Similar to the French concept of *patrie*, it also includes political rights and freedoms crucial to facilitate one's patriotic sense of belonging to it. *ʿAṣabiyya*, central for Ibn Khaldun in the success of a dynasty, is reinterpreted as patriotism (*waṭaniyya*) and becomes the ideological foundation of the state.

ʿAbduh's engagement with politics illustrates his ability to engage in different types of intellectual discourses at the same time. When ʿAbduh started writing for the newspaper *al-Ahrām* in 1876, he also produced his two earliest substantial scholarly works: his mystical *Risālat al-Wāridāt* and the theological-cum-philosophical commentary on the *Sharḥ al-ʿAqāʾid al-ʿAḍudiyya*. For ʿAbduh there was no contradiction between both activities as he considered his engagement with discursive theology (*al-ʿulūm al-kalāmiyya*) as preparation for adopting contemporary sciences (*al-ʿulūm al-ʿaṣriyya*)[161] from Europe which not only comprise technological and scientific knowledge but also 'political science and the history of the development of civilization'.[162] The co-existence of these different discourses – scholarly Islamic and political-utilitarian – reflects the culture of ambiguity of Islamic intellectual traditions into which Afghani introduced 'Abduh. The intellectual versatility this ambiguity cultivates allowed 'Abduh to teach orthodox Sunni theology at al-Azhar, to venerate Afghani as his quasi-divine spiritual master and to argue for the centrality of state law (*qānūn*) in ensuring the prosperity of a country in line with pre-modern Islamic genres of practical philosophy. This range of different activities and discourses was not contradictory for 'Abduh but sprung from a sense of the universality of reason which crosses civilizations and societies and provides universal rules for individual and collective human conduct. Such an intellectual outlook is informed by the capaciousness of pre-modern Islamic thought and its diverse intellectual traditions, manifestations of which are clearly observable in 'Abduh's earliest scholarly, political and journalistic writings.

This culture of ambiguity also allowed 'Abduh to navigate his journalistic interventions through political repression and autocracy and couch his calls for social and political reforms in a language that did not challenge the ruling authority directly, given 'Abduh's position as editor of the government's official mouthpiece. One needs to read between the lines to discover the fuller implications of 'Abduh's arguments, illustrating his mastery of intellectual ambiguity to communicate different messages to diverse readers at the same time. The reforms implemented during the 'Urabi Revolution and the popular momentum that carried it provided a brief discursive space for 'Abduh and other activists to articulate these ideas more openly. The failure of the 'Urabi Revolution and the restoration of autocratic rule – this time backed by a European occupying power – required a more forceful response to European imperialism that would shape 'Abduh's activism in the first years of his exile.

Notes

1 Quoted in Mustafa 'Abd al-Raziq, *Muḥammad 'Abduh* (Cairo: Dar al-Ma'arif, 1946), 74–5.

2 'Ali Al-e Dawud, 'Coffeehouse', in *Encyclopaedia Iranica*, 6, fasc. 1, 1–4.

3 For a comprehensive discussion of his life and thought, see Daniel Newman, *Rifa'a Al-Tahtawi: A 19th Century Egyptian Educationalist and Reformer* (Edinburgh: Edinburgh University Press, 2020).

4 Gilbert Delanoue, *Moralistes et politiques musulmans dans l'Egypte de XIXe siècle (1798–1882)*, vol. 2 (Cairo: Institut Français de l'Achéologie Orientale du Caire, 1982).
5 Elizabeth S. Kassab, *Contemporary Arab Thought: Cultural Critique in Comparative Perspective* (New York: Columbia University Press, 2010), 24.
6 Scholarship mostly uses the designation 'Urabi Revolt. Such a translation does not communicate the meaning of the Arabic term *thawra* which means revolution. Designating it as a mere revolt is also used to delegitimize the revolutionary movement led by 'Urabi. See Donald M. Reid, 'The 'Urabi Revolution and the British Conquest, 1879–1882', in *The Cambridge History of Egypt*, ed. Martin W. Daly, vol. 2 (Cambridge: Cambridge University Press, 1998), 217.
7 Khaled Fahmy, 'The Era of Muhammad 'Ali Pasha, 1805–1848', in *The Cambridge History of Egypt*, ed. Martin W. Daly, vol. 2 (Cambridge: Cambridge University Press, 1998), 139–79; Khaled Fahmy, *All the Pasha's Men: Mehmed Ali, His Army and the Making of Modern Egypt* (Cairo: The American University in Cairo Press, 2002).
8 In literature these new state schools that emerged in Egypt and in the Ottoman Empire are often characterizd as being 'secular' in character. Benjamin C. Fortna, however, questions such designation as being too simplistic as their curricula equally sought to foster an Islamic ethos. See Benjamin C. Fortna, 'Islamic Morality in Late Ottoman "Secular" Schools', *International Journal of Middle East Studies*, 32 (2000): 369–93.
9 Fahmy, 'Muhammad 'Ali Pasha', 178–9.
10 Robert F. Hunter, 'Egypt under the Successors of Muhammad 'Ali', in *The Cambridge History of Egypt*, ed. Martin W. Daly, vol. 2 (Cambridge: Cambridge University Press, 1998), 193.
11 Nevill Barbour, 'The Arabic Theatre in Egypt', *Bulletin of the School of Oriental and African Studies*, 8(1) (1935): 172–3.
12 Hunter, 'Successors of Muhammad 'Ali', 186–7.
13 Reid, "Urabi Revolution', 220.
14 Albert A. Kudsi-Zadeh, 'The Emergence of Political Journalism in Egypt', *The Muslim World*, 70(1) (1980): 47–8.
15 'Abd al-Mun'im Hamada, *al-Ustādh al-Imām Muḥammad 'Abduh* (Cairo: al-Maktaba al-Tijariyya, 1945), 53.
16 Muhammad Rashid Rida, *Ta'rīkh al-Ustādh al-Imām al-Shaykh Muḥammad 'Abduh*, vol. 1 (Cairo: al-Manar, 1931), 133.
17 Ibid., 135–7.
18 Muhammad 'Abduh, 'al-Kitāba wa-l-Qalam', in *al-A'māl al-Kāmila li-l-Imām Muḥammad 'Abduh*, ed. Muhammad 'Imara, vol. 3 (Beirut: Dar al-Shuruq, 1993), 15.

19 Ibid., 18.

20 Ibid., 20.

21 Ibid., 21.

22 Based on these lessons, ʿAbduh penned a book on the science of society and civilization (*ʿilm al-ijtimāʿ wa-l-ʿumrān*) which however has been lost. See Ahmad Amin, *Zuʿamāʾ al-Iṣlāḥ fī-l-ʿAṣr al-Ḥadīth* (Beirut: Dar al-Kitab al-ʿArabi, 1948), 292.

23 Ibn Khaldun, *Muqaddimat ibn Khaldūn*, vol. 1 (Damascus: Dar Yaʿrib, 2003), 115.

24 Ibid., 254–73.

25 Antony Black, *The History of Islamic Political Thought: From the Prophet to the Present*, 2nd edn (Edinburgh: Edinburgh University Press, 2011), 182.

26 Bruce B. Lawrence, 'Introduction to 2005 Edition', in *The Muqaddimah: An Introduction to History*, trans. Franz Rosenthal, abridged and ed. Nessim Joseph Dawood (Princeton: Princeton University Press, 2015), x–xi.

27 Rida, *Taʾrīkh*, vol. 1, 136.

28 For examples in Ottoman Syria see Fruma Zachs, *The Making of a Syrian Identity: Intellectuals and Merchants in Nineteenth Century Beirut* (Leiden: Brill, 2006), 67–77.

29 Delanoue, *Moralistes et politiques musulmans*; Mohamed Haddad, *Muḥammad ʿAbduh: Qarāʾa Jadīda fī Khiṭāb al-Iṣlāḥ al-Dīnī* (Beirut: Dar al-Taliʿa li-l-Tabaʿa wa-l-Nashr, 2003), 169–70.

30 Muhammad ʿAbduh, 'al-Tamaddun', in *al-Aʿmāl al-Kāmila li-l-Imām Muḥammad ʿAbduh*, ed. Muhammad ʿImara, vol. 2 (Beirut: Dar al-Shuruq, 1993), 38–41.

31 Muhammad ʿAbduh, 'al-ʿUlūm al-Kalāmiyya wa-l-Daʿwa ilā-l-ʿUlūm al-ʿAṣriyya', in *al-Aʿmāl al-Kāmila li-l-Imām Muḥammad ʿAbduh*, ed. Muhammad ʿImara, vol. 3 (Beirut: Dar al-Shuruq, 1993), 19.

32 Ibid., 18.

33 Ibn Khaldun, *Muqaddima*, vol. 1, 85.

34 Nasir al-Din Tusi, *Akhlāq-i Nāṣirī* (Tehran: Khwarizmi, 1356 SH [1977/1978]), 251–2; Shahab Ahmed, *What Is Islam?: The Importance of Being Islamic* (Princeton: Princeton University Press, 2016), 463–4.

35 François Guizot, *The History of Civilization in Europe* (New York: Colonial Press, 1899).

36 Muhammad ʿAbduh, 'al-Tuḥfa al-Adabiyya', in *al-Aʿmāl al-Kāmila li-l-Imām Muḥammad ʿAbduh*, ed. Muhammad ʿImara, vol. 3 (Beirut: Dar al-Shuruq, 1993), 23–4.

37 Guizot, *History of Civilization*, 29.

38 Ibid., 21–36; Margaret Kohn, 'Afghānī on Empire, Islam, and Civilization', *Political Theory*, 37(3) (2009): 412–13.

39 Muhammad ʿAbduh, 'al-Quwwa wa-l-Qānūn', in *al-Aʿmāl al-Kāmila li-l-Imām Muḥammad ʿAbduh*, ed. Muhammad ʿImara, vol. 1 (Beirut: Dar al-Shuruq, 1993), 308–9.

40 Ibid., 309.
41 Ibid., 310; Tusi, *Akhlāq-i Nāṣirī*, 252–4; Ahmed, *What Is Islam?*, 464–7.
42 Albert A. Kudsi-Zadeh, 'Islamic Reform in Egypt: Some Observations on the Role of Afghānī', *The Muslim World*, 61(1) (1971): 5.
43 Salim 'Anhuri, *Siḥr Hārūt* (Damascus: al-Matba'a al-Hanafiyya, 1885), 179–80; J. R. I. Cole, *Colonialism and Revolution in the Middle East: Social and Cultural Origins of Egypt's 'Urabi Revolt* (Princeton: Princeton University Press, 1993), 141.
44 Kudsi-Zadeh, 'Emergence of Political Journalism', 51.
45 Ibid., 50.
46 Ibid., 48–54.
47 Tahir Tanahi, ed., *Mudhakkirāt al-Imām Muḥammad 'Abduh* (Cairo: Dar al-Hilal, n.d.), 47.
48 For the rise of the printing press in the 1870s in Egypt and its political significance see Cole, *Colonialism and Revolution*, 110–32.
49 Muhammad 'Abduh, 'Taqrīẓ al-Ahrām', in *al-A'māl al-Kāmila li-l-Imām Muḥammad 'Abduh*, ed. Muhammad 'Imara, vol. 3 (Beirut: Dar al-Shuruq, 1993), 7–8; Ibrahim 'Abduh, *Jarīdat al-Ahrām: Ta'rīkh wa-Fann (1875–1964)* (Cairo: Mu'assasat Sajall al-'Arab, 196), 32–7.
50 'Abduh, 'al-Kitāba wa-l-Qalam', vol. 3, 13.
51 Israfil is one of the archangels who will blow his trumpet to announce the Day of Judgement.
52 'Abduh, 'al-Kitāba wa-l-Qalam', vol. 3, 14.
53 Kudsi-Zadeh, 'Emergence of Political Journalism', 54–5.
54 'Abduh, 'al-'Ulūm al-Kalāmiyya', vol. 3, 15–22.
55 For a similar involvement of Syrian reformers with a Sufi background in literary and journalistic activities, see Itzhak Weismann, *Taste of Modernity: Sufism, Salafiyya and Arabism in Late Ottoman Damascus* (Leiden: Brill, 2001), 227–34.
56 Robert Devereux, *The First Ottoman Constitutional Period: A Study of the Midhat Constitution and Parliament* (Baltimore: Johns Hopkins University Press, 1963).
57 Amin, *Zu'amā' al-Iṣlāḥ*, 300–1.
58 Adib Ishaq, *al-Durar: wa-Hiya Muntakhabāt al-Ṭayyib al-Dhikr al-Khālid al-Athar al-Marḥūm Adīb Ishaq* (Alexandria: Matba'at Jaridat al-Mahrusa, 1886), 50.
59 Ibid.
60 Cole, *Colonialism and Revolution*, 144.
61 Namık Kemal, 'And Seek Their Counsel in the Matter [Qur'an, Sura 3, Verse 159]', in *Modernist Islam, 1840–1940: A Sourcebook*, ed. Charles Kurzman (Oxford: Oxford University Press, 2002), 144–8.
62 L. M. Kenny, 'Al-Afghānī on the Types of Despotism', *Journal of the American Oriental Society*, 86(1) (1966): 25.
63 'Anhuri, *Siḥr Hārūt*, 180.

64 Kudsi-Zadeh, 'Emergence of Political Journalism', 51.
65 Kudsi-Zadeh, 'Islamic Reform in Egypt', 4.
66 Barbara De Poli, 'Italians, Freemasons and the Dawn of Egyptian Nationalism', *The Journal of North African Studies* (2021), DOI: 10.1080/13629387.2021.1891533, 6.
67 In 1864, Halim, one of the sons of Muhammad 'Ali, became one of the first Muslims in Egypt to be elected as grand master of a Masonic Lodge. See ibid., 8.
68 'Ali Shalash, *al-Māsūniyya fī Miṣr* (Cairo: Misr al-Nahda, 1994), 30–5.
69 Cole, *Colonialism and Revolution*, 137–8.
70 Shalash, *al-Māsūniyya*, 32; Di Poli, 'Italians, Freemasons and the Dawn of Egyptian Nationalism', 8–9.
71 Muhammad Rashid Rida, 'Mulakhkhaṣ Sīrat al-Ustādh al-Imām', *al-Manār*, 8 (1905): 401–3; Albert A. Kudsi-Zadeh, 'Afghānī and Freemasonry in Egypt', *Journal of the American Oriental Society*, 92(1) (1972): 27.
72 'Anhuri, *Siḥr Hārūt*, 181.
73 Ibid., 183.
74 Kudsi-Zadeh, 'Afghānī and Freemasonry', 31.
75 Wilfrid S. Blunt, *Secret History of the English Occupation of Egypt: Being a Personal Narrative of Events*, 2nd edn (London: Fisher Unwin, 1907), 489; Elie Kedourie, *Afghani and 'Abduh: An Essay on Religious Unbelief and Political Activism in Modern Islam* (London: Frank Cass, 1966), 25.
76 Kudsi-Zadeh, 'Afghānī and Freemasonry', 29–30; Rida, 'Mulakhkhaṣ', 402–3.
77 Cole sees Ismail's deposition in favour of his son Tawfiq as a result of European interference, as Britain and France intended to alleviate increasing grievances against the Egyptian regime and its European backers within several constituencies of Egyptian society. See Cole, *Colonialism and Revolution*, 106.
78 Muhammad 'Abduh, "Īd Miṣr wa-Maṭla' Sa'ādatihā', in *al-A'māl al-Kāmila li-l-Imām Muḥammad 'Abduh*, ed. Muhammad 'Imara, vol. 1 (Beirut: Dar al-Shuruq, 1993), 299.
79 Ibid.
80 Rida, 'Mulakhkhaṣ', 405.
81 Amin, *Zu'amā' al-Iṣlāḥ*, 296.
82 Cole, *Colonialism and Revolution*, 229–30.
83 Rida, *Ta'rīkh*, vol. 1, 175–81; Hamada, *'Abduh*, 65.
84 Muhammad 'Abduh, 'Tanbīh Rasmī Baṭlān al-Dūsa'; 'al-Dūsa', in *al-A'māl al-Kāmila li-l-Imām Muḥammad 'Abduh*, ed. Muhammad 'Imara, vol. 2 (Beirut: Dar al-Shuruq, 1993), 51–7.
85 Muhammad 'Abduh, 'Ḥukm al-Sharī'a fī Ta'addud al-Zawjāt', in *al-A'māl al-Kāmila li-l-Imām Muḥammad 'Abduh*, ed. Muhammad 'Imara, vol. 2 (Beirut: Dar al-Shuruq, 1993), 76–81.
86 Muhammad 'Abduh, 'Iḥtirām Qawānīn al-Ḥukūma wa-Awāmirihā min Sa'ādat al-Umma', in *al-A'māl al-Kāmila li-l-Imām Muḥammad 'Abduh*, ed. Muhammad 'Imara, vol. 1 (Beirut: Dar al-Shuruq, 1993), 304.

87 'Abduh, 'al-Quwwa wa-l-Qānūn', vol. 1, 311.

88 Muhammad 'Abduh, 'Khaṭā' al-'Uqalā'', in *al-A'māl al-Kāmila li-l-Imām Muḥammad 'Abduh*, ed. Muhammad 'Imara, vol. 1 (Beirut: Dar al-Shuruq, 1993), 323.

89 Ibid., 326.

90 Christopher Radler, *Eine Biographie als politisches Mittel: Muḥammad 'Abduh (1849–1905) und die Rebellion des Aḥmad 'Urābī in der Rezeption Ṭāhir aṭ-Ṭanāḥīs (Muḏakkirāt al-Imām Muḥammad 'Abduh)* (Berlin: Klaus Schwarz, 2010), 109–10.

91 Muhammad 'Abduh, 'Ikhtilāf al-Qawānīn bi-Ikhtilāf Aḥwāl al-Umam', in *al-A'māl al-Kāmila li-l-Imām Muḥammad 'Abduh*, ed. Muhammad 'Imara, vol. 1 (Beirut: Dar al-Shuruq, 1993), 337.

92 'Abduh, 'Kalām fī Khaṭā' al-'Uqalā'', in *al-A'māl al-Kāmila li-l-Imām Muḥammad 'Abduh*, ed. Muhammad 'Imara, vol. 1 (Beirut: Dar al-Shuruq, 1993), 329; Malcolm H. Kerr, *Islamic Reform: The Legal and Political Theories of Muhammad 'Abduh and Rashid Rida* (Berkeley: University of California Press, 1966), 135.

93 'Abduh, 'Ikhtilāf al-Qawānīn', vol. 1, 338.

94 Albert Hourani, *Arabic Thought in the Liberal Age: 1798–1939* (Cambridge: Cambridge University Press, 1983), 137.

95 'Abduh, 'Kalām fī Khaṭā'', vol. 1, 335.

96 Ibid; Qur'an 3:7 and 4:162.

97 Muhammad 'Abduh, 'al-Waṭaniyya', in *al-A'māl al-Kāmila li-l-Imām Muḥammad 'Abduh*, ed. Muhammad 'Imara, vol. 1 (Beirut: Dar al-Shuruq, 1993), 319.

98 'Abduh, 'Kalām fī Khaṭā'', vol. 1, 332.

99 'Abduh, 'al-Quwwa wa-l-Qānūn', vol. 1, 309.

100 Haddad, *Qarā'a Jadīda*, 129–30. On Ibn Miskawayh's understanding of complete happiness (*sa'āda tāmma*), see Ibn Miskawayh, *Tahdhīb al-Akhlāq* (Cairo: Matba'at al-Taraqqi, 1317 H [1900/1901]), 65–71. On the role of the ruler to provide the foundations of his subjects' happiness, see ibid., 61–2, 121–2. On his paternalistic understanding of political leadership, see ibid., 149–51; Franz Rosenthal, *Knowledge Triumphant: The Concept of Knowledge in Medieval Islam* (Leiden: Brill, 2007), 288–9; Majid F. Fakhry, 'Ethics in Islamic Philosophy', in *Routledge Encyclopedia of Philosophy*, ed. Edward Craig (London: Routledge, 1998).

101 'Abduh, 'al-Waṭaniyya', vol. 1, 315, 320.

102 'Abduh, 'al-Quwwa wa-l-Qānūn', vol. 1, 311. Ibn Miskawayh uses these concepts as being central to achieving social cohesion. Ibn Miskawayh, *Tahdhīb al-Akhlāq*, 111.

103 Haddad, *Qarā'a Jadīda*, 141–7.

104 Ahmed, *What Is Islam?*, 460.

105 'Abduh, 'Ikhtilāf al-Qawānīn', vol. 1, 342.

106 'Abduh, 'al-Quwwa wa-l-Qānūn', vol. 1, 311. On the relationship between *qānūn* and shari'a see Ahmed, *What Is Islam?*, 456–61.

107 Zachs, *Making of Syrian Identity*, 72–3.

108 'Abduh, 'al-Waṭaniyya', vol. 1, 318.

109 'Abduh, 'Kalām fī Khaṭā', vol. 1, 331.
110 'Abduh, 'al-Quwwa wa-l-Qānūn', vol. 1, 312.
111 'Abduh, 'Ikhtilāf al-Qawānīn', vol. 1, 338.
112 Ibid., 341.
113 Ibid., 342.
114 Reid, "Urabi Revolution', 224.
115 Ibid., 225–6.
116 Amin, *Zu'amā' al-Iṣlāḥ*, 298–9.
117 Muhamad 'Abduh, 'al-Ḥayāt al-Siyāsiyya', in *al-A'māl al-Kāmila li-l-Imām Muḥammad 'Abduh*, ed. Muhammad 'Imara, vol. 1 (Beirut: Dar al-Shuruq, 1993), 365.
118 Ibid.
119 Ibid; Tusi, *Akhlāq-i Nāṣirī*, 251–4.
120 'Abduh, 'al-Ḥayāt al-Siyāsiyya', vol. 1, 365.
121 Ibid.
122 Ibid., 366–7.
123 Ibid., 373.
124 Ibid. 'Abduh paraphrases here statements of the French philosopher Jean de la Bruyère (1645–1696) from his book *Les Caractères.*
125 Muhammad 'Abduh, 'Fī-l-Shūrā wa-l-Istibdād, in *al-A'māl al-Kāmila li-l-Imām Muḥammad 'Abduh*, ed. Muhammad 'Imara, vol. 1 (Beirut: Dar al-Shuruq, 1993), 382.
126 Kemal, 'And Seek Their Counsel', 144–8.
127 'Abduh, 'Fī-l-Shūrā', vol. 1, 385.
128 Ibid., 386.
129 Ibid., 389.
130 Ibid., 391.
131 Muhammad 'Abduh, 'al-Shūrā wa-l-Qānūn', in *al-A'māl al-Kāmila li-l-Imām Muḥammad 'Abduh*, ed. Muhammad 'Imara, vol. 1 (Beirut: Dar al-Shuruq, 1993), 398.
132 Ibid., 399.
133 Reid, "Urabi Revolution', 229–31.
134 Muhammad 'Abduh, 'Iḥtifāl Jam'iyya al-Maqāṣid bi-Taṣdīq 'alā Lā'iḥat al-Nawwāb', in *al-A'māl al-Kāmila li-l-Imām Muḥammad 'Abduh*, ed. Muhammad 'Imara, vol. 1 (Beirut: Dar al-Shuruq, 1993), 416.
135 Muhammad 'Abduh, 'al-Ittiḥād fī-l-Ra'ī Qarīn al-Ittiḥād fī-l-'Amal', in *al-A'māl al-Kāmila li-l-Imām Muḥammad 'Abduh*, ed. Muhammad 'Imara, vol. 1 (Beirut: Dar al-Shuruq, 1993), 424.
136 Ibid., 426.
137 Alexander M. Broadley, *How We Defended Arabi and His Friends: A Story of Egypt and the Egyptians* (London: Chapman and Hall, 1884), 233–6.
138 Reid, "Urabi Revolution', 233–4.
139 Ibid., 237–8.

140 Ahmad H. Al-Sawi, 'Muhammad 'Abduh and al-Waqa'i' al-Misriyyah', MSc diss. (Montreal, 1954), 55–78.
141 Tanahi, *Mudhakkirāt 'Abduh*, 172.
142 Rida, *Ta'rīkh*, vol. 1, 261–5.
143 Blunt, *Secret History*, 105.
144 Ibid., Appendix II, 383–7.
145 Ibid., 173.
146 Evelyn Baring, Earl of Cromer, *Modern Egypt*, vol. 2 (London: Macmillan, 1908), 179.
147 Quoted in Cole, *Colonialism and Revolution*, 244.
148 Amin, *Zu'amā' al-Iṣlāḥ*, 304.
149 Tanahi, *Mudhakkirāt 'Abduh*, 111–15.
150 Ibid., 124.
151 For his account of the court proceedings and assessment of main actors, see Broadley, *How We Defended Arabi*.
152 'Abduh's letter to Broadley in 'Abduh, *al-A'māl al-Kāmila*, vol. 1, 647.
153 Ibid.
154 Broadley, *How We Defended Arabi*, 230.
155 Ibid., 230–3. Tanahi equally considers popular support for the constitutional changes as having led 'Abduh to reassess his attitude towards the 'Urabi revolutionaries. See Tanahi, *Mudhakkirāt 'Abduh*, 10.
156 Cole, *Colonialism and Revolution*, 235.
157 Tanahi, *Mudhakkirāt 'Abduh*, 46–8.
158 Ahmed, *What Is Islam?*, 462.
159 For conceptual shifts of the term in pre-modern Ottoman contexts, see Nikos Sigalas, '*Devlet* et État: Du glissement sémantique d'un ancien concept du pouvoir au début du XVIIIe siècle ottoman', in *Byzantina et Moderna: Mélanges en l'honneur d'Helène Antoniades-Bibicou*, ed. Gilles Grivaud and Sokratis Petmezas (Athens: Ekdoseis Alexandreia, 2007), 385–415; Nikos Sigalas, 'Des histoires des sultans á l'histoire de l'état: Une enquête sur le temps du pouvoir ottoman (XVIe – XVIIIe siècle)', in *Les Ottomans et le temps*, ed. François Georgeon and Frédéric Hitzel (Leiden: Brill, 2012), 99–127; Florian Zemmin, 'The Janus Face of Kātib Çelebi', *Turcica*, 50 (2019): 327–54.
160 See Ami Ayalon, *Language and Change in the Arab Middle East: The Evolution of Modern Political Discourse* (New York: Oxford University Press, 1987), 16–28; Florian Zemmin, 'Modernity without Society? Observations on the Term *mujtama'* in the Islamic Journal "al-Manār" (Cairo, 1898–1940)', *Die Welt des Islams*, 56(2) (2016): 223–47. For a general discussion, see Helga Rebhan, *Geschichte und Funktion einiger politischer Termini im Arabischen des 19. Jahrhunderts* (1798–1882) (Wiesbaden: Otto Harrassowitz, 1986).
161 'Abduh, 'al-'Ulūm al-Kalāmiyya', vol. 3, 15.
162 'Abduh, 'al-Tuḥfa', vol. 3, 24.

4

Exile: From Paris to Beirut

Introduction

After Jamal al-Din al-Afghani was expelled from Egypt in 1879 for his opposition to the new Khedive Tawfiq, he spent three years in India and continued his nativist agitation against British rule of the subcontinent. In Cairo, Afghani had encouraged his disciples – which included Muslims, Christians and Jews – to promote a proto-nationalist sense of Egyptian patriotism against the country's foreign dependency. Likewise in India, he advocated an Indian notion of nationalism (*jinsiyya*) that included both Hindus and Muslims who should unite against British rule.[1] 'Abduh in his political articles before his exile articulated a nascent sense of Egyptian patriotism (*waṭaniyya*), that was directed against the Anglo-French dual control regime, and characterized the 'Urabi Revolution as 'a national one when men of all races and creeds – Mussulmans, Copts, and Jews – rushed to join it with enthusiasm'.[2] When 'Abduh was reunited with his mentor Afghani in Paris in 1884, both produced the highly influential journal *al-'Urwa al-Wuthqā* (The Firmest Bond) whose articles promote Islamic unity or, what has been termed, Pan-Islamism. Their promotion of Islamic unity against European imperialism in the journal appears to contradict their earlier advocacy of Egyptian or Indian forms of nationalism to counter foreign dependency or rule.[3]

However, this apparent contradiction results from the assumption that regional forms of nationalism that seek to include members of different religious communities are bound to be non-religious and secular while a Pan-Islamist appeal to Muslim unity suggests the exclusion of non-Muslims. Neither Afghani nor 'Abduh worked on these assumptions. Both like other Muslim reformers experimented with a new vocabulary to translate European discourses on nation and national identity into Islamic idioms. Terms such as community *as* nation (*umma*), country *as* nation (*waṭan*) or race *as* nation (*jins*) were just in the process of acquiring new meanings and were not necessarily conceived as denoting mutually exclusive sets of identities. Equally, emphasizing different identity markers in the common struggle against European imperialism reflects the expectations and backgrounds of the audiences such discourse seeks to reach. What appears contradictory can be explained by Islam's intellectual culture of ambiguity in which different discourses are not necessarily seen as contrary but reflecting the capacity of one's interlocutors and a skilful response to external contingencies. Both Afghani and ʿAbduh were familiar and entertained such ambiguity.

ʿAbduh's promotion of Egyptian proto-nationalism in his articles before his exile and his support for and participation in the ʿUrabi Revolution aimed at curbing his country's foreign dependency and ultimately preventing its occupation by Britain. Given the further momentum the colonial penetration of the Muslim world had reached in the early 1880s, Afghani and ʿAbduh broadened the direction of their anti-imperialist agitation by addressing all Muslims and highlighting the sources of Muslim communal solidarity without invalidating other forms of communal solidarity. A closer look at ʿAbduh's article in the journal *al-ʿUrwa al-Wuthqā* reveals that themes which have marked his religious and socio-political discourse in Egypt are still dominant but this time clothed in Islamic tropes. ʿAbduh's views on the development of human societies are still shaped by Ibn Khaldun's philosophy of history. His emphasis on Muslim unity, defined in doctrinal terms, is already evident in his early mystical treatise and in his theological commentary. In the articles of *al-ʿUrwa al-Wuthqā* the implications of Muslim unity are further articulated to encourage Muslims to take a united stand against European imperialism.

The full complexity of ʿAbduh's intellectual personality comes to the fore during his stay in Beirut where he continued his political, educational and journalistic activities engaging with a variety of audiences: students at local schools, intellectuals, notables and scholars from different religious communities, Ottoman government officials and local politicians. The image of ʿAbduh that emerges is that of an astute observer of the social and political realities of Syrian society, a person with significant political acumen and an irenic outlook towards religious difference. ʿAbduh not only sought relations with representatives from different religious communities but often entertained warm and close rapports with them. He showed little regard for their conformity with narrow definitions of Sunni orthodoxy but engaged and socialized with Christians, Shiis, Druze or Bahaʾis openly. His interest in the religious 'Other' and his cosmopolitan attitude is visible in writing and publishing a commentary on a key text of Shii Islam, *Nahj al-Balāgha* (The Peak of Eloquence), containing statements, sermons and letters attributed to Prophet Muhammad's son-in-law and first Shii Imam, 'Ali ibn Abi Talib.

The Firmest Bond

In December 1882, 'Abduh was ordered to go into exile in Beirut. After his stay in India, Afghani went to Paris in 1881 where attacks on the British colonial policy were welcomed, as France and Britain had been competing for supremacy in the Middle East for decades. Afghani sought French support for his opposition of British colonial intrusion in the Muslim world. In Arabic journals which were published in Paris, Afghani advocated the Ottoman caliphate as the only political entity which was able to launch a successful response to British colonialism. Not only was the Ottoman Empire quite successful in maintaining its independence as the remaining indigenous superpower in the region, but Afghani also envisioned the symbolic power of the Sunni caliphate claimed by the Ottoman sultan to become the religious motivation for a united effort of Muslims against European colonialism.[4]

In 1884, 'Abduh left Beirut and joined his mentor in the 'free city'[5] of Paris where they founded the secret society *al-'Urwa al-Wuthqā* (The Firmest Bond) and used a Qur'anic term to name it.[6] As part of the society's activities a journal was published under the same title which became the vehicle of their anti-colonial discourse. After the publication of the first issue in March 1884, it ceased only eight months later in October.[7] Whereas Rida attributed its discontinuation to British censorship in Egypt and India where the publication was soon prohibited,[8] it seems more likely that both editors ran out of money after the sources of income – Ottoman, Egyptian and Tunisian notables and government officials – had stopped funding the journal.[9] During its short life, the journal was sent to *'ulamā'*, notables, government officials and intellectuals in the entire Muslim world.[10]

A closer look at the features of the society which published the journal reveals patterns which have already been observed in regard to Afghani's and 'Abduh's endeavours in Egypt and resemble more the secrecy of Freemasonry and Islamic esotericism. Rida himself admits that 'Abduh did not reveal anything to him about the society.[11] Similar to initiation processes of esoteric traditions in Islam and Freemasonry, 'Abduh formulated a code of conduct incumbent for all members and an oath of allegiance which initiated new members and which required them to be secretive about the activities of the society and its members.[12] They had to swear to base their actions on the Qur'an, to promote its doctrines and laws, to defend Islam against its opponents and not to contradict other members of the society or to contravene their actions:

> I swear by the divine covenant (*ʿahd allāh wa-mithāqihī*) that I seek the means to strengthen Islam and the Muslims in their mind and in their power in every aspect I know, and of what I am ignorant of I seek knowledge from those who know (*min al-ʿārifīn*).[13]

ʿAbduh assumed different mediating roles depending on the audience he was addressing. In the journal's articles, British colonialism was denounced and Muslims were encouraged to pursue all means to counter the intrusion into their countries. ʿAbduh also undertook diplomatic missions meeting British politicians and government officials. In conversations with them, he criticized the British occupation of his country.[14] The Arabophile British politician Wilfrid S. Blunt invited ʿAbduh to London in 1884, where he met members of parliament and of the British government to lobby for a withdrawal of British troops from Egypt (Figure 2).[15]

In a meeting with the British war minister Spencer Hartington (1833–1908) ʿAbduh opposed the minister's position that the whole purpose of British colonial policy was to bring progress and prosperity to the country and to replace the despotism of the Turkish pashas with stable British rule. ʿAbduh denied the civilizing rationales for British colonialism and replied that it was against human nature to be ruled by a foreign power. Despite his distance to the khedivial family and his criticism of the Turkish-Circassian elite and of superficial modernizing reforms he had articulated on several occasions, in his meeting with a British government minister, ʿAbduh referred to the modernization policy of the Khedive Muhammad ʿAli and the intellectual and cultural achievements of his reign and that of his successors as success. The conversations with Hartington and other government officials revealed to ʿAbduh the colonizing intentions of the British government and the different theoretical pretexts provided for their justification based on the assumption that Egypt is unable to modernize itself without British help. ʿAbduh gained the impression that British government officials like Hartington consider Egyptians to be ignorant savages who require the civilizing force of British colonialism – a charge he responded to by pointing at the successful modernizing reforms since the first half of the nineteenth century.[16]

ʿAbduh's multiple activities also included efforts to secure support and financial contributions to ensure the continuous publication and wide

الاستاذ الامام الشيخ محمد عبده يصلي في لندن

Figure 2. Muhammad ʿAbduh in London, 1884.

dissemination of the journal. He wrote numerous letters to *ʿulamāʾ*, notables and officials making requests in this regard.[17] Apart from the journal, the Arabic translation of Afghani's *al-Radd ʿalā al-Dahriyyīn* (Refutation of the Materialists) is presented in ʿAbduh's letters as a major achievement of the society. In this book, Afghani denounces the reformist school of the South Asian Muslim reformer Sayyid Ahmad Khan (1817–1898) for his collaboration with British colonialism.[18]

When the publication of the journal was stopped and the society ran out of funding, Afghani sent 'Abduh to Tunis to establish a branch of the society and to raise money. During his mission to Tunis, 'Abduh adopted the pseudonym 'al-'Arabi Basis'[19] and met with *'ulamā'* to win them as new members. In a letter dated 24 December 1884, to Afghani, he reports about the outcome of his activities:

> I told them that the Bond is not the name of a journal but the name of a society which the Sayyid [Afghani] founded in Hyderabad. It has branches in many regions. Each of the branches does not know anything about the other and only the head knows all of them. Likewise, I told them that we intend today the foundation of a new branch in this country.[20]

Although he managed to do so in Tunis, the new members apparently could not provide the financial revenues Afghani and 'Abduh hoped to gain. In concluding the letter, 'Abduh can still find some amusing sides in his mission despite its failure in raising money: 'They believe we possess a great fortune! There is an unknown power which aids us in what we want. Their beliefs delight me more than the possession of the fortune would do.'[21]

'Abduh travelled further incognito to Egypt with the hope to meet Muhammad Ahmad ibn 'Abdallah (1844–1885) in Sudan who claimed to be the promised Islamic saviour (*mahdī*) in 1881 and managed to repel British troops during the Siege of Khartoum (March 1884–January 1885) and established the Mahdist state in Sudan afterwards. The journal *al-'Urwa al-Wuthqā* covered the Mahdist revolt as a successful indigenous revolt against increasing British colonial intrusion into the Muslim world.[22] However, his plans to meet the Mahdi of Sudan did not materialize, and 'Abduh returned to Beirut in early 1885.[23]

Colonial context of the journal

The colonial context of the journal *al-'Urwa al-Wuthqā* is important and constantly referred to throughout the various articles of the journal. In 1884, the political landscape of the Middle East had changed quite radically. The reform attempts undertaken in Egypt under 'Urabi and the constitutionalist revolution in the Ottoman Empire had failed resulting in the restoration of absolutist rule in both countries. Furthermore, the colonial intrusion into the Middle East gained further momentum. French troops began the conquest of Tunisia in 1881 and British troops occupied Egypt in 1882. The articles in *al-'Urwa al-Wuthqā* are devised as a response to colonialism addressing the elites of the Muslim world. The journal aims at illustrating the reasons for the current inferiority and weakness of the Muslim world, and 'the East' more generally, and at showing ways out of its crisis. It urges Muslims to seek the progress and prosperity of their civilization and to unite against the colonial intrusion by European powers.[24] Themes that are central to 'Abduh's discourses as editor of *al-Waqā'i' al-Miṣriyya* before his exile are still dominant: the promotion of social, cultural, political and educational reforms and opposition to foreign domination – now not just restricted to Egypt but addressing the entire Muslim world.

The journal contains two types of articles. A number of pieces seek to reveal the *modus operandi* of British colonialism, whether in Egypt, India, Sudan or Ireland[25] and the various modes of resistance to it which had emerged at the same time. Discussions are often based on translations of British newspaper articles, provided by Afghani's and 'Abduh's Iranian associate in Paris, Muhammad Baqir Bawanati (d. 1892/3), who translated these articles into Arabic with further commentary, reflection and analysis added by 'Abduh.[26] Apart from various articles covering current affairs and interpreting them in light of the journal's anti-British and anti-imperialist agenda, the journal also included some more programmatic articles setting out its vision of Islamic unity to counter European imperialism. These articles had a long-term impact on the Muslim world in providing a prototype of a Muslim anti-imperialist discourse and serving as the ideological precursor to twentieth-century iterations of Pan-Islamism.

Ancient glories and current challenges

'Abduh's programmatic articles work with a juxtaposition of Islam's ancient glories and its current malaise. In early Islamic history the authentic ethos of Islam had become manifest, while its current state betrays this original ethos and allowed the decline of Muslim societies and their foreign domination. Certain themes that shaped his political discourse in Egypt are still evident such as the need for unity, progress and civilizational development, but in *al-'Urwa al-Wuthqā* these themes are framed by Islamic tropes using the Qur'an and examples of early Islamic history to appeal to a global Muslim readership in response to the immediate threat of European imperialism.

Early Islamic history, particularly its first formative centuries, provides a role model which 'Abduh employs, reading it in particular as a prime example of the transition of an uncivilized tribal society to one of the most advanced and powerful civilizations at its time. Recuperating a theme from his earliest journalistic writings, ʿAbduh affirms that nations undergo an organic and dynamic development of growth and decline. History teaches the lesson that every nation experiences a period of growth during which its unity is well established, and its strong leadership manages to maintain its integrity and strength. Such a nation becomes an example for other nations. However, history also shows that the period of growth is followed by a period of decline. The unity of the nation is lost and it disintegrates when its members do not follow its shared beliefs and pursue their own egoistic interests.[27] Such discourse clearly mirrors Ibn Khaldun's philosophy of history on the cause for the rise and fall of dynasties. Religion is presented by ʿAbduh as the essential instrument to identify the causes for moral and cultural decline and to prescribe a remedy.

The classical juxtaposition in Muslim historical consciousness between the pre-Islamic Arab society, which was barbaric and backward and lived in a state of ignorance (*jāhiliyya*), and the rise of Islam is used by ʿAbduh to present Islam as one of the prime civilizing forces in world history. ʿAbduh's reference to Islamic history intends to show that Islam transformed a barbaric and ignorant nation like the Arabs to one of the most powerful and most developed nations in the world:

> Have you forgotten the history of the Arab nation (*umma*) and its characteristics before the rise of religion, its savagery and fragmentation, its looming abasement and reprehensible customs? When religion came, it united, strengthened and purified the nation, enlightened its intellects, made its morals firm and guided its rules.[28]

In political and military terms, early Islam emerged as a global power. The Muslim empire occupied a vast territory stretching from 'the far west to the Gulf of Tonkin on the borders of China and from Kazan in the north to Ceylon beneath the equator'.[29] At this time, 'their ʿAbbasid caliph uttered a word and the emperor of China obeyed and the greatest kings in Europe trembled for fear'.[30]

ʿAbduh's evocation of the former political and military supremacy of Muslims has to be seen in the light of the colonial threat. While Muslim territories today are threatened by military occupation and colonial subjugation, in the past Muslims were the ultimate imperial power of the world. ʿAbduh establishes a correspondence between the ancient glory of Islam and the need to revive this political ethos to counter European imperialism. According to him, the military power of the early Islamic empire and its rapid expansion illustrates that Muslims by their religious conviction are unwilling to accept foreign domination.[31]

What were the reasons for the success of the early Muslim community? For ʿAbduh, the specific nature of the Islamic religion needs to be taken into account:

> The Islamic religion is based on the quest for invasion, power, expansion and glory. It is based on the opposition to every secular law (*qānūn*) which contradicts its own religious law (*sharīʿatahā*) and the rejection of authority whose owner does not rise to implement the principles of religious law.[32]

Political domination and militant expansion form the ethos of the Islamic religion which motivated the early Muslims to undertake the military conquest of the Middle East, North Africa and Asia. For this reason, Islam as a religion is also more in line with the innate drive of communities to seek power (*mulk*) and dominion (*siyāda*)[33] – two terms Ibn Khaldun uses to describe the formation of dynastic rule.

One of the central reasons why the early Islamic empire projected such immense power lies in the open intellectual outlook the Islamic religion brought to the Arabs. It not only encouraged them to conquer the world but also to seek different branches of knowledge which they imported into their societies:

> They brought to their lands the medicine of Hippocrates and Galen, the geometry of Euclid, the geography of Ptolemy, the philosophy of Plato and Aristotle and what existed of it before Islam (*dīn*). Every nation attains mastery under this banner when its strength and civilisation lie in the adherence to the fundamental principles of its religion.[34]

ʿAbduh argues that the Arabs would never have acquired excellence in the fields of knowledge without their Islamic beliefs which encouraged them to acquire various fields of knowledge. This historical claim is linked to the contemporary need to acquire modern sciences. ʿAbduh had emphasized earlier the necessity to appropriate modern sciences but this time, this is connected with an inherent civilizational force within Islam which is evident in its early history. Such historical references to the civilizational progress Islam brought conflates Ibn Khaldun's philosophy of history and Guizot's understanding of the roots of European civilization. For the latter, Europeans were civilized through both the spiritual and moral vision of Christianity and the socio-political and legal order of the Roman Empire. Similarly, ʿAbduh argues the moral vision and legal order brought by Islam enabled the ferocious and tribal Arabs to absorb the intellectual and cultural legacy of the pre-Islamic Mediterranean world and turned Arabs into a major engine of civilizational progress.

Authentic Islam that 'Abduh constructs seeks political power and military expansion and stimulates unity to achieve these purposes. It is this political unity that allowed the early Arab Muslims to defeat the major empires at that time. At the same time, Islam not only channelled the Arabs' drive to military expansion but also reoriented their intellectual endeavours. A crucial element of their historical success was their active engagement with the pre-Islamic intellectual heritage of the Middle East and the wider Mediterranean world which early Muslims successfully appropriated not only to build a massive empire but also one of the world's leading civilizations. Authentic Islam, tangible in its early history, ought to be revived in light of the current threat of European colonialism. Like their ancestors, Muslims cannot accept foreign domination and legal regimes as their religion compels them to resistance. Similarly, Muslims today need to engage with modern sciences and appropriate them in order to secure the civilizational progress of their societies as early Muslims had done.

'Abduh admits that a look at the present situation in the Muslim world seems to contradict his depiction of the original spirit of Islam. Despite the intrinsic resistance of foreign domination in the Islamic ethos, Muslims seem to accept the European conquest of their territories. How can this reversal be explained? For 'Abduh, Muslims failed to understand the actual nature of their religion and to translate it into action.[35] Some Muslims took the doctrine of divine predestination to the extreme assumption that everything that happens in the world is decreed by God in advance and human interventions cannot prevent it. The original activist nature of Islam was thus destroyed and made its followers passive and apathic.[36] The second more salient factor in undermining Muslim power was increasing disunity: both politically and religiously. Muslim rulers competed and fought for supremacy rather than constituting a united front against foreign domination. Sectarian differences emerged that set one school of thought against another, equally weakening Muslim unity. As a consequence, Islam's strength will only be retrieved by regaining political unity and adopting an activist understanding of Islam as force for individual and collective transformation. Religious scholarship has a role to play in overcoming the spirit of sectarian partisanship and replacing it with sense of Muslim unity.[37]

'Abduh's call for restoring a united and activist understanding of Islam does not preclude engaging with non-Islamic sources of knowledge. His account of the intellectual and cultural blossoming of early Islamic civilization acknowledges how Muslims embraced Greek philosophy, medicine and science and the wider Middle Eastern intellectual and cultural heritage. Hence, 'Abduh's discourse of restoring authentic Islam involves two elements: he provides a politically activist, expansionist and militant reading of Islam – as exemplified by the early Arab-Muslim conquests – and acknowledges the multiple roots of Islamic civilization that included pre-Islamic elements. Similarly, Muslims today need to withstand intellectual trends that suggest subjugation to European imperialism while equally embracing modern science from Europe to restore the civilizational force of Islam. In this sense, tropes around the spread of knowledge, modern science and civilizational progress that shaped 'Abduh's early journalist pieces are still central to his discourse in the articles of *al-'Urwa al-Wuthqā*.

The latter-day agents causing Muslim disunity are for 'Abduh the self-labelled 'champions of freedom'.[38] They deem the blind imitation of Europe sufficient to achieve progress and civilization and emulate European eating habits and dress codes to become apparently cultured and civilized. For 'Abduh, the uncritical adoption of European knowledge and institutions has an imperialist dimension, as it serves to strengthen and facilitate European domination and undermines Muslim unity. Those 'imitators'[39] who adopt European concepts and institutions pave the way for colonial intrusion:

> Whenever foreigners find their way into the territory of any nation, they look out for these collaborators, approach them and turn them to their service after they had rejoiced over their arrival. Thereby, the foreigners sneak amidst them and win their trust as if they belonged to them.[40]

'Abduh warns of the spread of ideologies which Europeans have introduced to undermine Muslim solidarity and unity pointing in particular at the rise of ethnic identity markers that separate Arabs, Turks, Kurds and Iranians from one another. For 'Abduh, ethnicity or ethnic nationalism (*jinsiyya*) is not inherent in human nature as some of its promoters suggest but socially constructed, as his explanation for the formation of communities and nations illustrates. There is a natural human drive to seek one's own profit. As this profit can be better achieved in a group, humans form communities based on a shared territory they inhabit. This pragmatic and geographical construction of a community creates communal solidarity which serves as an ideological foundation for the social cohesion of a nation and its drive to dominate other nations.[41] 'Abduh's expositions on the origins of nations and communities resemble Ibn Khaldun's understanding and his concept of *'aṣabiyya* as the root of social cohesion and foundation of political power. In his discussion of the term solidarity (*ta'aṣṣub*), 'Abduh seeks to disconnect it from its identification with fanaticism (*fanātīk*)[42] by tracing its etymological roots back to Ibn Khaldun's concept of *'aṣabiyya* as denoting social cohesion and identity – a sense of belonging to a particular community.[43] Equally, ʿAbduh distinguishes two types: solidarity defined by ethnicity, which can reap benefits for a community but has a divisive impact on Muslims, and a more superior form defined by religion (*al-taʿaṣṣub al-dīnī*).[44]

ʿAbduh sees the harmful side of European forms of nationalism in the divisive character of an ethnically defined sense of solidarity. For him, the diffusion of modern notions of nationalism and their reception in the Muslim world are part of a colonialist plot to weaken the unity of the Muslim community by exaggerating their ethnic differences. In order to divide Muslims, Europeans provide ethnicity as an alternative source of communal identity and blame the religious orientation of society in the past as being responsible for its decline. Those Muslims who willingly adopt an ethnic sense of national identity become an instrument of colonial domination, as they destroy the unity of the Muslim community and facilitate its foreign invasion.[45] In reality, Islam is beyond all ethnic distinctions and creates a universal identity based on the belief in one God:

> This is the secret why Muslims reject in all regions they inhabit the consideration of ethnicities (*jinsiyyāt*) and dismiss any sense of communal solidarities (*ʿaṣabiyyāt*) which contradict their Islamic communal solidarity (*ʿaṣabiyyatahum al-islāmiyya*).[46]

A European type of ethnic nationalism is rejected as being foreign to the universal and supra-national Islamic religion. What ʿAbduh does not reject is the ideological spirit of modern nationalism which he identifies with Ibn Khaldun's concept of *ʿaṣabiyya*: a worldview which generates social cohesion among members of a group. Being bound together, they strive to increase the welfare of their community or nation, spread its power and reject any foreign attack. Islam provides a more superior sense of communal solidarity which unites members of the same religion to resist the imperialist threat posed by European powers.

ʿAbduh's Islamic reading of *ʿaṣabiyya* and his outright rejection of ethnic nationalism (*jinsiyya*) seem to contradict his earlier support for an Egyptian version of patriotism (*waṭaniyya*). In his earliest journalistic pieces, ʿAbduh defines patriotism as both a sense of allegiance to one's place of birth or residence and as a political identity based on rights and obligations that the state secures and provides. However, ʿAbduh does not denounce patriotism (*waṭaniyya*) in the articles in *al-ʿUrwa al-Wuthqā* but refers to ethnic nationalism (*jinsiyya*) as colonial instrument to divide the Muslim world. He criticizes those intellectuals who misuse the legitimate 'love for one's country (*maḥabbat al-waṭan*)'[47] to argue for an ethnic sense of nationalism. His rejection of such ethnically defined communal identities does not contradict his earlier articles on patriotism which he defines more in a sense of a civic nationalism: a communal sense of belonging that encourages the individual to work for the common good and to reject despotic rule and foreign domination. 'Abduh uses Ibn Khaldun's concept of *'aṣabiyya* to argue for patriotic connection to one's country in his Egyptian articles to counter European imperialism. In *al-'Urwa al-Wuthqā*, he conceives the derivation from Ibn Khaldun's term, *ta'aṣṣub*, as communal solidarity in order to introduce Islam as ultimate source of social cohesion in the struggle against European colonialism. Such a conception also mirrors Ibn Khaldun's argument that Islam provided Arab tribes with a higher and more effective sense of *'aṣabiyya* which transcended their tribal allegiances and allowed them to conquer the Middle East and to defeat its major empires.[48] For 'Abduh, it is this type of *'aṣabiyya* that Muslims need to revive today in order to defeat European imperialism.

Hence, 'Abduh's articles in terms of their fundamental intellectual orientation are not that different to his earlier approaches to a proto-nationalist sense of Egyptian patriotism but play with discursive and semantic ambiguity to address different audiences and to respond to quite different contexts. In his exile following the British occupation of Egypt, his priority was to counter European imperialism.[49] That the different layers of communal identities and subsequent loyalties that 'Abduh addresses in these articles are not mutually exclusive is evident, for example, in an article the Syrian Christian Adib Ishaq penned for his newspaper *Miṣr* in the late 1870s. This article provides a good example of attempts by reformist intellectuals to translate European concepts of the nation and nationalism into Islamic idioms. Ishaq distinguishes between community (*umma*) and country (*waṭan*). For Ishaq, *umma* is understood as a trans-ethnic communal entity as it exists in the United States of America or in the Ottoman Empire. Ishaq does not see a sense of loyalty to an *umma* to be in contradiction to the particular allegiance to a place of residence (*waṭan*), in his case Egypt. Ishaq considers himself a member of the Ottoman *umma* who has taken residence in Egypt as his adopted country (*waṭan*).[50] Both allegiances are not contradictory for an Ottoman (and Christian) intellectual like Ishaq but denote different layers of allegiance. Hence, in his articles in *al-'Urwa al-Wuthqā*, 'Abduh refers to a particular type of allegiance that encompasses the entire *umma* and is only concerned about the adoption of ethnic nationalism (*jinsiyyya*) insofar it is meant to undermine Muslim unity and is used to weaken the Muslim world as part of European colonial schemes. Similar to Ishaq's argument, allegiance to the *umma* does not invalidate a sense of loyalty to one's country. 'Abduh makes it also quite clear in one article that the journal's emphasis on Muslim unity does not promote a statist sense of Pan-Islamic nationalism. The political unification of the Muslim world in one state or under one leader is unrealistic. For him, the Qur'an is the actual ruler (*sulṭān*) over all Muslims.[51]

'Abduh's articles in *al-'Urwa al-Wuthqā* encourage Muslims to translate their faith into action and to adopt an activist understanding of their religion as it was prevalent in the early history of Islam when it constituted one of the greatest civilizations of the world.[52] One of his articles is prefaced by Qur'an 13:11: 'Indeed, God will not change the conditions of a people until they change it themselves' to further emphasize the need for communities to become agents of change themselves in order to achieve historical success.[53] As such, the articles resonate with the anthropocentric view of history Ibn Khaldun expounds.[54] For Ibn Khaldun, the causes for the success or failure of a community are human-made and not controlled by God. The success of a community is made in human history by humans dependent on certain factors and causes. History shows that the good governance of a ruler is measured by his success to reach, expand and sustain power. This paradigm is applied to the current situation of Muslims and juxtaposed to the historical success of Islam in its first centuries: once Muslims have retrieved their unity and regained their original strength, they will be in a position to counter European imperialism. This requires overcoming the spirit of sectarian differences and the implementation of Islam's socio-political teachings: a socio-political order based on Islamic law (shari'a) and not on legal regimes and ideologies imported from Europe.

This anthropocentric rationale for the rise (*nuhūḍ*) and decline (*hubūṭ*) of communities or nations (*umam*)[55] emphasizes human agency and is based on trans-historical laws as identified by Ibn Khaldun.[56] At the same time, such a de-sacralized view of history stands in tension with another term 'Abduh introduces to define these historical processes. Qur'anic stories of past communities outline how their decline began when they rejected a divine prophet or messenger or abandoned their teachings.[57] The rise of and fall of communities in the past, as presented in the Qur'an, inform its readers about 'the customs of God (*sunan allāh*)'. This is a key term in the Ash'ari school of theology to denote its theological occasionalism. An occasionalist reading of human history suggests that particular social conditions are not the cause for historical phenomena, as Ibn Khaldun argues, but God creates habitual relationships between specific social conditions and concomitant historical phenomena causing both to occur at the same time. Equally, pre-modern Islamic historiography uses the notion of 'the customs of God' to signify God's intervention throughout history. God is immanent in history, and the rise and fall of communities gives evidence of how

God operates throughout human history which is one of the divine signs visible in the world.[58] Such a theocentric view appears to contradict Ibn Khaldun's human-centred approach to history and has been used to suggest a fatalistic acceptance of realities, a mindset 'Abduh seeks to combat with his articles.[59]

The articles in *al-'Urwa al-Wuthqā* do not mention Ibn Khaldun, yet his imprint is visible in the way how the articles frame Islamic history. By equating Ibn Khaldun's philosophy of history with the concept of 'the customs of God', 'Abduh expresses Ibn Khaldun's anthropocentric and de-sacralized view of history in the idiom of Sunni theology and pre-modern Islamic historiography. Such terminology bears more authority in the Muslim world than references to the north African historian would. However, 'Abduh's discourse is not just an orthodox cladding of an anthropocentric view of history to overcome an apathic acquiescence of Muslims to European domination. His framing is part of a larger discourse in Islamic political philosophy which suggests that 'the ultimate *empirical test* of the success of the ruler's *siyāsat* [politics] is the *maṣlaḥat*-welfare of the community'.[60] The same manner by which one can identify a competent physician – a correct diagnosis and the prescription of a suitable remedy – so can one identify a competent ruler by the extent to which their policies promote the welfare of a community. This common analogy between physician and competent ruler in Islamic political philosophy is also rehearsed by 'Abduh when he creates an analogy between the current political, social and intellectual malaise of Islam and physical ailments that require medical treatment: 'for any grave matter that causes pain there is an experienced physician (*naṭāsī*) for its remedy and an insightful sage (*ḥakīm*) who can respond to it.'[61] The cure for the current condition of Islam can be retrieved by studying its history and prescribing a remedy that follows successful models of the socio-political organization of Muslim societies that achieved unity, strength and domination in the past. Retrieving the underlying socio-political principles of such a model in the present will also reveal 'God's intent'[62] and establish an order which is based on laws and principles that, because they promote the welfare of a community, are aligned with the shari'a. In this sense, state law (*qānūn*) derived from welfare-driven policies does not stand in opposition to Islamic law but is in accordance with it, as Islamic political philosopher asserted in the past[63] and 'Abduh equally argues in his earlier Egyptian articles. 'Abduh promotes neither replicating a historical precedent or recreating a golden past nor re-contextualizing an extracted 'Islamic essence'[64] in the present. He rather suggests an eclectic appropriation of the diverse Islamic intellectual traditions to understand the principles of successful governance.

Hence, the articles in *al-'Urwa al-Wuthqā* – despite a different target audience and discursive ductus – conflate the same intellectual traditions that inform 'Abduh's earlier political articles before his exile: Ibn Khaldun's philosophy of history, Islamic genres of practical and political philosophy and European concepts of evolutionary development and civilization. Ambiguities remain around different types of communal solidarity and allegiance or the relationship between anthropocentric and theocentric views of history: 'Abduh does not seek to reconcile these ambiguities intellectually but assumes their inherent confluence and harmony, based on the supposition in pre-modern Islamic political philosophy that policies which bring welfare to society are aligned with the shari'a. Shari'a is understood here not just as the sum of Islamic normative practices, a set of legal prescriptions and proscriptions deduced from the scriptural sources of Islam, but more philosophically as the underlying divine principles – God's intent or His customs – that undergird how the world functions.[65]

Return to Beirut

'Abduh returned to Beirut in early 1885 having failed to meet the Mahdi of Sudan or to secure more funding in order to continue publishing the journal *al-'Urwa al-Wuthqā*. He would stay for the next three years in the city before returning to Egypt. His reputation as an intellectual and political activist preceded him, as he received a constant stream of visitors from Beirut and the wider Ottoman province of Syria, including Ottoman government officials and religious scholars coming from both Sunni and Shii communities, Christian notables and merchants as well as European and American missionaries. Intellectually, 'Abduh entered quite familiar cultural and intellectual terrain. Similar to Cairo, Beirut emerged as major urban cosmopolitan hub in which discourses around progress (*tarqiyya*) and civilization (*tamaddun*) had taken deep roots since the 1860s. The Arab Christian man of letters Butrus al-Bustani (1819–1883) had published the first Arab encyclopaedia, *Dā'ira al-Ma'ārif* (1875–83), to which Afghani had contributed.[66] In its entry on Beirut, Bustani describes the city as a bridge between East and West and its inhabitants as particularly 'civilised' (*mutamaddinun*).[67] Hence, the intellectual climate resonated with the cosmopolitan environment 'Abduh was involved with in Cairo before his exile which transcended religious and sectarian boundaries which were more visible in Beirut given its religious heterogeneity. Together with other Egyptian exiles who were associated with Afghani, 'Abduh also became involved in one of the local Masonic lodges in Beirut, the Lebanon Lodge (*maḥfil lubnān*) where he established links with many local notables and Ottoman officials as well as the American envoy to Syria.[68] Similar to his involvement in Masonic lodges in Cairo, the Beirut lodge provided a social environment for elite members of Beirut society to interact with foreigners and followers of different religions.

'Abduh stayed at the invitation of the city's mayor Muhyi al-Din Bay Hamada whom he had met during his first sojourn in Beirut and whose niece he married after the death of his first wife.[69] Hamada stemming from the city's Sunni Muslim elite exhibited reformist tendencies and supported his approach and was willing to patronize his activities. 'Abduh initially stayed in the Bashura neighbourhood of the city before he moved to Zuqaq al-Balat in which many leading educationalists, writers and intellectuals were based who played a central role in the Arabic Revival (*al-nahḍa al-'arabiyya*) in the late nineteenth century. The most important educational institutions of the city – missionary and otherwise – were also based in this religiously diverse neighbourhood which had become 'an education quarter'.[70]

'Abduh began to engage in teaching at various schools in Beirut covering subjects such as the life of the Prophet Muhammad and Qur'anic exegesis. In late 1885, he was approached by the patrons of the Madrasa Sultaniyya to start teaching at the institution, located in the Zuqaq al-Balat neighbourhood, and to oversee some reforms in its curriculum. As a new secondary school, the Madrasa Sultaniyya had been established in 1883 by the Islamic Society for Benevolent Objectives (*jam'iyyat al-maqāṣid al-khayriyya al-islāmiyya*) and was headed by a Muslim scholar from Beirut who had graduated from al-Azhar and had studied under Afghani and 'Abduh in Cairo, Ahmad 'Abbas al-Azhari (1852/3–1926).[71] The institution was modelled after modern schools in order to compete with the increasing number of European missionary schools that had opened in Beirut and the wider Mount Lebanon region of Ottoman Syria. The Madrasa Sultaniyya used Arabic as language of instruction and combined Islamic education with modern subjects including teaching different languages such as Turkish, French and English. In light of wider educational reforms in the Ottoman Empire and the Middle East, the school was meant to educate a new indigenous Arab-Muslim elite that mastered modern scientific and administrative knowledge as well as Arabic and Turkish to assume careers in the Ottoman civil service while at the same ensuring their adherence to Islam and minimizing the influence of missionary schools on the young elite of the Beirut region. 'Abduh shared this concern for creating a modern Muslim education, as he had witnessed the educational bifurcation in Egypt and the appeal of foreign missionary schools. The objectives of the Madrasa Sultaniyya equally resonated with his anti-colonial agenda.

'Abduh was initially tasked to oversee and develop the Arabic language instruction and Islamic education of the school. When he started teaching, the school offered only foundational instruction into Arabic grammar and a basic introduction to the jurisprudence around Islamic ritual practices. 'Abduh expanded the curriculum, teaching the jurisprudence of the Hanafi legal school, the official legal school of the Ottoman Empire and most widely followed among Sunni Muslims in the Syrian province. He also introduced classes in logic and Islamic theology. His theology lectures at the Madrasa Sultaniyya would later be published in Egypt as his most influential work – *Risālat al-Tawḥīd* (Treatise on Divine Unity).[72] Some of the philosophical and theological content of this book and the lectures is based on the *Tahdhīb al-Manṭiq wa-l-Kalām* (The Refinement of Logic and Theology), a textbook on logic and the fundamentals of Islamic theology by Sa'd al-Din al-Taftazani (1322–1390) whom he had already studied and taught at al-Azhar.[73] 'Abduh also taught some more advanced Islamic philosophy such as the *Ishārāt* by Ibn Sina and used the *Maqāmāt* of Badi' al-Zaman al-Hamadani (969–1007), an anthology of aphorisms on human conduct, when teaching Arabic.[74] 'Abduh also used a Shii text to teach Arabic language and rhetoric. *Nahj al-Balāgha* (The Peak of Eloquence) is a collection of statements, sayings and letters attributed to the first Shii Imam and son-in-law of the Prophet Muhammad, 'Ali ibn Abi Talib, which was compiled by the Shii scholar al-Sharif al-Radi (970–1015).

'Abduh continued his eclectic approach in teaching, following the inspiration by his teacher Afghani, including a mix of rationalist Sunni theology, Islamic philosophy and pre-modern Arabic literature and a Shii anthology of sayings of 'Ali ibn Abi Talib in his curricular approach to teach Arabic and Islam. According to the memoirs of his associates in Beirut, 'Abduh equally emphasized the moral dimension of education and encouraged the students to work for the common welfare and assume responsibility for their societies – reflecting themes that had emerged earlier in his socio-political articles. 'Abduh equally continued his journalistic work contributing several articles to the Beirut-based journal *Thamarāt al-Funūn* (The Fruits of the Arts).[75]

'Abduh's unconventional approach to developing an Islamic education and Arabic language curriculum, his lively and engaging teaching style and his reputation as a reformist intellectual and political activist also drew opposition. He was also connected via marriage to influential notable families in Beirut and also victim of feuds between them. As opposition to him grew, a number of military officers associated with the Madrasa Sultaniyya secured his removal from his teaching position. They feared that his reformist approach to teaching would undermine the authority of the Ottoman sultan and his representatives in the Syrian province but probably were dismayed by ʿAbduh's unconventional educational and intellectual approach for which he had found both supporters and detractors in the past.[76] After his dismissal, ʿAbduh continued to teach in his private residence and also held public lectures on the Qur'an in one of the city's mosques that attracted the wider public and formed the nucleus of his later Qur'anic commentary.[77] Despite the restrictions ʿAbduh faced – an experience not novel to him – he managed to exercise influence on a number of reformist scholars and activists. The Syrian man of letters Muhammad ʿAli Kurdi (1876–1958), though never having met him, recounts the political acumen of ʿAbduh that has left a lasting impact on Syrian reformist intellectual scene.[78] Muhammad Rashid Rida would later become ʿAbduh's most influential disciple, though they only met briefly once when ʿAbduh visited his hometown Tripoli.[79] Another important Lebanese follower of ʿAbduh was Shakib Arslan (1869–1946), a graduate from the Madrasa Sultaniyya. Originally, from a notable Druze family, he would later become an important Arab nationalist statesman, activist and intellectual.[80]

Involvement in Ottoman educational politics

During his exile in Beirut, ʿAbduh was not an apolitical figure but an astute observer of local politics and equally commenting on educational reforms that were undertaken in the Ottoman Empire at that time. The demand for modern education, modelled after European schools and curricula, was evident given the popularity of European Christian missionary schools in Syria and the creation of private Islamic schools such as the Madrasa Sultaniyya. The Ottoman authorities themselves had initiated educational reforms earlier with the aim of yielding loyal Ottoman subjects that possessed at the same time the necessary scientific expertise to turn the Ottoman Empire into a modern state that can withstand European colonial pressure.[81]

ʿAbduh contributed to these debates in articles to the journal *Thamarāt al-Funūn* and also penned two petitions: one sent to the *shaykh al-islām*, the highest Islamic religious authority in the Ottoman Empire,[82] and the other to the Ottoman governor in the city of Beirut in 1887. Both petitions despite their different addressees and approaches share certain themes. They are driven by an anti-colonial agenda pointing at the danger of European missionary schools in moving young people away from Islam and thereby undermining their loyalty to the Ottoman state. Hence, both petitions resonate with his anti-colonial activism against the British occupation of Egypt and the anti-imperialist articles in the journal *al-ʿUrwa al-Wuthqā*. In both petitions, ʿAbduh requests the expansion of Islamic education in state schools as he deems current provisions, particularly in military schools, minimal. Both petitions equally emphasize the central role of the Ottoman state in overseeing and centralizing education given the various foreign actors which had emerged and whose educational provisions had proven quite popular. It is not clear what actual impact ʿAbduh's petitions had – there is no evidence that they had any. However, they show his awareness of the local situation in Syria and his continuous concern for bridging the gap between modern forms of education offered in foreign or state schools and traditional religious education that has remained dominant in Islamic seminaries and did not engage with modern ideas and sciences. ʿAbduh's concern for the negative impact of Christian missionary schools was not new. Already in 1881, as editor for the official journal *al-Waqāʾiʿ al-Miṣriyya*, he wrote an article warning of the dangers of American Protestant schools in Cairo and Alexandria in enticing young Egyptian Muslims away from their religion.[83]

This particular concern also emerges in ʿAbduh's two petitions. In both, he presents himself as a loyal servant to the Ottoman sultan describing himself as 'a Muslim by creed, an Ottoman by persuasion and an Arab in tongue'.[84] In the petition to the Ottoman *shaykh al-islām*, ʿAbduh applauds recent initiatives to reform the educational system in the empire but is also critical of the basic religious instruction which is provided in state schools such as the military academies and only provides a superficial grasp of some laws and rituals without an inner, ethical understanding (*fiqh bāṭinī*) needed to initiate individual moral transformation.[85] ʿAbduh suggests a systematic three-tier approach towards Islamic education addressing the specific religious needs of the general populace, future Ottoman bureaucrats and religious scholars.[86] This distinction between three educational levels also reflects the approach taken by the Madrasa Sultaniyya. The general populace only needs instruction into the basic tenets of Islam and an understanding of early Islamic history, in particular the biography of the Prophet Muhammad to acquire the virtues early Muslims represented and to understand the sources of the power of the early Islamic empire. Future governmental officials and civil servants should in addition be trained in logic and modern sciences and develop the necessary intellectual and argumentative skills to counter arguments of Christian missionaries and other detractors of Islam. Finally, future religious scholars need to be educated in the whole spectrum of traditional Islamic branches of knowledge but also acquire an understanding of pre-modern and modern history to perceive the reasons for the rise and decline of communities and the current condition of Muslims. Their theological training should also include the contributions of Islamic philosophy in order to acquire rational arguments for Islamic doctrines.[87]

In this petition, ʿAbduh connects Islamic education with political loyalty to the Ottoman sultan. The more the Islamic component in state education is strengthened, the more likely is the creation of loyal subjects to the Ottoman ruler. ʿAbduh resonates here with a main agenda of Ottoman educational reforms and connects it with his own concern: the fear that a new modern-educated elite will emerge with little attachment to Islam because of weak Islamic provisions in state schools or their complete education in European missionary schools in which students do not receive any Islamic education. European Christian missionary schools 'graduate Christians by creed and Muslims by name or materialists (*dahriyyīn*) without any creed'.[88] In order to strengthen new Muslim elite's commitment to Islam, they need to be educated in order to develop an ethical understanding of their religion. The education should provide students the intellectual means to understand, internalize and defend Islam rather than just becoming its superficial adherents.

ʿAbduh's second petition exhibits his acute awareness of the complex sectarian demographics of the Ottoman province of Syria and the district of Mount Lebanon (*mutaṣarrifiyyat jabal lubnān*) which had been separated from the Syrian province in 1860 following European diplomatic pressure, given its majority Christian population. In the second petition, ʿAbduh addresses the particular educational needs of the different sectarian groups in Syria and measures the extent of their loyalty to the Ottoman sultan. While Sunnis are the most loyal supporters of the Ottoman state and of the caliphate held by the sultan, their loyalty should not be taken for granted, in particular if their understanding of Islam remains superficial and their religious commitment to the Ottoman state is not sufficiently developed as part of their education. ʿAbduh seeks to rehabilitate the activities of Muslim benevolent societies and their private schools in particular which have been attacked as undermining Ottoman educational policies. ʿAbduh presents them as the best bulwark against the corrupting influence of missionary schools. According to ʿAbduh, Shiis unlike their Sunni counterparts do not possess any inherent theological affinity to the Ottoman sultan as they do not believe in the caliphate. However, given their views on the ritual impurity of Christians, the majority of Shiis do not send their children to European schools and do not pose a particular political threat to Ottoman suzerainty either. However, their passive loyalty cannot be assumed without reservations, in particular if European missionaries make inroads into this community.

The Druze were the strongest allies of the Ottoman state but have felt disempowered with Christian dominance established in the autonomous Mount Lebanon district and alienated from the empire as a consequence. Given this distance of the younger generation of Druze to the Ottoman state, British and French educational institutions have successfully reached out to them. Christians in Lebanon are presented by 'Abduh as though most likely to disengage with the Ottoman state, though he distinguishes between different Christian denominations and their political attitudes. Greek-Orthodox Christians are closest to the Ottoman state and less likely to be under the influence of Christian missionary schools. Of particular concern for 'Abduh are the Maronite Christians of Mount Lebanon whose educational system is dominated by French institutions and financial support which has entirely undermined their allegiance to the Ottoman Empire: 'The Maronites consider themselves to be French, are inclined and devoted to the French state and believe that it protects them and safeguards their rights.'[89]

'Abduh in line with his anti-colonial attitudes observes how European powers exploit the complex sectarian geography of Syria and Mount Lebanon to undermine the social and political reach of the Ottoman state to its diverse communities. He seems to suggest that it is almost too late to counter the French orientation of Maronite Christians, given the political protection and financial support they receive from the French state. However, other Christian dominations are not under the sway of European missionaries to that extent and certainly Druze and Shiis can be co-opted with the state if it develops a systematic and centralized plan to extend state education to these communities. A unified educational system under Ottoman state control will establish schools that foster 'the revival of religion and love for the state'.[90]

To what extent, 'Abduh's analysis would have added any new insights to Ottoman authorities is questionable. The types of reforms he suggested in both petitions reflect educational policies already implemented by the Ottomans in their state schools. Islam was already conceived as the foundation of individual morality that included the teachings of morals (*akhlāq*), Islamic jurisprudence (*fiqh*) and the biography of the Prophet Muhammad (*sīra*).[91] His motivation for writing these petitions was perhaps to position himself as an important voice within debates around educational reforms in the Ottoman Empire and to assume an advisory role in some official capacity. 'Abduh also defends the educational activities of Muslim benevolent societies and their private schools which had been placed under government control because of suspicions they had tried to undermine the Ottoman state.

Both petitions were means for 'Abduh to make himself known towards Ottoman authorities while underlying his allegiance to the sultan after allegations have been made against him accusing him of disloyalty.[92] They also gave him a platform to communicate his approach towards a reformed understanding of Islamic education that aligns itself with the primary objective of educational reforms in the Ottoman Empire: to create loyal Ottoman subjects in the imperial classroom. He also hints at the potential shortcomings of an approach to educational reforms that is primarily concerned with securing political loyalty and does not sufficiently envision the intellectual and moral transformation of Muslim students. In a speech given in 1886 at the Madrasa Sultaniyya, 'Abduh summarizes his educational philosophy and repeats core tropes of his intellectual approach towards Islam. While praising educational reforms undertaken by the Ottoman authorities, he is equally critical of the sole promotion of technological and scientific knowledge without an intrinsic understanding of the intellectual roots of the development made by European countries: 'We seek the knowledge behind these sciences which is nothing else than knowledge that touches the human soul – knowledge of human life.'[93] Such knowledge needs to be based on 'deep understanding of religion'[94] to develop human ethical capabilities and to be translated into moral human conduct. Rather than blindly imitating European cultural traditions, Islam's own intellectual resources should be revived to develop an understanding of Islam as an individual and social transformative power.

Irenic engagement with the religious 'Other'

The urban context of Beirut and the wider Syrian province was different to the religious composition of Egyptian society in which 'Abduh grew up. The complex and diverse sectarian make-up of Syrian society was obvious. All the associates of 'Abduh who have written about his stay in Beirut – Rida includes three accounts in his biography – attest to his appeal across religious boundaries. In Beirut, 'Abduh met representatives from different religions, and his lectures on the Qur'an were attended by Christians as well.[95] His involvement in a local Masonic lodge allowed him to establish links to reformist notables of different religious backgrounds and foreign residents in the city. The account provided by Shakib Arslan emphasizes 'Abduh's irenic engagement with the religious 'Other' – whether within Islam or outside of it. Arslan describes how 'Abduh welcomed scholars from different Muslim denominations and other religions at his home and engaged in theological debates within them. While these debates did not always lead to agreements, participants left with an impression of 'Abduh's intellectual generosity. Investigating the roots of 'Abduh's cosmopolitan and irenic intellectual outlook, Arslan attributes it to his immersion in mystical philosophy: 'This insight descended upon me: how exalted philosophy (*falsafa*) is among the branches of knowledge (*'ulūm*); how it facilitates the understanding of everything; how excellent the intellectual acumen is that wisdom (*ḥikma*)[96] bestows and Sufism (*taṣawwuf*) fashions.'[97]

To underline 'Abduh's irenic attitude, Arslan not only mentions his regular contacts with Christian dignitaries but also the esteem in which he held his own Druze community. 'Abduh comes across in his account as somebody who was more impressed by a person's erudition and cosmopolitan outlook than their religious background. Arslan highlights this attitude in particular when he introduces 'Abduh's relationship with 'Abbas Effendi. Also known as 'Abd al-Baha' (1844–1921), 'Abbas Effendi was the son of Husayn 'Ali Nuri Baha' Allah (1817–1892), an Iranian aristocrat who was then exiled in 'Akka, Palestine, at that time leader of the Babi movement out of which the Baha'i Faith emerged. Arslan mentions the particular enmity 'Abduh's teacher Afghani exhibited towards the Babis in order to point that despite the doctrinal differences that might have existed between the two, 'Abduh held 'Abbas Effendi in high esteem and enjoyed his company and erudition.[98] That 'Abbas Effendi's father as founding figure of a new religious movement made claims to post-Qur'anic revelation did not concern 'Abduh in particular. In a conversation with his disciple Rida later in his life, 'Abduh appears unaware of the nature of the Baha'i Faith and the prophetic claims of its founder and rather praises 'Abbas Effendi's character.[99]

Another Iranian of a Muslim background whose conduct did not conform with narrow notions of orthodoxy and with whom 'Abduh collaborated in Beirut was Muhammad Baqir Bawanati.[100] He had translated English press articles into Arabic for the journal *al-'Urwa al-Wuthqā* and had moved to Beirut in 1884.[101] Bawanati had a complex religious biography having experimented with different religions, once a wandering dervish, Christian, Jew and atheist, and working on a synthesis between Christianity and Islam which he named 'Islamo-Christianity'[102] while based in London. Perhaps because of Bawanati's own ventures into bringing Christianity and Islam together in a new religious synthesis, Rida suggests that, while in Beirut, ʿAbduh headed an association for the rapprochement between Islam, Christianity and Judaism (*jamʿiyyat al-taʾlīf wa-l-taqrīb*) working together with Bawanati who acted as the society's secretary. According to Rida, the society included a number of Iranian residents in Beirut and Ottoman officials and also had two British members. Its representative in Britain was the Anglican clergyman and Canon of York, Isaac Taylor (1829–1901).[103] Apart from Rida's account which was uncritically adopted by later biographers and some academic scholarship, there is no evidence that ʿAbduh established or was part of such a formal association.[104] Even the suggestion that it was 'a global correspondence network'[105] seems an overstatement.

Bawanati's religious experimentations did not lead into any formal organization around his syncretic beliefs but only found expression in his Persian poetry.[106] His conformity to standard practices of Muslim piety appeared to be weak. Another Iranian living in Beirut states that 'Mirza Baqir is not an observant Muslim (*musalmān-i mutasharriʿ nīst*)'.[107] Nevertheless, ʿAbduh engaged and associated with intellectuals and scholars of a wide variety of religious persuasions and exchanged extensive correspondence while in Beirut – even if they did not conform to narrow definitions of Islamic orthodoxy as the cases of the religious 'free thinker'[108] Bawanati and the Babi-Bahaʾi leader ʿAbbas Effendi illustrate.[109] Rida might have wanted to legitimize his teacher's unconventional contacts in the framework of a secret society whose apparent agenda was achieving a rapprochement among Judaism, Christianity and Islam while in reality it was meant as an instrument for 'the defence of and call to Islam'.[110] Perhaps, Rida used his references to the secret society uniting the three Abrahamic religions as a cover to conceal ʿAbduh's wide-ranging contacts and associates and for his involvement in the Beirut Masonic lodge which included members of different religions and resembled a secretive interfaith organization. The manner which Rida describes the purpose of the alleged association, its cultural activities and its political orientation is reminiscent of the cosmopolitan and trans-sectarian remit of Middle Eastern branches of Freemasonry.[111]

ʿAbduh exchanged two letters with the alleged British representative of the society, Isaac Taylor. Taylor caused a public stir that ensured for several years after his address to the annual congress of the Anglican Church, held in Wolverhampton in 1887. In his speech, Taylor suggested that Islam was more successful in its missionary activities in Africa than Christianity. His arguments were based on racial assumptions of cultural superiority: Islam as a cruder form of religion was better in appealing to abase instincts that dominated Africans while Christianity was 'too spiritual, to lofty … unintelligible to savages'.[112] Because of its appeal to Africans, Islam was a more promising avenue towards civilizing the African continent and a stepping stone towards Christianity by gradually leading Africans to its purer and more spiritual form after they had initially converted to Islam. Given his racist view of the inherent intellectual and moral inferiority of Africans, Taylor argued that Islam was the best option to elevate their morality and civilization. In line with evolutionary social thought at that time, Taylor advanced a progressive understanding of religious maturation: the question is not which religion is true or truer but which religion is more appropriate for the next step in the religious, intellectual and civilizational development of Africa. For Taylor, this was clearly Islam. Despite the explicit racism in Taylor's line of thought, his views were perceived as pro-Islamic in the ensuring public debate led by representative of various missionary societies.[113]

News of Taylor's positive assessment of Islam as a civilizational power *en par* with Christianity also reached Beirut, with ʿAbduh publishing a translation of this talk in the journal *Thamarāt al-Funūn*.[114] ʿAbduh wrote a letter to Taylor, congratulating him for perceiving 'Islam in its original nature'[115] and for inviting 'the sons of your community to "a common word (*kalīma sawā*')"[116] between them and Muslims'.[117] ʿAbduh affirms the divine origin of all Biblical prophets and their scriptures and their fundamental unity and concludes that this 'sound approach'[118] should be taught in the schools of Syria given its religious diversity. Taylor responded to his letter and asked about different Islamic views on divorce, polygamy and slavery. His questions suggest that his view of Islam did not transcend Orientalist stereotypes as they were common in Victorian Britain at that time and revolved around the status of women and polygamy in particular. ʿAbduh does not really engage with Taylor's questions in his second letter to him but considers them of secondary relevance in light of the fundamental theological unity of both Christianity and Islam. Nevertheless, ʿAbduh – perhaps out of disappointment about Taylor's response to his initial irenic letter – exhibits certain triumphalist tone presenting Islam as the culmination of salvation history and the purest articulation of monotheism.[119]

It is not known whether there was any further correspondence between Taylor and ʿAbduh. The exchange of letters certainly does not warrant the conclusion that both were involved in an organized form of interfaith dialogue bringing both Christianity and Islam together. Taylor himself quotes from ʿAbduh's first letter – without mentioning him by name – and supportive letters he had received from other Muslims residing in Iran and the Ottoman Empire.[120] There is no suggestion in Taylor's account that he was part of an interfaith association that included Christians and Muslims. ʿAbduh was probably excited about a British clergyman attesting to the civilizational force of Islam in a public lecture and being placed under severe public criticism as a consequence. Taylor's approach to Islam and civilization appeared to resonate with 'Abduh's own arguments of the inherent civilizational force of Islam. The racial connotations in Taylor's line of argument and his depiction of Islam as somehow more primitive than Christianity escaped 'Abduh's attention. Nevertheless, the public discourse following Taylor's 1887 Wolverhampton framed him as a defender of Islam in Britain, and it was this image that encouraged 'Abduh to engage with Taylor and to conclude in a letter to another person that Taylor had become a Muslim but 'calls to Islam under a veil'[121] to eschew persecution by his countrymen.

The Peak of Eloquence

In Beirut, 'Abduh also engaged with Shiis, though little is known about individuals from the Shii community in Lebanon with whom he interacted. Bawanati's Iranian Shii background was obvious but did not perturb 'Abduh in particular. His close relationship to Afghani must have made 'Abduh aware of his mentor's Iranian Shii background. He also engaged with other Iranians residing in Beirut. In Beirut he also began to engage with an important Shii text, *Nahj al-Balāgha* which contains sermons, statements and letters attributed to the first Shii Imam, 'Ali ibn Abi Talib. 'Abduh used the *Nahj al-Balāgha* as a textbook to teach Arabic rhetoric at the Madrasa Sultaniyya. This is an odd choice from the rich corpus of Arabic literature he could have used to familiarize his students with the finesse of the Arabic language. While 'Ali is also revered in the Sunni tradition as the fourth of the rightly guided caliphs (*al-khulāfa' al-rāshidūn*), *Nahj al-Balāgha* is a Shii text. It contains more general homiletic statements on the nature of God, creation, eschatology and ethics. Equally, it includes statements by 'Ali that support a sectarian narrative in support of the Shii view on the succession of the Prophet Muhammad. 'Ali's accounts of how his right to the caliphate was usurped by Abu Bakr and 'Umar, of his confrontation with Muhammad's wife Aisha and the Prophet's Companions Talha and Zubayr during the Battle of the Camel and of his struggle with Mu'awiya of the Umayyad clan who also rejected 'Ali's caliphate are included in the collection. Using such a text to teach Arabic rhetoric is unconventional to say the least, but 'Abduh made a core Shii text accessible to his mostly Sunni students at the Madrasa Sultaniyya. Using a Shii collection to teach Arabic language and rhetoric constituted a safe route in advancing understanding between Sunnis and Shiis. Including such a text in an

Arabic language class was more secure and aroused less suspicion than using it when teaching early Islamic history.

'Abduh not only used the text as a teaching tool but also published a commentary on it, making this text available in print. His engagement with the text in the classroom and as its commentator and editor reflects his objective to alert Muslim readers to various sources and genres of Islamic literature and to avert narrow-minded notions of Islamic orthodoxy that exclude certain Islamic epistemes and genres by declaring them as standing outside the fold of Islam. In the introduction, 'Abduh lays out his agenda as non-sectarian: his commentary is not about the question of the succession of the Prophet and does not use controversial traditions or interpretations to vindicate the view of a particular school of thought (*madhhab*) against others. Rather his commentary is interested in the meaning of words and expression and seeks to highlight the sublime style of the compilations based on the agreement shared by all scholars of the Arabic language that 'the words of Imam 'Ali ibn Abi Talib are the most noble and the most eloquent words after the Word of God, the Exalted, and of His Prophet'.[122] His various commentaries on the different parts of the *Nahj al-Balāgha* focus on linguistic questions and, if they provide historical contextual information, steer away from controversy.

'Ali's accounts of the resistance he experienced to his claim to the caliphate are dealt with by discussing the meaning of words or geographical references these statements contain. When 'Ali complains how Abu Bakr and 'Umar usurped the caliphate and how a committee was appointed by 'Umar to choose his successor as a further attempt to undermine his legitimate right to lead the Islamic community, 'Abduh provides a factual account of the consultation process that followed 'Umar's death and appointed 'Uthman as his successor without further assessment.[123] In a sermon in which 'Ali attacked Aisha, Talha and Zubayr for their rejection of his own caliphate during the Battle of the Camel, 'Abduh provides an account of the battle, including the overall death toll on both sides, and explains the linguistic meaning of the various derogatory terms 'Ali uses when referring to the partisans of Talha and Zubayr.[124] 'Ali's attacks on Mu'awiya and the Umayyad clan are left uncommented by 'Abduh: neither does he suggest any agreement with 'Ali's assessment of Mu'awiya's character and the corrupt conduct of members of the Umayyad clan, nor does he seek to defend the Umayyad dynasty or exonerate Mu'awiya to vindicate the early caliphate from a Sunni perspective.[125] 'Abduh suggests that the enmity between the Umayyad and Hashmid clans, from which 'Ali stemmed, dated back to the pre-Islamic period as a remnant of the tribal nature of Arab society.[126]

When 'Ali outlines the station of the Shii Imams vis-à-vis their followers or points at the special position of the family of the Prophet Muhammad (*ahl al-bayt*) in leading the Islamic community, 'Abduh is solely occupied with the meaning of certain terms he uses.[127] The contents of 'Ali's prominent letter to Malik al-Ashtar when he appointed him as governor of Egypt which lays out his political philosophy in quite some detail is also left uncommented for the most part. 'Ali's admonition to Malik not to wage war against God is interpreted as meaning not to contradict Islamic law (shari'a) by being oppressive.[128] When 'Ali emphasizes in his letter that good conduct towards his subjects is the source of their loyalty to him, 'Abduh argues that the best form of obedience towards political authority stems from the inner conviction and the trust of the subjects in their ruler.[129] The rest of his comments delve on linguistic details.

The only occasions where 'Abduh engages in sectarian arguments is when commenting on 'Ali's attacks on another movement that opposed his caliphate: the Kharijites. 'Abduh concurs with 'Ali's rejection of the Kharjite position that any sinner ceases to be a Muslim and becomes an apostate as contradicting the Prophet Muhammad's teachings.[130] The Kharijites defected from 'Ali's camp when he was prepared to negotiate with Mu'awiya. They deserted (and one of their followers later assassinated him) with the slogan: 'Judgement belongs to God alone (*lā-ḥukm illā li-llāh*).'[131] In his refutation, 'Ali deconstructs their slogan as being theologically true but politically misconstrued. The Kharijites failed to distinguish between the transcendental sovereignty of God and the practical question of political leadership (*imra*) in this world. While God is the only judge in this world from a theological point of view, this doctrine needs to be separated from the question of political leadership in this world: without a ruler (*amīr*) society would descend into anarchy. 'Abduh in a brief commentary concurs with this assessment arguing that leadership is necessary in a society and the moral standing of the ruler does not have any bearings on the Islamic community fulfilling the requirements of their religion: Muslims can be good Muslims, even under an immoral ruler.[132]

'Abduh, in his commentary, neither suggests any agreement with 'Ali's accounts of the struggle of succession which present the Shii view of early Islamic history nor defends the Sunni point of view but leaves the more controversial aspects of *Nahj al-Balāgha* uncommented and seeks to make this core Shii text and its historical, doctrinal and ethical views accessible to modern Muslim readers by focussing on its linguistic and homiletic characteristics and without pursuing an apologetic sectarian agenda. The irenic approach that characterizes his personal interaction with Muslims of different sectarian backgrounds finds a literary articulation in his commentary that also mirrors his advocacy for Islamic unity. The only exception are the Kharijites where 'Abduh takes sides and explicitly supports 'Ali's refutations and attacks on them: they are an unproblematic target as their political stance and theological views are rejected by Sunnis and Shiis alike. By targeting the Kharijites, 'Abduh asserts one area of common ground between Sunnis and Shiis and also attacks a sectarian group in early Islam, known for its zealotry and intolerance towards divergent doctrinal and political views.

Conclusion

'Abduh's exile is characterized by diverse political and intellectual engagements and literary outputs. He was engaged in anti-imperialist agitation, calling for the restoration of Islam as an activist religion and engine of civilizational progress, and advocated educational reforms in the Ottoman Empire to form loyal Muslim subjects. He equally socialized with notables, scholars and intellectuals of very diverse religious backgrounds and disregarded questions of orthodoxy in his interaction with them and rather praised the intellectual erudition and moral character of his interlocutors. On the one hand, 'Abduh argued for the essential unity of all religions and engaged with individuals and movements espousing similar ideas such as 'Abbas Effendi or Muhammad Baqir Bawanati while, on the other hand, he retained a triumphalist understanding of Islam and its crucial role in forming anti-colonial attitudes and activism among Muslims. At first sight, 'Abduh's diverse personal interactions and varied intellectual outputs from journalistic articles promoting Islamic unity to petitions to Ottoman authorities and commentaries on a central text of Shii Islam appear random. However, in his engagement with different audiences during his exile, certain intellectual continuities can be observed: his recourse to pre-modern Islamic genres of practical and political philosophy, his ethical understanding of Islam as a force for individual and collective transformation, his rejection of the blind imitation of Europe and the need to revive Islam's own intellectual traditions to counter encroaching European colonialism.

The trope of unity equally runs through these different activities: similar to his promotion of a proto-nationalist sense of Egyptian patriotism before his exile, his advocacy for Muslim unity in the articles of *al-'Urwa al-Wuthqā* are meant to instil solidarity that transcends sectarian differences to counter European imperialism successfully. Unity is presented as the source of strength for any community and nation, as both history and the Qur'an illustrate. Islamic unity is not achieved by narrow and exclusionary definitions of Islamic orthodoxy – reducing Islam to some essential beliefs and practices – but by adopting an irenic attitude towards inner-Islamic diversity which appreciates and engages with its manifold literary and intellectual manifestations. As his student in Beirut Shakib Arslan notes, it was 'Abduh's immersion in philosophy and Sufism that allowed him to adopt such an irenic attitude and to seek common ground with people of diverse and often contradictory religious persuasions: behind the apparent diversity observable in the world there is an essential unity overcoming and encompassing all these ostensible differences. As 'Abduh confirms in a letter to the Anglican clergyman Isaac Taylor as well: 'Everything has its origin in the One. Then, it multiplies until it cannot be limited.'[133]

Equally, 'Abduh's engagement with mystical philosophy allowed him to refine the ambiguity of his intellectual persona and to frame his discourse in accordance to the different expectations of diverse audiences. The clandestine activism against European imperialism as part of the secret society named like the journal *al-'Urwa al-Wuthqā* resembled more the approach of esoteric Islamic movements or Freemasonry. At the same time, there was a public side of his activism: teaching Islam and Arabic in Beirut and engaging with Ottoman authorities to lobby for educational reforms. The discourses and conduct of 'Abduh differed between the covert and visible side of his various activities but both served the purpose of countering European imperialism. His more conspicuous activities suggest loyalty to the Ottoman sultan and affirm orthodox notions of Sunni theology. 'Abduh remained a political figure seeking patronage from reform-oriented members of the Muslim elite. While his efforts failed to secure further financial support for the journal *al-'Urwa al-Wuthqā* and shaping Ottoman educational policies, he was more successful in receiving patronage for his educational and intellectual activities from the Sunni elite in Beirut. Sustaining intellectual ambiguity and shaping a particular public image and role as Muslim reformist intellectual would prove crucial when 'Abduh returned to Egypt in 1888.

Notes

1 Nikki R. Keddie, *Sayyid Jamāl ad-Dīn 'al-Afghānī': A Political Biography* (Berkeley: University of California Press, 1972), 155–60.

2 'Abduh quoted in Alexander M. Broadley, *How We Defended Arabi and His Friends: A Story of Egypt and the Egyptians* (London: Chapman and Hall, 1884), 231.

3 Keddie, *'al-Afghānī'*, 159.
4 Ibid., 184–6.
5 Muhammad 'Abduh, 'Li-Mādhā Ṣadarat al-Jarīda', in *al-'Urwa al-Wuthqā wa-l-Thawra al-Taḥrīriyya al-Kubrā*, Jamal al-Din al-Afghani and Muhammad 'Abduh, (Cairo: Dar al-'Arab, 1958), 6.
6 Qur'an 2:256 and 31:22.
7 For a French translation of the most influential articles, see Marcel Colombe, trans., 'Pages choisies de Djamal al-Din al-Afghani', *Orient*, 21 (1962): 87–115; *Orient*, 22 (1962): 125–59; *Orient*, 23 (1962): 169–90; *Orient*, 24 (1962): 125–51; *Orient*, 25 (1963): 141–52. For a discussion of the articles, see Josep P. Montada, 'Al-Afghânî, a Case of Religious Unbelief?', *Studia Islamica*, 100 (2005): 203–20.
8 Muhammad Rashid Rida, 'Mulakhkhaṣ Sīrat al-Ustādh al-Imām', *al-Manār*, 8 (1905): 462.
9 Keddie, *'al-Afghani'*, 215–19.
10 Muhammad Rashid Rida, *Ta'rīkh al-Ustādh al-Imām al-Shaykh Muḥammad 'Abduh*, vol. 1 (Cairo: al-Manar, 1931), 283.
11 Ibid.
12 For the constitution of the society, see Muhammad 'Abduh, in *al-A'māl al-Kāmila li-l-Imām Muḥammad 'Abduh*, ed. Muhammad 'Imara, vol. 1 (Beirut: Dar al-Shuruq, 1993), 664.
13 Quoted in ibid., 660.
14 Ahmad Amin, *Zu'amā' al-Iṣlāḥ fī-l-'Aṣr al-Ḥadīth* (Cairo: Maktabat al-Nahda al-Misriyya, 1948), 307.
15 Rida, *Ta'rīkh*, vol. 1, 336.
16 Rida, 'Mulakhkhaṣ', 460–1.
17 Various letters are reprinted in 'Abduh, *al-A'māl al-Kāmila*, vol. 1, 667–701. See in particular pages 686 and 694–5.
18 For a translation in English, see Nikki R. Keddie, *An Islamic Response to Imperialism: Political and Religious Writings of Sayyid Jamāl ad-Dīn 'al-Afghānī'* (Berkeley: University of California Press, 1968).
19 'Ali Shalash, *Silsilat al-A'māl al-Majhūla Muḥammad 'Abduh* (London: Riad al-Rayyes, 1987), 46.
20 Letter quoted in ibid., 45–6.
21 Ibid., 46.
22 Muhammad 'Abduh, 'Ṣidā Da'wat al-Sūdān', in *al-'Urwa al-Wuthqā wa-l-Thawra al-Taḥrīriyya al-Kubrā*, Jamal al-Din al-Afghani and Muhammad 'Abduh (Cairo: Dar al-'Arab, 1958), 179–80.
23 'Abd al-Mun'im Hamada, *al-Ustādh al-Imām Muḥammad 'Abduh* (Cairo: al-Maktaba al-Tijariyya, 1945), 102–3.

24 Jacques Jomier, 'La revue al-'Orwa al-Wothqa (13 mars – 16 octobre 1884) et l'autorité du Coran', *Mélanges d'Institut Dominicain d'Etudes Orientales du Caire*, 17 (1986): 13–14
25 Muhammad Abduh, 'Īrlandā', in *al-'Urwa al-Wuthqā wa-l-Thawra al-Taḥrīriyya al-Kubrā*, Jamal al-Din al-Afghani and Muhammad 'Abduh (Cairo: Dar al-'Arab, 1958), 187.
26 Mahmud Qasim, 'Ahdāf al-'Urwa al-Wuthqā', in *al-'Urwa al-Wuthqā wa-l-Thawra al-Taḥrīriyya al-Kubrā*, Jamal al-Din al-Afghani and Muhammad 'Abduh (Cairo: Dar al-'Arab, 1958), xxxiii.
27 Muhammad 'Abduh, 'Māḍī al-Umma wa-Ḥāḍiruhā wa-'Ilāj 'Ilalihā', in *al-'Urwa al-Wuthqā wa-l-Thawra al-Taḥrīriyya al-Kubrā*, Jamal al-Din al-Afghani and Muhammad 'Abduh (Cairo: Dar al-'Arab, 1958), 13–14.
28 Ibid. 21.
29 Muhammad 'Abduh, 'al-Waḥda al-Islāmiyya', in *al-'Urwa al-Wuthqā wa-l-Thawra al-Taḥrīriyya al-Kubrā*, Jamal al-Din al-Afghani and Muhammad 'Abduh (Cairo: Dar al-'Arab, 1958), 67.
30 Ibid.
31 Ibid., 67–8.
32 Muhammad 'Abduh, 'al-Naṣrāniyya wa-l-Islām wa-Ahluhumā', in *al-'Urwa al-Wuthqā wa-l-Thawra al-Taḥrīriyya al-Kubrā*, Jamal al-Din al-Afghani and Muhammad 'Abduh (Cairo: Dar al-'Arab, 1958), 26.
33 'Abduh, 'Māḍī al-Umma', 21.
34 Ibid.
35 Erez Naaman, 'Nurture over Nature: Habitus from al-Fārābī through Ibn Khaldūn to 'Abduh', *Journal of the American Oriental Society*, 137(1) (2017): 22.
36 'Abduh, 'al-Naṣrāniyya wa-l-Islām', 28–9.
37 Muhammad 'Abduh, 'Inḥiṭāṭ al-Muslimīn wa-Sukūnuhum wa-Sabab Dhālika', in *al-'Urwa al-Wuthqā wa-l-Thawra al-Taḥrīriyya al-Kubrā*, Jamal al-Din al-Afghani and Muhammad 'Abduh (Cairo: Dar al-'Arab, 1958), 34–5.
38 'Abduh, 'Māḍī al-Umma', 18.
39 Ibid., 19.
40 Ibid.
41 Muhammad 'Abduh, 'al-Jinsiyya wa-l-Diyāna al-Islāmiyya', in *al-'Urwa al-Wuthqā wa-l-Thawra al-Taḥrīriyya al-Kubrā*, Jamal al-Din al-Afghani and Muhammad 'Abduh (Cairo: Dar al-'Arab, 1958), 9–10.
42 Muhammad 'Abduh, 'al-Ta'aṣṣub', in *al-'Urwa al-Wuthqā wa-l-Thawra al-Taḥrīriyya al-Kubrā*, Jamal al-Din al-Afghani and Muhammad 'Abduh (Cairo: Dar al-'Arab, 1958), 39.
43 Ibid., 40; Malcolm H. Kerr, *Islamic Reform: The Legal and Political Theories of Muhammad 'Abduh and Rashid Rida* (Berkeley: University of California Press, 1966), 137–8.

44 'Abduh, 'al-Ta'aṣṣub', 42.
45 Ibid., 45–7.
46 'Abduh, 'al-Jinsiyya', 10.
47 'Abduh, 'al-Ta'aṣṣub', 45.
48 Ibn Khaldun, *Muqaddimat ibn Khaldūn*, vol. 1 (Damascus: Dar Ya'rib, 2003), 289.
49 Amin, *Zu'amā' al-Iṣlāḥ*, 306.
50 Adib Ishaq, *al-Durar: wa-Hiya Muntakhabāt al-Ṭayyib al-Dhikr al-Khālid al-Athar al-Marḥūm Adīb Ishaq* (Alexandria: Matba'at Jaridat al-Mahrusa, 1886), 53–5.
51 'Abduh, 'al-Waḥda al-Islāmiyya', 72.
52 Other modern Muslim reformers engaged in a similar argumentation. See Monica M. Ringer, *Islamic Modernism and the Re-Enchantment of the Sacred in the Age of History* (Edinburgh: Edinburgh University Press, 2020), 113–14.
53 Muhammad 'Abduh, 'Sunan Allāh fī-l-Umam', in *al-'Urwa al-Wuthqā wa-l-Thawra al-Taḥrīriyya al-Kubrā*, Jamal al-Din al-Afghani and Muhammad 'Abduh (Cairo: Dar al-'Arab, 1958), 128.
54 Thomas Bauer, *Die Kultur der Ambiguität: Eine andere Geschichte des Islams* (Berlin: Verlag der Weltreligionen, 2011), 337–8.
55 'Abduh, 'Māḍī al-Umma', 20.
56 For a similar understanding of human history, equally influenced by Ibn Khaldun, see the discussion of the prominent Ottoman scholar Katib Çelebi (1609–1657) in Florian Zemmin, 'The Janus Face of Kātib Çelebi', *Turcica*, 50 (2019): 339–47.
57 'Abduh, 'Sunan Allāh fī-l-Umam', 128–30.
58 Ringer, *Islamic Modernism*, 98–104.
59 Muhammad 'Abduh, 'al-Qiḍā' wa-l-Qadar', in *al-'Urwa al-Wuthqā wa-l-Thawra al-Taḥrīriyya al-Kubrā*, Jamal al-Din al-Afghani and Muhammad 'Abduh (Cairo: Dar al-'Arab, 1958), 67–73.
60 Shahab Ahmed, *What Is Islam?: The Importance of Being Islamic* (Princeton: Princeton University Press, 2016), 470 [emphasis in the original].
61 'Abduh, 'Māḍī al-Umma', 14. 'Abduh plays here with the different meanings of the term *hakīm* which can mean sage or philosopher but was also used for practitioners of pre-modern medicine.
62 Ringer, *Islamic Modernism*, 107. Ringer attributes this re-reading of 'the customs of God' to a historicist shift among modern Muslim reformers. However, understanding *sunan allāh* as referring to what God intends for humanity more generally is part of pre-modern Islamic political philosophy.
63 Ahmed, *What Is Islam?*, 482–4.
64 Ringer, *Islamic Modernism*, 108.
65 Ahmed, *What Is Islam?*, 484.

66 Juan R. I. Cole, 'New Perspectives on Sayyid Jamal al-Din al-Afghani in Egypt', in *Iran and Beyond: Essays in Middle Eastern History in Honor of Nikki R. Keddie*, ed. Rudi Mathee and Beth Baron (Costa Mesa: Mazda, 2000), 23.

67 Fruma Zachs, *The Making of a Syrian Identity: Intellectuals and Merchants in Nineteenth Century Beirut* (Leiden: Brill, 2006), 69–72.

68 Shahin Makariyus, *Kitāb Faḍā'il al-Māsūniyya*, 2nd edn (Cairo: al-Muqattam, 1900), 121–5; Ammeke Kateman, *Muḥammad 'Abduh and His Interlocutors: Conceptualizing Religion in a Globalizing World* (Leiden: Brill, 2019), 88.

69 Uthman Amin, *Muḥammad 'Abduh* (Cairo: Dar Ajya' al-Kutub al-'Arabiyya, 1944), 71; Richard Amin Gottheil, 'Mohammad 'Abdu: Late Mufti of Egypt', *Journal of the American Oriental Society*, 28 (1907): 194.

70 Jens Hanssen, 'The Birth of an Education Qarter: Zokak el-Blat as the Cradle of Cultural Revival in the Arab World', in *History, Space and Social Conflict in Beirut: The Quarter of Zokak el-Blat*, ed. Hans Gebhard (Würzburg: Ergon-Verlag, 2005), 143.

71 For a brief biographical sketch, see ibid., 172–3.

72 Amin, *Zu'amā' al-Iṣlāḥ*, 308.

73 Ibid., 288.

74 On this work, see Franz Rosenthal, *Knowledge Triumphant: The Concept of Knowledge in Medieval Islam* (Leiden: Brill, 2007), 267–8.

75 Hamada, *'Abduh*, 110.

76 Ibid., 108; Amin, *Zu'amā' al-Iṣlāḥ*, 309.

77 Hamada, *'Abduh*, 109.

78 Kaïs Ezzerelli, 'Muhammad 'Abduh et les réformistes syro-libanais: influence, image, postérité', in *Modernités islamiques: Actes du colloque organisé à Alep à l'occasion du centenaire de la disparition de l'imam Muḥammad 'Abduh, 9–10 novembre 2005*, ed. Maher Al-Charif and Sabrina Mervin (Damascus: IFPO, 2006), 93–4.

79 Rida, *Ta'rīkh*, vol. 1, 390.

80 Ezzerelli, 'Muhammad 'Abduh et les réformistes syro-libanais', 95–8.

81 Benjamin C. Fortna, *Imperial Classroom: Islam, the State, and Education in the Late Ottoman Empire* (Oxford: Oxford University Press, 2002), 43–86.

82 For a French translation of this petition, see Gilbert Delanoue, 'Endoctrinement religieux et idéologie ottmane: l'adresse de Muh'ammad [!] 'Abduh au Cheikh al-Islam, Beyrouth, 1887', *Revue de l'Occident musulman et de la Méditerranée* 13–14 (1973): 293–312.

83 Muhammad 'Abduh, 'Ta'thīr al-Ta'līm fī-l-Dīn wa-l-'Aqīda', in *al-A'māl al-Kāmila li-l-Imām Muḥammad 'Abduh*, ed. Muhammad 'Imara, vol. 3 (Beirut: Dar al-Shuruq, 1993), 58–61.

84 Muhammad 'Abduh, 'Lā'iḥa Iṣlāḥ al-Qaṭar al-Sūrī', in *al-A'māl al-Kāmila li-l-Imām Muḥammad 'Abduh*, ed. Muhammad 'Imara, vol. 3 (Beirut: Dar al-Shuruq, 1993), 93.

85 Muhammad 'Abduh, "Lā'iḥa Iṣlāḥ al-Ta'līm al-'Uthmānī', in *al-A'māl al-Kāmila li-l-Imām Muḥammad 'Abduh*, ed. Muhammad 'Imara, vol. 3 (Beirut: Dar al-Shuruq, 1993), 77–81.

86 Albert Hourani, *Arabic Thought in the Liberal Age: 1798–1939* (Cambridge: Cambridge University Press, 1983), 153–4.

87 'Abduh, 'al-Ta'līm al-'Uthmānī', vol. 3, 81–6.

88 Abduh, 'al-Qaṭar al-Sūrī', vol. 3, 103.

89 Ibid., 97.

90 Ibid., 103–4.

91 Benjamin C. Fortna, 'Islamic Morality in Late Ottoman "Secular" Schools', *International Journal of Middle East Studies*, 32 (2000): 369–93.

92 Muhammad 'Abduh, 'Murāsilāt', in *al-A'māl al-Kāmila li-l-Imām Muḥammad 'Abduh*, ed. Muhammad 'Imara, vol. 1 (Beirut: Dar al-Shuruq, 1993), 743.

93 Ibid., 744.

94 Ibid., 745.

95 Rida, 'Mulakhkhaṣ', 462–4.

96 The term *ḥikma* also connotes philosophy (*falsafa*). See Ahmed, *What Is Islam?*, 15–19.

97 Rida, *Ta'rīkh*, vol. 1, 402.

98 For a conversation between 'Abduh and Rida on 'Abbas Effendi and Baha'ism, see ibid., 930–6.

99 For 'Abbas Effendi's account of his relationship with 'Abduh, see Fazil Mazandarani, *Ta'rīkh-i Ẓuhūr al-Ḥaqq*, vol. 6, 766–7. Available online: http://www.h-net.org/~bahai/arabic/vol3/tzh6/tzh6.htm (accessed 11 May 2021).

100 For a portrait provided by one of his Ottoman disciples, see Johann Strauss, 'Nineteenth-Century Ottoman and Iranian Encounters: Ahmed Midhat Effendi and Ebrāhīm Jān Mo'aṭṭar (Moḥammad Bāqer Bawānātī)', in *The Twelver Shia in Modern Times: Religious Culture and Political History*, ed. Rainer Brunner and Werner Ende (Leiden: Brill, 2001), 97–113.

101 Edward G. Browne, *A Year amongst the Persians* (Cambridge: Cambridge University Press, [1893] 1927), 15–16. The Cambridge Orientalist Edward G. Browne (1862–1926) was a student of Bawanati while he was in London.

102 For a poster in which Bawanati visualizes his religious synthesis between Christianity and Islam, see Iraj Afshar, *Sawād-u Bayāḍ: Majmū'a-yi Maqālāt*, vol. 1 (Tehran: Dehkhoda, 1344 SH [1966]), 30; Browne, *Year amongst the Persians*, 14.

103 Rida, *Ta'rīkh*, vol. 1, 819–20.

104 Mohammad 'Ali Pirzadeh Na'ini (*c.* 1835–1904), an Iranian itinerant Sufi who lived in Beirut and, according to Rida, was one of the members of the society, provides a detailed account of Bawanati's religious activities in Beirut and his relationship to 'Abduh without mentioning the existence of such a society. Pirzadeh discusses Bawanati's diverse religious interests and his lax attitude towards the requirements of Islamic law and hence does not have a particular reason to conceal his involvement in such a secretive society. For an excerpt from his *Safarnāma* discussing Bawanati's activities in Beirut, see Afshar, *Sawād-u Bayāḍ*, 38–43.

105 Kateman, *'Abduh and His Interlocutors*, 89.

106 For examples, see Afshar, *Sawād-u Bayāḍ*, 17–18; Browne, *Year amongst the Persians*, 14; Edward G. Brown, *The Press and Poetry of Modern Persia* (Cambridge: Cambridge University Press, 1914), 168.

107 Pirzadeh Na'ini, Mohammad 'Ali, *Safarnāma*, in Afshar, *Sawād-u Bayāḍ*, 42.

108 Afshar, *Sawād-u Bayāḍ*, 1.

109 Rida devotes a few pages in his *Ta'rīkh* to restore Bawanati's orthodox reputation. Apparently, he was successful in strengthening the Islamic re-commitment of the Ottoman Sultan Abdül-Hamid II who suffered from religious doubts. See Rida, *Ta'rīkh*, vol. 1, 817–19.

110 Ibid., 817.

111 See in particular ibid., 828–9.

112 Quoted in Thomas Prasch, 'Which God for Africa: The Islamic-Christian Missionary Debate in Late-Victorian England', *Victorian Studies*, 33(1) (1989): 51.

113 Ibid., 51–73.

114 Rida, *Ta'rīkh*, vol. 1, 822–4.

115 Muhammad 'Abduh's first letter to Isaac Taylor in *al-A'māl al-Kāmila li-l-Imām Muḥammad 'Abduh*, ed. Muhammad 'Imara, vol. 2 (Beirut: Dar al-Shuruq, 1993), 355.

116 Qur'an 3:64.

117 'Abduh's first letter to Taylor in *al-A'māl al-Kāmila li-l-Imām Muḥammad 'Abduh*, vol. 2, 355.

118 Ibid., 356.

119 Ibid., 357.

120 Isaac Taylor, *Leaves from an Egyptian Note-Book* (London: Kegan Paul, 1888), 127–130.

121 Letter by 'Abduh in *al-A'māl al-Kāmila li-l-Imām Muḥammad 'Abduh*, ed. Muhammad 'Imara, vol. 1 (Beirut: Dar al-Shuruq, 1993), 679.

122 Muhammad 'Abduh, *Nahj al-Balāgha: Sharḥ al-Ustādh al-Imām al-Shaykh Muḥammad 'Abduh*, vol. 1 (Beirut: Dar al-Ma'rifa, n.d.), 6. 'Abduh uses the Shii designation of *imām* for 'Ali rather than referring to him as Commander of the

Believers (*amīr al-mu'minīn*) or caliph (*khalīfa*) as it is more common in Sunni contexts.

123 Ibid., 35.

124 Ibid., 45.

125 Ibid., 91, 190.

126 Ibid., 47.

127 Muhammad 'Abduh, *Nahj al-Balāgha: Sharḥ al-Ustādh al-Imām al-Shaykh Muḥammad 'Abduh*, vol. 2 (Beirut: Dar al-Ma'rifa, n.d.), 13, 27.

128 Muhammad 'Abduh, *Nahj al-Balāgha: Sharḥ al-Ustādh al-Imām al-Shaykh Muḥammad 'Abduh*, vol. 3 (Beirut: Dar al-Ma'rifa, n.d.), 84.

129 Ibid., 88.

130 Abduh, *Nahj al-Balāgha*, vol. 2, 7–8.

131 Gerald R. Hawting, 'The Significance of the Slogan *lā ḥukm*[a] *illā lillāh* and the References to the *ḥudūd* in the Traditions about the *fitna* and the Murder of 'Uthmān', *Bulletin of the School of Oriental and African Studies*, 61 (1978): 453–63.

132 Abduh, *Nahj al-Balāgha*, vol. 1, 91.

133 'Abduh's first letter to Taylor in *al-A'māl al-Kāmila*, vol. 2, 356.

5

Return to Egypt: A new approach

Introduction

After six years in exile, Muhammad 'Abduh returned to Egypt in 1888. However, his exile continued despite his permission to move back to his native country, as the Khedive Tawfiq whom he tried to oust during the 'Urabi Revolution prevented his return to public life. 'Abduh initially had to withdraw to inner exile, being banned from Cairo, and only re-emerged in public life after the death of Tawfiq and the ascension to the throne of his son and successor 'Abbas Hilmi II (1874–1920) in 1892. 'Abduh managed initially to establish a better rapport with the new khedive and became an important public figure in the political, intellectual and cultural life of fin-de-siècle Egypt. He was appointed to a number of public positions such as chair of a committee to reform the organization and curriculum of al-Azhar in 1895, as member of the consultative assembly (*majlis al-shūrā*) and, most importantly, as grand mufti of Egypt in 1899, the highest Islamic authority in the country. Despite these significant positions, 'Abduh grew increasingly alienated from 'Abbas Hilmi II and still entertained a difficult relationship with the conservative establishment of al-Azhar that sought to undermine his political, intellectual and religious standing.

'Abduh's return to Egypt also required re-evaluating his relationship to his erstwhile mentor Jamal al-Din al-Afghani. The final available correspondence between both suggests a complete alienation. Back in Egypt, 'Abduh dissociated from his staunch anti-imperialist activism and adopted a pragmatic attitude: as resistance was futile, it was better to use European colonial rule to modernize Muslim societies. In his conflicts with the establishment of al-Azhar and the new Khedive 'Abbas Hilmi II, it was the British colonial authorities, in the person of the consul general Lord Cromer, that provided most support for 'Abduh's public activities at that time. 'Abduh remained politically active playing a leading role in substantial organizational reforms of al-Azhar and other public institutions of

Islamic life in Egypt, laying the groundwork for increasing state control over the religious sector. With his involvement in grassroots Muslim social activism and his aim to popularize Islamic discourse, he also laid the foundation for a new understanding of a modern Muslim scholar-cum-activist.

Return to Egypt and alienation from Afghani

'Abduh's exile was supposed to last for only three years until 1885. However, his direct involvement in the publication of *al-'Urwa al-Wuthqā* and its anti-British orientation did not allow for a return to Egypt that quickly, as both the British occupying authorities and his chief nemesis, Khedive Tawfiq, feared that 'Abduh's presence in Egypt might destabilize the regime. The return of his long-standing political ally Riyad Pasha as prime minister of Egypt in 1888 and the latter's intercession at the khedivial court as well as the mediating role of supporters like Ahmad Mukhtar Pasha (1839–1919), the Ottoman representative in Egypt, and the politically active Egyptian socialite Princess Zaynab Nazli Hanim (1853–1913) achieved a pardon by the khedive so that 'Abduh could return to Egypt in 1888.[1] While Rida downplays the importance of Lord Cromer in the khedive's decision and emphasizes the mediation of local intercessors, Lord Cromer admits that Tawfiq pardoned 'Abduh 'under British pressure'.[2]

The khedive might have issued the official decree allowing 'Abduh's return to Egypt but given his earlier association with Afghani and his anti-British agitation, the khedive could only have pardoned 'Abduh with British approval.[3] 'Abduh's Egyptian friends received the assurance from him that he would abstain from any direct involvement in politics after his return and only engage in religious reform in such a way as it would not threaten the authority of the British occupying powers.[4] Despite the khedive's pardon 'Abduh's public influence was curbed immediately after his return to Egypt. Although 'Abduh intended to resume teaching at Dar al-'Ulum, the khedive feared that this would give him a strong platform to exercise public influence. Therefore, he ordered 'Abduh to become judge at a court outside the capital, an order which can be considered to mean a further exile within the country.[5]

'Abduh's acquittal also required his dissociation from Afghani. 'Abduh's break with Afghani was to some extent necessary in order to live and work in British-occupied Egypt. However, there are some indications that this break was not just fabricated to appease Lord Cromer and the khedive but that it reflected 'Abduh's genuine disillusionment with the style of activism Afghani embodied. Rida indicates that particularly after the failure and end of the society of *al-'Urwa al-Wuthqā* and its journal, 'Abduh increasingly felt the futility of Afghani's political schemes. Rida's biography contains a conversation in which 'Abduh suggests to Afghani a strategy change and an idealistic educational scheme as an alternative to their hitherto ineffective political activities:

> 'I think', he said to Afghani, 'we should abandon politics and should go to a completely unknown place on the earth where we don't know anybody. We should then choose among the people of this place ten young men or more who are bright and in good condition. We should educate them in our way and draw their attention to our purpose. When for each one of them the further education of ten others is destined, it will only take some years and we have one hundred sons who are firm in the struggle (*jihād*) on the path of reform.'... But Afghani replied: 'You are hesitant. We have been proceeding in this way and it is necessary to continue. As long as we persevere, we will see its effect.[6]

In the first meeting 'Abduh had with Rida in Cairo in 1898, he expressed regrets over how Afghani wasted his energy and talents in futile political struggles, though 'Sayyid Jamal al-Din possessed extraordinary power. If he had changed and had devoted his attention to teaching and education (*al-ta'līm wa-l-tarbiyya*), Islam would have gained immense benefits'.[7] However, Afghani was too impatient a person to devise long-term plans for a profound reform of Muslim societies via education: 'Sayyid Jamal al-Din thought that the path of education is long and that quicker reform is achieved by the reform of the ruler and the government.'[8] 'Abduh bemoaned the fact that instead of using his contacts with the Ottoman sultan to lobby for educational reforms as he did while in Beirut, Afghani associated with people in Istanbul who pursued despicable activities. Rather than seeking the cooperation of influential religious leaders in Istanbul to increase the funding for religious colleges and universities, Afghani embarked on political schemes which were not only futile but also corrupt and ultimately frustrated any reform attempts.[9]

The last correspondence between Afghani and 'Abduh expresses the rift between the two. Their final exchange of letters cannot be completely reproduced and dated but must have occurred in the early 1890s. Rida only summarizes the contents of 'Abduh's letter and quotes a few sentences from Afghani's reply. According to Rida, 'Abduh wrote a rather allusive letter to Afghani in which he explains his disillusionment with their political activities. 'Abduh chose an esoteric style as he feared that the police might read all mail sent to Afghani. Likewise he did not sign the letter, knowing that Afghani would recognize his handwriting.[10] Such secretive methods were a sign of 'Abduh's fear that the khedive and the British authorities might interpret their correspondence as a sign of their continuing association. Afghani in reply rebukes him for such secretive measures and accuses him of being a coward who lives

> in dark abodes where the evil is not distinguished from the good, the honourable from the despicable and the prudent from the reckless ... Death is before you, so caution does not avail you in the first place. If you were covetous of your standing, fear would not save you in the second place. Don't restrain yourself! Be a philosopher who sees the deficient world. Don't be an anxious little boy![11]

For Afghani, 'Abduh's decision to seek pardon from their chief opponent, Khedive Tawfiq, and from their former common enemy, the British colonial authorities, must have felt like a betrayal. When Afghani died quite isolated and alone in Istanbul in 1897, 'Abduh did not write any commemorative article or eulogy to his former master whom he had adored so much as a young man.[12]

Hence, 'Abduh's break with Afghani represents a different understanding of renewal between the two. While Afghani and 'Abduh prior to his return to Egypt believed in indigenous reform attempts and saw in the 'Urabi Revolution an expression of this possibility, the failure of the 'Urabi Revolution and all other reform attempts in the Middle East and the consequent colonial policy of European powers led to a re-adjustment of their strategies. In the articles of *al-'Urwa al-Wuthqā*, the liberation from and struggle against European colonialism possess priority over political reforms. Afghani believed that his political agitation and cooperation with Middle Eastern rulers like the Ottoman Sultan Abdül-Hamid II would eventually be successful in driving European powers out of the Muslim world. As 'Abduh saw the failure of Afghani's anti-imperialist activism and the inability of Middle Eastern regimes to introduce reforms, he realized that reforms can only be achieved with the colonial powers and not against them.[13] Since the British occupying powers in Egypt controlled every aspect of public life and even the khedive depended on them, 'Abduh decided to cooperate with the British. It is obvious that the relationship between the two deteriorated as 'Abduh decided to pursue a path which Afghani utterly detested. However, 'Abduh's acquiescence to British colonial rule only marked a change in strategy. For him, colonial rule had to be temporary and was a necessary evil to prepare the ground for an Egypt that overcomes oppression (*ẓulm*) and despotism (*istibdād*) and achieves reform (*iṣlāḥ*) and freedom (*ḥurriyya*).[14]

Colonialism as a tool to modernization

Initially, ʿAbduh found the new Khedive ʿAbbas Hilmi II a strong supporter for his reformist agenda. The khedive appointed ʿAbduh to various positions in order to enforce reforms. ʿAbduh in return produced an article in this time pointing at the benefits of ʿa just despot (*mustabidd ʿādil*)ʾ[15] and at the need for a gradual approach to political reforms in different stages. ʿAbduh's discourse echoes an article Afghani had written twenty years earlier with a similar argument. Afghani in 1879, like ʿAbduh in the 1890s, was under the patronage of Riyad Pasha who favoured the model of an enlightened autocrat and gradual reforms. Hence, ʿAbduh adopted a discourse which favoured Riyad's political agenda and sought to win his support and that of the new khedive. Similar to British colonial rule, despotism was a temporary condition to be accepted if leading to the establishment of a free and independent Egypt.

Despite ʿAbduh's efforts to forge a good rapport with the new khedive, their relationship deteriorated when ʿAbduh contravened on several occasions the khedive's interests.[16] Consequently, the khedive countered ʿAbduh's reform initiatives and allied with the conservative *ʿulamāʾ* of al-Azhar to curtail his public influence. ʿAbduh developed a hostile attitude towards the khedive stressing his foreign origin and attempting to decrease his political influence – in line with the hostile attitudes towards the dynasty of Muhammad ʿAli he had expressed earlier. As the khedive failed to provide political patronage for his projects, ʿAbduh turned towards the British colonial authorities and their chief representative Lord Cromer in whom he found a reliable supporter whenever he faced the opposition of the political and religious establishment of the country.[17]

While the *ʿulamāʾ* and the khedive turned into his enemies, for the British authorities ʿAbduh was ʿan ʿAlimʾ of … a superior typeʾ and ʿa man of broad and enlightened viewsʾ.[18] He not only found in the chief representative Lord Cromer an ally but he also developed a good rapport with him. The British occupying powers were the driving force behind Abduh's appointment as grand mufti of Egypt in 1899.[19] When ʿAbduh's position was threatened due to his controversial fatwas, it was Cromer's backing which ensured that ʿAbduh could retain this office.[20] Legal reforms affecting the shariʿa courts and reforms in the central administration of pious endowments (*waqf*, pl. *awqāf*) and the network of mosques were initiated by ʿAbduh as grand mufti of Egypt. They could only be achieved against the resistance of the *ʿulamāʾ* and the khedive because of Cromer's support for these reforms.

In Cromer, 'Abduh found a kind of political authority which shared his scepticism toward and distance from the religious and political establishment and was keen on curbing the influence of the conservative *'ulamā'* and the khedive. Cromer was rather sceptical of the prospect that Egyptians would gain a degree of political maturity which would allow self-rule in the foreseeable future. For him, it would take many years until an educational system could be established creating an intellectual and political elite capable of governing the country, as he generally assumed an inherent inferiority of the 'Oriental' mind.[21] 'Abduh shared the view of Egyptian elite as being incapable of modernizing the country on their own. Before self-rule could be established an elite would have to be created with the necessary educational standard to provide effective and moral leadership.[22] 'Abduh agreed with Cromer that British colonial rule was required in order to prepare the Egyptians for self-government. Contemporary biographers and observers of 'Abduh compared him with Sayyid Ahmad Khan who laboured for political, social and religious reforms among Muslims in India with British support.[23]

The British authorities were for 'Abduh an important counter-pole to the khedive limiting his obstructive policies against reforms. When, in 1904, Wilfrid Scawen Blunt asked his friend 'Abduh about the conditions under which Egyptian independence could be achieved, 'Abduh clearly expresses his resentments against the khedive in the letter he wrote in response. For him,

> the first and fundamental rule of administration must be that the Khedive shall have no power of interference in the executive of any of the Ministerial Departments, nor yet in the *Awkaf*, nor in the Azhar, nor in the religious Courts. His personal intervention in the Egyptian Administration should be done away with, once and for all.[24]

Blunt sent another letter to 'Abduh in which he asks him to develop a post-independence draft constitution for Egypt. In light of the khedive's opposition to such a constitution, Blunt suggested that he should be replaced by a European prince who would support a constitutional government. Although 'Abduh rejected the idea of installing a European ruler in Egypt, he stressed the need of British rule in preparation of independence, as 'the British Government shall watch over the maintenance of order and the safeguarding of the Constitution to be granted, and not leave it exposed to interference by the Khedives'.[25]

That 'Abduh saw in European colonialism an agent of modernization can also be seen in his journey to Tunisia and Algeria in 1903 which were under French colonial rule. Contacts with reformist *'ulamā'* in this region had already been established, as they received copies of the journal a*l-Manār*, the reformist Islamic journal he started publishing with Rida from 1898 onwards. 'Abduh's journey had the purpose of meeting those *'ulamā'* who felt attracted to his reformist interpretation of Islam. 'Abduh was aware that he had to avoid the impression that his journey was an attempt to mobilize Muslims in Algeria and Tunisia against French colonial rule. As soon as some of 'Abduh's opponents in Egypt heard about his plans to travel to North Africa, they sent letters to the colonial authorities in Algeria warning them of 'Abduh's future arrival and his alleged plans to stir up unrest and disorder.[26] Therefore, 'Abduh had to present his journey as having merely an educational and religious mission for the reform of Islam and the revival of the Arabic language. In April 1903, he published an article in *al-Manār* which provided a favourable description of French colonial policy in order to prepare his visit to North Africa and to receive French backing.[27] As 'Abduh stayed in France prior to his departure to Algeria, he required the permission of the French government to enter its colony. It is not unlikely that the permission was granted under the condition that 'Abduh did not touch upon political questions during his stay in Algeria and Tunisia.[28]

At first sight, 'Abduh's journey appeared to be completely apolitical (Figure 3). He met reformist *'ulamā'*, discussed with them the need for educational reforms, urged them to ensure the application of the shari'a and gave a commentary on the Qur'anic *sūrat al-'aṣr* (The Declining Day) in several lectures. However, he chose to undertake a politically inconspicuous exercise like writing a Qur'anic commentary to convey a political message to his addressees which was sympathetic to French colonial rule. The full text of the *sūra* is as follows:

> I swear by the declining day that man is in [deep] loss, except for those who believe, do good deeds (*ṣāliḥat*), urge one another to the truth (*ḥaqq*) and urge one another to patience (*ṣabr*).[29]

According to 'Abduh, the very short *sūra* contains the notion that salvation depends on the adherence to truth. As the political pendant to truth is justice, the *sūra* implies that justice will triumph in the world if people exhibit patience (*ṣabr*).[30] This interpretation – though not spelled out explicitly but understood by his audience implicitly – reflects 'Abduh's pragmatic stance in relation to European colonialism. The foreign occupation of Muslim countries might be an undesirable state but the imperative of political patience dictates that it is more beneficial to abstain from violent opposition to European imperialism and to accept it as a tool for the modernization of Muslim societies.[31]

Figure 3. Muhammad ʿAbduh in Tunis, 1903.

In his public lectures, ʿAbduh advised the Muslim elite in the colonies to acquire a quietist stance towards their colonisers and to seek cooperation with them. As long as the colonial authorities feel that their subjects oppose them, they will suppress them. Therefore, Muslims should abstain from anti-colonialist activities in order to gain material support for the modernization of their countries. Acquiescence to colonial rule does not mean that attempts should not be made to influence the policies of the colonial authorities and to affect their legislation.[32] 'Abduh envisioned a pacifist and loyal cooperation of Muslims with their colonisers as a necessary condition for the development of Muslim societies. The civilizing mission of European colonialism is implicitly acknowledged as 'Abduh believed that indigenous reform attempts would fail outside the colonial context.[33]

His journeys to Europe similarly document how much European countries remained to be a role model for Middle Eastern societies, for 'the freedom and civilization'[34] they have achieved. He started learning French in the 1890s and had become fluent by the early 1900s, 'almost Parisian in its intonation',[35] according to one contemporary observer. Whenever he travelled to Europe, in particular to Geneva for holidays, he gained the inspiration and motivation for the reform of Islam and Muslim societies. Asked by Rida, what he is expecting from his European journeys, 'Abduh replied: 'I go there to renew myself'[36]:

> The journeys to Europe had the effect that they strengthened my hope in the reform of the conditions of Muslims. Whenever I travelled to Europe, it renewed my hope in changing the state of Muslims for the better, achieved through the reform of what they have corrupted in their religion … This hope always turned weak whenever I returned to my country … But when I returned to Europe and stayed there for a month or two that hope came back to me.[37]

The purpose of 'Abduh's European journeys as expressed in his own words provides evidence of his view that the modernization of Muslim societies could only be achieved in cooperation with European nations. 'Abduh still considered Europe a role-model to be emulated, similar to his discourse as a young journalist and journal editor when he supported state-led modernization and reforms. He still held the view that 'the welfare of Muslims is intertwined with the welfare of Europeans in all the quarters of the earth'.[38] Yet, Europe remained an ambivalent role-model to which he equally maintained a critical distance. While he admired its cultural, political and economic achievements, he remained critical of the superficial imitators of European mannerisms within the elites of Muslim societies who dress and eat like Europeans to appear modern but lack any intrinsic understanding of the intellectual foundations of European progress. 'Abduh is equally aware of the Janus-faced nature of European colonial policies: while colonial powers are needed to reform Muslim societies they equally exploit their colonies economically[39] and endanger alienating indigenous colonial elites from their history, culture and religion.

The public role of a modern Muslim intellectual

Rida provides a quasi-hagiographical account of a typical day in 'Abduh's life giving an insight in the vast array of activities in which he was involved as a public Muslim intellectual and activist:

> He used to get up and leave for the consultative assembly (*majlis al-shūrā*) early in the morning, for example. He would shed light on presented issues based on research, whether they were judicial, administrative or financial, align them with the welfare of the country and support them with legal and rational proofs which convinced the government after being approved by the members of the consultative assembly. Then, he would leave the assembly. He would have lunch and go to al-Azhar afterwards. If it was a day in which the administrative council would meet, he would work there. Then, he would move on to the Mufti's office where people with various welfare needs from the government or otherwise, people requesting his legal opinion, visitors, teachers from schools of the Benevolent Society, *'ulamā'* and students from al-Azhar would already be waiting for him. He would attend to their matters until the afternoon. Then, he would leave for the office of pious endowments (*diwān al-awqāf*) if it was the day when its high council met. Or he would leave for the administrative council of the Benevolent Society if it was the day when it met. At the time of sunset, he would leave for al-Azhar and teach there. He would depart after the night prayer heading to his house. He would find people with needs and requests already waiting for him in the vicinity of his house and presenting them to him. On the train back home, he would have already read the evening papers. And after all this, his house was rarely free from evening conversations on science, literature and general and individual welfare.[40]

The various fields of 'Abduh's activities as outlined by Rida occurred in changing patterns of the religious field in Egypt and the wider Muslim world which followed two major trends: first, the rise of a new educational elite outside the religious sector. 'Abduh responded to this development with his vision of a new type of religious scholar-cum-public intellectual who has command over a synthesis of traditional religious and modern knowledge, engages in various fields of activities and adopts strategies to disseminate it among the new elite. The second major development was the gradual *étatisation* of religion. The state assumed more control of public institutions of Islamic life and limited the autonomy of the *'ulamā'*.[41] With Muhammad 'Ali's rise to power in Egypt in 1805, a process was initiated attempting to bring all sectors of society including Islam and its various expressions under state control.

State interference in the religious sector manifested itself primarily in legal reforms. Under Muhammad ʿAli's rule the competence of shariʿa courts was reduced to questions of personal status and property among Muslims. Foreign residents in Egypt enjoyed special legal privileges, being under the jurisdiction of their home countries. Mixed courts were introduced in 1876, being responsible for commercial, civil and criminal litigation involving Egyptians and foreigners. During the British occupation of Egypt, further attempts were made to secularize the legal system. So-called national courts (*al-maḥākim al-ahliyya*) were introduced which dealt with all civil, commercial and criminal matters and followed the French code of law.[42] Judges for these courts were trained at state-sponsored schools of law. Hence, there existed several parallel legal systems in late nineteenth-century Egypt resulting in a marginalization of shariʿa courts and consequently of the *ʿulamā*'s legal authority. Finally, the shariʿa courts were placed under the supervision of the ministry of justice and their legal procedures became codified and formalized.[43]

Efforts to centralize and control the religious sphere in Egypt were also reflected in the creation of the Mufti's office (*dār al-iftā*') in 1895. The Egyptian state appointed a body of official muftis who served as reference points for the shariʿa courts. There was an official mufti appointed from all the four legal school of Sunni Islam. The Hanafi mufti possessed special importance as head of the official legal school of the state and was gradually elevated to the rank of grand mufti of Egypt.[44] The government reduced the number of muftis and centralized authority in the religio-legal system of the country in the office of the grand mufti.[45] The grand mufti was concerned with legal matters referred to him by the different government departments and had to deal with issues around the administration of pious endowments. He also had to respond to complaints against decisions of shariʿa courts and to confirm death penalties.[46]

ʿAbduh supported governmental reforms in the religious sector. He was one of the governmental representatives in the administrative council, overseeing the reform of al-Azhar[47] and produced a report on the reform of the shariʿa courts in his position as grand mufti.[48] His suggestions sought to systematize and professionalize the functioning of the shariʿa courts: a school should be established to train judges at the courts, a legal compendium should be produced as guide to ensure that judges prioritize the general welfare of people in their judgements and the restriction of courts to adjudicate according to the Hanafi legal school alone should be lifted.[49] ʿAbduh was also responsible for the administration of pious endowments and the nationwide network of mosques. One of his objectives was to centralize the administration of mosques which were under-funded and whose staff tended to lack proper education. He petitioned to reform the mosque system in order to provide the personnel of mosques with a regular salary and to make their education at al-Azhar compulsory.[50] As the khedive feared that such reforms would increase the influence of ʿAbduh,[51] he opposed these attempts to centralize and systematize the administration of pious endowments under the authority of the grand mufti. Cromer's intervention ended the khedive's obstruction and implemented ʿAbduh's petition.[52]

In addition to his activities to centralize and to professionalize religious authority and to minimize political interference in its functioning, ʿAbduh assumed further political roles. The khedive chose him as new member of the consultative assembly (*majlis al-shūrā*) in 1899.[53] He considered his membership in the assembly and the responsibilities involved with it as a continuation of his other reformist activities.[54] Although he abhorred politics and did not consider it to be an agent of change,[55] he still saw his membership in the consultative assembly as a useful tool to exercise influence on the educational policies of the state without being directly associated with the government. As member of the assembly, ʿAbduh often acted as an intermediary between its members and the government seeking compromises if there were disagreements between both bodies.[56]

While initially the rapport between ʿAbduh and the Khedive ʿAbbas Hilmi II was quite cordial as both shared a common desire to reform and centralize Islamic public institutions in Egypt, ʿAbduh's amicable relationship with the British authorities and his lack of respect for the khedive resulted in an antagonistic relationship. On several occasions, ʿAbduh contravened the khedive. Under ʿAbduh's instigation, the administrative council of al-Azhar contradicted the khedive in its decision to bestow honorary robes to well-respected professors. On the occasion of celebrating the solemn bestowal of these robes which the khedive also attended, ʿAbduh embarrassed the khedive publicly by mentioning that the ceremony was taking place despite his opposition.[57] The khedive was also irritated by ʿAbduh's meeting with ʿUrabi after he returned from exile.[58] Then, ʿAbduh supported a group of blind *ʿulamāʾ* at al-Azhar in their legal case to receive money from pious endowments. During the trial, the suspicion was raised that the khedive had defrauded the *waqf* money originally destined for the blind *ʿulamāʾ*.[59] The ultimate break between ʿAbduh and the khedive is attributed to a conflict about the administration of pious endowments. As the British representative Cromer wanted to regulate their administration and distribution, a council was created of which ʿAbduh as grand mufti of Egypt became member. ʿAbduh intervened when the khedive attempted to exchange land under his possession with more lucrative *waqf*-land in Giza administered by the council. Apart from the financial loss 'Abduh's refusal meant for the khedive, the conflict also documents a general disagreement over the control of pious endowments. While 'Abduh as member of the council intended to exclude the khedive from administering them, the khedive wanted to secure government control over them.[60] Calling 'Abduh 'a pharaoh', the khedive attempted to minimize his public influence and frustrated his reform initiatives.[61] While 'Abduh was willing to become part of state-sponsored reforms after his return to Egypt, his attitude towards religious reforms under the auspices of the khedive changed when the latter came under the sway of conservative *'ulamā'*. 'Abduh felt confirmed in his negative assessment of Middle Eastern regimes and their inability to instigate reforms. While supporting the centralization of public institutions of Islamic life in Egypt, he equally wanted to make sure that the state does not interfere in their organization and operation.

Given the failure of the religious and political establishment to reform Islam, 'Abduh created forms of religious and social organization outside established institutions. In 1892, he founded the Muslim Benevolent Society (*al-jam'iyya al-khayriyya al-islāmiyya*) – whose president he became in 1900 – and a literary association, the Society for the Revival of Arabic Literature (*al-jam'iyya li-iḥyā' al-kutub al-'arabiyya*) in 1900. In other parts of the Ottoman Empire similar organizations had been founded like in Syria where Tahir al-Jaza'iri (1851–1920),[62] with whom 'Abduh was also in contact, established a benevolent society in the late 1870s under the support of the then governor Midhat Pasha (1822–84) in order to provide funding and organization for mosques, schools and religious colleges.[63] 'Abduh also taught in Beirut at the Madrasa Sultaniyya which was formed by the local Muslim benevolent society and defended its activities in his petition to the local Ottoman governor in Beirut. The formation of a similar Muslim benevolent society in Egypt not only expressed 'Abduh's understanding of the social responsibility of a religious scholar but also his attempt to create networks for socio-religious activism outside the state. As the state remained uninterested in the social plight of the people and traditional religious institutions only sporadically engaged in charitable activities, the society aimed at providing systematic and constant charitable support and educational services.[64] One of the core activities of the society was to establish schools for disadvantaged children who would otherwise not receive any education.[65] The foundation of such an organization outside the state apparatus raised the suspicion of 'Abduh's opponents among the *'ulamā'* and the political leadership who spread rumours that the society actually had political aims – allegations he had already encountered during his exile in Beirut. In their attempt to discredit 'Abduh and his society in the eyes of the British colonial authorities, they accused the society of providing funding for militant insurgents like the Mahdi and his followers in Sudan.[66] For the *'ulamā'*, the establishment of religious institutions outside their control was an infringement of their religious monopoly.

In the long term, 'Abduh's Muslim charitable organization foreshadowed the move of Islam into the private sector and the further undermining of the religious authority of the *'ulamā'* with a proliferation of religious organizations with charitable, educational and political aims in the twentieth century. Given the increasing marginalization of the *'ulamā'* in traditional spheres of their authority – be it in the legal or educational system – 'Abduh sought alternative avenues for how *'ulamā'* in the modern world could exercise their influence. The private sector offered this opportunity. The mushrooming of such private Islamic organizations in the twentieth century would also fill a gap left after the demise of Sufi orders as the mainstream religious organizations of Muslim world, when lacking political patronage and the financial support of the urban middle-class minimized their socio-political influence.[67] As private religious organizations with social outreach such benevolent societies, like the one founded by 'Abduh, continued the role earlier fulfilled by Sufi orders in providing social and educational services, spiritual guidance and later also political mobilization for the urban middle-class.

In his interaction with the political authorities in Egypt, 'Abduh was a modern manifestation of the ambivalent attitude *'ulamā'* had to the centre of power. 'Abduh was willing to become politically active as long as this involvement did not compromise his independence from the government. On the one hand, he revealed a sceptical view of politics in general and the political performance of Middle Eastern regimes but, on the other, he did not abstain from politics and sought alternative forms of socio-political activism which would ensure his influence on society but at the same time allow him to stand aloof of the vicissitudes of *realpolitik*. 'Abduh had to realize that religious reforms cannot be achieved by relying on the political elites of Middle Eastern countries, be they in the form of an indigenous autocracy or of a foreign colonial power. Hence, state interference in religious questions would only corrupt religion itself.[68]

For 'Abduh, the unhealthy cooperation between political leaders and the *'ulamā'* led to the decline of Islam. Most *'ulamā'* remained apolitical and failed in their duty to oversee the policies of the ruler and to make them accountable for them. Either they were complacent and became willingly instrumentalized by the political authorities to provide religious legitimacy for their inefficient and incompetent leadership or they attempted to obstruct any attempts of modernizing Muslim societies. In addition, they lost all connection to the people and became unable to relate to them and make Islamic discourse relevant to them.[69] The aloofness, passivity and conservatism of the religious establishment were for ʿAbduh responsible for the demise of the *ʿulamāʾ* class. ʿAbduh's aim was to create 'a new kind of religious leadership'[70] whose religious and intellectual authority is based on both traditional scholarship and modern knowledge. More important than a thorough knowledge of the scholarly tradition of Islam would be their ability to relate the teachings of Islam to the modern world.[71]

During a visit to Istanbul in 1901, ʿAbduh met the *shaykh al-islām* of the Ottoman Empire, the highest religious authority of the empire, Jamal al-Din Effendi (1848–1917).[72] During the meeting, they discussed the state of the *ʿulamāʾ* class. Both agreed on the demise of the class of the learned ones in Islam and on their inability to relate to the modern world and to provide guidance to the common people. In the course of their conversation, ʿAbduh provides an outline of the characteristics of a true scholar (*ʿālim*) – a vision of a new form of religious leadership:

> The scholar (*ʿālim*) is not a scholar unless he is an expert (*ʿārif*) through his knowledge. An expert is someone who can combine religion with that which benefits the people in every age in his reckoning. The one who is proficient in the fields of religious knowledge but is not acquainted with the condition of the people in his age and does not keep an eye on the principles of his time cannot be called a scholar but is a narrow-minded and one-sided specialist (*mutafannin*). I mean, he knows the discipline (*fann*) of grammar or jurisprudence and similar ones but cannot be called a scholar in reality unless he leaves a mark of his knowledge among his people. He only achieves this, after he has known their conditions and has become aware of their needs.[73]

ʿAbduh finds this understanding of the role of the *ʿulamāʾ* not only 'common among the first generations of our *ʿulamāʾ*'[74] but also necessary in order to reach out to the new group of Western educated Muslims. Being a member of the national assembly, establishing private charitable and educational institutions and exercising public influence by publishing articles and books, ʿAbduh set a modern example of the activist religious scholar (*al-ʿālim al-ʿāmil*) who is socially active and politically conscious without becoming too closely associated with governmental policies. Muslim leaders would imitate ʿAbduh in the twentieth century by creating a space for Islamic discourse in society outside the realm of traditional religious scholarship and independent of, if not in competition with, the state.

Reform of al-Azhar

'Abduh stood outside the religious establishment of al-Azhar and was critical of its intellectual traditionalism. Because of his lacking association with the Egyptian religious nomenclature, his reform attempts were hampered from the beginning. Initially, 'Abduh found in the new Khedive 'Abbas Hilmi II an ally in the reform of al-Azhar. Aware of the obstacles he had to face in his attempts to introduce changes to this long-established institution, 'Abduh knew that the only way of modernizing al-Azhar was by winning the support of the new khedive.[75] 'Abbas Hilmi II shared with 'Abduh the desire to modernize the institutions. He agreed to set up a new administrative committee (*majlis idārat al-azhar*) in 1895 and appointed 'Abduh as one of its members.[76]

The committee initiated significant institutional reforms gradually turning al-Azhar into a modern educational establishment: admission criteria for students were specified as well as the length of study and required examinations formalized. In 1896, a law was passed stipulating that an *'ālim* needs to pass examinations in twelve subjects in order to graduate. A central library for al-Azhar was inaugurated by the khedive in 1897. The certification process was also formalized in 1899, with the introduction of different degree levels and determining the length of study to graduate. Other changes initially suggested by 'Abduh were implemented after his death between 1908 and 1911.[77] *'Ulamā'* received fixed salaries, a council was established representing *'ulamā'* of all four legal schools and different *madrasas* across the country were placed under the central authority of al-Azhar.[78] These modernization initiatives, to 'Abduh's frustration, did not affect curricular reform to the extent he had hoped for. A thorough intellectual reorientation of the institution was not achieved.[79] Although 'Abduh was successful in introducing geometry, algebra, geography, arithmetic and Islamic history into the curriculum and in putting primary texts rather than commentaries in the centre of the syllabus, his aspiration to include modern sciences failed.[80]

One of the most significant reforms was the establishment of the position of *shaykh al-azhar* as government-appointed head of the institution in 1899. The creation of this position marked the pinnacle of the institutional modernization of al-Azhar. 'Abduh suggested this position to modernize and centralize the administration of al-Azhar – facing the opposition of conservative *'ulamā'* as a consequence. These significant organizational reforms implemented by the administrate council under the leadership of 'Abduh were quite successful and had a lasting impact on the management of the institution and its relationship to the state – with consequences that were not entirely intended by ʿAbduh. He hoped the centralization and modernization of the institution would create a bulwark against state control and political interference[81] while in effect they institutionalized state control further and undermined the institutional autonomy of al-Azhar and the religious sector as whole in Egypt. The state appointment of the head of al-Azhar, for example, meant in the long-term that this position became an instrument to control the institution and to subordinate it to the state as part of 'la nationalisation de l'islam égyptien'.[82]

His relationship with the Khedive ʿAbbas Hilmi II deteriorated at the end of his life and the conservative forces in al-Azhar could use their good connections with the court to prevent further reforms. To undermine his public standing, ʿAbduh became the victim of an extensive press campaign that culminated in 1902 in the publication of a photograph of a smiling ʿAbduh surrounded by European women who were, however, modestly dressed and chaperoned by other men.[83] ʿAbduh had to realize that further initiatives from his side to modernize the curriculum were destined to fail. He was dismissed or pressured to resign from the administrative council in 1905.[84] While he praised Dar al-ʿUlum and its teaching of Arabic as exemplary,[85] ʿAbduh ultimately came to the conclusion that existing educational institutions were insufficient and hoped a new *madrasa* or university would offer modern subjects in addition to religious instruction and create a new intellectual elite. He started making plans for the foundation of new *madrasa* in the outskirts of Cairo and managed to secure funding for its formation.[86] However, ʿAbduh's premature death in 1905 prevented the realization of these plans.[87]

Mufti of the Egyptian realms

The apex of ʿAbduh's personal career was reached with his appointment as grand mufti of Egypt (*muftī al-diyār al-miṣriyya*) in 1899. However, it seems that ʿAbduh became mufti by accident as neither appointer nor appointee were very happy with the nomination. A statement by the khedive indicates that the British occupying powers played an important role in ʿAbduh's nomination. As the khedive feared that ʿAbduh would reject the offer, he told two of ʿAbduh's friends that 'if he does not accept the position of grand mufti now, I reckon that I will fall in personal difficulties with the occupying powers'.[88] To limit ʿAbduh's influence, the khedive separated the two positions of grand mufti and *shaykh al-azhar* both of which 'Abduh hoped to hold jointly.[89] Furthermore, 'Abduh felt that this new responsibility would deter him from his actual interest in and activities for the intellectual reform of Islam. According to Rida, he, however, managed to convince 'Abduh that 'he would make the greatest religious office an instrument for the general reform of Islam'.[90] As grand mufti of Egypt, 'Abduh was also a member of the council managing pious endowments. While pursuing a centralization of various pious endowments under the management of the office to regulate their operation consistently across the country, 'Abduh also managed to increase the endowment for al-Azhar to ensure financial support for the various institutional reforms he wished to implement.

'Abduh produced almost 1,000 fatwas during his tenure.[91] While Rida suggested that he used his position as an agent of religious reform, the majority of his fatwas are quite conventional. Most of them deal with mundane and technical questions, in particular as they pertain to the administration of pious endowments due to his oversight as mufti over them. Despite his rejection of the imitation of scholarly conventions of the past (*taqlīd*), such official matters required him to follow the rulings of the official Hanafi legal school limiting thereby his interpretative freedom.[92] Therefore, 'Abduh does not provide original interpretations but seeks to create organizational conformity and consistency in the management of these endowments. The second largest body of fatwas pertains to inheritance law where his interpretative scope was equally limited by the jurisprudence of the Hanafi school he had to adhere to. In these fatwas, 'Abduh follows traditional rulings of division of the inheritance and the order of precedence of relatives as laid out in Islamic jurisprudence. In one fatwa, he also denies that person bequeathing can freely distribute their inheritance as they wish but are bound by the requirements of Islamic law.[93] He also confirms that a non-Muslim cannot inherit from a Muslim, citing the example of a Christian woman who had converted to Islam before her death and had a daughter from her first marriage with a Coptic husband who apparently remained Christian because she was still a minor. While the Christian daughter could receive inheritance from her Christian father, that of her Muslim mother was not available to her.[94] In many fatwas, 'Abduh makes references to standard Hanafi legal compendia that address such technical issues in more detail.

Other fatwas respond to issues around business transactions, the ownership of land or marital issues. Given the practical remit of most of these questions, they did not invite creative and radically different approaches but often required quite practical solutions that conform to standards set in Hanafi jurisprudence in particular. For instance, 'Abduh issued a number of fatwas that supported the state opening of various banking operations. While he was heavily criticized by some of his opponents for allegedly permitting usury or taking interest (*ribā*), his fatwas follow profit-sharing models, known as *muḍāraba*, that are considered permissible in pre-modern Islamic jurisprudence.[95] In questions of marital law, 'Abduh confirms that if a Muslim husband converts to another religion his marriage to his Muslim wife becomes void and his wife can remarry.[96] In another case, a half-brother who was the legal guardian over his younger half-sister after their parents' death married her off against her will at the age of fifteen. 'Abduh argues that the forced marriage is invalid, because it was conducted against her will and, given that she had already reached maturity (*bulūgh*) at the age of fifteen, the legal guardianship of her half-brother had ceased.[97] Such an interpretation which suggests the legal guardianship over a half-sister ends after she had reached maturity is in line with interpretations provided by scholars in the Hanafi and Shafi'i legal schools. Despite not containing radical reinterpretations of previous jurisprudence for the most part, some requests for fatwas give evidence of modern and unprecedent problems. One enquirer refers to the marriage between an Egyptian Muslim man and a Christian woman that occurred in Germany asking whether conducting an Islamic marriage with a foreign woman in a foreign country is permissible and recognized. 'Abduh provides a pragmatic answer that is entirely in line with traditional jurisprudence: marriages with women from the People of the Book (*ahl al-kitāb*, Jews and Christians) are permissible for Muslim men and valid as long as requirements for marriage ceremony – the presence of two witnesses who do not have to be Muslims themselves – are met. The location where the marriage ceremony is conducted is irrelevant.[98]

His fatwas on questions of ritual practices (*'ibādāt*) such as prayer or fasting are not particularly innovative either but urge enquirers to follow practices as determined by Islamic jurisprudence, referring again in particular to the jurisprudence of the Hanafi legal school.[99] One enquiry asks whether Muslims need to see the crescent in order to determine the start of Ramadan or whether astronomical calculations are permissible. 'Abduh does not commit himself to a particular answer but refers to different views on this concluding however, that 'the principles of the Islamic religion are built on what is the simplest and the easiest for the people'.[100] While 'Abduh does not deviate from standard Islamic jurisprudence for the most part, his legal approach is determined by finding a simple and practical solution to a problem.

A number of fatwas address issues Muslim face in the modern world: the rise of nation-states and their legal autonomy, the relationship between the

Qur'an and modern science and Muslim religious life under colonial rule or in a minority status.[101] Among these new issues more innovative solutions are required and 'Abduh's reformist approach is most visible. The most interesting fatwas were produced as responses to requests coming from outside of Egypt which gives evidence that 'Abduh had acquired some international reputation as a scholar.[102] These more challenging and often unprecedented questions allowed him to develop his creative approach that defies traditional conventions more effectively.[103] In these fatwas, he also moved outside of the parameters of the Hanafi legal school to which he had to adhere when issuing fatwas in the domestic context of Egypt. By addressing more diverse Muslim constituencies in other parts of the Middle East, Africa and South Asia he incorporated the view of different legal schools to increase the appeal of his fatwas beyond Hanafi jurisprudence.

The rise of proto-national identities, the emergence of institutional structures within colonial states and the centralization of legal systems within their jurisdiction are addressed in one enquiry that asks about the connection between nationality (*jinsiyya*) and the type of Islamic law one needs to follow: is an Egyptian who follows the Hanafi school and resident in Morocco bound to follow the jurisprudence of the Maliki school as prevalent in that country? 'Abduh's response resonates with themes articulated earlier. He affirms that 'there is no nationality (*jinsiyya*) in Islam'[104] and that national origins do not have any bearings on which school of Islamic law one should adhere to, even if a particular school is prevalent in one's country of origin. The concept of nationality originated with European countries and resembles the type of tribal solidarity (*'aṣabiyya*) that existed among the Arabs before the rise of Islam. Islam came to eradicate tribalism and its contemporaneous manifestation in competing national identities. In reality, 'Islamic law (*sharī'a*) is one and the rights are one, treating everyone equal in any place they may be within the Islamic countries (*al-bilād al-islāmiyya*)'.[105] In practice, this means however that an Egyptian Hanafi Muslim living in Morocco must accept the legal and judicial authority of Islamic courts that follow Maliki jurisprudence and cannot deny the validity of their legal judgements by referring to his Hanafi allegiance.

While 'Abduh's argument comes across as a defence of the universality of Islamic law and a Pan-Islamic rejection of different national identities, in reality he accepts the legal autonomy of emergent Muslim colonial states and their right to establish a centralized legal system in line with the prevalent school of jurisprudence – a development he himself advanced in Egypt. In pre-modern

Muslim societies, Muslims could move between different legal traditions and approach judges representing them with relative ease. 'Abduh's response negates this opportunity by pointing at the prerogative of the state to implement its version of Islamic law and the requirement of all Muslim residents regardless of their legal background to adhere to it. No other state possesses any right to interfere in the internal legal system of another country. To suggest how absurd such an interference would be, 'Abduh compares this to the election of local municipal councils. The inhabitants of Alexandria do not have the right to determine who represents the people of Cairo in their elected local council.[106] Not even the Ottoman state with its head claiming to be the Sunni caliph possesses nominal suzerainty over the legislation of other Muslim countries: 'This country is Morocco, this country is Afghanistan and both countries have governments that are independent from one another. Both governments are independent of the Ottoman state.'[107] The nationalization of Islam that 'Abduh facilitated in the Egyptian context by centralizing shari'a courts, establishing the office of the *shaykh al-azhar*, streamlining the administration of pious endowments and holding the office of grand mufti is equally valid in other Muslim countries that should do similar. Creating domesticated forms of Islam – that are independent from the Ottoman Empire in their jurisprudence and legal system – was also in the interest of European colonial powers, whether the French in Morocco or the British in Egypt.

Another question from outside of Egypt 'Abduh received dealt with the compatibility of religious beliefs with theories of modern science. An Islamic scholar from Nablus approached 'Abduh with a question that occurred to him after he had read in recent historical essays that the flood of Noah did not cover the whole surface of the earth but was restricted to the region Noah and his people inhabited. For the enquirer, such an assertion would lead to the problematic theological conclusion that Noah was not a prophet sent to the whole of humanity but that his mission was restricted to his own people.[108] 'Abduh in his response favours the Qur'anic account over other interpretations. He criticizes historians who deny the global scale of the deluge and thereby the universality of Noah's prophetic mission, as this stands in contradiction to the text of the Qur'an that the flood covered the whole earth.[109] It also contravenes statements found in authenticated hadith reports that confirm that, indeed, 'Noah – peace be on him – was the first messenger that God sent to the people of the world (*ahl al-arḍ*)'.[110] In response, the historians 'ridicule hadith scholars and rely on stories attributed to the people of China'.[111] They argue that the respective Qur'anic passages 'are prone to allegorical interpretation (*ta'wīl*) and that there is no proof in them'.[112] ʿAbduh explains to the Islamic scholar from Nablus the basic methodology of historians and its possible conflicts with religious beliefs:

> Regarding the historian or the researcher, he has the right to acquire an opinion of what carries greater weight for him based on the trustworthiness of a transmitter, a historian and anyone else. What the historians and commentators consider in this question is limited to the extent of the existence of reliable historical sources or the lack of it. They do not take strong evidence from the religious believer.[113]

ʿAbduh admits that in the question of the flood there is a gap between historical researchers and what Muslims, Jews and Christians believe. Nevertheless, he seems to express the hope that in the future, after intensive research, the religious point of view will also be vindicated through historical evidence, as he refers to some historians who agree with both the Biblical and Qur'anic accounts of the flood and use fossils of fishes found on mountains as possible evidence for the global scale of the flood. In conclusion, ʿAbduh reaffirms that scientific investigation cannot be isolated from religious beliefs.[114]

However, his fatwa is replete with semantic ambiguity. On the one hand, he is clearly aware of the vantage point of the enquirer who expects the Qur'anic account to be vindicated. He appears to confirm that the Qur'anic account takes precedence over any historical and scientific investigation and thereby anticipates a trend in modern Qur'anic exegesis that attempts to prove the scientific character of the Qur'an either by showing how Qur'anic verses predict modern scientific discoveries or by explaining away scientific theories in conflict with Muslim beliefs.[115] On the other hand, his fatwa equally seeks to illustrate the intellectual validity of the approach taken by historians by explaining the fundamental theoretical and methodological assumptions under which historical research operates and which lead to particular conclusions on events about which clear historical records do not exist. Such an assertion implies that the Bible and the Qur'an cannot count as reliable historical sources and are therefore irrelevant as sources for historical research. While ʿAbduh reassures *prima facie* the enquirer by addressing his concerns and hoping for a future reconciliation of the historical and Qur'anic views on Noah's flood, he equally seeks to legitimize the approach taken by historians and does not dismiss their methods and assumptions as illegitimate *per se*. On the contrary, he shows understanding for the reasons why historians cannot take the Bible or the Qur'an as reliable historical records.

Another request ʿAbduh received reflects the experience of Muslims in minority and colonial contexts. Some Sunni *ʿulamā* in India strove to improve the educational level of Muslims on the subcontinent and by doing so,

> they ask unbelievers and followers of heretical and deviant sects (*al-kuffār wa-ahl al-bidaʿ wa-l-ahwā*) for assistance in order to support the Muslim community, to preserve its property, to achieve its reunion and to join its forces. Is such a request for assistance permissible, according to the shariʿa?[116]

These *ʿulamā* probably crossed sectarian lines and sought collaborations with Shiis and possibly also Ismailis in order to promote Muslim interests in India. Furthermore, they might have also approached Hindus for assistance or the British colonial authorities. ʿAbduh sent this request to four leading *ʿulamā* at al-Azhar, each representing one of the four legal schools. All agreed that 'regarding the effort to achieve harmony and understanding among Muslims, it is undisputable that this belongs to the most virtuous and greatest religious acts in the sight of God'.[117] Likewise the cooperation with unbelievers and deviant heretics is considered permissible as long as 'it pertains to using their wealth and it is for religious welfare and worldly benefit and does not contain humiliation and the denial of political authority'.[118] All four *ʿulamā* also reprimand inter-sectarian intolerance among Muslims, recommending their coreligionists in India to be cautious with declaring other Muslims infidels in spite of their innovations and deviations.[119] All four responses are filled with references to Qur'anic passages, hadith reports and similar judgements of eminent scholars of the past in order to support their conclusions.

ʿAbduh, in his own response to the question, concurs with his colleagues at al-Azhar and declares cooperation with non-Sunni Muslims and non-Muslims in general permissible for the outlined purposes. He differs, however, in his methodology to reach this conclusion. His only reference points are the Qur'an, the *sunna* of the Prophet and the practices of the pious ancestors (*al-salaf al-ṣāliḥ*). References to the judgements of other *ʿulamā* are missing, illustrating ʿAbduh's insistence on a direct engagement with the primary sources and his rejection of the blind emulation of past authorities. He does not quote from the standard hadith collections but just refers to examples of interaction between Muslims and non-Muslims in early Islamic history. Muhammad, the first caliphs and the Umayyads and ʿAbbasids cooperated and used the expertise of non-Muslims for the benefits of the Muslim community. ʿAbduh uses a rather unusual authority to prove his judgement and quotes at length from Ibn Khaldun and his discussion of how non-Muslims were employed by Muslim rulers as civil servants and ministers throughout Islamic history.[120] While in this particular matter, ʿAbduh found himself in agreement with his colleagues at al-Azhar, he differs in the approach he takes from them, ignoring scholarly conventions, using solely the primary sources of Islam and using figures like Ibn Khaldun to support his argument.

The so-called Transvaal Fatwa written in response to questions of a Muslim diaspora community in South Africa became most notorious, as the following outcry among the *ʿulamāʾ* of al-Azhar reflected their opposition towards his reformist ideas and his isolation among the political and religious establishment of Egypt.[121] The khedive himself became part of the opposition to ʿAbduh's rulings during a press campaign in 1903 which he instigated.[122] No other fatwa had ever received such attention in Egypt and other parts of the Muslim world. A member of the Muslim community in the South African province of Transvaal asked ʿAbduh whether it is permissible for Muslims to wear European hats during their business transactions with non-Muslims, whether it is allowed to eat meat slaughtered by Christians, and whether followers of the Shafiʿi school can pray behind a Hanafi imam.[123] ʿAbduh declared all three permissible. For ʿAbduh, wearing European hats does not constitute an act of apostasy if they are worn for practical reasons like protection against the sun or increasing success in business activities. The connection between dress and one's religious affiliation is irrelevant – what counts is the intention of the wearer. ʿAbduh does not ground his response on any reference to the Qur'an or the *sunna* of the Prophet but uses the legal criterion of welfare (*maṣlaḥa*) as guiding principle.

As for the second question, ʿAbduh refers to a Qur'anic verse which allows Muslims to eat the food of the People of the Book.[124] Although there is a complex legal discussion in Islamic jurisprudence on whether and to what extent food of Jews and Christians is allowed for consumption, ʿAbduh keeps his response as simple as possible ignoring the whole legal tradition around this problem by referring solely to the Qur'an. For him, any meat slaughtered by Christians and Jews is permissible for consumption as long as both slaughter their animals in accordance with their own religious rites. Furthermore, despite his position as Hanafi mufti, he includes the approval of a Maliki jurist as another authority to justify his opinion.[125] ʿAbduh not only ignores judgements of previous scholars on this issue but also the legal distinctions between the different Sunni schools of law aiming at their rapprochement (*talfiq*).[126] Regarding the third question, ʿAbduh again simplifies his answer and does not enter a discussion of the detailed differences in the ritual practices of the different legal schools. He confirms the validity of any prayer according to any school of law and allows the followers of one school to join the prayer of another. Insisting on the differences between the legal schools endangers the inherent unity of Islam and treats the four legal schools like four different religions. For 'Abduh, it is particularly necessary for Muslims in a minority status to reduce the differences among them and to stress their commonalities.[127]

'Abduh's responses illustrate his general approach to resolving the problems Muslims face in following their religion in the modern world. He intended to offer pragmatic and simple solutions and is completely disinterested in the detailed technicalities of casuistic legal discussions among Muslim jurisprudents. Furthermore, 'Abduh was willing to combine and utilize rulings of different legal schools if appropriate and useful to arrive at verdicts in the best interests of Muslims. 'Abduh's disregard for such complex discussions and for a strict adherence to one of the legal schools in the Transvaal Fatwa led his opponents among the conservative *'ulamā'* to discredit him by accusing him to claim the rank of a *mujtahid* and the same status as the founders of the four canonical schools.[128] In particular his position as Hanafi mufti was questioned, as his legal ruling on the permissibility of meat slaughtered by Christians and Jews contradicted the consensus of the Hanafi school on this issue.[129] The opposition of conservative *'ulamā'* was to some extent politically motivated aiming at undermining the public influence of 'Abduh.[130] The outcry appears particularly fabricated as the vast majority of his fatwas are remarkably conventional and follow Hanafi jurisprudence.

In his role as mufti as in his other positions, 'Abduh was able to move between different discourses and to address diverse audiences. As the official Hanafi mufti of Egypt, he produced fatwas on the administration of pious endowments, commercial transactions, landownership and issues around personal status law which enforce the jurisprudence of the official Hanafi legal school of Egypt. However, when addressing issues coming from outside of Egypt, he engaged in a fresh and highly eclectic approach to Islamic jurisprudence. He defied scholarly conventions to achieve more flexibility, combined rulings from different legal schools to broaden the appeal of his fatwas and ignored previous legal rulings if they appeared impractical for modern Muslims living under colonial rule or in a minority status.[131] In his fatwas addressing a more global Muslim audience, 'Abduh followed his new understanding of the role of the *'ālim*. Rather than being the custodian and preserver of a scholarly tradition, he should become an agent of change and development in the Islamic tradition.

Conclusion

Upon his return to Egypt in 1888 and certainly after the ascension of Khedive 'Abbas Hilmi II in 1892, 'Abduh became an influential public figure holding various offices and roles that allowed him to actively influence the direction of key institutions of Islamic life in Egypt. As in the past, 'Abduh assumed different discourses and approaches, this time navigating carefully between a hostile political and religious establishment in Egypt and the more supportive British colonial authorities. This explains why in his role as grand mufti the majority of his fatwas are quite conventional often confirming previous rulings. There are only a few instances where his approach or rulings are more innovative, in particular when responding to enquires coming from outside of Egypt. Both the nature of their requests and their location allowed 'Abduh to be more reformist, as he did not need to fear the repercussions coming from the opposition of his domestic opponents. His ability to employ the genre of Islamic legal responsa literature for very different purposes also illustrates his immersion into the intellectual culture of ambiguity and his ability to adapt discourses accordingly: affirming Hanafi jurisprudence when required while also using fatwas to simplify Islamic law if possible. The public outcry resulting from his Transvaal Fatwa however illustrated the precarious position he was in given the enmity he faced from both the khedive and conservative religious scholars, based at al-Azhar. Hence, 'Abduh's public role required his self-portrayal as Islamic reformer within the Sunni tradition and to couch his reformist discourse in prevailing notions of orthodoxy to avoid further antagonism.

For 'Abduh to assume these new roles required a significant re-adjustment of his politics. Most significantly, he undertook a complete re-appraisal of colonialism and accepted it as a temporary condition that will prove beneficial for the modernization of Muslim societies. This re-adjustment meant a complete dissociation from Afghani and his staunch anti-imperialism. However, his re-positioning towards colonialism remained ambivalent. He acquiesced to colonial rule as a means to lay the foundations for later freedom and independence. While he needed British support for many of his initiatives and often to retain his official positions and influence in Egypt and commended French colonial policies in North Africa, he was equally critical of the economic motivations behind European imperialism and the exploitation of colonized countries. Colonialism was for him a necessary evil, providing temporary advantages.

In redefining the relationship between the institutions of Islamic life and the state, 'Abduh equally played an ambivalent role. He furthered the development of Muslims charitable and civic activism outside of the state with the formation of the Muslim Benevolent Society and cultural activities for the revival of the Arabic language. His support for the centralization of shari'a courts and the codification of their rulings, for the organizational consolidation of pious endowments and for the institutional modernization of al-Azhar was meant to create powerful institutions that could withstand the khedive's interference and state control. Inadvertently, however, by supporting these organizational and operational reforms that centralized these institutions, 'Abduh became an agent of the colonial state. These reforms laid the groundwork for the nationalization of Egyptian Islam and the subordination of public institutions of Islamic life under government control that would become particularly manifest in the twentieth century – in Egypt and in other Muslim-majority countries.

Many tropes identified earlier in his intellectual and political activism remained constant but were articulated differently. 'Abduh operated as a public intellectual within two distinct understandings of politics. On a descriptive level, he viewed current politics as corrupt and appealing to the lower nature of humans.[132] His distance to ruling authorities, his apparently apolitical stance in contradistinction to Afghani's approach and his emphasis on educational reforms over political change stem from this negative view of politics. However, 'Abduh did not turn into an apolitical figure after he had returned to Egypt. His involvement was based on a normative understanding of politics conceiving it as a means for communal cooperation in order to achieve individual moral perfection and common welfare.[133] This required educational reform to yield a new intellectual elite, combining Islamic and modern knowledge and guiding the rest of society. His major intellectual outputs produced in this period of life aimed at achieving this.

Notes

1 Muhammad Rashid Rida, *Ta'rīkh al-Ustādh al-Imām al-Shaykh Muḥammad 'Abduh*, vol. 1 (Cairo: al-Manar, 1931), 418.

2 Evelyn Baring (Earl of Cromer), *Modern Egypt*, vol. 2 (London: Macmillan, 1908), 179.

3 Ahmad Amin, *Zu'amā' al-Iṣlāḥ fī-l-'Aṣr al-Ḥadīth* (Cairo: Maktabat al-Nahda al-Misriyya, 1948), 310.

4 Ibid., 337.
5 Rida, *Ta'rīkh*, vol. 1, 420; 'Abd al-Mun'im Hamada, *al-Ustādh al-Imām Muḥammad 'Abduh* (Cairo: al-Maktaba al-Tijariyya, 1945), 148.
6 Rida, *Ta'rīkh*, vol. 1, 416–17.
7 Ibid., 894.
8 Ibid., 896.
9 Ibid. 'Abduh is probably referring to Afghani's association with Ottoman and Iranian political dissidents and his efforts to overthrow the Qajar dynasty which found its climax in the assassination of Nasir al-Din Shah in 1896 by one of Afghani's followers. See Nikki R. Keddie, *Sayyid Jamāl ad-Dīn 'al-Afghānī': A Political Biography* (Berkeley: University of California Press, 1972), 373–423.
10 Rida, *Ta'rīkh*, vol. 1, 896.
11 Ibid., 897.
12 'Abd al-Rahman Rafi'i, *al-Thawra al-'Urābiyya wa-l-Iḥtilāl al-Injilīzī* (Cairo: Maktabat al-Nahda al-Misriyya, 1949), 158.
13 For 'Abduh's critical reflection on the failure of indigenous reform attempts, written in 1892, see Muhammad 'Abduh, 'al-Ḥaqq al-Murr', in *al-A'māl al-Kāmila li-l-Imām Muḥammad 'Abduh*, ed. Muhammad 'Imara, vol. 1 (Beirut: Dar al-Shuruq, 1993), 781–4.
14 Ibid., 781–5.
15 Muhammad 'Abduh, 'Innamā Yunhiḍa bi-l-Sharq Mustabidd 'Ādil', in *al-A'māl al-Kāmila li-l-Imām Muḥammad 'Abduh*, ed. Muhammad 'Imara, vol. 1 (Beirut: Dar al-Shuruq, 1993), 845–6.
16 Amin, *Zu'amā' al-Iṣlāḥ*, 319–20; Achille Sékaly, 'Le Problème des Wakfs en Egypte', *Revue des Etudes Islamiques*, 3 (1929): 115–16.
17 Rida, *Ta'rīkh*, vol. 1, 572–5; Amin, *Zu'amā' al-Iṣlāḥ*, 313.
18 Baring, *Modern Egypt*, vol. 2, 179.
19 Rida, *Ta'rīkh*, vol. 1, 602.
20 Baring, *Modern Egypt*, vol. 2, note 1, 180–1.
21 For Cromer's use of Orientalist stereotypes in order to justify British rule of Egypt see his description of 'The Englishman's mission' in *Modern Egypt*, vol. 2, 123–6.
22 Muhammad Rashid Rida, 'Mulakhkhaṣ Sīrat al-Ustādh al-Imām', *al-Manār*, 8 (1905): 489; Ali Merad, 'L'enseignement politique de Muhammad 'Abduh aux algériens (1903)', *Confluent*, 42–3 (1964): 674–89.
23 Amin, Ahmad, *Zu'amā' al-Iṣlāḥ*, 314; Baring, *Modern Egypt*, vol. 2, 180; Rida, *Ta'rīkh* 1, 717–18.
24 Quoted in Wilfrid S. Blunt, *Secret History of the English Occupation of Egypt: Being a Personal Narrative of Events*, 2nd edn (London: Fisher Unwin, 1907), 625.
25 Quoted in ibid., 626.
26 Rida, *Ta'rīkh*, vol. 1, 781.

27 Muhammad ʻAbduh, ʻFaransā wa-l-Jazāʼir, *al-Manār* 6 (1903): 79–80.
28 Merad, ʻEnseignement politiqueʼ, 659–63.
29 Qurʼan 103:1–3.
30 Muhammad ʻAbduh, ʻSūrat al-ʻAṣrʼ, in *al-Aʻmāl al-Kāmila li-l-Imām Muḥammad ʻAbduh*, ed. Muhammad ʻImara, vol. 5 (Beirut: Dar al-Shuruq, 1993), 487–8.
31 Merad, ʻEnseignement politiqueʼ, 671–3.
32 See Muhammad ʻAbduhʼs letter to an Algerian scholar in *al-Aʻmāl al-Kāmila*, vol. 1, 836.
33 Rida, *Taʼrīkh*, vol. 1, 873–4.
34 ʻAbduh, ʻal-Ḥaqq al-Murrʼ, vol. 1, 776.
35 Richard Gottheil, ʻMohammad ʻAbdu: Late Mufti of Egyptʼ, *Journal of the American Oriental Society*, 28 (1907): 196.
36 Rida, *Taʼrīkh*, vol. 1, 847.
37 Ibid., 846–7.
38 Ibid., 105.
39 See ʻAbduhʼs conversation with Rida in ʻAbduh, *al-Aʻmāl al-Kāmila*, vol. 1, 811.
40 Rida, *Taʼrīkh*, vol. 1, 1030–1.
41 Jakob Skovgaard-Petersen, *Defining Islam for the Egyptian State: Muftis and Fatwas of the Dar al-Ifta* (Leiden: Brill, 1997), 77–9.
42 On the development of the legal system in Egypt in the nineteenth century see also Andreas H. E. Kemke, *Stiftungen im muslimischen Rechtsleben des neuzeitlichen Ägypten: Die shariarechtlichen Gutachten (Fatwas) von Muhammad ʻAbduh (st. 1905) zum Wakf* (Frankfurt A.M.: Peter Lang, 1991), 8–10.
43 Skovgaard-Petersen, *Defining Islam*, 56–65.
44 Ibid., 100–6.
45 Kemke, *Stiftungen*, 11–18.
46 Rida, *Taʼrīkh*, vol. 1, 646; Charles C. Adams, ʻMuhammad ʻAbduh and the Transvaal Fatwaʼ, in *The MacDonald Presentation Volume* (Princeton: Princeton University Press, 1933), 13–14.
47 Rida, *Taʼrīkh*, vol. 1, 430–2.
48 Ibid., 605–10.
49 Hamada, *ʻAbduh*, 180–1; Samira Haj, *Reconfiguring Islamic Tradition: Reform, Rationality, and Modernity* (Stanford: Stanford University Press, 2009), 136–43.
50 Rida, Rida, *Taʼrīkh*, vol. 1, 631–42.
51 Hamada, *ʻAbduh*, 184.
52 Rida, *Taʼrīkh* vol. 1, 630–45.
53 Ibid., 719.
54 Ibid., 722.
55 Ibid., 891.
56 Amin, *Zuʻamāʼ al-Iṣlāḥ*, 334–5; Hamada, *ʻAbduh*, 188–9.

57 Amin, *Zu'amā' al-Iṣlāḥ*, 320; Hamada, *'Abduh*, 202–3.
58 'Abduh, *al-A'māl al-Kāmila*, vol. 1, 34, note 9.
59 Sékaly, 'Le Problème des Wakfs', 115–16.
60 Amin, *Zu'amā' al-Iṣlāḥ*, 320; Hamada, *'Abduh*, 203–4.
61 Ibid., 205–8.
62 Joseph H. Escovitz, '"He was the Muhammad 'Abduh of Syria": A Study of Tahir al-Jaza'iri and His Influence', *International Journal of Middle East Studies*, 18 (1986): 293–310.
63 Itzhak Weismann, *Taste of Modernity: Sufism, Salafiyya and Arabism in Late Ottoman Damascus* (Leiden: Brill, 2001), 283–4.
64 Charles C. Adams, *Islam and Modernism in Egypt: A Study of the Modern Reform Movement Inaugurated by Muhammad 'Abduh* (London: Oxford University Press, 1933), 83–4.
65 Hamada, *'Abduh*, 192. By 1905, the society had established seven schools teaching around 770 children. See Rida, *Ta'rīkh*, vol. 1, 730–8, 744–6.
66 Ibid., 729.
67 For the reasons of the socio-political decline of Sufi orders in modern Egypt see Michael Gilsenan, *Saint and Sufi in Modern Egypt: An Essay in the Sociology of Religion* (Oxford: Clarendon Press, 1973), 188–207.
68 Rida, *Ta'rīkh*, vol. 1, 891–2.
69 See 'Abduh's conversation with the *shaykh al-islām* of the Ottoman Empire, published in ibid., 851–3.
70 Yvonne Y. Haddad, 'Muhammad Abduh: Pioneer of Islamic Reform', in *Pioneers of Islamic Revival*, ed. Ali Rahnema, 2nd edn (London: Zed Books, [1994] 2005), 49.
71 Rida, *Ta'rīkh*, vol. 1, 851–3.
72 Ibid., 848–50.
73 Ibid., 851–2.
74 Ibid., 852.
75 Rida, 'Mulakhkhaṣ', 472; Adams, *Islam and Modernism*, 71.
76 Rida, *Ta'rīkh*, vol. 1, 569.
77 Indira Falk Gesinck, *Islamic Reform and Conservatism: Al-Azhar and the Evolution of Modern Sunni Islam* (London: I.B. Tauris, 2010), 211–30.
78 Pierre-Jean Luizard, 'Muhammad 'Abduh et la réforme d'Al-Azhar', in *Modernités islamiques: Actes du colloque organisé à Alep à l'occasion du centenaire de la disparition de l'imam Muḥammad 'Abduh, 9–10 novembre 2005*, ed. Maher Al-Charif and Sabrina Mervin (Damascus: IFPO, 2006), 17–18; Adams, *Islam and Modernism*, 73–6.
79 Rida, *Ta'rīkh*, vol. 1, 570.
80 Adams, *Islam and Modernism*, 75.
81 See conversation between 'Abduh and Rida in 'Abduh, *al-A'māl al-Kāmila*, vol. 3, 194–5.

82 Luizard, "Abduh et la réforme d'Al-Azhar', 27; Haj, *Reconfiguring Islamic Tradition*, 103–4.

83 Gesinck, *Islamic Reform and Conservatism*, 183–6. Raising questions around 'Abduh's moral propriety was also used by his opponents in Beirut who accused him of dancing with 'Christian women'. See Fazil Mazandarani, *Ta'rīkh-i Ẓuhūr al-Ḥaqq*, vol. 6, 766–7. Available online: http://www.h-net.org/~bahai/arabic/vol3/tzh6/tzh6.htm (accessed 11 May 2021).

84 Amin, *Zu'amā' al-Iṣlāḥ*, 324; Gesinck, *Islamic Reform and Conservatism*, 210.

85 Hillary Kalmbach, *Islamic Knowledge and the Making of Modern Egypt* (Cambridge: Cambridge University Press, 2020), 127–8.

86 Donald M. Reid, *Cairo University and the Making of Modern Egypt* (Cambridge: Cambridge University Press, 1990), 24–5.

87 Rida, *Ta'rīkh*, vol. 1, 946–7.

88 Ibid., 602.

89 Amin, *Zu'amā' al-Iṣlāḥ*, 318–19; Kemke, *Stiftungen*, 30.

90 Rida, *Ta'rīkh*, vol. 1, 602.

91 Dietrich Jung, 'Islamic Reform and the Global Public Sphere: Muhammad Abduh and Islamic Modernity', in *The Middle East and Globalization: Encounters and Horizons*, ed. Stephan Stetter (New York: Palgrave Macmillan, 2012), 157.

92 Hamada, *'Abduh*, 171; Albert Hourani, *Arabic Thought in the Liberal Age: 1798–1939* (Cambridge: Cambridge University Press, 1983), 152.

93 Muhammad 'Abduh, *Fatāwa al-Imām Muḥammad 'Abduh* (Cairo: al-Jam'iyya al-Khayriyya al-Islamiyya, 2005), 185.

94 Ibid., 164.

95 Gesinck, *Islamic Reform and Conservatism*, 175–6.

96 'Abduh, *Fatāwa 'Abduh*, 230–1.

97 Ibid., 200.

98 Ibid., 196.

99 Ibid., 11–16.

100 Ibid., 20–1.

101 Adams, 'Transvaal Fatwa', 79–81.

102 Skovgaard-Petersen, *Defining Islam*, 126–7.

103 Muhammad Rashid Rida, 'Ta'yīd al-Fatwā wa-Ḥaqīqatuhā wa-mā bihī-l-Iftā'', *al-Manār*, 6 (1904): 784–5; Muhammad Rashid Rida, 'Qawl fī-l-Muftī wa-Taqlīdihī', *al-Manār*, 6 (1904): 785–6; Hamada, *'Abduh*, 171; Gesinck, *Islamic Reform and Conservatism*, 194.

104 'Abduh, *Fatāwa 'Abduh*, 227.

105 Ibid., 225.

106 Ibid., 227.

107 Ibid., 226.

108 Rida, *Ta'rīkh*, vol. 1, 666.
109 Qur'an 54:12.
110 Rida, *Ta'rīkh*, vol. 1, 666.
111 Ibid., 667.
112 Ibid., 666.
113 Ibid., 667.
114 Ibid.
115 See the influential scientific commentary of Tantawi Jawhari (1862–1940), *al-Jawāhir fī Tafsīr al-Qur'ān al-Karīm al-Mushtamil 'alā 'Ajā'ib Badā'i' al-Mukawwināt wa-Gharā'ib al-Āyāt al-Bāhirāt*, 13 vols (Beirut: Dar al-Kutub al-'Ilmiyya, 2005).
116 Rida, *Ta'rīkh*, vol. 1, 648.
117 Ibid.
118 Ibid., 652.
119 Ibid., 657–61.
120 Ibid., 662–6.
121 For a discussion on the press coverage of the controversy in Egypt see Rida, *Ta'rīkh*, vol. 1, 694–5, 704–12.
122 Ibid., 668–9; Gesinck, *Islamic Reform and Conservatism*, 169–96.
123 Muhammad 'Abduh, *al-Fatāwa fī-l-Tajdīd wa-l-Iṣlāḥ al-Dīnī* (Tunis: Dar al-Ma'arif, 1989), 20.
124 Qur'an 5:5.
125 For the *fatwa* of the Maliki jurist Abu Bakr ibn 'Arabi, cited by 'Abduh, and discussions among Muslim jurists about this question see Rida, *Ta'rīkh*, vol. 1, 683–9.
126 Hourani, *Arabic Thought*, 152.
127 'Abduh, *Fatāwa fī-l-Tajdīd*, 20–1; Adams, 'Transvaal Fatwa', 16–28.
128 Rida, *Ta'rīkh*, vol. 1, 712–13; Adams, 'Transvaal Fatwa', 28–9.
129 Rida, *Ta'rīkh*, vol. 1, 689–90.
130 Haj, *Reconfiguring Islamic Tradition*, 149–50.
131 For Rida's defence of 'Abduh's general use of *ijtihād*, see Rida, *Ta'rīkh*, vol. 1, 690–1.
132 Muhammad 'Abduh, 'al-Radd 'alā Faraḥ Anṭūn,' in *al-A'māl al-Kāmila li-l-Imām Muḥammad 'Abduh*, ed. Muhammad 'Imara, vol. 3 (Beirut: Dar al-Shuruq, 1993), 334.
133 On this distinction between these two types of politics, see Mohamed Haddad, *Muḥammad 'Abduh: Qarā'a Jadīda fī Khiṭāb al-Iṣlāḥ al-Dīnī* (Beirut: Dar al-Tali'a li-l-Taba'a wa-l-Nashr, 2003), 154.

6

ʿAbduh and the discourse of Islamic reform

Introduction

After his return to Egypt, ʿAbduh assumed various public roles and established his fame both in the country but also in the wider Muslim world. This was also the period when he produced his most influential works that would shape his intellectual legacy and define his reputation as a Muslim reformer, such as his *Risālat al-Tawḥīd* (Treatise on Divine Unity), his Qur'an commentary *Tafsīr al-Manār* (The Lighthouse Commentary) and various apologetic works. As seen in the previous chapter, ʿAbduh also developed and embodied a new model of intellectual leadership in Islam that engaged with contemporary problems Muslim societies faced. This reformed understanding of religious authority was based on intellectual foundations laid earlier in his life and sought to synthesize the diverse heritage of Islamic intellectual life and to make it relevant to the lives of Muslims in the modern world. In addition, ʿAbduh continued to use non-scholarly avenues to disseminate ideas in order to increase the appeal of Islamic knowledge traditions outside of scholarly circles.

Although ʿAbduh distanced himself from the anti-colonial activism of his teacher Afghani, the mystico-philosophical instructions he received as a young man still shaped the doctrinal discourse at this stage of his life. ʿAbduh incorporated Islam's philosophical heritage to argue for the inherent rationality of Islam and to attack in particular the mindset of *taqlīd*, the blind imitation of scholarly authorities that sidelined the authority of the primary sources of Islam and undercut intellectual independence which ʿAbduh considered crucial for making Islam relevant to the modern world. In his theological works he faced a similar dilemma as in his role of mufti: he had to adhere to a particular restrictive approach to Islamic jurisprudence by implementing the rulings of the Hanafi school as its official mufti. Yet, he also wanted to use his role to provide flexible and pragmatic solutions to contemporary problems which utilize the broad field of Islamic jurisprudence in its fullness. As a writer in Islamic theology, ʿAbduh also realized that his theological discourse had to conform to certain parameters which define orthodoxy in a Sunni context. Despite his references to authority figures in Sunni Islam like Abu al-Hasan al-Ashʿari (873–936) whose school would define mainstream Sunni theology, his writings still engage with a wide range of intellectual traditions and continue to bear the imprint of Ibn Sina, Ibn Khaldun, Ibn Miskawayh and other philosophers to a significant extent.

In his articles in the journal *al-ʿUrwa al-Wuthqā*, ʿAbduh refers to the pious ancestors (*al-salaf al-ṣāliḥ*) as the historical role model in early Islamic history who embodied the true ethos of Islam. References to the pious ancestors also occur frequently in his writings at this time and were meant to strengthen the orthodox credentials of his reformist project. However, the manner in which he employs this term to describe his approach to Islamic reform includes several ambiguities which previous scholarship has not recognized. The Salafi label disguises the nature of his reforms more than it adequately describes them and obscures his complex engagement with the capaciousness of Islamic intellectual traditions.

ʿAbduh and the pious ancestors (*al-salaf al-ṣāliḥ*)

In the beginning of his autobiographical remarks, ʿAbduh describes the objectives of his reformist project:

> First, to liberate thought from the shackles of blind imitation (*taqlīd*) and understand religion in the way of the ancestors of the community (*salaf al-umma*) before disagreements appeared; to return in the acquisition of religious knowledge to its first sources and to weigh them in the scales of reason which God has created in order to prevent excess and to lessen delusion and adulteration in religion, so that the wisdom of God may be fulfilled in preserving the order of the human world. Religion in this respect can be counted as a friend of science, investigating the secrets of existence, summoning respect for established truths and demanding reliance on them in one's moral life and in the reform of one's conduct. All this, I count as one matter, and in my advocacy for them, I stood in opposition to the opinion of two great groups of which the body of the community is constituted – the students of the different fields of religious knowledge, and those who are like them, and the students of the arts of this age, and those who are on their side.[1]

The primary target of ʿAbduh's reformist work is opposing the ethos of *taqlīd*, the blind imitation of previous scholarly authorities that has caused the intellectual stagnation of Islamic scholarship and undermines the authority of the primary sources of Islam. In addition, he emphasizes the centrality of reason in this reformist endeavour. Reason is a human capability bestowed by God and necessary to avoid irrational readings of Islam and to ensure openness towards the insights of modern science. Equally important: such rational underpinning of a rediscovery of the foundations of Islam encourage an ethical reading of the religion whose primary objective is to reform human conduct (*iṣlāḥ al-ʿamal*).

The historical manifestation of this particular type of Islam are for ʿAbduh the ancestors of the community (*salaf al-umma*), an ambiguous term that invites different interpretations. In other contexts he also refers to 'the pious ancestors (*al-salaf al-ṣāliḥ*)',[2] 'the first ancestors (*al-salaf al-awwalūn*)'[3] or just 'the ancestors (*al-salaf*)'.[4] References such as these to early Muslims have led to the designation of ʿAbduh's reform movement as Salafiyya, a term he did not use himself but goes back to his disciple Rida.[5] To distinguish ʿAbduh's school of thought from contemporary puritanical forms of Salafism, that originated in the Wahhabi movement, scholars also refer to it as '*modernist Salafism*'.[6] Modernist Salafism is characterized by advocating a return to the primary sources of Islam, the Qur'an and the *sunna* of the Prophet, the rejection of *taqlīd* and the essential conformity of Islam with reason and its alignment with modern science.[7] ʿAbduh's description of his reformist project confirms such a reading. However, both the most influential works he produced in this period and his use of the term *salaf* suggest a more complex and ambiguous appropriation of Islam's intellectual heritage which combines different strands of Islamic thought he had studied and engaged with earlier in his life.

The pious ancestors (*al-salaf al-ṣāliḥ*) is understood in Sunni Islam as the designation for the first three generations of Muslims: the Prophet Muhammad and his Companions, their successors (*tābiʿūn*) and the successors of the successors (*tābiʿ al-tābiʿīn*). This distinction is based on a hadith attributed to the Prophet Muhammad[8] and also denotes the period of Islamic intellectual history before Greek philosophy impacted Islamic fields of scholarship. Previous scholarship – with the exception of Haddad[9] – has not recognized ʿAbduh's equivocal use of the term *salaf*. ʿAbduh includes quite different groups under the label of *salaf* and uses the term in at least four different ways. In a brief outline of the place of reason and the reception of Greek philosophy in early Islamic scholarship, he presents 'the school of the ancestors (*madhhab al-salaf*)'[10] as those who rejected the use of reason altogether. ʿAbduh employs the term here in reference to the people of tradition (*ahl al-ḥadīth*), the group of early Islamic scholars around Ahmad ibn Hanbal (780–855) which argued against the use of philosophical discourse in Islamic theology and demanded all articles of faith to be based on scriptural evidence alone.[11] However, 'Abduh does not subscribe to this approach but presents the theological approach of Abu al-Hasan al-Ash'ari and his school as a middle position between two extremes: Hanbali scripturalism and the overreliance on reason of theological schools like the Mu'tazila. He is also critical of the scholars of the Hanbali school who declared al-Ash'ari an infidel and demanded his execution.[12] Given his overall broad irenic intellectual approach, it is very difficult to argue that 'Abduh adhered to the strict scripturalism of the Hanbali school of thought in doctrinal matters, as Rida suggests.[13] One is hard-pressed to find many references to prophetic traditions (*aḥādīth*) in 'Abduh's writings – an important element to qualify as Salafi scholar for whom – next to the Qur'an – the *sunna* of the Prophet and its collection in *aḥādīth* is the most authoritative source to define Islamic doctrines and practices. Important scholarly figures of the Hanbali tradition, such as Ibn Taymiyya (1263–1328), are also missing as reference points in his writings.

'Abduh also uses the term to refer to different generations of early Muslim scholars and includes the influential scholar Hasan al-Basri (641–728) among the *salaf*. Al-Basri is considered to be part of the second generation after the Prophet Muhammad and his Companions, the so-called successors (*tābi'ūn*). In his other writings, 'Abduh employs the label *salaf* in much broader terms. Bemoaning the poor status of Islamic education, he urges the students of Islamic scholarship to study directly 'the works of the ancestors (*āthār al-salaf*)',[14] which for him includes the Qur'an commentaries of al-Tabari (839–923), Abu Muslim al-Isfahani (869–934) and al-Qurtubi (1214–1273). While all these figures are crucial in shaping exegetical traditions in Sunni Islam, they are not part of the pious ancestors. Likewise, Abu Hamid al-Ghazali (1058–1111) is presented as one of the pious ancestors[15] despite living more than two hundred years after their demise. 'Abduh also includes the theologians Abu al-Hasan al-Ash'ari, Abu Mansur al-Maturidi (853–944) and Abu Bakr al-Baqillani (940–1013) – figures that shaped Sunni theology substantially but were not of the pious ancestors. 'Abduh's more wide-ranging use of the label *salaf* comprises Islamic scholars of the first sixth centuries of Islam.[16]

This more inclusive understanding of the *salaf* might be informed by the more technical distinction between different periods in the development of Islamic theology before and after the thirteenth century that goes back to Ibn Khaldun.[17]

Ibn Khaldun refers to theologians until al-Ghazali as ancestors (*salaf* – later also known as *mutaqaddimūn*) and includes figures like al-Ash'ari who laid the foundation of theology as a discursive discipline in Islamic thought and al-Ghazali who engaged in a critique of philosophy. Theologians that appeared after al-Ghazali Ibn Khaldun designates as successors (*muta'akhkhirūn*). They sought to broaden the intellectual remit of Islamic theology: it was not just to define, defend and rationalize matters of creed (*'aqā'id*) but to become the epistemological foundation of all Islamic fields of knowledge, incorporating metaphysics, science and logic. Ash'ari theologians like Fakhr al-Din al-Razi (1150–1210) represent the latter generation of theologians that moved closer to rationalist approaches in theology like the Mu'tazila with a metaphorical interpretation of divine attributes and the priority of reason over revelation in providing absolute proof.[18]

'Abduh was sceptical of the conflation of philosophy and theology[19] and suggests that his theology 'uses the approach of the ancestors (*al-salaf*) in matters of creed (*'aqā'id*) and does not indulge in the way of the successors (*al-khalaf*) after the disagreement of different schools of thought'.[20] 'Abduh follows here Ibn Khaldun's specific distinction: he designates as *salaf* pre-Ghazalian theologians like al-Ash'ari who focussed in their theological discussions on matters of creed. These *salaf* in Islamic theology were not opposed to philosophy as such but limited its epistemological scope in Islamic knowledge traditions. In contrast, their successors (*khalaf*) blurred the boundaries between philosophy and theology.[21] By claiming to follow the *salaf* in matters of creed, 'Abduh suggests only to follow early Ash'ari theologians.

There are at least four different ways in which 'Abduh uses the term *salaf* in his writings: in reference to the anti-rationalist and scripturalist Hanbali school (*madhhab al-salaf*), very early Muslim scholars like Hasan al-Basri, Muslim theologians and Qur'an commentators until the thirteenth century and pre-Ghazalian Muslim theologians. He dissociates himself from the Salafi approach of the Hanbali school, as his critical remarks of its scripturalism and intolerance illustrate. Even the more technical understanding of the term to distinguish between pre- and post-Ghazalian Sunni-Ash'ari theology does not entirely apply to 'Abduh. While he criticizes the fusion of theology and philosophy, 'Abduh's theological expositions include elements of Avicennan philosophy and of later Ash'ari theologians. Ultimately, he undertakes a synthesis of different strands of Islamic thought in his writings to allow for a creative engagement with modern ideas and the rise of a new model of religious leadership.

'Abduh positions himself between two groups: the representatives of traditional Islamic scholarship who remained untouched by the emergence of Western modernity and intellectuals who have studied modern sciences and dismiss Islam as inherently backward. From the time of his early educational career, 'Abduh was uneasy with the first group as his frustration with traditional scholarship and modes of instruction indicated. At the same time, he rejected the blind imitation of European modernity as advocated by European educated intellectuals and members of the ruling elite. The new educated elite outside the *'ulamā'* milieu was 'Abduh's target group of his theological and apologetic writings at the end of his life. Members of this group had benefited from a modern education and viewed traditional Islamic scholarship as obscurantist and irrelevant to the needs of the modern world. Journalism remained one of the instruments to reach out to the new educated Muslim elite. Together with Rida, he published the journal *al-Manār* (The Lighthouse) from 1898 onwards which became one of the chief outlets to disseminate his and Rida's reformist ideas. He also continued to publish regularly in other Egyptian journals and newspapers. In 1899, 'Abduh began to provide a comprehensive commentary on the Qur'an in the form of public lectures at al-Azhar, developing further earlier public lectures he had given in Beirut.[22] These lectures were written down and later published in the journal *al-Manār*, giving 'Abduh's commentary the name under which it was known, *Tafsīr al-Manār*.[23] By targeting lay Muslims, 'Abduh made non-scholarly approaches to the Qur'an possible and 'initiated the twentieth-century trend of individual interaction with and interpretation of the Qur'an'.[24]

A new theology?

The various writings at the final stage of 'Abduh's life are usually seen as central to his intellectual legacy. They are presented as genuine to his reformist ideas and containing his original intellectual contribution. His early mystical and theological writings have often been ignored with the argument that they primarily or solely contain Afghani's philosophical instructions and not 'Abduh's own ideas.[25] However, such a reception is implicitly based on the dichotomy between normative and marginal discourses in Islam. The former includes theological and jurisprudential discourses that define 'Sunni orthodoxy' while the latter refers to mystical, esoteric and rationalistic traditions that are often perceived as marginal to normative mainstream (Sunni-)Islam. The works of Bauer and

Ahmed point at these artificial distinctions between genres, discourses and epistemes that are presented as 'properly' Islamic while marginalizing others as peripheral.[26] Hence, the exclusion of 'Abduh's earlier mystical and philosophical writings is based on a particular image created of him as an 'orthodox' Sunni reformer. However, his later theological writings contain important continuities to mystical and philosophical tropes that mark his earlier contributions. These writings reveal the same fundamental concerns of mystical philosophy and Islamic traditions of *ādāb* literature and historiography but are couched more explicitly in the language of Sunni-Ash'ari theology. Given his public role and experience of opposition from conservative religious establishment, 'Abduh was particularly conscious not to antagonize them further. In reality, 'Abduh did not just provide a rationalized and modernist reading of Sunni theology but brought together different strands of intellectual traditions to reconceive Islam and its moral, social and political role in the modern world.

This is obvious when considering his most influential work first published in 1897, the *Risālat al-Tawḥīd* (Treatise on Divine Unity) which is often characterized as the ultimate summary of his reformist theological ideas.[27] Based on the notes of his theology lectures at the Madrasa Sultaniyya, the *Risālat al-Tawḥīd* is not a scholarly work like his early theological commentary on the *Sharḥ al-'Aqā'id al-'Aḍudiyya*. Addressing the general public, it seeks to simplify complex theological debates. The treatise addresses core theological questions, the nature of God and His attributes, the nature of human beings, the relationship between human free will and divine predestination and the scope of human ability to distinguish different moral categories. The connection between God and humanity are the prophets and messengers whose purpose and mission the treatise equally outlines and the necessity of whose revelations it justifies. It concludes with an outline of the mission of the Prophet Muhammad, the Qur'an as the ultimate proof of his prophecy and the nature and purpose of the Islamic religion as the final revelation of God and the ultimate climax of salvation history. A superficial look at the structure, contents and discourse of the treatise suggests that it provides a modernist Sunni theological catechism, enriched with 'arguments from history and the social sciences'.[28] A closer look, however, reveals the continuation and re-articulation of mystical and philosophical ideas that had preoccupied 'Abduh since his encounter with Afghani. By focussing on the common features of Islam, the treatise seeks to instil the reader with an irenic attitude towards its doctrinal and sectarian diversity. It is, as Haddad suggests, a pedagogical document to achieve Muslim doctrinal unity.[29]

The continuous relevance of philosophy is most evident at the start of the treatise when 'Abduh recounts three different philosophical proofs of God's existence which had been articulated for the first time in this form by Ibn Sina. These proofs are already laid out in 'Abduh's *Risālat al-Wāridāt* and paraphrase discussions from other theological catechisms such as Taftazani's *Tahdhīb al-Manṭiq wa-l-Kalām* which he also used as a textbook when teaching theology at the Madrasa Sultaniyya in Beirut.[30] While 'Abduh criticizes certain excesses of Islamic philosophers and their often blind imitation (*taqlīduhum*) of Plato and Aristotle, he equally underlines that the objectives of philosophical enquiry – using reason as a means to acquire knowledge about human nature and the world, to distinguish truth from falsehood and to achieve happiness (*sa'āda*) – are encouraged in Islam.[31] However, the benefits that philosophy has brought to Islamic intellectual life have been overshadowed by certain factors: the validity of the rational approach was undermined by the intellectual excesses of some philosophers, their critical and speculative thought at times, by which they lost the support of other scholars and the wider Muslim community. Ultimately, philosophy merged with theology,[32] a process that led to 'intellectual chaos among Muslims, protected by the ignorance of their political leaders'.[33]

In line with his previous ethical reading of Islam, 'Abduh also emphasizes the ethical mandate of religion. Prophets and messengers are primarily spiritual and ethical teachers, relaying to their communities 'what contains their happiness (*sa'ādatuhā*) in both lives'[34] – this world and the hereafter. Similarly, the Prophet Muhammad's mission was to reform morals (*akhlāq*) and customs (*'awā'id*).[35] This outline of the moral vision of religions in general and Islam in particular and the need to translate beliefs into action to achieve happiness resonates with the philosophical concerns of figures like al-Ghazali and Ibn Miskawayh. Identifying the means to achieve happiness is one of the primary objectives in Islamic philosophy[36] and is the central feature in classical *ādāb* literature.[37] The pairing of knowledge (*'ilm*) and action (*'amal*) is a necessary preparation for the hereafter and the only way to achieve happiness, for al-Ghazali.[38] The latter's confluence of knowledge, which also includes divinely revealed knowledge, and its translation into rightful human conduct to secure happiness goes back to Ibn Miskawayh. In his *Tahdhīb al-Akhlāq*, he emphasizes the nexus between knowledge and action as necessary to achieve human perfection and happiness and presents it as a key insight provided by philosophy.[39]

'Abduh discusses the nature of divine revelation and of prophecy which conforms to standard definitions of Ash'ari theology in the *Risālat al-Tawḥīd*. Prophets are chosen by God and receive His word via revelations which are aurally transmitted.[40] This exposition appears to stand opposite to the more rationalized account 'Abduh provides in his *Risālat al-Wāridāt* in which he recounts Ibn Sina's philosophical prophetology: prophets are individuals that have achieved intellectual, spiritual and moral excellence by their innate disposition (*fiṭra*) and receive divine revelations qua their inherent perfection. The different accounts of the nature and sources of prophecy in both works suggest a shift of his theological stance from conceptions informed by Afghani's mystical philosophy to an understanding in line with Ash'ari theology.[41] Such an argumentation, however, overlooks that 'Abduh addresses very different audiences in both works: the mystical *Risālat al-Wāridāt* includes an account of Afghani's teaching sessions while the *Risālat al-Tawḥīd* provides a summary of 'Abduh's classes on theology at an Islamic secondary school published for the wider Muslim public. The different audiences required the adoption of different idioms.

Elements of philosophical conceptions of prophecy are still evident in the *Risālat al-Tawḥīd* when 'Abduh seeks to make the concept of revelation plausible. For 'Abduh, it is obvious that humans differ in their intellectual abilities and that these differences are not solely the result of the type of education (*ta'līm*) they have received. Rather these differences result from how 'disparate innate dispositions (*fiṭar*) are which are not determined by human choice or acquisition'.[42] Certain humans are intellectually more advanced than others by their innate abilities and have insights to knowledge other people do not possess. As consequence, 'Abduh concludes that

> among human souls there are those who have a pure essence based on their innate disposition (*fiṭra*) and who have been thereby prepared to receive direct divine effulgence (*al-fayḍ al-ilāhī*) in order to reach the most sublime horizons and to attain the highest peak of humanity. They witness by divine command things with their own eyes which others cannot obtain, even if they use reason and their senses, with the aid of evidence and proof.[43]

Such a conceptualization of prophecy echoes Ibn Sina's philosophical prophethology: prophets possess the innate disposition to gain access to knowledge other humans cannot reach. Embodying 'the highest peak of humanity', prophets appear more like the perfect human (*al-insān al-kāmil*) whose inherent perfection allows them to receive unmediated divine guidance. Revelation (*waḥī*) now becomes divine effulgence (*fayḍ ilāhī*), a key term in Islamic mystical philosophy, closely associated with the concept of emanation, to denote how God bestows knowledge on prophets, saints and philosophers.

As creation is a perpetual process, so God constantly illuminates perfect human beings with his knowledge. In this case, 'Abduh adopts the approach to prophecy articulated in *Risālat al-Wāridāt* – without mentioning Ibn Sina or emanation theology directly – in order to make the possibility of revelation plausible to a modern Muslim reader.

Some of the ramifications of this more mystical and philosophical conception of prophecy are explored further. In line with Ash'ari theology, 'Abduh distinguishes between revelation (*waḥī*) and inspiration (*ilhām*), the latter being more like an intuition (*wijdān*) whose source is unknown.[44] However, following his more philosophical conception of prophecy, 'Abduh also confirms the reality of saints, though admitting that most who claim this status are imposters and charlatans. However,

> the sublime leaders and heavenly intellects from amongst the gnostics (*'urafā'*) have not reached the level of prophets but are content to be their saints (*awliyā'*) and the trustees of their revelation and mission. Many of them receive a portion of proximity to the prophetic status in type and sort. In some of their states, they reach something in the hidden world (*'ālam al-ghayb*). They truly witness things in the world of images (*'ālam al-mithāl*) which does not deny them to attain its realities in this world. Therefore, they are not that far away from what prophets experience.[45]

This section is replete with Sufi terms and suggests that saints partake in the prophetic charisma. Their status is close to that of prophets and their mystical experiences akin to them. They have some access to the hidden knowledge which is only fully revealed to the prophets, but have visions of the world of images which is an intermediary realm between physical reality and the hidden spiritual world, inhabited by angels and jinn and the location of heaven and hell – beings and places Sufis saints encounter in their visions.[46] The access of saints to different worlds also resonates with a Sufi cosmology that distinguishes between different cosmic ranks, as discussed in 'Abduh's *Risālat al-Wāridāt*.

In his discussion of core issues of Islamic theology, 'Abduh equally merges the approaches and conclusions of different schools of thought. Several authors have observed that 'Abduh's understanding of the objective reality of good and evil and the inherent human ability to distinguish between both, without the aid of divine revelation, comes from the Mu'tazila school of theology.[47] Basic moral categories, like the aesthetic categories of beauty (*ḥusn*) and repugnance (*qubḥ*), are not determined by revelation but exist as objective realities. The role of revelation is merely to confirm these categories that humans can intuitively arrive at.[48] The Maturidi school adopts a similar approach to this question which stands in opposition to the approach of the Ash'ari school which argues that it is the act of revelation that determines what is morally good and what is morally reprehensible. While 'Abduh's adoption of the Mu'tazila or Maturidi approach[49] does not suggest he was a 'neo-Mu'tazilite'[50] or a follower of the Maturidi school, it illustrates his approach to bring different theological schools together, in particular if their arguments are helpful in demonstrating the inherent rationality of Islam.[51] His immersion in the intellectual culture of ambiguity of pre-modern Islam allowed him to disregard potential contradictions and inconsistencies between different theological schools as irrelevant and purely resulting from an exaggeration of their theological differences.

In other theological questions, he also moves between or combines perspectives of different theological schools. One of the earliest theological controversies in Islam revolved around the relationship between human free will and divine predestination. While Hasan al-Basri and the Mu'tazila argue that human moral accountability necessitates humans choosing their actions by their own free will, other schools such as the *jabariyya* maintain complete divine determinism: everything in the world, including human actions, are predestined by God. Al-Ash'ari developed a middle position arguing that human actions are created by God while humans acquire these actions out of which results their moral responsibility. 'Abduh already reveals certain closeness to this Ash'ari position in his early theological commentary[52] and reiterates his support for the Ash'ari doctrine of acquisition (*kasb*). 'Abduh advises against dwelling on such issues too much as the relationship between divine predestination and human free will transcends rational understanding and only leads to theological divisions which he seeks to overcome.[53] Equally, 'Abduh is eager to overcome the fatalistic mindset he attributes to most Muslims at his time who do not engage in activism based on a passive submission to divine providence.[54] 'Abduh adds another component to human action not contained in Ash'ari theology by suggesting that 'actions in all their conditions are derived from acquisition (*kasb*) *and* choice (*ikhtiyār*)'.[55] The concept of choice plays a significant role in *ādāb* literature but is also central to Shi'i theology with which 'Abduh was acquainted through Afghani[56] and is an important contribution of Maturidi to these discussions.[57] By adding the element of choice, 'Abduh does not resolve the theological conundrum, he considers to be unresolvable in any case, but adds an element of human agency which the Ash'ari notion of acquisition and its fatalistic interpretation does not entail.

In relation to another theological controversy, 'Abduh equally adopts elements from different schools. In the *Risālat al-Tawḥīd*, he returns to the question of the createdness of the Qur'an as a major site of controversy between the Mu'tazila and Ash'ari schools of theology – a topic he discusses in detail in his first theological commentary. The Mu'tazila maintains that the Qur'an as the Word of God is created (*makhlūq*) in time and not eternal. The Ash'ari school in contrast argues that the Qur'an as the World of God is uncreated (*ghayr makhlūq*) and pre-existent (*qadīm*). In his discussion of the question, 'Abduh appears to endorse the Mu'tazila understanding of the createdness of the Qur'an which stands in clear opposition to the Ash'ari view and Rida found so problematic that he omitted this section from the second edition of the treatise, published after 'Abduh's death.[58] A closer reading of the relevant passage, however, reveals that 'Abduh does not really endorse the Mu'tazila point of view, as some have suggested,[59] but reiterates the argument he already made in his earlier theological commentary on this question.[60] The Word of God in Itself is pre-existent (*qadīm*) but 'there is no disagreement that the heard Word [of God] (*al-kalām al-masmū'*) itself, the articulation of that pre-existent attribute, is contingent (*ḥudūth*) and a creation (*khalq*) of God'.[61] 'Abduh castigates those believing in the eternity of the recited Qur'an (*al-qur'ān al-maqrū'*) as misguided and ridicules in particular Ahmad ibn Hanbal, one of the staunchest defender of the uncreatedness of the Qur'an.[62] However, 'Abduh's reading does not conform to the Mu'tazila position either: he maintains that the Qur'an as the Word of God in Itself is eternal and distinguishes it from the recited Word of God which is created – a position that resembles the approach of the Maturidi school of theology and also of al-Ghazali on that matter.[63]

On other questions, 'Abduh incorporates contemporaneous evolutionary views of history or a utilitarian approach to the formation of societies. This evident in his evolutionary account of salvation history with Judaism, Christianity and Islam representing different stages in the spiritual and intellectual maturation of humanity. Judaism as the religion of humanity's infancy introduced a paternalistic understanding of God and provided 'restrains or constraints'.[64] Christianity emerged as humanity matured appealing to the emotional side of human nature and advocating compassion. Islam, however, as the religion of human maturity engages in a discourse of reason and brings the material and spiritual needs of humans into harmony.[65] Such an evolutionary reading of salvation history appears innovative in an Islamic context[66] but reflects progressive conceptions of the intellectual and spiritual maturation of humanity in esoteric and mystical traditions of Islamic philosophy such as the Shaykhi School in Shia Islam to which Afghani was attracted. This scheme has also been compared with the 'law of the three stages' by the French social philosopher August Comte (1798–1857).[67] For

Comte, the final mature stage of human history is marked by replacing the search for supranatural and theological explanations for phenomena in the world with the use of reason, science and empirical observation. While Comte suggests the ultimate substitution of religion with science at this stage, for 'Abduh, Islam, at least, need not be replaced: it is the religion of reason and science.

Similar apologetic arguments emerge when 'Abduh provides a utilitarian account for the need of prophets and divine guidance – an approach that resonates with Ibn Sina's argument for the necessity of prophethood.[68] Divine messengers and prophets not only teach about the realities of the hereafter which cannot be rationally grasped, they equally play a crucial role in forging social cohesion. Societies form out of the human need to provide subsistence which is easier to achieve in collectives. However, for societies to remain sustainable they need to be based on moral and spiritual principles that move beyond pragmatic notions of cooperation to fulfil the material needs of its members. Genuine connections among human beings, leading to peace and tranquillity, are based on love or affection (*maḥabba*) which creates social bonds as no other force. The socio-political manifestation of love is justice (*'adl*) which is the most central principle on which any society needs to be built[69] and as a concept plays an important role in Islamic political philosophy.[70] While a few people with sufficient intellectual insight realize these pre-conditions for the successful and sustainable formation of a society, the majority does not. For this reason, God sends prophets and messengers as religion is the most powerful force to create social bonds and to preserve 'the order of society'.[71] 'Abduh's emphasis on the need to establish ideational foundations of social cohesion mirrors Ibn Khaldun's understanding of *'aṣabiyya*, this sense of group solidary that creates and sustains socio-political orders. The nexus between love and justice equally reflects Ibn Miskawayh's exposition of how societies create cohesion and what role religion plays in this process.[72]

'Abduh reaches out to a newly educated Muslim elite who is not necessarily convinced of the benefits of Islam in the modern world. By pointing out how religion facilitates the successful functioning of a society and its sustainability and basing his argument on intellectual sources coming from Islam as well as contemporaneous European social thought, he seeks to prove that Islam has not become obsolete in the modern world. 'Abduh's *Risālat al-Tawḥīd* combines different intellectual traditions of Islam with the aim of grounding modern Islamic thought in philosophy: the mystical philosophies of Ibn Sina and al-Ghazali, practical philosophy of Ibn Miskawayh and other authors of *ādāb* literature and the history of philosophy of Ibn Khaldun. While 'Abduh hails Abu al-Hasan al-Ash'ari as developing an important theological middle-position, not many of the creedal points the *Risālat al-Tawḥīd* puts forward are really Ash'ari: many basic theological questions represent the views of Ibn Sina, the Mu'tazila or Maturidi schools of theology while questions of ethics and society are informed by French historians and sociologists and by moral and social philosopher of the Islamic tradition such as Ibn Miskawayh and Ibn Khaldun. Their names do not appear but shape the theological discourse of the treatise more than Abu al-Hasan al-Ash'ari.

Untypical for a theological catechism, 'Abduh's treatise lacks any detailed discussion of eschatology, the reward and punishment that await the believer in the hereafter, the possibility divine forgiveness and the nature of resurrection.[73] 'Abduh makes only a brief reference to these matters in one paragraph and presents them as well-known (*ma'rūf*).[74] 'Abduh intends to introduce a different model of Islamic religiosity that bears the imprint of Islamic philosophy more so than of Ash'ari theology. Muslims should develop a strong faith commitment not out of imitation of their ancestors but accept Islam out of an inner conviction in its inherent rationality and intelligibility. Such a faith commitment is informed by two sources: reason (*'aql*) and revelation (*naql*).[75] Equally, the knowledge acquired by both sources needs to be translated into moral human conduct – not out of fear for eternal punishment in the hereafter. Muslims should translate their beliefs into action as such conduct will lead to happiness for the individual – both in this world and the hereafter – and 'the general welfare'[76] of society.

'Abduh's apologetics

Similar concerns and arguments also mark 'Abduh's apologetic works of that time. He engaged in two debates in the press: one in response to several articles on Islam by the former French foreign minister Gabriel Hanotaux (1853–1944) and the other in response to articles by the Lebanese Christian author Farah Antun (1874–1922), a friend of Rida. Antun and Rida had moved together from Tripoli to Egypt in 1897. When discussing the contents of 'Abduh's apologetics, the discursive parameters of this genre need to be taken into account, as well as their publication in newspapers. Apologetics simplify and polemicize – in the case of 'Abduh to defend Islam against criticisms that were informed by Orientalist and racial stereotypes and articulated the common notion of European cultural superiority that also affected Arab writers like Antun. However, beneath the surface of the more apologetic presentation, 'Abduh articulates similar themes that shape the discourses of his other works.

Hanotaux published two articles in French in *Le Journal* in 1900. In these articles, he argues that Semitic and Aryan peoples possess different conceptions of divinity: Semites emphasize divine transcendence which assumes an inherent gap between humanity and God, encourages a fatalistic submission to God's will and discourages engagement in the world. Islam as a Semitic religion exhibits these features explaining its civilisational inferiority. Christianity, in contrast, managed to overcome its Semitic roots and adopted an Aryan conception of God which emphasizes divine immanence in the world and the close connection between God and humanity. This is articulated in the Christian belief in Jesus Christ being the incarnate son of God. Such an understanding of God becoming human creates an attitude towards the world that is characterized by activism, explaining the superiority of European civilization.[77] Hanotaux's articles were translated and published in Arabic and led to a wider debate in the Egyptian and Arab press in which 'Abduh was just one of many participants.[78] The editor of the Egyptian *al-Ahrām* newspaper also conducted an interview with Hanotaux in the course of the debate to which 'Abduh responded.

'Abduh deconstructs both the racial assumptions and the simplistic connection between theological convictions and civilizational progress. Hanotaux's assumption of a gulf between Semites and Aryans is artificial, as both peoples have interacted and mixed throughout history; in reality, 'there are no differences between Aryans and Semites'.[79] 'Abduh cites examples of Semitic peoples that have been industrious and successful in trade or developed great civilizations such as Jews or ancient Phoenicians.[80] In contrast, Indians today, although being Aryans, are considered to be backward.[81] Islam despite its belief in divine transcendence developed a great civilization in its early days by incorporating 'the sciences of the Persians, Egyptians, Romans and Greeks'.[82] Hence, historical evidence suggests that neither one's race nor one's theology have an impact on civilizational progress. A fatalistic or activist attitude does not depend on whether one believes in divine transcendence or immanence but how one conceptualizes 'the extent of divine knowledge of everything and the completeness of His power over everything contingent'.[83] In these questions, neither Christians nor Muslims have developed uniform responses but a range of different views in their theologies.[84]

The colonial context of these debates is crucial. Hanotaux justified French colonialism to bring civilization to Muslim societies as they need support because of their Semitic nature and recommended the model of French colonial rule in Tunisia where French authority was supplanted on existing political structures. In an interview with the newspaper *al-Ahrām*, Hanotaux points out that European societies only advanced once their states had secularized and political and religious authority was separated: 'And this is what we French want to support in our colonies: that absolute power belongs to the ruling authority while respecting the beliefs of the people who are under our jurisdiction and authority. And this is how we have proceeded in Algeria, Tunisia and other French colonies.'[85] This separation between religion and politics that French colonialism seeks to establish aims to change the parameters of Muslim politics for their own benefit: moving away from 'the necessity of Islamic unity'[86] and from determining political alliances by religious affiliation. European nations, in contrast, offer a model of international relations which are determined by what advances 'their economic and political welfare'[87] and not by religious considerations. The separation of religion and politics will lead to progress and a more pragmatic approach to international relations among Muslims and allow them to appreciate the benefits of French colonialism.

ʿAbduh at that time had adopted a pragmatic attitude towards British colonial rule in Egypt and cooperated with Cromer and the British authorities when he needed their support against the khedive and the conservative religious establishment at al-Azhar. However, in his response to Hanotaux's justification of European imperialism he reverts back to his anti-colonial stance and rejects the suggestion that Muslims should acquiesce to foreign domination.[88] He also makes a more subtle point about the need to secularize political authority which French colonialism seeks to facilitate in the Muslim world by pointing at several misunderstandings. Hanotaux's assertion about the primacy of Islam in Muslim politics is erroneous. Muslims might express solidarity with the Ottoman sultan as last remaining indigenous regional power and holder of the Sunni caliphate, but the religious policies of the Ottoman state reveal a pragmatic stance. Christians are employed in senior positions within the Ottoman state bureaucracy and do not face any discrimination. Hanotaux presents the orientation to *realpolitik* as a particular achievement of modern Europe that disregards religious affiliation. For ʿAbduh, the Ottoman Empire is not different at all, as its alliances with European nations such as Germany illustrate:

> The politics of the Ottoman state with European states is not based on religious politics. It was not religious at all when it was founded and is not until today. In the past, it was a state of conquest and victory, and lately it has become a state of diplomacy (*siyāsa*) and defence. Religion has nothing to do with its interaction with European nations.[89]

According to 'Abduh, a more serious misinterpretation lies in Hanotaux's projection of the particular experience of Christian Europe onto the relationship between religion and state in Islam.[90] It is true, for 'Abduh, that Islam as a religion not only provides guidance on spiritual matters but also brings a law, a social order and political authority. However, this does not mean that spiritual and secular authority are fused. There is no papacy in Islam which exercised immense power over secular rulers in Europe in the Middle Ages. Islamic law bestows 'to the supreme ruler, whether he is caliph or sultan'[91] the right to rule but he does not have any religious mandate: 'The sultan directs (*mudabbir*) the country in domestic politics and defends it in war and in foreign politics.'[92] This mandate of the ruler as outlined here is informed by discussions in Islamic political philosophy. For the Persianate Islamic philosopher Nasir al-Din Tusi, 'such directing (*tadbīr*) is called political leadership (*siyāsat*)'[93] and foundational to the formation of a polity (*tamaddun*). The creation of more complex socio-political forms of human organization occurred first in cities (*mudun* – hence the process is denoted as *tamaddun*) and requires law (*nāmūs*/*qānūn*) and a ruler to function.[94] Based on such conceptualizations in political philosophy, 'Abduh conceives the caliph as 'a civil ruler (*ḥākim madanī*) in every respect'[95] who, like state-appointed religious officiaries such as judges and muftis, only possesses 'civil authority (*sulṭa madaniyya*)'.[96] Their mandate does not extend to matters of belief but solely pertains to those of the state, designated here as civil (*madanī*). 'Abduh's designation of caliphal or sultanic authority as civil denotes neither a secular reading of Islamic modes of governance, as suggested by Haddad,[97] nor the primacy and comprehensive nature of Islamic law, as argued by Rida.[98] His understanding bears the imprint of pre-modern Islamic political philosophy. For society to function and prosper, the ruler needs to enforce the law which consists of both, the legal discretion of the ruler (*qānūn*) and divine law (shari'a). However, neither caliph and sultan nor religious officiaries appointed by them to assist in the implementation of law possess any authority over creedal matters. Hence, requesting a secular separation between political and religious authority in Islam, as it has occurred in European history, is irrelevant to modes of governance and their relation to religion in Islamic history. For 'Abduh, one cannot separate what has never been combined.

The opposition between Islam and Christianity was also central in the apologetic debate between 'Abduh and Farah Antun which resonates with many of the issues touched upon in the debate with Hanotaux. Antun published an article in his own journal *al-Jāmi'a*[99] in 1902 on the lack of tolerance (*tasāmuḥ*) in Islam arguing that it led to hostility towards the scholarship of followers of other religions, religious wars among Muslims and the rejection of philosophy and science. Christians, in contrast, adopted a more tolerant attitude towards philosophy and science which explains its current advancements and civilizational superiority. 'Abduh counters Antun's argument with several historical examples and his own particular reading of early Islamic history. Antun fails to mention 'the philosophers and sages from different religions whom the heart of Islam embraced'.[100] Jews, Christians and Zoroastrians held important government positions in Muslim empires and their scholarly activities were not only tolerated but they were employed by Muslim rulers as scientists, physicians, teachers and translators to disseminate their knowledge.[101] Muslim societies adopted a universal approach to different fields of knowledge which disregarded religious affiliation: 'Islam used to embrace in its heart the stranger and the friend by using the same criterion which is the criterion of respect of scholars for knowledge.'[102]

Antun's second evidence for the lack of tolerance in Islam is the sectarian warfare that its history has witnessed. 'Abduh counters this argument by minimizing the religious nature of these conflicts. The early sectarian conflicts were not caused by creedal differences but by 'political views on the way the community (*umma*) should be ruled. They fought the caliphs not to vindicate their creed but to change the form of government'.[103] The conflict between the Umayyad caliphs and 'Ali and his sons was not a sectarian war but a power struggle between two tribes: the Hashimids to which 'Ali and his descendants belonged and the Umayyads. More recent conflicts between Muslim empires are also 'political wars'.[104] Christianity, in contrast, exhibited a much lower degree of tolerance throughout its history. Sectarian wars between Protestants and Catholics marred European history. The Catholic Church suppressed scientific investigation and persecuted scientists.[105] Jews and Muslims were expelled from Spain after Christians had conquered it.[106] European nations only managed to develop modern civilization not because of Christianity but in spite of it.[107] The intellectual roots of modern European civilization lie in the philosophical and scientific transmission work of Muslims in Spain. Political upheaval such as the French Revolution countered the power of Christian churches, and science only began to flourish once European societies had turned their back on Christianity.[108]

'Abduh's portrayal of Christianity in opposition to Islam is part of the apologetic exchange between him and Antun. As Antun simplifies the nature of Islam in his article, so does 'Abduh reduce both religions to certain immutable features which determine their social, cultural and political role throughout history. 'Abduh distinguishes between the fundamental principles that determine the nature (*ṭabīʿa*) of both religions: Christianity is irrational, intolerant and other-worldly while Islam is presented as rational, tolerant and finds a better balance between human welfare in this life and in the hereafter.[109] His response to Hanotaux was in this regard more nuanced, as it rejected simplistic causal relations between doctrinal beliefs and social and historical realities. 'Abduh's juxtaposition of Christianity and Islam is part of the apologetic rhetoric to suggest to Muslim readers that it is not Islam that has a particular problem with modern science but rather Christianity.[110]

'Abduh also uses apologetics as vehicle to criticizse contemporary Muslim societies and their attitudes towards intellectual investigation and scientific knowledge. In his portrayal of Christianity, 'Abduh projects many of the elements of the cultural and intellectual malaise of Muslim societies: the intolerance of Muslims towards other opinions, their rejection of modern science, their recourse to revelation as sole source of knowledge and their bigotry and fanaticism. 'Abduh reveals more about how he viewed the state of Muslim societies at his time than Christianity and polemicizes against the followers of both religions who think that 'ignorance is the source of piety'.[111] In his apologetic responses to both Hanotaux and Antun, he does not deny the current intellectual and cultural inferiority of Muslims and the need to reform Islam. However, he intends to demonstrate that this inferiority is not due to some inherent theological features of Islam – determined by race or doctrine – but due to the corruption Muslims have undertaken of their religion and to the incompetency of their political leaders. 'Abduh seeks to introduce a different vision of Islam as a religion of reason and tolerance that was once a major civilizational power because of its openness to knowledge, its interaction with different cultures and religions and its tolerance towards followers of other religions and acceptance of internal diversity. Therefore, Muslims today do not need to imitate Europeans, as Hanotaux and Antun suggest, but retrieve those intellectual and cultural values their civilization possessed in the past. These values are universal and based on human reason and fixed laws of history and unfold in the interaction between different civilizations.[112]

For Muslims today, this means rediscovering the capaciousness of Islamic intellectual traditions which included different branches of knowledge and encouraged the concurrent engagement with them. The tolerant co-existence of different Islamic discourses and epistemes was part of traditional institutions of Islamic education which approaches their diversity without fostering intellectual hostility or supremacy to one another. For 'Abduh, Muslims need to embrace the culture of ambiguity that marks their intellectual heritage:

> In a mosque or seminary belonging to a mosque teaching sessions of the jurisprudent, the theologian, the scholar of hadith, the grammarian, the ethicist, the philosopher, the astronomer and the geometrician were conducted. The student moved freely from the jurisprudent to the session of the philosopher and from the session on hadith to the session on ethics. If a debate occurred among them on a particular issue, freedom (*ḥurriyya*) prevailed based on persuasion and compelling argument. The standing of zealotry (*ghulūw*) was diminished in the deliberations and tolerance (*tasāmuḥ*) prevailed among them.[113]

For 'Abduh, this universality and comprehensiveness of Islamic knowledge traditions need to be recuperated, rather than seeing different branches of knowledge in opposition to another. Retrieving and synthesizing different intellectual traditions of Islam to focus on individual and collective moral transformation and civilizational progress reflects themes 'Abduh articulates in his early theological commentary on the *Sharḥ al-'Aqā'id al-'Aḍudiyya* and is also central to his *Risālat al-Tawḥīd*. 'Abduh sought to anchor these objectives in his Qur'an commentaries as well.

'Abduh's Qur'an commentaries

'Abduh sought to move exegetical discourses around the Qur'an out of the scholarly domain by providing accessible interpretations for an educated modern Muslim audience, emphasizing that 'it is necessary for every Muslim to partake in its understanding according to their ability and capacity'.[114] The aim to widen Muslim engagement with the Qur'an is evident in the methods he used to interpret it and the manner in which he disseminated his interpretation in journals. He never produced a complete scholarly commentary but his more systematic engagement with the Qur'anic text occurred during public lectures in Beirut and Cairo which were attended by the wider public, including non-Muslims, and became known as *Tafsīr al-Manār*. His other commentary *Tafsīr Juz' 'Amma* on the last 37 *sūras* of the Qur'an was written for teachers at schools run by his Muslim Benevolent Society in 1903.[115] Although written initially as a teachers' training tool, the commentary was published for a wider readership and, according to Rida, at the time of its publication in 1904 the most prominent and most widely read of 'Abduh's works.[116]

The question of authorship is important in Abduh's Qur'an commentaries. *Tafsīr al-Manār* was published based on notes taken by Rida which ʿAbduh reviewed and approved prior to their publication. His premature death in 1905 meant that ʿAbduh could not complete his lectures on the Qur'an and only reached up to verse 4:125. Rida then completed the exegesis without ʿAbduh. ʿAbduh's death also meant that he was only able to review Rida's notes until the middle of *sūra* 2 which were published during his lifetime (Figure 4). Hence, the commentaries on the latter half of *sūra* 2 and *sūras* 3 and 4 cannot be attributed with absolute certainty to ʿAbduh, as he was not able to ensure that they reflected his ideas. Even those transcripts ʿAbduh was able to review and which were published during his

Figure 4. Muhammad Rashid Rida in Egypt, 1909.

lifetime do not solely contain his own words but are intermixed with Rida's own reflections. In particular from the latter half of the second *sūra* onwards, Rida's interventions dominate the discourse. For this reason, Pink suggests that around 15 per cent of the *Tafsīr al-Manār* can be attributed to 'Abduh while the *Tafsīr Juz' 'Amma* is the only commentary solely authored by him.[117]

'Abduh's *Risālat al-Tawḥīd*, contains a chapter on the Qur'an which presents its inimitability (*i'jāz*) as proof of its divine origin.[118] While this argument reflects standard Islamic doctrines, 'Abduh sees the uniqueness of the Qur'an not only in its literary and rhetorical eloquence (*balāgha*) but also in its argumentative cogency that compels the intellect to believe in its divine origin. In his apologetics with Antun, 'Abduh emphasizes more explicitly – restating a view of the Mu'tazila school –[119] that 'the miracle of the Qur'ān (*mu'jizat al-qur'ān*) lies in its combination of speech and knowledge (*al-qawl wa-l-'ilm*) both of which lead the intellect (*'aql*) to understanding'.[120] Accepting the Qur'an and its recipient Muhammad yielded the civilisational transformation of the Arabs and other peoples that accepted Islam, as these peoples internalized the agenda of moral and intellectual progress expounded by the Qur'an.[121]

'Abduh's exegetical works align with this understanding and seek to make the Qur'anic message accessible and to use hermeneutics as a tool for the socio-moral transformation of Muslim societies. Therefore, he avoids complex linguistic discussions and rejects the use of Judeo-Christian sources (known as *isrā'īliyyāt*)[122] to shed further light on Biblical figures and events that are mentioned in the Qur'an.[123] Comparing and contrasting Qur'anic stories with accounts contained in other books of ancient history is pointless, as 'the Qur'an is not history or stories but guidance and exhortation. It does not mention a story to explain historical events'.[124] His approach to synthesize different Islamic knowledge traditions that characterizes most of 'Abduh's intellectual output is also evident in his approach to Qur'anic exegesis, as he is disinterested in the consistent application of the technical apparatus traditional commentators would use. There is a conspicuous disregard for past authorities and a dearth of references to Prophetic traditions (*aḥādīth*) as sources of interpretation.[125]

Both his *Tafsīr al-Manār* and *Tafsīr Juz' 'Amma* share similar objectives with his other writings: opposing the spirit of blind obedience to scholarly authorities of the past (*taqlīd*), extracting the moral message of the Qur'an and rationalizing it. 'Abduh discusses the polemics of the Qur'an against different groups opposing Muhammad's revelation, such as the Arab polytheists (*mushrikūn*) and the People of the Book (*ahl al-kitāb*, Jews and Christians). 'Abduh, however, uses these polemics to make a general point about *taqlīd*. The deviation of Jews and

Christians was the result of 'the imitation (*taqlīd*) of their forefathers'.[126] Likewise, he defines an unbeliever (*kāfir*) as someone who rejects the clear evidence of truth if it contradicts their own beliefs and clings onto 'the imitation (*taqlīd*) of his ancestors'.[127] Another example 'Abduh uses to attack the spirit of *taqlīd* are the so-called hypocrites (*munāfiqūn*), a Qur'anic term for the opponents of Muhammad in Medina who had accepted Islam but secretly conspired against him. Pretending to be loyal Muslims, they were 'putting forward corruption caused by the evil of blind imitation (*taqlīd*) which is not able to distinguish between what is righteous and what is corrupt'.[128] 'Abduh makes it very clear that the mind-set of the hypocrites was not restricted to their time, but 'the verses describe a group of people that exists in every community'.[129] When discussing the refusal of these various groups to embrace Islam, 'Abduh presents their adherence to past authorities as the main reason and equates their ritualistic and formalistic approach to their religion with the manner in which his contemporaries practise Islam.[130] As 'imitators who do not use their intellects (*'uqūl*)' they prefer inherited 'traditions and customs (*al-taqālīd wa-l-'ādāt*)'[131] over divine commandments.

This slavish adherence to the past is contrasted by 'Abduh to an intellectual engagement with Islam that uses independent reasoning (*ijtihād*). Similar to his other works, 'Abduh maintains that, via their rational faculty, humans possess the innate ability to distinguish between right and wrong. This ability precedes revelation[132] and is the result of innate human disposition (*al-fiṭra al-insāniyya*)[133] or innate intuition (*al-wijdān al-fiṭrī*).[134] In discussing the Qur'anic term 'those who are pious (*al-muttaqūn*)',[135] 'Abduh interprets it as a reference to those Arabs before the rise of Islam who rejected polytheism and developed a monotheistic conviction by the use of reason (*'aql*)[136] alone and possessed 'an intuitive knowledge of the creator (*wijdān ma'rifat al-khāliq*)'.[137] 'Abduh's commentary conceives humans as rational beings who are encouraged to use their intellect to understand and interpret their religion, as the Qur'an itself emphasizes the rational intelligibility of its theological and moral teachings.

The term 'Abduh employs here to denote the innate ability of humans to acquire knowledge of the truth and to make moral judgements is *fiṭra*, usually translated as nature or innate disposition. 'Abduh's use of the term *fiṭra* reflects his earlier exposure to the discussion of the concept within Islamic philosophy.[138] Ibn Sina considered *fiṭra* as an innate epistemic disposition rather than innate knowledge humans possess. *Fiṭra* allows humans to understand certain general premises, to make judgements on certain issues, based on these premises, observations and estimations, and to use these to develop arguments. For Ibn Sina, *fiṭra* denotes the *modus operandi* of the intellect[139] whose judgements need not be correct.[140] Equally, *fiṭra* does not include the ability to undertake right moral judgements.[141] Developing the idea of *fiṭra* further, al-Ghazali does not approach *fiṭra* 'as an innate repository of knowledge but as the human disposition toward truth and the capacity to arrive at it'.[142] Equally, he considers monotheism to be part of the human innate disposition and in this sense, ingrained in the human soul naturally.[143] In line with Sunni-Ash'ari theology, al-Ghazali rejects the notion that *fiṭra* can determine morality whose sole source for him is the shari'a.[144] Early Muslim philosopher al-Farabi (872–950), on the other hand, adduces an ethical dimensions to *fiṭra* by suggesting an innate human disposition towards morality which instigates the human realization and acquisition of virtues.[145]

'Abduh does not really define *fiṭra* but his framing of the concept and its use suggests a conflation of these different philosophical approaches additionally informed by the view of the Mu'tazila school of theology.[146] Such views equally reflect nineteenth-century European discourses on 'natural religion' as an 'anthropological constant'.[147] Similar to Ibn Sina, he comprehends it as the manner in which the intellect operates while being closer to al-Ghazali and al-Farabi in the understanding that in its intellectual operation it is naturally disposed towards realizing the unity of God and arriving at right moral judgements. 'Abduh suggests that by bestowing humans with this innate disposition, God inspires knowledge to humans leading them to truth and morality.[148] At the same time, following Ibn Sina, 'Abduh also includes an empirical element: human innate disposition includes the ability to measure the moral values of certain actions by observing their consequences. By assessing actions through their impact, God facilitates the human process of arriving at correct moral judgements.[149]

'Abduh's commentary covers *sūras* that contain references to the signs announcing the Day of Judgement and descriptions of the hereafter – in particular in his *Tafsīr Juz' 'Amma* that includes the earliest revelations during Muhammad's Meccan period.[150] 'Abduh adheres to the literal meaning of these eschatological descriptions and does not explain them away by adopting an allegorical approach. The opening of the sky, the eclipse of the sun, the falling of the stars, the setting in motion of mountains and the resurrection of the bodies are understood as literal occurrences, based on 'Abduh's premise that 'we believe in what God, the Exalted, tells us about it. Neither do we add or take anything away nor do we research about its particulars'.[151] In a similar vein, it is necessary to believe in the reality of hellfire as punishment for the unbelievers and sinners[152] and the promise that the believers will be joined by 'pure spouses'[153] in paradise. 'Abduh, however, emphasizes the difference between this life and the hereafter pointing out that 'the joy of spousal companionship will be loftier there'.[154]

'Abduh's approach to Qur'anic depictions of the Day of Judgement and the hereafter accepts its literal meaning and suggests a suspension of disbelief: these descriptions should be accepted at face-value without any further investigation – an attitude that resembles the Ash'ari position of 'not asking how' (*bi-lā-kayfa*) of certain theological questions. In his *Risālat al-Tawḥīd*, 'Abduh exhibits reluctance to discuss Islamic eschatology and just devotes one paragraph to it. In his earlier theological commentary, he defends the philosophers' understanding of resurrection as not being physical. In his Qur'an commentary, he oscillates between two positions and thereby adopts an approach similar to the Sufi philosopher Ibn 'Arabi[155]: 'Abduh demands faithful adherence to its literal meaning in the Qur'an. At the same time, he stresses – in a vein similar to mystical philosophy – the complete otherness of the hereafter and seeks to steer the attention away from its sensorial descriptions as a place that is spiritual (*rūḥānī*).[156] The moral message behind these verses that outline in detail the punishment or reward that humans await on the Day of Judgement is more important. They intend to communicate the ultimate purpose of religion which is to promote justice (*'adl*), truthfulness (*ṣidq*), good actions (*'amal khayr*) and general welfare (*maṣaliḥ 'āmma*).[157]

'Abduh exhibits an ambivalent attitude to the scientific exegesis of the Qur'an (*tafsīr 'ilmī*) which suggests various ways how the Qur'an anticipates or conforms to the discoveries of modern science. There are a few examples in his commentaries where 'Abduh draws analogies between supernatural beings or events and phenomena discovered by modern science. For instance, he suggests that microbes are a type of jinn.[158] Qur'anic descriptions of the signs of the Day of Judgement are equally related to scientific evidence. That 'the seas boil over'[159] is equated with earthquakes and volcanos showing that tectonic shifts push hot magma from beneath the ground to the surface of the earth and could heat up the seas on the Day of Judgement.[160] However, 'Abduh appears sceptical of a scientific exegesis of the Qur'an, since he emphasizes that the prophets are not meant to be experts and teachers in history and sciences.[161] His observations of possible analogies are often qualified. He uses his equation of jinn with microbes as an opportunity to emphasize the need to follow the insights of medical experts[162] and to criticize efforts to understand the nature of jinn in more detail.[163] Rather than suggesting that the Qur'an is in conformity with modern science, he attempts to make some Qur'anic tropes plausible by proposing their similarities with modern scientific discoveries.

A similar approach becomes evident when 'Abduh discusses the meaning of miracles and magic. For 'Abduh, the belief in miracles as such is not irrational. It is possible that God suspends the laws of nature to cause a miraculous occurrence, although it is not a doctrinal requirement to believe in the miracles (*karamāt*) attributed to Sufi saints.[164] He confirms the miracles performed by other prophets[165] but presents the miracle of Muhammad's prophecy as being of a superior nature: the Qur'an itself and its rhetorical and argumentative perfection provide clear evidence for the truth of his mission which is, in this sense, not really a suspension of natural law. As miracles can occur, so does 'Abduh not deny the reality of magic (*siḥr*). He does not explain away the Qur'anic references to magical practices among the Arabs before the rise of Islam but emphasizes that the Qur'an must not be used to suggest a divine sanction of magic.[166] 'Abduh opens up possibilities for alternative readings of Qur'anic references to magic at the same time: 'The evil of those who blow knots'[167] – a reference to sorcerers who used knots to cast spells on people – might describe how insincerity and viciousness can destroy the bond of friendship and other human relations.[168]

'Abduh's approach to rationalize passages and concepts that seem to contradict a modern scientific worldview is multifaceted and ambiguous. While he relates some Qur'anic passages to discoveries in modern science, he neither endorses fully a scientific exegesis of the Qur'an nor employs allegorical interpretations consistently to explain away issues and statements potentially contradictory to modern science. In interpreting supernatural descriptions as they are meant to occur on the Day of Judgement, he attempts to adhere to the literal meaning of the Qur'an as much as possible and to keep its understanding simple and argues against further specification as distracting from the moral message of the Qur'an. Equally, 'Abduh alludes to certain pathways for an allegorical interpretation of such passages while maintaining the validity of their literal meaning. Pre-modern traditions of Qur'anic exegesis conceived the Qur'an as a deliberately ambiguous and open to a variety of interpretations.[169] 'Abduh does not attempt to resolve these ambiguities and postulates a certain intellectual relativism: both a literal and an allegorical interpretation of eschatological Qur'anic verses are equally true. Such an attitude aligns with exegetical approaches in mystical philosophy which assumes that the Qur'anic text as divine scripture possesses multiple layers of meaning. 'Abduh's approach is also shaped by intellectual caution: he does not deny the validity of the verses' literal meaning to avoid being accused of undermining the scriptural authority of the Qur'an while equally suggesting interpretative approaches that prioritize the moral message of the Qur'an and appear more modern.

'Abduh's approach to Qur'anic exegesis is defined by one central objective: to extract the intellectual and moral universe from the Qur'an and to use the text as a means to arrive at a rationally founded and defensible religious and moral worldview. In his constant rejection of *taqlīd* and his emphasis on the faculties that human innate disposition (*fiṭra*) provides, 'Abduh emphasizes the intellectual and moral autonomy of humans which is always threatened by social and cultural forces that pressurize individuals into conformity and cloud their rational and moral judgement. In his understanding of *fiṭra*, 'Abduh does not follow a clear definition but combines approaches to its understanding from different Islamic philosophers and theologians. Overcoming the ethos of *taqlīd* includes for 'Abduh not to articulate his allegiance to a particular school of thought and also to combine their approaches creatively. He intends to encourage critical reflection of the Qur'an rather than blindly adhering to traditional interpretations and religious conventions. As 'Abduh argues, *taqlīd* prevents Muslims from becoming sincere believers and – as the example of Arab polytheists and the People of the Book suggests – leads to disbelief (*kufr*). True and sincere faith is built, however, on 'sound evidence derived from innate intuition (*al-dalīl al-ṣaḥīḥ al-mustamad min al-wijdān al-fiṭrī*)'.[170] Such a plea for overcoming *taqlīd* in understanding Islam and its foundational text suggests the need for a constant re-interpretation via *ijtihād* to retrieve the core theological and moral message of the Qur'an. With a concern for 'the general meaning'[171] of the Qur'anic text, 'Abduh's approach facilitates separating the particular from the universal, ethicizing the Qur'anic text by distracting universal values out of its comprehensive message and approaching the Qur'an as a holistic document that purports a coherent and intelligible doctrinal and moral worldview. This method would significantly influence literary and contextual exegetical approaches in the twentieth century.[172]

Conclusion

'Abduh's intellectual output in the final stage of his life shows that a label like Salafi does not sufficiently encompass the various intellectual traditions he synthesizes in his writings and he engaged with throughout his life. The Salafi label does not do justice to his approach even if 'modernist' is attached to it. Designating 'Abduh as an Islamic modernist is equally problematic as it suggests an attempt to transplant modern ideas into a novel reconstruction of an Islamic essence. His earliest journalistic articles, his anti-colonial agitation and his apologetic works appeal to the civilizational strength of Islam in the past which is not based on the role-model of a golden age or the actualization of an immutable Islamic essence but resulted from the capaciousness of its intellectual traditions. Muslim societies do not need to emulate a model of modernity as imposed on them by European colonialism. Islamic knowledge traditions provide sufficient intellectual resources for an indigenous engagement with modernity which does not reduce its diversity to minimalist essential features.

Despite 'Abduh's combination of a variety of sources which at times appear random and inconsistent, certain themes that were informed by Islamic philosophical traditions and had been central to his thought before his return to Egypt remain constant. He emphasizes the social and moral progress that Islam seeks to achieve as a civilizational force. The laws of history explain the factors that lead to the rise and decline of communities. Unity and social cohesion remain the main sources of strength combined with competent political leadership and intellectual freedom. While he sees the need to articulate these ideas in the idiom of Sunni notions of orthodoxy in his later writings, he equally wants to ensure that humans use their rational faculties to explore the laws of history and nature and adopt methods of scientific investigation for that matter.

A key theme is his critique of the intellectual stagnation of the contemporary Muslim world, caused by the slavish adherence to scholarly authorities of the past (*taqlīd*). 'Abduh's own ideas are certainly influenced by previous scholars but he combines their contributions in a creative synthesis that converses with modern European historical and social theories, in particular nineteenth-century notion of the evolutionary progression of societies. The opposite of *taqlīd* is the notion of *ijtihād*, independent reasoning – an opposition which receives a particular reading by 'Abduh. Traditionally *ijtihād* denotes the personal effort of a religious scholar to arrive at a legal ruling using the primary sources as well as the whole repertoire of jurisprudential scholarship. *Taqlīd* refers to the adherence of a scholar to the scholarship of their own legal school (*madhhab*). 'Abduh however provides these terms with a new meaning. The *mujtahid*, the scholar practising *ijtihād*, is identified with a new model of Islamic intellectual leadership: the *mujtahid* re-interprets the primary sources in the light of current problems and circumstances and historicizes the accumulated scholarly knowledge.[173] The *muqallid*, in contrast, meticulously preserves the medieval scholarly heritage and is presented as a traditionalist out of touch with the modern world.[174] 'Abduh – steeped in Islam's culture of ambiguity – does not always adhere to this idealized dichotomy between *ijtihād* and *taqlīd*. As grand mufti of Egypt he had to ensure that his official fatwas followed the jurisprudence of the Hanafi school of law. He was equally conscious that a hostile religious and political environment required him to couch his re-assertion of rationalist traditions of Islam in the idiom of Sunni orthodoxy. Such an orthodox cladding of Islamic philosophical traditions yields ambiguity and potentially delimits the innovative potential of his call for *ijtihād*, as the subsequent reception history of his ideas illustrates.

'Abduh also contrasts *taqlīd* to *fiṭra*, the innate human disposition to arrive at true theological and ethical insights which has been clouded by social conventions and scholarly traditions. 'Abduh adopts the well-known designation, put forward by the Hanbali scholar Ibn Taymiyya that Islam is the religion of innate disposition or the religion of nature (*dīn al-fiṭra*).[175] However, unlike Ibn Taymiyya, 'Abduh does not understand this term in the sense that every human being is naturally born Muslim and then taken away from their original disposition by the corrupting religious education of their parents and society. For 'Abduh, Islam is *dīn al-fiṭra*, as its basic doctrinal and ethical principles can be attained by the use of reason. A proper use of the human intellect (*'aql*) will lead to a realization of divine truths.[176] However, blind imitation disables this innate disposition and inhibits human reason to achieve its full intellectual potential. In his Qur'an commentary, 'Abduh refers to a group of people who were known as *hanīf* in the pre-Islamic period of *jāhiliyya*. They had abandoned imitating the polytheistic practices of their society and, of their own accord, began to believe in and worship one God:

> They are those whose innate disposition was sound (*salamat fiṭratuhum*). Their intellects (*'uqūl*) acquired some sort of right understanding and some capacity (*isti'dād*) was present in their souls to reach the light of truth that leads them to avoid the displeasure of God, the Exalted, and to seek His pleasure. This is due to what their knowledge (*'ilmuhum*) gave them and what their contemplation (*naẓaruhum*) and independent reasoning (*ijtihāduhum*) brought them.[177]

These individuals who turned towards monotheism by their own effort and without following a revealed religion were capable of doing so because they overcame the mindset of *taqlīd* and did not blindly imitate the customs, traditions, beliefs and practices of their ancestors and societies but kept their innate disposition intact to arrive at the realization that there can only be one God. 'Abduh's reform was to retrieve this original disposition among his Muslim contemporaries to arrive at an understanding of Islam in tune with the modern world.

'Abduh's reformist oeuvre does not suggest a resolution of theological, sectarian and jurisprudential controversies of the past nor does it seek to reconcile Islam with modernity by translating modern ideas into an Islamic idiom. Rather he undertakes a selective synthesis of diverse intellectual traditions of Islam whose tensions he does not resolve. Equally, he does not disambiguate the ambivalences created by aligning certain concepts with modern intellectual paradigms. His anti-colonial intellectual outlook is visible, for example, in rejecting calls by European intellectuals and their Muslim emulators to secularize Islamic modes of governance in order to achieve progress and freedom. For ʿAbduh, such an assumption imposes the European historical experience on Muslims and reveals a lack of understanding of the relationship between political and religious authority in Islamic history which Islamic political philosophy and jurisprudence has more adequately theorized. For ʿAbduh, positioning Islam intellectually, culturally and politically in the modern world is not achieved by emulating European societies and their values completely or vindicating a particular school of thought in Islam as constituting orthodoxy. ʿAbduh suggests adopting an irenic attitude towards the diversity of Islamic thought and fully utilizing it in its plurality to provide the most suitable and pragmatic answers to the challenges Muslim face in the modern world. His theological commentary on the *Sharḥ al-ʿAqāʾid al-ʿAḍudiyya* seeks to nurture such an outlook by arguing that all sects of Islam are saved because their fundamental commonalities outweigh their differences. Such an approach can be characterized as eclectic, inconsistent and contradictory but is informed by the intellectual culture of ambiguity that shaped the pre-modern Muslim world and ʿAbduh employs in his own effort to reform Islam. His legacy is characterized by a certain incompleteness as a consequence. He did not want to and could not address all ambiguities. His plans to establish a new educational institution in Egypt that combines Islamic with modern knowledge never materialized. His Qurʾan commentary remains incomplete, as his premature death in 1905 prevented pursuing these and other projects further.

Notes

1 Muhammad Rashid Rida, *Taʾrīkh al-Ustādh al-Imām al-Shaykh Muḥammad ʿAbduh*, vol. 1 (Cairo: al-Manar, 1931), 11; Albert Hourani, *Arabic Thought in the Liberal Age: 1798–1939* (Cambridge: Cambridge University Press, 1983), 140–1.

2 Jamal al-Din al-Afghani and Muhammad ʿAbduh, *al-ʿUrwa al-Wuthqā wa-l-Thawra al-Taḥrīriyya al-Kubrā*, 2nd edn (Cairo: Dar al-ʿArab, 1958), 56, 131, 133.

3 Muhammad ʿAbduh, ʿal-Radd ʿalā Hānūtūʾ, in *al-Aʿmāl al-Kāmila li-l-Imām Muḥammad ʿAbduh*, ed. Muhammad ʿImara, vol. 3 (Beirut: Dar al-Shuruq, 1993), 226.

4 Muhammad 'Abduh, *Risālat al-Tawḥīd*, 17th edn (Cairo: Yousif Sulayman, 1960), 15.
5 Henri Lauzière, *The Making of Salafism: Islamic Reform in the Twentieth Century* (New York: Columbia University Press, 2016), 5, 36.
6 Ibid., 4.
7 Ibid., 4–5.
8 'The best generation is my generation, then those who come after them, then those who come after them.'
9 Mohamed Haddad, *Muḥammad 'Abduh: Qarā'a Jadīda fī Khiṭāb al-Iṣlāḥ al-Dīnī* (Beirut: Dar al-Tali'a li-l-Taba'a wa-l-Nashr, 2003), 84.
10 'Abduh, *Tawḥīd*, 16.
11 Muhammad 'Abduh, 'al-Radd 'alā Faraḥ Anṭūn', in *al-A'māl al-Kāmila li-l-Imām Muḥammad 'Abduh*, ed. Muhammad 'Imara, vol. 3 (Beirut: Dar al-Shuruq, 1993), 267; Muhammad 'Abduh, 'Nafī al-Qitāl bayna-l-Muslimīn li-Ajall al-I'tiqād', *al-Manār*, 5 (1902): 405.
12 'Abduh, *Tawḥīd*, 18–19; Ibn Khaldun, *Muqaddimat ibn Khaldūn*, vol. 2 (Damascus: Dar Ya'rib, 2003), 212.
13 'Abduh, *Tawḥīd*, 19, n. 2.
14 'Abduh, 'Radd 'alā Anṭūn', vol. 3, 359.
15 'Abduh Muhammad, 'al-Qiḍā' wa-l-Qadar', in *al-'Urwa al-Wuthqā wa-l-Thawra al-Taḥrīriyya al-Kubrā*, Jamal al-Din al-Afghani and Muhammad 'Abduh (Cairo: Dar al-'Arab, 1958), 56.
16 'Abduh, 'Radd 'alā Anṭūn', vol. 3, 359; Hourani, *Arabic Thought*, 149.
17 Ibn Khaldun, *Muqaddima*, vol. 2, 212–14.
18 Ovamir Anjum, *Politics, Law, and Community in Islamic Thought: The Taymiyyan Moment* (Cambridge: Cambridge University Press, 2012), 148–9. 'Abduh adopts al-Razi's preference for allegorical interpretations in case of a contradiction between reason and revelation. See 'Abduh, 'Radd 'alā Anṭūn', vol. 3, 301.
19 'Abduh, *Tawḥīd*, 22.
20 Ibid., 4.
21 Haddad, *Qarā'a Jadīda*, 73–4.
22 Jacques Jomier, *Le Commentaire Coranique du Manâr: tendances modernes de l'exégèse en Egypte* (Paris: Maisonneuve, 1954), 50–1.
23 Rida, *Ta'rīkh*, vol. 1, 768–9.
24 Yvonne Y. Haddad, 'Muhammad Abduh: Pioneer of Islamic Reform', in *Pioneers of Islamic Revival*, ed. Ali Rahnema, 2nd edn (London: Zed Books, [1994] 2005), 46.
25 Rotraud Wielandt, 'Main Trends of Islamic Theological Thought from the Late Nineteenth Century to Present Times', in *The Oxford Handbook of Islamic Theology*, ed. Sabine Schmidtke (Oxford: Oxford University Press, 2016), 718.

26 Thomas Bauer, *Die Kultur der Ambiguität: Eine andere Geschichte des Islams* (Berlin: Verlag der Weltreligionen, 2011), 192–223; Shahab Ahmed, *What Is Islam?: The Importance of Being Islamic* (Princeton: Princeton University Press, 2016), 10–31.
27 Wielandt, 'Main Trends of Islamic Theological Thought', 719.
28 Johann Buessow, 'Re-imagining Islam in the Period of the First Modern Globalization: Muhammad 'Abduh and His *Theology of Unity*', in *A Global Middle East: Mobility, Materiality and Culture in the Modern Age, 1880–1940*, ed. Liat Kozma, Cyrus Schayegh and Avner Wishnitzer (London: I.B. Tauris, 2015), 284.
29 Haddad, *Qarā'a Jadīda*, 82–3.
30 Sa'd al-Din al-Taftazani, *Tahdhīb al-Manṭiq wa-l-Kalām* (Cairo: Matba'at al-Sa'ada, 1912), 7–35, 77–104; Ibn Khaldun, *Muqaddima*, vol. 2, 205–7.
31 'Abduh, *Tawḥīd*, 20.
32 'Abduh's account of the conflation of both mirrors Ibn Khaldun's description. Compare 'Abduh, *Tawḥīd*, 19–20, with Ibn Khaldun, *Muqaddima*, vol. 2, 213.
33 'Abduh, *Tawḥīd*, 23.
34 Ibid., 119, 129–30, 200.
35 Ibid., 140.
36 Franz Rosenthal, *Knowledge Triumphant: The Concept of Knowledge in Medieval Islam* (Leiden: Brill, 2007), 248.
37 Ibn Miskawayh, *al-Sa'āda li-bn Miskawayh fī Falsafat al-Akhlāq* (Cairo: al-Matba'a al-'Arabiyya, 1928). On similar discussion on what constitutes happiness, see Ibn Miskawayh, *Tahdhīb al-Akhlāq* (Cairo: Matba'at al-Taraqqi, 1318 H [1900/1901]), 65–6.
38 al-Ghazali, *Mizān al-'Amal* (Cairo: Dar al-Ma'arif, 1964), 193–7. See also his Persian work focussing on the philosophical and spiritual means to achieve happiness, al-Ghazali, *Kīmīyā-yi Sa'ādat*, 2 vols (Tehran: Intisharat-i 'Ilmi wa-Farhangi, 1380 SH [2001/2002]). On how 'Abduh's discourse is shaped by al-Ghazali, see Samira Haj, *Reconfiguring Islamic Tradition: Reform, Rationalist, and Modernity* (Stanford: Stanford University Press, 2009), 110–12.
39 Ibn Miskawayh, *Tahdhīb al-Akhlāq*, 32–3; Majid F. Fakhry, 'Ethics in Islamic Philosophy', in *Routledge Encyclopedia of Philosophy*, ed. Edward Craig (London: Routledge, 1998).
40 'Abduh, *Tawḥīd*, 109.
41 Muhammad 'Imara, 'al-Muqaddima', in *al-Ta'līqāt 'alā Sharḥ al-'Aqā'id al-'Aḍudiyya*, Jamal al-Din al-Afghani and Muhammad 'Abduh (Cairo: Maktabat al-Shuruq al-Duwwaliyya, 2002), 16.
42 'Abduh, *Tawḥīd*, 111.
43 Ibid., 112; R. Caspar, 'Le Renouveau mo'tazilite', *Mélanges d'Institut Dominicain d'Etudes Orientales du Caire*, 4 (1957): 169–70.
44 'Abduh, *Tawḥīd*, 109.

45 Ibid., 115.
46 On the understanding of *'ālam al-mithāl* in mystical philosophy, see Fazlur Rahman, 'Dream, Imagination and *'ālam al-mit͟hāl*', *Islamic Studies*, 3(2) (1964): 167–80.
47 Caspar, 'Le Renouveau mo'tazilite', 157–69.
48 'Abduh, *Tawḥīd*, 67–75; al-Afghani and 'Abduh, *al-Ta'līqāt*, 476.
49 Hourani, *Arabic Thought*, 142.
50 Thomas Hildebrandt, 'Waren Ǧamāl ad-Dīn al-Afghānī und Muḥammad 'Abduh Neo-Mu'taziliten?', *Die Welt des Islams*, 42(2) (2002): 207–62.
51 Hourani, *Arabic Thought*, 142.
52 Haddad, *Qarā'a Jadīda*, 105–6.
53 'Abduh, *Tawḥīd*, 62.
54 Ibid., 62–3. See also detailed discussion in 'Abduh, 'al-Qiḍā' wa-l-Qadar', 49–58.
55 'Abduh, *Tawḥīd*, 65 [emphasis added].
56 Vincent J. Cornell, 'Muḥammad 'Abduh: A Sufi-Inspired Modernist?', in *Tradition and Modernity: Christian and Muslim Perspectives*, ed. David Marshall (Washington, DC: Georgetown University Press, 2009), 110
57 Meric J. Pessagno, 'Irāda, Ikhtiyār, Qudra, Kasb: The View of Abū Manṣur al-Māturīdī', *Journal of the American Oriental Society*, 104(1) (1984): 177–91; Ulrich Rudolph, *Al-Māturīdī and die sunnitische Theologie in Samarkand* (Leiden: Brill, 1997), 340. For the Maturidi roots of 'Abduh's understanding, see Ulrich, *Al-Māturīdī*, 340, note 360; Wielandt, 'Main Trends of Islamic Theological Thought', 723–4.
58 Mohamed Haddad, 'Les Oeuvres de 'Abduh: histoire d'une manipulation', *Revue de l'Institut des Belles Lettres Arabes*, 180 (1997): 197–222.
59 Caspar, 'Le Renouveau mo'tazilite', 157–69.
60 al-Afghani and 'Abduh, *al-Ta'līqāt*, 490–2.
61 Muhammad 'Abduh, 'Risālat al-Tawḥīd', in *al-A'māl al-Kāmila li-l-Imām Muḥammad 'Abduh*, ed. Muhammad 'Imara, vol. 3 (Beirut: Dar al-Shuruq, 1993), 393. Volume 3 of 'Imara's collected works by 'Abduh contains the first edition of the *Risālat al-Tawḥīd.*
62 Ibid., 394.
63 Ahmad S. Dallal, 'Review: Ghazali and the Perils of Interpretation', *Journal of the American Oriental Society*, 122(4) (2002): 780.
64 'Abduh, *Tawḥīd*, 167.
65 Ibid., 168–71.
66 Wielandt, 'Main Trends of Islamic Theological Thought', 721.
67 Buessow, 'Re-imagining Islam', 287; Hourani, *Arabic Thought*, 138.
68 Frank Griffel, 'Al-Ġazālī's Concept of Prophecy: The Introduction of Avicennan Psychology into Aš'arite Theology', *Arabic Sciences and Philosophy*, 14 (2004): 110.
69 'Abduh, *Tawḥīd*, 99–103.

70 Ahmed, *What Is Islam?*, 478–81.
71 ʿAbduh, *Tawḥīd*, 107.
72 Ibn Miskawayh, *Tahdhīb al-Akhlāq*, 109–16.
73 Taftazani, *Tahdhīb al-Manṭiq*, 107–13.
74 ʿAbduh, *Tawḥīd*, 202.
75 Ibid., 24.
76 Ibid., 157; Haddad, *Qarāʾa Jadīda*, 128–9.
77 Gabriel Hanotaux, 'L'islam', *Le Journal*, 9(2730) (1900): 1; Gabriel Hanotaux, 'L'islam. II', *Le Journal*, 9(2737) (1900): 1; Ammeke Kateman, *Muḥammad ʿAbduh and His Interlocutors: Conceptualizing Religion in a Globalizing World* (Leiden: Brill, 2019), 167–8.
78 Kateman, *ʿAbduh and His Interlocutors*, 168–73.
79 ʿAbduh, 'Radd ʿalā Hānūtū', vol. 3, 223.
80 Ibid., 223, 226.
81 Ibid., 221.
82 Ibid.
83 Ibid., 225.
84 Ibid., 226.
85 'Ḥadīth maʿa Hānūtū li-Ṣāḥib Jarīdat al-Ahrām', in *al-Islām bayna-l-ʿIlm wa-l-Madaniyya*, M. ʿAbduh (Damascus: Dar al-Sida li-l-Thaqafa wa-l-Nashr, 2002), 36.
86 Ibid., 39.
87 Ibid.
88 ʿAbduh, 'Radd ʿalā Hānūtū', vol. 3, 238.
89 Ibid., 254.
90 Ibid., 308–9; Haj, *Reconfiguring Islamic Tradition*, 92–6.
91 ʿAbduh, 'Radd ʿalā Hānūtū', vol. 3, 250.
92 Ibid.
93 Nasir al-Din Tusi, *Akhlāq-i Nāṣirī* (Tehran: Khwarizmi, 1356 SH [1977/1978]), 252.
94 Ahmed, *What Is Islam?*, 462–8.
95 ʿAbduh, 'Radd ʿalā Anṭūn', vol. 3, 308.
96 Ibid., 309; Haj, *Reconfiguring Islamic Tradition*, 96–7.
97 Haddad, *Qarāʾa Jadīda*, 22–3.
98 Muhammad Rashid Rida, *al-Khilāfa* [*aw al-Imāma al-ʿUẓmā*] (Cairo: Hindawi [1922] 2015), 68, 87–99; Andrew F. March, *The Caliphate of Man: Popular Sovereignty in Modern Islamic Thought* (Cambridge, MA: Harvard University Press, 2019), 53–7.
99 *Al-Jāmiʿa* was a journal published by the Syrian Christian Farah Antun to familiarize the Egyptian reading public with French Enlightenment thought. See Donald M. Reid, 'Farah Antun: The Life and Times of a Syrian Christian Journalist in Egypt' (PhD diss., Princeton, 1969), 99–126.

100 'Abduh, 'Radd 'alā Anṭūn', vol. 3, 275.
101 Ibid., 273–5.
102 Ibid., 275–6.
103 Ibid., 267.
104 Ibid.
105 Ibid., 285.
106 Ibid., 289–90.
107 Haj, *Reconfiguring Islamic Tradition*, 97.
108 'Abduh, 'Radd 'alā Anṭūn', vol. 3, 354–6.
109 Ibid., 276–315.
110 Ayyub, M., 'Islam and Christianity: A Study of Muhammad Abduh's View of the Two Religions', *Humaniora Islamica*, 2 (1974): 121–37.
111 Abduh, 'Radd 'alā Anṭūn', vol. 3, 284.
112 Ibid., 250.
113 Ibid., 328.
114 Muhammad 'Abduh, *Tafsīr al-Fātiḥa* (Cairo: Isma'il Hafiz, 1901), 5; J. J. G. Jansen, *The Interpretation of the Koran in Modern Egypt* (Leiden: Brill, 1974), 18–19.
115 Muhammad 'Abduh, *Tafsīr Juz' 'Amma*, 3rd edn (Cairo: Matba'at Misr, 1341H [1922–3]), 2.
116 Rida, *Ta'rīkh*, vol. 1, 788.
117 Johanna Pink, "Abduh, Muḥammad', in *Encyclopedia of the Qur'ān*, ed. Jane Dammen McAuliffe (Leiden: Brill, 2001); Jomier, *Commentaire coranique*, 50–1. Naguib disagrees and argues that the volumes published during 'Abduh's lifetime reflect his ideas despite Rida's significant editorial role. See Shuruq Naguib, 'The Hermeneutics of Miracle: Evolution, Eloquence, and the Critique of Scientific Exegesis in the Literary School of *tafsīr*. Part I: From Muḥammad 'Abduh to Amīn al-Khūlī', *Journal of Qur'ānic Studies*, 21(3) (2019): 62.
118 'Abduh, *Tawḥīd*, 146–7.
119 Nasr Hamid Abu Zayd, 'The Dilemma of the Literary Approach to the Qur'an', *Alif: Journal of Comparative Poetics*, 23 (2003): 10–18.
120 'Abduh, 'Radd 'alā Anṭūn', vol. 3, 299; Naguib, 'Hermeneutics of Miracle', 63–4.
121 'Abduh, *Tawḥīd*, 134–5.
122 On *isrā'īliyyāt*, see Roberto Tottoli, 'Origin and Use of the Term *Isrā'īliyyāt* in Muslim Literature', *Arabica*, vol. 46 (1999): 193–210.
123 Muhammad 'Abduh and Muhammad Rashid Rida, *Tafsīr al-Qur'ān al-Ḥakīm al-Mushtahīr bi-sm Tafsīr al-Manār*, 2nd edn, vol. 1 (Cairo: al-Manar, 1947), 174; Jomier, *Commentaire coranique*, 112; Jansen, *Interpretation of the Koran*, 27.
124 Muhammad 'Abduh and Muhammad Rashid Rida, *Tafsīr al-Qur'ān al-Ḥakīm al-Mushtahīr bi-sm Tafsīr al-Manār*, 2nd edn, vol. 2 (Cairo: al-Manar, 1947), 471; Abu Zayd, 'Literary Approach to the Qur'an', 19–20.

125 Jomier, *Commentaire coranique*, 59, 62.
126 'Abduh, *Tafsīr Juz' 'Amma*, 133.
127 Ibid., 169, 136–7; 'Abduh and Rida, *Tafsīr al-Manār*, vol. 1, 430; Hourani, *Arabic Thought*, 148.
128 'Abduh and Rida, *Tafsīr al-Manār*, vol. 1, 157; 'Abduh, *Tafsīr Juz' 'Amma*, 184–5.
129 'Abduh and Rida, *Tafsīr al-Manār*, vol. 1, 157.
130 'Abduh, *Tafsīr Juz' 'Amma*, 163–4.
131 'Abduh and Rida, *Tafsīr al-Manār*, vol. 1, 154.
132 'Abduh, *Tafsīr Juz' 'Amma*, 90–1.
133 Ibid., 101.
134 Ibid., 56; Jomier, *Commentaire coranique*, 133–5.
135 Qur'an 2:1.
136 'Abduh and Rida, *Tafsīr al-Manār*, vol. 1, 126. This is a reference to Arabs who have rejected polytheism before the rise of Islam and are known as *ḥanīf*. See ibid., 338.
137 'Abduh, *Tafsīr Juz' 'Amma*, 17.
138 Frank Griffel, 'The Harmony of Natural Law and Shari'a in Islamist Theology', in *Shari'a: Islamic Law in the Contemporary Context*, ed. Abbas Amanat and Frank Griffel (Stanford: Stanford University Press, 2007), 49.
139 Dimitri Gutas, 'The Empiricism of Avicenna', *Oriens*, 40(2) (2012): 404–10.
140 Frank Griffel, 'Al-Ghazālī's Use of 'Original Human Disposition' (*Fiṭra*) and Its Background in the Teachings of al-Fārābī and Avicenna', *The Muslim World* 102 (2012): 14.
141 Ibid., 24–5.
142 Andrew F. March, 'Naturalizing *Sharī'a*: Foundationalist Ambiguities in Modern Islamic Apologetics', *Islamic Law and Society*, 22 (2015): 59.
143 Griffel, 'Al-Ghazālī's Use of "Original Human Disposition"', 5–6; 30–31.
144 Griffel, 'The Harmony of Natural Law and Shari'a', 45.
145 March, 'Naturalizing *Sharī'a*', 61–2.
146 Haddad, *Qarā'a Jadīda*, 132–4.
147 For a discussion of this concept in relation to 'Abduh's *Risālat al-Tawḥīd*, see Buessow, 'Re-imagining Islam', 293.
148 'Abduh, *Tawḥīd*, 127.
149 'Abduh, *Tafsīr Juz' 'Amma*, 101–2; 'Abduh, *Tawḥīd*, 60; 70–2.
150 All *sūras* are attributed to the Meccan period with the exception of *sūras* 98, 99 and 110 which are considered to be Medinan.
151 'Abduh and Rida, *Tafsīr al-Manār*, vol. 1, 233; 'Abduh, *Tafsīr Juz' 'Amma*, 5.
152 Ibid., 28.
153 Qur'an 2:25.
154 'Abduh and Rida, *Tafsīr al-Manār*, vol. 1, 234. 'Abduh equates the spouses in paradise with the *ḥūriyy* who are equally promised as a reward. See ibid., 233.

155 Ahmed, *What Is Islam?*, 29.

156 'Abduh, *Tafsīr Juz' 'Amma*, 73.

157 Ibid., 24.

158 Muhammad 'Abduh and Muhammad Rashid Rida, *Tafsīr al-Qur'ān al-Ḥakīm al-Mushtahīr bi-sm Tafsīr al-Manār*, 2nd edn, vol. 3 (Cairo: al-Manar, 1947), 96; Lutz Berger, 'Esprits et microbes: l'interpretation des ğinn-s dans quelques commentaires coraniques du XXe siècle', *Arabica*, 47(3) (2000): 557.

159 Qur'an 81:6.

160 'Abduh, *Tafsīr Juz' 'Amma*, 26; Jomier, *Commentaire coranique*, 152.

161 'Abduh, *Tawḥīd*, 123–4; Jacques Jomier, 'La raison et l'histoire dans le commentaire du Manār', *Mélanges de l'Institut dominicain d'études orientales du Caire*, 19 (1989): 25.

162 'Abduh and Rida, *Tafsīr al-Manār*, vol. 2, 96.

163 'Abduh, *Tafsīr Juz' 'Amma*, 186–7.

164 'Abduh, *Tawḥīd*, 206–7; Naguib, 'Hermeneutics of Miracle', 61–6.

165 'Abduh, *Tafsīr Juz' 'Amma*, 11–13.

166 Ibid., 181–3.

167 Qur'an 113:4.

168 'Abduh, *Tafsīr Juz' 'Amma*, 181; Jansen, *Interpretation of the Koran*, 31.

169 Bauer, *Kultur der Ambiguität*, 46–7.

170 'Abduh, *Tafsīr Juz' 'Amma*, 56, 152–3; al-Afghani and 'Abduh, *al-Ta'līqāt*, 164.

171 'Abduh, *Tafsīr Juz' 'Amma*, 21.

172 See Naguib, 'Hermeneutics of Miracle', 57–88.

173 Haj, *Reconfiguring Islamic Tradition*, 79–84. On broadening the scope of *ijtihād* and the rejection of *taqlīd* among eighteenth-century Muslim reformers, see Ahmad S. Dallal, *Islam without Europe: Traditions of Reform in Eighteenth Century Islamic Thought* (Chapel Hill: University of North Carolina Press, 2018), 68–93.

174 Muhammad 'Abduh, 'al-Fiqh wa-l-Fuqahā'', in *al-A'māl al-Kāmila li-l-Imām Muḥammad 'Abduh*, ed. Muhammad 'Imara, vol. 3 (Beirut: Dar al-Shuruq, 1993), 212–15; Jakob Skovgaard-Petersen, *Defining Islam for the Egyptian State: Muftis and Fatwas of the Dar al-Ifta* (Leiden: Brill, 1997), 65–8.

175 'Abduh, 'Radd 'alā Hānūtū', vol. 3, 242.

176 Haddad, *Qarā'a Jadīda*, 85.

177 'Abduh and Rida, *Tafsīr al-Manār*, vol. 1, 126.

7

Conclusion: ʿAbduh's contested legacy

Introduction

The prominent liberal Egyptian scholar Nasr Hamid Abu Zayd (1943–2010) characterizes ʿAbduh's approach as follows:

> He decided to select out of the classical theological discourse what is considered 'best' and 'useful' for modern Muslims. He, therefore, combined together dogmas from different theological schools and synthesized them without being aware of the conflict between some of these chosen doctrines.[1]

For Abu Zayd, ʿAbduh's synthesis remains incomplete as he sought to combine incongruent intellectual traditions, being unaware of their inherent contradictions. ʿAbduh's primary pragmatic concerns let him ignore or be oblivious to their fundamental differences. Placing ʿAbduh, however, in the pre-modern culture of ambiguity explains why he was not concerned about them. The works of Bauer and Ahmed alert their readers to the culture of ambiguity that dominated the intellectual and cultural life of pre-modern Muslim societies and make a crucial contribution to the starting point of reformist endeavours undertaken by figures like ʿAbduh. However, their assertion that modern Islam has lost its appreciation of ambiguity and falls short of the intellectual richness of pre-modern Muslim societies needs to be contested. ʿAbduh's own complex intellectual trajectory illustrates a creative re-articulation of this diversity and a selective appropriation that is also communicated differently to various audiences. His intellectual biography illustrates how the capaciousness of Islamic thought – with all its contradictions, inconsistencies and ambiguities – remains relevant in the modern world.

Coming from a culture of ambiguity, ʿAbduh was comfortable in re-articulating the rich texture of Islamic thought in a modern context. As such this book seeks to overcome the notion of inadequacy that is usually associated with Muslim modern reform projects such as those 'Abduh undertook. Scholarship perceives them as intellectually impoverished recipients of Western modernity and its ideological luggage which they approach from a position of cultural and intellectual inferiority. Their approach is often presented as apologetic, being caught between contrarian intellectual and cultural forces – Islam and Western modernity. Their responses are viewed as inconsistent and contradictory, not resolving the inherent tensions that exist between traditional Islam and modernity – tensions that Europe appears to have resolved more consistently by compartmentalizing Christianity as distinct from the domains of science and politics, for example. Muslim reformers assert the harmony of Islam with modern science, define Islam as an anti-imperialist ideology, conceive it as both a religion and civilization and source of both private and public morality, and maintain it as a cultural resource to counter complete Europeanization (*tafarrunj*).[2] For this reason, they failed to resolve the tension between religion and modernity and to relegate the former to particular domains in order to free science, politics and public life from its constraints.[3] Such an approach is not just replete with Orientalist tropes but also misunderstands the intellectual and cultural vantage point of modern Muslim thinkers like 'Abduh: the pre-modern culture of ambiguity that accepted different registers of truth and knowledge regimes as complementary and mutually beneficent. Islamic jurisprudence and theology, practical, political and natural philosophy, mysticism and esotericism were not compartmentalized as contradictory and exclusive but as part of the capacious intellectual heritage of Islam. 'Abduh's intellectual formation nurtured such respect for this diversity, an understanding of how to communicate it in different contexts and the motivation to revive it in the modern world.

The reception history of his ideas spells out contradictions and ambiguities of 'Abduh's intellectual legacy more fully. One branch of his disciples became involved in Egyptian nationalist politics, paving the way for the country's nominal independence from Britain in 1922, and developed a liberal and secular sense of Egyptian nationalism. Within this particular intellectual trajectory 'Abduh became the precursor of, what has been called, liberal or progressive Islam.[4] Within the influential reading of his intellectual legacy by Rida, 'Abduh became a Salafi reformer, more aligned with Sunni traditions of renewal (*tajdīd*) than with mystical philosophy, and also an inspiration for nascent political Islam in Egypt and other parts of the Muslim world in the first decades of the twentieth century.

'Abduh and the culture of ambiguity

'Abduh believed that Islam has the intellectual resources to accommodate modern values so that Muslim societies can find their place in the modern world. He did not try to make Islam more flexible but believed in its inherent flexibility because of its rich and diverse intellectual traditions whose plurality he sought to revive and to combine in his reformed vision of Islam. He identified the need to develop Islam's own alternative model of modernity, which is not based on a historical template that needs to be revived or on a constructed essence of Islam but on the strength and capaciousness of its diverse intellectual traditions. 'Abduh sought to bring this rich and diverse, ambiguous and contradictory heritage together in a synthesis – not in the sense of Hegelian dialectic to resolve contradictions for the sake of achieving intellectual consistency. Historical figures like al-Ghazali harmonized Sufism with Sunni notions of orthodoxy and orthopraxy and delimited the role of philosophy. Yet, al-Ghazali's complex intellectual legacy and posterior efforts to read sense into it illustrate that placing figures like him and 'Abduh in a corset of intellectual consistency not only does them injustice but also fails to appreciate the intellectual culture of pre-modern societies that al-Ghazali shaped and from which 'Abduh stemmed.

The convergence of different strands of intellectual history in Islam is particularly manifest in mystical philosophy from Ibn Sina to the School of Isfahan in Safavid Iran and found in the nineteenth century its latest articulation in the esoteric Shaykhi School. Afghani was attracted in his youth to the Shaykhi School whose founder Ahmad al-Ahsa'i sought to integrate Shii theology and jurisprudence with Sufism and Peripatetic philosophy. All these schools assumed the inherent harmony of reason and revelation as two complementary avenues of divine self-disclosure to humanity. For this reason, 'Abduh does not see the necessity of harmonising reason and revelation, as his approach is informed by Islamic intellectual traditions that assume their conformity and unity. When he states that Islam is in harmony with reason and science, then he does not solely make an apologetic assertion often associated with Islamic modernism but re-articulates an attitude central to esoteric and mystical traditions of Islamic philosophy. At the same time, he is sufficiently skilful to articulate this synthesis in different idioms: whether in the language of Sufism in his earliest *Risālat al-Wāridāt* or in the idiom of philosophy in his first theological commentary on the *Sharḥ al-'Aqā'id al-'Aḍudiyya* or in line with Sunni notions of orthodoxy in his *Risālat al-Tawḥīd*. Reason is universal and becomes manifest in the underlying ordering structure of an Avicennan 'necessitarian cosmos'.[5] 'The nature of existence (*ṭabīʿat al-wujūd*) or the order of the universe (*niẓām al-kawn*)'[6] that science seeks to discover and the laws of history that practical philosophy identifies are equally universal and accessible via human rational faculty. Understanding both is necessary for the advancement of civilization as a universal historical process.

ʿAbduh also knows how to articulate these ideas in the idiom of Sunni orthodoxy when he identifies these universal laws with the customs of God (*sunan allāh*). In Sunni Ashʿari theology the customs of God are used to undergird divine occasionalism: phenomena in creation do not occur out of necessity but because God customarily creates them in conjunction with one another. Fire burns – not out of an inherent necessity but because God creates fire so that it burns but could also create fire that does not burn if He wanted to. By identifying universal laws of nature and history with the customs of God, ʿAbduh translates the understanding of a necessitarian cosmos into the language of mainstream Sunni theology. Both views of the world do not contradict one another but articulate the same reality in different semantics. ʿAbduh wants to encourage Muslims to study sciences and to understand the laws of history and society to advance Muslim civilization. These laws are immutable – whether they are because of an inherent necessary structure of creation or because of divine customs does not matter. The deliberate ambiguity leaves the reader with different options: ʿAbduh can be interpreted as rearticulating both Ashʿari divine occasionalism and therefore Sunni notions of orthodoxy or a view of nature and history informed by Ibn Sina and Ibn Khaldun – or, in fact, both.

Similar dynamics become manifest when he discusses the relationship between free will and divine predestination. Throughout his writings, ʿAbduh considers a fatalistic belief in divine predestination to be the main source for the intellectual, political and civilizational decline of Islam. In a similar manner as he encourages the study of science and history to apply scientific and historical insights for the advancement of civilization, he wants Muslims to become active agents in shaping their social and political lives: whether this is in the creation of a new Egypt, fighting against European imperialism or reforming Islamic education. At the same time, ʿAbduh confirms the Ashʿari doctrine of acquisition (*kasb*): human acts are created by God alone and not humans themselves, who only acquire these acts. ʿAbduh is aware that this doctrine has been made responsible for widespread fatalism in Muslim societies, in particular in Orientalist scholarship. However, he does not openly challenge the Ashʿari concept of *kasb* but adds the Maturidi notion of choice (*ikhtiyār*) to emphasize human agency. Rather than challenging Ash'ari theology openly, 'Abduh adds a concept from another Sunni theological tradition, which is equally central to Shii theology and Islamic practical philosophy, to leave sufficient ambiguity for the reader: he introduces philosophical concepts of agency in the idiom of orthodoxy.

Ambiguities also appear when it comes to the discussion of the relationship between reason (*'aql*) and religion (*dīn*) where several, often contradictory, statements occur in his writings. 'Abduh employs the term *'aql* in different ways: in his earliest theological commentary it denotes the laws of logic, is the instrument to acquire intuitive knowledge and describes the Avicennan cosmic rank of the First and Second Intellect from which creation emanated.[7] In his later theological and exegetical works *'aql* is described as the locus of intellectual activity, of thought and thinking, which though universal to human beings requires to be aligned with an unadulterated innate disposition (*fiṭra*) to fully reach its potential. Only then can the human intellect arrive at the belief in one God and know good and evil intuitively.[8] The role of revelation is then to confirm these insights and to provide guidance on the hereafter which is not attainable by the use of human reason alone. This attitude reflects the intellectual elitism of Islamic philosophy, but 'Abduh seeks to popularize these notions in his theological works. In contradiction to this prioritization of reason, 'Abduh also states in his Qur'an commentary that God has only given reason to humanity as a means to organize the division of labour which characterizes complex societies.[9] Religion (*dīn*) is the most important divine source of guidance and the only one external to human beings which provides the necessary moral corrective to steer reason as human faculty into the right direction.[10] 'Abduh in his own Qur'an commentary provides different definitions of the relationship between reason and religion. He states at the same time that human reason, if attuned to its innate disposition, can discover fundamental divine and moral truths while pointing at its insufficiency and the necessity to be guided by religion as well.

For 'Abduh, the conflict between religion and science is solely a problem of Christianity and not relevant to Islamic intellectual history. Islam is not only a rational religion because of the intelligibility of its core doctrines, Islamic history itself provides ample evidence of how Muslim societies made significant scientific advancements. 'Abduh reaches such conclusions, as he does not differentiate between reason (*'aql*) and knowledge (*'ilm*) and often equates the latter with modern science. This equation betrays the continuous influence of pre-modern intellectual traditions[11] but also adds further ambiguity. In his apologetics against Antun, he prioritizes reason over revelation: if there is a contradiction between reason and revelation, the apparent meaning of revelation is mistaken and needs to be interpreted allegorically (*taʾwīl*) to harmonize it with reason.[12] In his fatwas and Qurʾanic exegesis he suggests the opposite: if there is a contradiction between Qurʾanic accounts on history and science, the assumption is that both accounts will ultimately be harmonized but the Qurʾanic narrative prevails in case of doubt.[13]

How can these contradictory approaches to defining the relationship between reason and revelation be explained? Considering ʿAbduh's intellectual background in the epistemology of mystical philosophy, he believed that there could not be any contradictions between reason and revelation, between science and religion. Access to reason is not equally shared among all human beings, leading to different perceptions of reality and contradictions, inconsistencies and ambiguities in human understandings of the world. Such an approach considers the different branches of Islamic knowledge, their disparate approaches and conclusions as well as the insights of modern science not as mutually exclusive but as different manifestations of and approximations to reality.[14] As such, it was not necessary that contradictions are resolved – they are just apparent in any case, resulting from the limited use of human reason. However, in an age of increasing demands towards intellectual consistency and the clear delineations of religious and scientific truths, such an ambiguous position proved untenable. Either the scientific nature of Islam had to be proven by reading, for example, scientific discoveries into the Qurʾan or irrational and unscientific statements had to be interpreted allegorically to overcome contradictions. ʿAbduh in his own approach to Qurʾanic exegesis suggested both options without committing himself to either of them explicitly.

In the question of Islam's relationship to politics, ʿAbduh also maintained an attitude of ambiguity. While his intellectual outlook was informed by pre-modern traditions of Islamic political thought, he equally endorsed the modernizing efforts of the colonial state and its increasing interference in and control of the religious sector. He conceives Islam as both religion and civilization and not only rejects the secular compartmentalization of society but also re-articulates the world view of pre-modern Muslim societies in which the distinction between religion and civilization or religion and politics would not have made much sense. In his apologetic works, ʿAbduh presents this separation as a particular problem in the history of Christianity in Europe which is not relevant to Islam. Religion and politics were always functionally separated in Muslim polities. Caliphs and sultans were civil (*madanī*) rulers while the *ʿulamāʾ* exercised religious authority. Therefore, ʿAbduh rejects the separation between religion and the secular as not applicable to Muslim societies. 'Abduh opposes the secularization of Muslim societies that relegates Islamic morality to the private sphere and does not consider the secular separation between religion and state applicable to Muslim conceptions of politics.[15] Such a separation was ultimately not needed. Informed by pre-modern models of Islamic governance, 'Abduh did not perceive a contradiction between state law (*qānūn*), based on reason, custom and the ruler's legal discretion, and Islamic law (shari'a). Like pre-modern Islamic political philosophers,[16] he viewed a socio-political order which – via the ruler's civic authority – promotes welfare (*maṣlaḥa*) and justice (*'adl*) not only as embodying good governance but also in harmony with the shari'a, based on the notion that a state achieving both must be aligned with its divine purpose. Hence, for 'Abduh *qānūn* and shari'a need not to be separated but are in confluence with one another if political leadership is just and concerned about the promotion of public welfare.

Ahmed asserts that demands for a secularization of Islamic modes of governance are mistaken because of the lack of a comparable church institution in Islam from which the state could be separated. 'Abduh makes a similar argument rejecting calls for the secularization of Muslim polities by European Orientalists and colonial powers, because there is no single institution in Islam which possesses a monopoly over the definition of religious truth but political authority, whether held by the caliph or sultan is civil in nature and does not require further secularization. As Ahmed points out, modern Muslim-majority states – given the modern paradigmatic religion/secular dichotomy – had to create institutional frameworks to facilitate the separation between religion and state: 'Indeed, one of the great inconveniences experienced by the projects of secularization undertaken by modern Muslim states has been the *absence* of a readily-available institution within which to sequester "religion/Islam" with the result that such an institution has had to be invented along with the concomitant re-making of the "religion" to be housed in.'[17] While 'Abduh rightly rejected the imposition of a secularist framework on Islamic modes of governance in his apologetic works, as a religious officiary employed by the Egyptian colonial state, he supported the institutionalization of Islamic public life. He suggested centralizing reforms of shari'a courts and pious endowments, the professionalization of Islamic education in the modern colonial state and the codification of Islamic law for the purpose of more uniform and reliable Islamic adjudication. While meant to protect Islamic public life from state interference by making it institutionally more robust and better organized, 'Abduh was ironically complicit in the complete nationalization of Islamic institutions in post-colonial state of the Arab Middle East and for the institutional sequestration of Islamic public life by the state.

A contested legacy – full of ambiguities

Bauer and Ahmed suggest that the ambiguity of pre-modern Islamic intellectual and cultural life has come to an end in the modern world. The rise of modern nation-states has undercut the traditional discursive diversity of Islamic jurisprudence by translating it into simplistic sets of positive laws. Sufism and Islamic philosophy have been marginalized in orthodox reconstitutions of Islam that have been mostly legalistic, literalist and scripturalist. The rich and diverse intellectual traditions of Islam have been reduced to dogmatic pietism and a set of normative practices. The spread of universal education and print also destroyed the spatio-social separation of different discursive engagements with Islam and facilitated a further homogenization of Islamic beliefs and practices around the world. True as these characterizations are in such broad contours, they do not sufficiently encapsulate that complex picture that a modern Muslim reformer like ʿAbduh provides. He leaves behind a contested and ambiguous legacy that is further accentuated by the often contradictory reception of his ideas that seek to steer him in a particular direction to resolve the contradictions and ambiguities that mark his thought. However, the diverse reception history gives equal testimony to the continuous capaciousness of modern Islamic thought.

Albert Hourani remarks how the tensions left in ʿAbduh's thought became manifest among his disciples. One group stressed the unchanging and eternal nature of Islam as embodied in the scriptural sources of the Islamic tradition and its ideal embodiment in the early community. This group made ʿAbduh Salafi, comparing him with figures like Ibn Taymiyya and taking Salafi-style scripturalism and anti-rationalism as guiding principles. The other group of his students emphasized ʿAbduh's notion of necessary social change and followed nineteenth-century ideas of freedom and progress. This group sought the separation of Islam from politics and its relegation to private morality, thereby becoming more secular. This group ignored Islam in ideological terms and rendered it irrelevant for the social and political organization of Muslim societies.[18]

Modern secular thought in Egypt has its origin in ʿAbduh, as he opened the door for a critical evaluation of the role of Islam in the modern world with his opposition towards the *ʿulamāʾ* and their conservatism. The secular branch of his disciples shifted away from the question of how Islam must be understood to give it a place in the modern world. The members of the secular branch were interested in the question of which values are important for the progress of a society in the modern world.[19] This group became organized in the People's Party (*ḥizb al-umma*) and used the journal *al-Jarīda* (The Magazine) edited by Ahmad Lutfi al-Sayyid (1872–1963) to articulate its ideas publicly. Lutfi al-Sayyid was an important figure in the foundation of the first modern Egyptian university and became one of its first professors and rectors.[20] For Lutfi al-Sayyid, education was important for social progress as it was for 'Abduh, but the religious element becomes secondary in his thought. Lutfi al-Sayyid attributed to Islam a role in providing general moral values but for the reconstruction of the Egyptian nation a cohesive nationalist ideology was most important.[21]

Nationalism and liberalism were the two central ideological frameworks around which the secular wing of 'Abduh's disciples centred their intellectual and political activities. While some of them became intellectuals and literati providing an ideological foundation for an independent and democratic Egypt, other disciples became important figures in Egyptian inter-bellum political life. Sa'd Zaghlul studied under Afghani and 'Abduh and became the leading figure in the post World War I independence movement as the founder of the *Wafd* Party which was to dominate Egyptian politics until the Free Officers' coup in 1952. Zaghlul became the first prime minister after Egypt had gained nominal independence from Britain in 1922.[22] Political figures like Zaghlul, despite their initial intellectual and political formation by 'Abduh, were pre-occupied with nationalist politics and the construction of an independent Egypt and hence disinterested in working towards a reform of Islamic thought. Priorities had changed, and 'Abduh's close rapport with the British colonial authorities in the last fifteen years of his life was equally problematic in the creation of a post-independence nationalist narrative.[23]

At the same time, the pre-occupation of Lutfi al-Sayyid and Zaghlul with creating the intellectual, cultural and political conditions for an independent and democratic Egypt reflected particular concerns of 'Abduh as well. In his early political articles written at the start of his publishing career in the 1870s and early 1880s, 'Abduh engages in a utilitarian and proto-nationalist discourse arguing for economic development, modern educational reforms, a public sphere to create political consciousness and the introduction of parliamentary and constitutional forms of government in Egypt. Islam as a frame of reference does not feature prominently in his early political pieces. After his return to Egypt, despite his acquiescence to British colonial rule, his long-term aspiration was the creation of an independent and democratic Egypt. When nationalist leaders engaged in these activities in the first two decades of the twentieth century leading up to Egyptian independence, they did not turn away from ʿAbduh's intellectual legacy but emphasized particular aspects of his thought.

For Rida, the rise of thinkers in Egyptian intellectual life proposing liberal and secular views on Islam were signs of the complete Europeanization of the political, intellectual and cultural elites of Muslim societies which ʿAbduh sought to prevent. That many of the proponents of these ideas stemmed from the circle of ʿAbduh's disciples who claimed to be faithful to the intellectual heritage of their teacher constituted a particular insult to Rida and led him to re-interpret ʿAbduh's ideas in sharp contrast to those secular intellectuals.[24] Rida reacted to this wave of Muslim liberalism by associating himself with the Hanbali tradition of Islam and its main representatives like Ahmad ibn Hanbal, Ibn Taymiyya and the eighteenth-century reformer Muhammad ibn ʿAbd al-Wahhab (1703–92) and their scripturalist and legalistic approaches. In particular, the successful establishment of the Saudi state on the Arab peninsula in the 1920s increased his interest and admiration for the Wahhabi movement and its religious puritanism as the sole successful Muslim response to both European imperialism and the secularization of Muslim societies and states.[25] Rida stressed the adherence to the scriptural sources of Islam, the Qur'an and hadith collections, and the role model of the early community (*al-salaf al-ṣāliḥ*) as the ideal embodiment of Islam. Although ʿAbduh is considered one of the founding figures of the Salafiyya movement, it was rather born out of Rida's association with the Hanbali tradition and its modern expression in Wahhabism. Rida's biography therefore gives ʿAbduh a Salafi twist, presenting him as a champion of Sunnism whose aim was to return to the earliest sources and the example of the early community and to cleanse Islam from alien elements as represented in Sufism, Shiism and Islamic philosophy.[26]

ʿAbduh's equivocal use of and identification with the pious ancestors allowed such a reading as well as his ambiguous employment of the language of Sunni orthodoxy in his later writings to reach a wider public. Rida's interventionist redaction of ʿAbduh's writings has given further credence to his Salafi reading. Completing ʿAbduh's Qur'anic exegesis *Tafsīr al-Manār* and using the journal under the same name to disseminate his particular reading of his teacher's ideas further cemented his reputation of being ʿAbduh's intellectual heir and made their different approaches to Islamic reform indistinguishable. Other disciples like Zaghlul who enjoyed a much longer association with ʿAbduh were busy in Egyptian national politics and did not or could not challenge Rida's reading.

Outside of Rida's circle, interest into 'Abduh only remerged in the 1940s in the context of new reform attempts at al-Azhar, led by its rector Mustafa 'Abd al-Raziq (1885–1947).[27]

Rida further buttressed 'Abduh's alignment with a narrow definition of Sunni scripturalism by referring to him as *mujaddid*. He thereby employed a very similar strategy as the disciples of the early Islamic jurisprudent and founding figure of one of the legal schools bearing his name, al-Shafi'i (767–820). Al-Shafi'i's opponents accused him of introducing innovation (*bid'a*) into Islam with his systematization of Islamic jurisprudence. His disciples used the *mujaddid* hadith to underpin his scholarly and religious authority by portraying him as the agent of cyclical reform in Islam as predicted in the hadith.[28] By characterizing 'Abduh as the Islamic renewer of the fourteenth century after the *hijra*, Rida attempted to deflect doubts about his Sunni credentials which were quite justified in the light of his interest in mystical philosophy. The label *mujaddid* not only sets them in line with the eminent Sunni scholars of the past like al-Shafi'i, al-Ghazali and Ibn Taymiyya but also gives his reformist work a specific doctrinal direction. Whatever he endeavoured to accomplish in the various fields of his activities, he always aimed at the restoration of authentic Islam, the return to the *sunna* of the Prophet and the example of the early community. This identification with the Sunni tradition of *tajdīd* led to a particular reception history of 'Abduh's reforms and gave his movement the label of modernist Salafism. However, such a reading invites misunderstandings and misrepresents his intellectual approach. The Hanbali tradition and its modern re-articulation in the Wahhabi movement did not play any role in his own reformist work. He rather rejected the Hanbali opposition to reason and philosophy. Ibn Taymiyya does not appear as a reference point in 'Abduh's writings and shapes much more Rida's approach.

'Abduh's and Rida's attitudes towards Europe differed as well. 'Abduh admired Europe for its achievements, an admiration that led him to travel as often as possible to Europe. Rida's opinions were more ambiguous respecting the political power, economic strength and technological achievements of European societies[29] but also being more sceptical of Europe because of the slavish imitation of European lifestyle he observed in the Egyptian middle class and intelligentsia. He argued for an adoption of modern civilization only as far as it was necessary for Muslim societies to regain strength. Adaptation to Europe should be restricted to scientific and technological borrowing and should not include the adoption of European cultural or ideological values.[30] 'Abduh was equally critical of superficially Europeanized Muslims who emulated European mannerisms and intellectual attitudes and considered Islam as backward and outdated. Such an approach to modernization would be not sustainable because of its superficiality and its lacking embeddedness in the Islamic tradition. Another approach is needed, anchored more in the rich and diverse intellectual heritage of Islam. ʿAbduh emphasized both the adoption of scientific achievements of Europe but also of the critical spirit behind it. Only adopting modern science and technology – as Rida suggested – would not be sufficient for an intellectual re-orientation of Muslim societies either.[31] Such an approach would be as superficial as imitating European mannerisms.

Liberal and Islamist trajectories

Wider geopolitical reconfigurations in the Middle East accentuated the dichotomy between these two different strands of his disciples and followers. In 1924, the National Assembly of newly founded Turkish republic abolished the caliphate held by the Ottoman sultan. An institution came to an end that claimed continuous existence since the death of the Prophet Muhammad and was seen as central to Sunni Islam as a political entity. Responses to the abolition also divided ʿAbduh's disciples and followers. The Islamic scholar and liberal Egyptian statesman ʿAli ʿAbd al-Raziq (1888–1966), the younger brother of Mustafa ʿAbd al-Raziq, provided one prominent response in his *al-Islām wa-Uṣūl al-Ḥukm* (Islam and the Foundations of Government),[32] published in 1925. He argues that the caliphate is not a religious but a political institution which emerged after the death of the Prophet.[33] There are no bases for it in the Qur'an or the *sunna* and, hence, no political system is associated with Islam *per se*.[34] While the book caused a public stir and resulted in ʿAli ʿAbd al-Raziq losing his teaching position in al-Azhar, his ideas are not that far removed from ʿAbduh's understanding. Despite public assertions to the contrary, ʿAbduh was not an ardent supporter of the Ottoman caliphate and denied that it had any particular religious role to play. For him, the Qur'an is the actual ruler (*sulṭān*)[35] and leader (*imām*) of Muslims.[36] Caliphate and sultanate are political institutions and possess civil (*madanī*) authority without any religious mandate.[37] ʿAbduh seems to imply with his statements about the caliphate that he does not see it as an institution that is religiously required. Equally, he restricts its mandate to matters of state. ʿAbd al-Raziq takes the implications of ʿAbduh arguments further and aligns them more with the modern religion/secular dichotomy: civil authority becomes secular power, meaning that the caliphate was first and foremost a political institution that accidentally emerged and evolved in Islamic history but is not essentially connected to the Islamic religion.

Rida, however, provided a different response. For him, a secularized reading of the caliphate does not only betray the intellectual legacy of 'Abduh but also deprives Islam of an essential institution to safeguard its integrity. If Islam was both a religion and a civilization, it would require a political system based on Islamic principles. On the eve of the abolition of the caliphate in 1922, Rida wrote a treatise on the institution entitled *al-Khilāfa aw al-Imāma al-'Uẓmā* (The Caliphate or the Supreme Leadership) which reiterates classical Sunni theories on the caliphate and seeks to apply them to a modern political context.[38] In 1922, the Turkish National Assembly effectively spiritualized the caliphate by abolishing the sultanate. 'Abdül-Mecid (1869–1944) was elected as caliph for all Muslims, devoid of any political power – a step that prefaced the eventual abolition of the caliphate two years later. Following discussions throughout the Muslim world on the future of the caliphate, Rida envisions a restoration of this institution adapted to notions of representative government and national sovereignty.[39] The caliph should be elected by popular consensus of the entire Islamic community. This is ensured if learned and prominent leaders of the Muslim world, namely the *'ulamā'*, acted as its representatives in a council either electing the caliph or approving his appointment by his predecessor.[40] Being composed of *'ulamā'*, the council would provide a comprehensive, unified and coherent Islamic code of law by which the entire Islamic community and the caliph would have to abide by.[41] However, Rida does not conceive the caliph to be the temporal ruler of a unified Islamic state. He accepts the division of the Islamic *umma* in several nation-states[42] and portrays the caliph as the personification of the legal unity of the Islamic *umma*. The caliph should be the chief *mujtahid* of the entire Islamic community who formulates the precepts of the shari'a in consultation with the *'ulamā'* represented in the council – a type of leadership that Rida compares to the Roman Catholic papacy and its global reach.[43] Rida conceives the caliph as the highest religious authority in the Muslim world, being both a symbol of its unity and guarantor of its legal and doctrinal cohesion.[44]

In addition, Rida demands a political system based on Islamic principles and laid the foundation for later formulations of an Islamic state. Rida's understanding of role of the shari'a in a modern state would particularly prove influential for later Islamist ideologues.[45] Reclaiming the all-comprehensive nature of Islam, Rida develops a notion of the shari'a which denies that it is merely an ideal which the jurisprudents should aspire to achieve or that it only deals with personal status laws. In theory, so Rida argues, the shari'a provides guidelines from which rules and regulations for all aspects of individual and social life could be deduced. His understanding of the shari'a as the sole foundation of Muslim societies countered the turn of secular thinkers and politicians towards European codes of law. He turns the shari'a into an equivalent to secular law whose formulation mimics the legislative process of modern nation-states. In contrast to secular law, the shari'a would provide Muslims with infallible divine guidance and be therefore superior to any temporal legislation.[46]

The modern religion/secular fault lines become apparent in this distinction which 'Abduh had left ambiguous: for him, both *qānūn* as the legal discretionary authority of the state and shari'a as divine law serve as legal foundations of an Islamic socio-political order and are not in conflict with one another, if *qānūn* is based on reason and promotes welfare and justice. For his disciples, drifting apart into secular and Islamic camps respectively, secular law and Islamic law now were clearly delineated: his secular-nationalist disciples as other Middle Eastern political elites intended to emulate liberal democratic regimes and transferred European legal systems into their countries which required minimizing the legal relevance of Islamic law in the modern state relegating it at best to matters of personal status. For Rida and his later Islamist followers, the shari'a becomes the sole legitimate legal foundation of a modern Islamic state: it is comprehensive and provides infallible guidance and a central anti-colonial bulwark against the Westernization of the political and legal culture of post-colonial Muslim-majority countries.

Rida's idea of the all-comprehensive nature of the shari'a as the foundation of an Islamic socio-political order and his opposition to the increasing secularization of Muslim societies inspired a new generation of Muslim intellectuals to formulate an oppositional attitude towards the liberal and secular orientation of Egyptian society[47] and to oppose the continuing presence of European powers in Egypt.[48] The most eminent among them was Hasan al-Banna (1906–1949)[49] who visited Rida frequently during his studies in Cairo and became editor of the journal *al-Manār* after Rida's death.[50] In 1928, al-Banna founded the Society of the Muslim Brothers (*jamā'at al-ikhwān al-muslimīn*) in the provincial town of Ismailiyya on the Suez Canal which would become one of the largest and most influential Islamist organizations in the world. Later on, similar organizations were founded throughout the Muslim world, and the Brotherhood established national sub-branches in several Middle Eastern countries in the 1940s.[51] The Muslim Brothers saw themselves in the tradition of modern Islamic reform initiated by Afghani, 'Abduh and Rida. Al-Banna considered these figures to be his predecessors who had paved the way for the activities of the Brotherhood.[52]

The indebtedness of the Muslim Brothers to ʿAbduh and Rida is also reflected in the materials which teachers of the Brotherhood used in their lectures and study sessions; among them the Qur'an commentary *al-Manār* and ʿAbduh's *Risālat al-Tawḥīd*.[53]

The aim of the early Muslim Brotherhood was not to establish an Islamic state, in fact, al-Banna had not developed such an ideological concept.[54] By ensuring the Islamic orientation of individual and collective morality with wide-ranging educational, literary and social activities, a truly Islamic society would gradually be established.[55] The breeding of a new Islamized cultural cadre would inaugurate the establishment of a true Islamic order (*niẓām islamī*) within Muslim societies. More important than the restoration of the caliphate was the creation of a society whose legal system is based on the shariʿa and whose public and individual morality is directed by Islamic principles.[56]

Hasan al-Banna created a direct intellectual lineage to Rida, ʿAbduh and Afghani presenting them as his predecessors in the struggle against European imperialism and for the Islamization of modern Egyptian society. Afghani's and ʿAbduh's articles in *al-ʿUrwa al-Wuthqā* were for the first to conceive Islam as an anti-imperialist ideology. Creating an Islamic organization for educational and charitable purposes was pioneered by ʿAbduh forty years earlier and reflected a general move of Islamic social activism into the private sphere and adopting a grassroots approach that involved lay Muslims in Islamic activism and intellectual discourses. Al-Banna was a trained secondary school teacher, and many other members of the Brotherhood had received secular education and were not religious scholars. Hence, al-Banna's claim to be a successor of ʿAbduh – though his reception was mediated by Rida – is plausible and possible because of the ambiguities in ʿAbduh's thought and his social and political activism.[57] ʿAbduh encouraged the social mobilization of Muslims and the laicization of Islamic discourse by making it accessible to educated Muslims with or without specific religious training. His legacy also includes anti-colonial agitation, despite his pragmatic cooperation with the British later in his life.

The concept of an Islamic state as anti-thesis to the secular nation-state entered the vocabulary of the Muslim Brotherhood in the 1950s in the writings of Sayyid Qutb (1906–1966). Qutb engaged in particular with the South Asian Islamist thinker and activist Abu al-Aʿla Mawdudi (1903–1979), the founder of the Jamaat-i Islami, and his understanding of how divine sovereignty (*ḥākimiyya*) needs to be operationalized in an Islamic state.[58] For Mawdudi, any political system that invests political authority to the people which includes their right to give themselves their own laws is un-Islamic and will yield injustice. Such a legislative prerogative, however operationalized, contravenes fundamental Islamic principles, as 'Islam admits of no sovereignty except that of God and, consequently, does not recognize any Law-giver other than Him'.[59] Qutb uses *ḥākimiyya* in his writings to emphasize the uniqueness of the Islamic socio-political order which 'is based on the premise that sovereignty (*ḥākimiyya*) belongs to God alone'[60] and demarcates it from 'a society of ignorance (*mujtama' jāhilī*)'[61] which 'is built on the premise to attack the power of God (*sulṭān allāh*) on earth'.[62] Any political order that does not implement *ḥākimiyya* constitutes idolatry (*shirk*).[63]

Such absolutist and exclusionary definitions of Islam as mandating one particular political system in the modern world appear far removed from 'Abduh's general disinterest in politics from an Islamic normative perspective and his irenic attitude towards religious diversity. However, first allusions of more politicized readings of Islam can be seen in his interpretation of the final *sūra* of the Qur'an. 'Abduh criticizes the reliance of Muslims on intermediaries, leaders and scholars who by claiming 'spiritual authority (*sulṭa ruḥiyya*)'[64] for themselves, usurp divine authority and turn Muslims away from the divine book and from God, 'the divine ruler (*al-sulṭān al-ilāhī*)'.[65] In reality, 'there is for humanity no lord, no king and no deity except God'.[66] While 'Abduh describes here the transcendental sovereignty of God, he uses terms (*sulṭa*, *sulṭān*) that denote political authority in Islam. Hence, the translation of divine sovereignty into the political sphere as conceived by Sayyid Qutb and Mawdudi finds in 'Abduh's reading a potential Qur'anic precedent.[67]

The trajectory of influence from 'Abduh to Rida to the Muslim Brotherhood is evident, because al-Banna himself creates an intellectual lineage back to Afghani and Rida provides the link between 'Abduh and later Egyptian Islamists because of his particular Salafi reading of his teachers' ideas. A similar connection to twentieth-century representatives of liberal or progressive Islam is also identifiable. 'Abduh's immediate disciples such as Zaghlul did not pick up the religious threads left by their teacher but engaged in nationalist politics. Possible influences of 'Abduh on 'Ali 'Abd al-Raziq's secular approach to Islam and political authority in particular have been identified. Another example of a direct lineage among 'Abduh's immediate disciples is Qasim Amin (1863–1908) to whose book *Taḥrīr al-Mar'a* (The Liberation of Women), published in 1899, 'Abduh likely contributed.[68] Together with his second book *al-Mar'a al-Jadīda* (The New Woman), published in 1901, Amin has been seen as a pioneer for promoting women's rights in the Arab world. Between both books, a discursive shift towards more secular paradigms is observable. While in the first book, Amin asserts the conformity of his suggestions with Islamic law and uses Qur'anic verses to support his re-interpretation of the status of women, his second book supports his advocacy based on utilitarian arguments.[69] Both ʿAli ʿAbd al-Raziq and Qasim Amin were amongst the most influential figures emerging out of ʿAbduh's liberal and secular disciples.

The generation following ʿAbduh's immediate disciples took his approach further and shaped the intellectual life of Egypt from post-independence to the coup of the Free Officers in 1952. The Egyptian writer and intellectual Taha Husayn (1889–1973) pursued similar interests as ʿAbduh, writing for example on Ibn Khaldun's philosophy, and admired him[70] but trajectories of influence have yet to be established through a comparative study. A clearer intellectual trajectory can be established which connects ʿAbduh with the literary approach (*manhaj adabī*) to Qur'anic exegesis which emerged in mid-twentieth-century Egypt. Amin al-Khuli (1895–1966) builds on ʿAbduh's exegesis to introduce a different model of Qur'anic interpretation. His starting point is the miraculous character of the Qur'an (*iʿjāz*) which for al-Khuli like ʿAbduh does not consist in its rhetorical features (*balāgha*) and its unique literary qualities alone but both in its form and contents. The style of the Qur'an and the rational intelligibility of its message constitute its miracle. Focussing on both the form of the text and its meaning is crucial to ensure its continuous relevance. For al-Khuli, the Qur'an only introduces general, spiritual and moral premises and rarely provides much detail on historical and scientific questions. In a lecture series on philosophy at al-Azhar he gave in the 1930s and dedicated to ʿAbduh, he warned the religious students that they should not fall into the trap of identifying contradictions between Islam and science. The Qur'an is not meant to be a scientific document or historical record. Assuming a contradiction between Islam and science transposes issues that existed in Christianity into Islam.[71]

Al-Khuli's approach to the Qur'an and its interpretation is informed by his understanding of religious renewal which – similar to ʿAbduh – is 'progressive not restorative'.[72] Religion does not exist outside of human interpretation and is, in fact, a constantly evolving interpretation which is bound to change as human societies develop and human ideas evolve. To ensure that the Qur'an remains relevant for different societies and moves with their evolutionary development, he introduces a contextual approach to its interpretation that a literary understanding facilitates. The exegete needs to combine both text and context in their interpretation: what form does the text have and what meaning does it convey and how are both shaped by the immediate context in which the text emerges? The direct addressees were the Arabs of the seventh century. For this reason, the Qur'an uses their language, Arabic, and a style to communicate its content that would make it intelligible to them. Yet, in order to avoid that the text remains frozen in the seventh century, it needs to be de-contextualized by extracting the moral and spiritual message the Qur'an contains – an objective central to 'Abduh exegetical approach.

Al-Khuli's student Muhammad Ahmad Khalafallah (1916–1998) applies these ideas further in his controversial PhD thesis in 1947 which caused a major public outcry in Egypt. Approaching the Qur'an as literary text means that the Qur'anic stories about prophets and communities of the past do not constitute historical facts. Both al-Khuli and Khalafallah refer to 'Abduh to support their approach to the mythico-historical contents of the Qur'an.[73] Khalafallah quotes in his thesis sections from the *Tafsīr al-Manār* in which 'Abduh argues that the Qur'an should not be treated as a book of history.[74] Both the concern for historical accuracy and conformity with science distract the reader from understanding the central spiritual and moral message of the Qur'an. Addressing the world view of seventh-century Arabs, the Qur'an contains metaphors and allegories meaningful to them in order to communicate its message. For Khalafallah, a literary approach distinguishes between the structure of a Qur'anic story and its meaning and thereby allows disregarding questions around their historicity by focussing on their meaning.[75]

Nasr Hamid Abu Zayd is the latest representative of the literary approach to the Qur'an who experienced even harsher opposition to his reading of the Qur'an. For his controversial theses, he was declared an apostate by a shari'a court in Egypt in 1995 and forced into exile to evade death threats. His approach takes the literary understanding of the Qur'an further by arguing that 'religious texts, though divine and revealed by God, are historically determined and culturally constructed'.[76] Contextualizing the Qur'an as a literary text in the environment it emerged allows the exegete to 'distinguish between circumstances and principles'[77] and to extract the latter from the contextual contingencies. Such an approach avoids affixing restrictive avenues to understanding the Qur'an and provides an opening for 'interpretative diversity because the endless process of interpretation and re-interpretation cannot but differ in time'.[78] Theologically, Abu Zayd aligns this understanding of the Qur'an with the doctrine of its createdness, as developed by the early Mu'tazila school of theology.[79] Considering the Qur'an as a literary document, created in time and therefore historical, creates sufficient exegetical flexibility to ensure the relevance of its message for different times and societies. 'Abduh himself addressed the question of the createdness of the Qur'an. While he criticized – like Abu Zayd – the Hanbali insistence on its eternity, he did not fully subscribe to the Mu'tazila doctrine of its createdness either and presented a middle-position that resembles the approach of the Maturidi school. 'Abduh did not want to re-open this debate and adopted a conciliatory attitude, leaving his own position ambiguous. For Abu Zayd, the issue of the nature of the Qur'an needs to be reconsidered in order to provide the literary approach that al-Khuli and Khalafallah pioneered with a solid theological foundation.

The contradictory reception histories of 'Abduh, from Islamists like Sayyid Qutb to liberal Muslim thinkers like Nasr Hamid Abu Zayd, from intellectual precursors of contemporary jihadist movements and of feminist exegetes alike, illustrates the diversity of interpretations caused by the very ambiguity of his intellectual legacy. It equally shows that the distinction between Islamic modernism and Islamism is tenuous and measures Islamic reform movements by how much they embrace modern values. Islamism not only emerged out of Islamic modernism. 'Abduh's complex reception history shows that the two major intellectual and ideological trends of modern Islam are closely intertwined. This overview just focussed on his reception within two different intellectual and ideological fields of twentieth century Egyptian Islamic discourse. 'Abduh, mostly through the mediation of his disciple Rida, influenced reform activities in North Africa,[80] South East Asia,[81] and Iran.[82] The journal *al-Manār*, edited by Rida, his commentary on the Qur'an and his *Risālat al-Tawḥīd* have been most influential. A closer look at the various reception histories in different parts of the Muslim world will equally reveal diverse readings and appropriations of his legacy.

Conclusion

Bauer's and Ahmed's works which have informed the approach this book has taken seek to highlight the cultural diversity and intellectual plurality of the pre-modern Muslim world, the co-existence of contradictory discourses and the variety of Islamic epistemes and literary genres in which they find their expressions. They also encourage researchers to unlearn the categorizations that have been applied to Islamic history and thought distinguishing between orthodox vs. heterodox, religious vs. secular and theological-jurisprudential vs. mystico-philosophical. Such dichotomies reveal modern conceptions of religion and are based on reductionist definitions of orthodoxy in Islam. For both Bauer and Ahmed, however, modern Islam has lost its tolerance towards ambiguity and its ability to diffuse different, apparently contradictory, discourses at the same time.

Has the culture of ambiguity come to an end in modern Islam? 'Abduh's intellectual biography suggests otherwise. While the reception history of 'Abduh reveals a desire to end the ambiguities and resolve contradictions in his thought, its diverse trajectories equally illustrate the continuous capaciousness of Islamic thought. Later followers mirrored the ideological disambiguation that the modern age with its orientation towards intellectual consistency and ideological conformity demands but, as 'Abduh illustrates, the pre-modern legacy of cultural ambiguity in Islamic intellectual and cultural life has survived in different iterations. Perhaps figures like 'Abduh, Taha Husayn or Amin al-Khuli operated in a more liberal age that tolerated diversity of opinions and allowed a more experimental approach to reforming Islamic thought. Muslim intellectuals and ideologues in the latter half of the twentieth century experienced the rise of autocratic regimes and the failure of different ideological experiments in the Muslim world, whether liberal democracy, Pan-Arabism or socialism. For Islamists like Sayyid Qutb, it meant embracing a more totalitarian reading of Islam, for liberal Muslims a more explicit adoption of liberal and secular paradigms. 'Abduh did not want to and did not have to position himself that clearly but maintained an approach of ambiguity.

This book seeks to make a broader contribution to re-considering the intellectual history of modern Islam by taking Bauer's and Ahmed's contributions to the study of modern Islam and by acknowledging the continuous capaciousness of its intellectual traditions. The book also seeks to apply their plea to avoid reductionist categorizations that centre certain articulations of Islamic religious life and de-centre others as marginal. Likewise, research on modern Islamic thought will ignore its continuous ambiguity when it attaches simplistic labels to particular thinkers, compartmentalizes Islamic discourses, favours certain intellectual outputs over others or takes the European trajectory of modernity as yardstick to measure the success of modern Islamic reform movements. 'Abduh was more than just an Islamic modernist who responded to Western modernity from a sense of intellectual and cultural inferiority or attempted to embed modern concepts in the Islamic tradition.[83] 'Abduh sought to indigenize modernity in Islam not by reducing it to narrow essentialized notions of legalism and scripturalism but by engaging creatively with the diversity of Islamic thought. He combined different intellectual traditions and re-articulated their contributions in the modern world and was not a Salafi of any sort who favoured a particularly restrictive trajectory. His biography and diverse intellectual interests reveal the complexity of nineteenth-century Middle Eastern *gedankenwelt* in which different trends of pre-modern Islamic thought are creatively re-articulated. Research on other figures of modern Islamic thought and its pre-modern precursors that avoids simplistic categorizations and essentializations will equally reveal the continuity of Islam's culture of ambiguity in the modern world.

Notes

1 Nasr Hamid Abu Zayd, 'The Dilemma of the Literary Approach to the Qur'an', *Alif: Journal of Comparative Poetics*, 23 (2003): 39–40.

2 Muhammad Rashid Rida, *al-Khilāfa [aw al-Imāma al-'Uẓmā]* (Cairo: Hindawi, [1922] 2015), 62–4.

3 Samira Haj, *Reconfiguring Islamic Tradition: Reform, Rationality, and Modernity* (Stanford: Stanford University Press, 2009), 1–6. For examples of such an approach, see P. J. Vatikiotis, 'Muḥammad 'Abduh and the Quest for a Muslim Humanism', *Arabica*, 4(1) (1957): 55–72; or Nadav Safran, *Egypt in Search of Political Community* (Cambridge, MA: Harvard University Press, 1961). For a critique of Safran, see Charles D. Smith, 'The "Crisis of Orientation": The Shift of Egyptian Intellectuals to Islamic Subjects in the 1930's', *International Journal of Middle East Studies*, 4(4) (1973): 382–410. For a critical self-reflection on this approach, see the preface to the 1983 edition of Albert Hourani, *Arabic Thought in the Liberal Age: 1798–1939* (Cambridge: Cambridge University Press, 1983), viii–ix.

4 Hourani, *Arabic Thought*, 161–92.

5 Ovamir Anjum, *Politics, Law, and Community in Islamic Thought: The Taymiyyan Moment* (Cambridge: Cambridge University Press, 2012), 150.

6 Muhammad 'Abduh, *Risālat al-Tawḥīd*, 17th edn (Cairo: Yousif Sulayman, 1960), 6.

7 Mohamed Haddad, *Muḥammad 'Abduh: Qarā'a Jadīda fī Khiṭāb al-Iṣlāḥ al-Dīnī* (Beirut: Dar al-Tali'a li-l-Taba'a wa-l-Nashr, 2003), 84–5.

8 'Abduh, *Tawḥīd*, 72–8; Muhammad 'Abduh, *Tafsīr Juz' 'Amma*, 3rd edn (Cairo: Matba'at Misr, 1341H [1922–3]), 126.

9 Muhammad 'Abduh, *Tafsīr al-Fātiḥa* (Cairo: Isma'il Hafiz, 1901), 48.

10 Ibid., 49.

11 Franz Rosenthal, *Knowledge Triumphant: The Concept of Knowledge in Medieval Islam* (Leiden: Brill, 2007), 252–3.

12 'Abduh adopts here the approach of late Ash'ari theologians like Fakhr al-Din al-Razi (1150–1210). See Muhammad 'Abduh, 'al-Radd 'alā Faraḥ Anṭūn', in *al-A'māl al-Kāmila li-l-Imām Muḥammad 'Abduh*, ed. Muhammad 'Imara, vol. 3 (Beirut: Dar al-Shuruq, 1993), 301.

13 Muhammad Rashid Rida, *Ta'rīkh al-Ustādh al-Imām al-Shaykh Muḥammad 'Abduh*, vol. 1 (Cairo: al-Manar, 1931), 666–7; 'Abduh, *Tafsīr Juz' 'Amma*, 44–5, 138.

14 Haddad, *Qarāʾa Jadīda*, 119–20.
15 Haj, *Reconfiguring Islamic Tradition*, 98–9.
16 Shahab Ahmed, *What Is Islam?: The Importance of Being Islamic* (Princeton: Princeton University Press, 2016), 482–9.
17 Ibid., 190 [emphasis in the original].
18 Hourani, *Arabic Thought*, 161.
19 Ibid., 161–70.
20 Donald M. Reid, *Cairo University and the Making of Modern Egypt* (Cambridge: Cambridge University Press, 1990).
21 Hourani, *Arabic Thought*, 171–82; Smith, 'Crisis of Orientation', 391–3.
22 Christina P. Harris, *Nationalism and Revolution in Egypt: The Role of the Muslim Brotherhood* (The Hague: Mouton, 1964), 89–100.
23 Haddad, *Qarāʾa Jadīda*, 57.
24 Malcolm H. Kerr, *Islamic Reform: The Legal and Political Theories of Muhammad ʿAbduh and Rashid Rida* (Berkeley: University of California Press, 1966), 205.
25 For Rida's own efforts to rehabilitate the Wahhabi movement in the eyes of his contemporaries and for his own support of the Saudi state on the Arab peninsula see Muhammad Rashid Rida, *al-Wahhābiyyūn wa-l-Ḥijāz* (Cairo: al-Manar, 1344H [1925–6]). On the influence of Wahhabism on Rida's reformist agenda, see Muhammad b. ʿAbdallah Al-Salman, *Rashīd Riḍā wa-Daʿwat al-Shaykh Muḥammad b. ʿAbd al-Wahhāb* (Kuwait: Maktabat al-Muʿalla, 1988); Hourani, *Arabic Thought*, 231–2; Henri Lauzière, *The Making of Salafism: Islamic Reform in the Twentieth Century* (New York: Columbia University Press, 2016), 61–70.
26 Mohamed Haddad, "Abduh et ses lecteurs: pour in histoire critique de "lectures" de Muhammad ʿAbduh', *Arabica*, 45 (1998): 29–30.
27 ʿAbduh, *Qarāʾa Jadīda*, 60–2.
28 Ella Landau-Tasseron, 'The "Cyclical Reform": A Study of the *Mujaddid* Tradition', *Studia Islamica*, 70 (1989): 79–117.
29 Muhammad Rashid Rida, 'Manāfiʿ al-Ūrubiyīn wa-Maḍāruhum fī-l-Sharq', *al-Manār*, 10 (1907) : 340–4.
30 Rida, *Taʾrīkh*, vol. 1, 235–6.
31 Muhammad ʿAbduh, 'Murāsilāt', in *al-Aʿmāl al-Kāmila li-l-Imām Muḥammad ʿAbduh*, ed. Muhammad ʿImara, vol. 1 (Beirut: Dar al-Shuruq, 1993), 743–4.
32 ʿAli Abd al-Raziq, *al-Islām wa-Uṣūl al-Ḥukm: Baḥth fī-l-Khilāfa wa-l-Ḥukūma fī-l-Islām* (Cairo: Matbaʿat Misr, 1925).
33 Hourani, *Arabic Thought*, 183–92.
34 For a summary of Sunni debates on the caliphate in the aftermath of its abolition see Hamid Enayat, *Modern Islamic Political Thought* (Austin: University of Texas Press, 1982), 52–68.

35 Muhammad 'Abduh, 'al-Waḥda al-Islāmiyya', in *al-'Urwa al-Wuthqā wa-l-Thawra al-Taḥrīriyya al-Kubrā*, Jamal al-Din al-Afghani and Muhammad 'Abduh (Cairo: Dar al-'Arab, 1958), 72.

36 Muhammad 'Abduh, 'al-Imām Huwwa-l-Qur'ān', in *al-A'māl al-Kāmila li-l-Imām Muḥammad 'Abduh*, ed. Muhammad 'Imara, vol. 1 (Beirut: Dar al-Shuruq, 1993), 865.

37 Muhammad 'Abduh, 'Radd 'alā Anṭūn', vol. 3, 308–9.

38 For a French translation see Henri Laoust, trans., *Le Califat dans la doctrine de Rašid Rida: Traduction annotée d'al-Hilâfa au al-Imâma al-'Uẓmâ (Le Califat ou l'Imama suprême)* (Beirut: Institute Français de Damas, 1938); M. O. Haddad, 'Rashid Rida and the Theory of the Caliphate: Medieval Themes and Modern Concerns' (PhD diss., New York, 1989).

39 Rida allows the possibility of a 'caliphate of necessity'. In case a candidate who meets all the required criteria to assume the caliphate cannot be found, the caliphate of an unqualified candidate who illegitimately usurped this position is permissible. Thereby, loyalty to the Ottoman caliphate becomes legitimate. See Rida, *al-Khilāfa*, 38–40.

40 Ibid., 36–7, 58–61. The Syrian reformist intellectual 'Abd al-Rahman al-Kawakibi (1848–1902) developed ideas similar to Rida. See Reinhard Schulze, *Islamischer Internationalismus im 20. Jahrhundert: Untersuchungen zur Geschichte der islamischen Weltliga* (Leiden: Brill, 1990), 57–8.

41 Rida, *al-Khilāfa*, 33–5; Kerr, *Islamic Reform*, 165.

42 Rida, *al-Khilāfa*, 53–8.

43 Ibid., 99.

44 Ibid., 30–2; Enayat, *Islamic Political Thought*, 76; Kerr, *Islamic Reform*, 176–86; Andrew F. March, *The Caliphate of Man: Popular Sovereignty in Modern Islamic Thought* (Cambridge, MA: Harvard University Press, 2019), 43–4.

45 Enayat, *Islamic Political Thought*, 76–80.

46 Rida, *al-Khilāfa*, 68, 87–99; March, *Caliphate of Man*, 53–7.

47 Schulze, *Islamischer Internationalismus*, 89–90.

48 Harris, *Nationalism and Revolution*, 145–9.

49 For a collection of his writings, see Hasan al-Banna, *Majmū'a Rasā'il al-Imām al-Shahīd Ḥasan al-Bannā* (n.p., n.d.). For his autobiography see Hasan al-Banna, *Mudhakkirāt al-Da'wa wa-l-Dā'iyya* (Kuwait: Maktabat Afaq, 2012).

50 Richard P. Mitchell, *The Society of the Muslim Brothers* (Oxford: Oxford University Press, 1969), 5; Brynjar Lia, *The Society of the Muslim Brothers in Egypt: The Rise of an Islamic Mass Movement, 1928–1942* (Reading: Ithaca Press, 1998), 29.

51 Mitchell, *Muslim Brothers*, 104–5.

52 Ibid., 321–2.

53 Ibid., 321–3.

54 On the priority of socio-moral change and religious education over the restoration of the caliphate, see Harris, *Nationalism and Revolution*, 62–3.

55 al-Banna, *Majmūʿa Rasāʾil*, 101–13; Nazih Ayubi, *Political Islam: Religion and Politics in the Arab World* (London: Routledge, 1991), 130–4; Mitchell, *Muslim Brothers*, 323.

56 al-Banna, *Majmūʿa Rasāʾil*, 249; Mitchell, *Muslim Brothers*, 232–59.

57 Al-Banna was, similar to ʿAbduh, also attracted to Sufism and incorporated certain Sufi elements in the organizational structure and activities of the Muslim Brotherhood. See Krämer Gudrun, *Hasan al-Banna* (Oxford: Oneworld, 2009).

58 Muhammad Qasim Zaman, 'The Sovereignty of God in Modern Islamic Thought', *Journal of the Royal Asiatic Society*, 25(3) (2015): 389–418; Humeira Iqtidar, 'Theorising Sovereignty in the Colony: Abul Aʿla Maududi's "Theodemocracy"', *Review of Politics*, 82(4) (2020): 595–617.

59 Sayyid Abul Aʿla Maududi, *The Islamic Law and Constitution*, trans. and ed. Khurshid Ahmad (Lahore: Islamic Publications, 1960), 72.

60 Ibid., 76.

61 Sayyid Qutb, *Maʿālim fī-l-Ṭarīq* (Beirut: Dar al-Shuruq, [1964] 1979), 105.

62 Ibid., 8.

63 Zaman, 'Sovereignty of God', 390; Khatab Sayed, 'Hakimiyyah and Jahiliyyah in the Thought of Sayyid Qutb', *Middle Eastern Studies*, 38 (2002): 145–70; William E. Shepard, 'Sayyid Qutb's Doctrine of *Jāhiliyya*', *International Journal of Middle East Studies*, 35 (2003): 521–45.

64 ʿAbduh, *Tafsīr Juzʾ ʿAmma*, 185.

65 Ibid.

66 Ibid.

67 Rida discusses the extent of the authority of God (*wilāyat allāh*) and gives it a similar quasi-political reading. Muhammad ʿAbduh and Muhammad Rashid Rida, *Tafsīr al-Qurʾān al-Ḥakīm al-Mushtahīr bi-sm Tafsīr al-Manār*, 2nd edn, vol. 3 (Cairo: al-Manar, 1947), 42–5.

68 Muhammad ʿImara, 'Taḥqīq Hādhihi-l-Aʿmāl', in *al-Aʿmāl al-Kāmila li-l-Imām Muḥammad ʿAbduh*, ed. Muhammad ʿImara, vol. 1 (Beirut: Dar al-Shuruq, 1993), 262–6; Haj, *Reconfiguring Islamic Tradition*, 155–6.

69 Qasim Amin, *Taḥrīr al-Marʾa* (Cairo: Hindawi, [1899] 2016); Qasim Amin, *al-Marʾa al-Jadīda* (Cairo: Hindawi, [1901] 2011).

70 Taha Husayn, *al-Ayyām* (Cairo: Hindawi, [1929] 2014), 142–5; Zahiye Kundos, 'The Loss of the Mufti: Muhammad ʿAbduh in Taha Husayn's Days', *Europe in the Middle East – The Middle East in Europe (EUME) Berliner Seminar* (2021). Available online: https://www.eume-berlin.de/en/events/calendar/details/the-loss-of-the-mufti-muhammad-abduh-in-taha-husseins-days.html (accessed 12 May 2021).

71 Shuruq Naguib, 'The Hermeneutics of Miracle: Evolution, Eloquence, and the Critique of Scientific Exegesis in the Literary School of *tafsīr*. Part I: From

Muḥammad 'Abduh to Amīn al-Khūlī', *Journal of Qur'ānic Studies*, 21(3) (2019): 67.

72 Ibid., 68.

73 Abu Zayd, 'Literary Approach to the Qur'an', 9.

74 Ibid., 20; Muhammad ʿAbduh and Muhammad Rashid Rida, *Tafsīr al-Qurʾān al-Ḥakīm al-Mushtahīr bi-sm Tafsīr al-Manār*, 2nd edn, vol. 2 (Cairo: al-Manar, 1947), 471.

75 Abu Zayd, 'Literary Approach to the Qur'an', 25.

76 Ibid., 34–5.

77 Ibid., 39.

78 Ibid.

79 Ibid., 35–6.

80 Ali Merad, 'L'enseignement politique de Muhammad 'Abduh aux algériens (1903)', *Confluent*, 42–3 (1964): 643–89; Chenoufi Moncef, 'Les deux séjours de Muhammad 'Abduh en Tunisie', *Les Cahiers de Tunisie*, 16 (1968): 57–96; Rachid Bencheneb, 'Le séjour du Šayẖ 'Abduh en Algérie (1903)', *Studia Islamica*, 53 (1981): 121–35.

81 Jutta Bluhm-Warn, 'A Preliminary Statement on the Dialogue Established between the Reform Magazine Al-Manar and the Malay-Indonesian World', *Indonesia Circle*, 32 (1983): 35–42; Mona Abaza, 'Southeast Asia and the Middle East: Al-Manār and Islamic Modernity', in *From the Mediterranean to the China Sea: Miscellaneous Notes*, ed. Claude Guillot, Denys Lombard and Roderick Ptak (Wiesbaden: Otto Harrassowitz, 1998), 93–111; Abushouk Ahmed Ibrahim, 'Al-Manār and the Ḥadhramī Elite in the Malay-Indonesian World: Challenge and Response', *Journal of the Royal Asiatic Society*, 17 (2007): 301–22; Hafiz Zakariya, 'From Cairo to the Straits Settlements: Modern *Salafiyyah* Reformist Ideas in Malay Peninsula', *Intellectual Discourse*, 15(2) (2007): 125–46.

82 Christopher Pooya Razavian, 'From *fiṭrah* to Perfectionism: The Development of Islamist Political Theory from Rashid Rida to Tabatabai and Motahari', Paper Presented at the Workshop 'Divine Sovereignty, Morality and the State: Maududi and His Influence', King's College London, 5 September 2019; Oliver Scharbrodt, and Mohammad Mesbahi, 'Maḥmūd Ṭāliqānī', in *The De Gruyter Handbook of Qur'ānic Hermeneutics*, ed. Georges Tamer (Berlin: De Gruyter, forthcoming).

83 Ammeke Kateman, *Muḥammad 'Abduh and His Interlocutors: Conceptualizing Religion in a Globalizing World* (Leiden: Brill, 2019), 239–40.

Bibliography

Primary sources

ʻAbd al-Raziq, ʻAli. *Al-Islām wa-Uṣūl al-Ḥukm: Baḥth fī-l-Khilāfa wa-l-Ḥukūma fī-l-Islām*. Cairo: Matbaʻat Misr, 1925.

ʻAbd al-Raziq, Mustafa. ʻDhikrā Rīnān fī-l-Jāmiʻa al-Miṣriyyaʼ. *al-Manār*, 24 (1923): 303–17.

ʻAbd al-Raziq, Mustafa. *Muḥammad ʻAbduh*. Cairo: Dar al-Maʻarif, 1946.

ʻAbduh, Muhammad. *Al-Aʻmāl al-Kāmila li-l-Imām Muḥammad ʻAbduh*, edited by Muhammad ʻImara. 5 vols, Beirut: Dar al-Shuruq, 1993.

ʻAbduh, Muhammad. *Al-Fatāwa fī-l-Tajdīd wa-l-Iṣlāḥ al-Dīnī*. Tunis: Dar al-Maʻarif, 1989.

ʻAbduh, Muhammad. *Al-Islām bayna-l-ʻIlm wa-l-Madaniyya*. Damascus: Dar al-Sida li-l-Thaqafa wa-l-Nashr, 2002.

ʻAbduh, Muhammad. ʻFaransā wa-l-Jazāʼirʼ, *al-Manār* 6 (1903): 79–80.

ʻAbduh, Muhammad. *Fatāwa al-Imām Muḥammad ʻAbduh*. Cairo: al-Jamʻiyya al-Khayriyya al-Islamiyya, 2005.

ʻAbduh, Muhammad. ʻNafī al-Qitāl bayna-l-Muslimīn li-Ajall al-Iʻtiqādʼ. *al-Manār*, 5 (1902): 405–7.

ʻAbduh, Muhammad. *Nahj al-Balāgha: Sharḥ al-Ustādh al-Imām al-Shaykh Muḥammad ʻAbduh*. 4 vols, Beirut: Dar al-Maʻrifa, n.d.

ʻAbduh, Muhammad. *Risālat al-Tawḥīd*. 17th edn, Cairo: Yousif Sulayman, 1960.

ʻAbduh, Muhammad. *Risālat al-Wāridāt: fī Naẓariyyāt al-Mutakallimīn wa-l-Ṣūfiyya fī-l-Falsafa al-Ilāhiyya*. 2nd edn, Cairo: al-Manar, 1925.

ʻAbduh, Muhammad. *Rissalat al tawhid: exposé de la religion musulmane*, traduite de l'arabe avec une introduction sur la vie et les idées du Cheikh Mohammed Abdou par B. Michel et Moustapha Abdel Razik. Paris: Geuthner, 1925.

ʻAbduh, Muhammad. *Tafsīr al-Fātiḥa*. Cairo: Ismaʻil Hafiz, 1901.

ʻAbduh, Muhammad. *Tafsīr Juzʼ ʻAmma*. 3rd edn, Cairo: Matbaʻat Misr, 1341H [1922–3].

ʻAbduh, Muhammad. *The Theology of Unity*, translated by Ishaq Musaʻad and Kenneth Cragg. London: George Allan and Unwin, 1966.

ʻAbduh, Muhammad, and Muhammad Rashid Rida. *Tafsīr al-Qurʾān al-Ḥakīm al-Mushtahīr bi-sm Tafsīr al-Manār*. 12 vols, 2nd edn, Cairo: al-Manar, 1947.

al-Afghani, Jamal al-Din. *Al-Aʻmāl al-Kāmila li-Jamāl al-Dīn al-Afghānī*, edited by Hadi Khosroshahi. 6 vols, Tehran: al-Majmaʻ al-ʻAlami li-l-Taqrib bayna-l-Madhahib al-Islamiyya, 2000.

al-Afghani, Jamal al-Din, and Muhammad ʿAbduh. *Al-Taʿlīqāt ʿalā Sharḥ al-ʿAqāʾid al-ʿAḍudiyya*. Cairo: Maktabat al-Shuruq al-Duwwaliyya, 2002.

al-Afghani, Jamal al-Din, and Muhammad ʿAbduh. *Al-ʿUrwa al-Wuthqā wa-l-Thawra al-Taḥrīriyya al-Kubrā*. 2nd edn, Cairo: Dar al-ʿArab, 1958.

Afshar, Iraj, and Asghar Mahdawi (eds). *Majmūʿa-yi Asnād wa-Madārik Chāp Nashuda Dar Barā-yi Sayyid Jamāl al-Dīn Mashhūr Ba Afghānī*. Tehran: University of Tehran, 1963.

Amin, Ahmad. *Zuʿamāʾ al-Iṣlāḥ fī-l-ʿAṣr al-Ḥadīth*. Beirut: Dar al-Kitab al-ʿArabi, 1948.

Amin, Qasim. *Al-Marʾa al-Jadīda*. Cairo: Hindawi, [1901] 2011.

Amin, Qasim. *Taḥrīr al-Marʾa*. Cairo: Hindawi, [1899] 2016.

Amin, ʿUthman. *Muḥammad ʿAbduh*. Cairo: Dar Ajyaʾ al-Kutub al-ʿArabiyya, 1944.

Amin, ʿUthman. *Muhammad ʿAbduh*, translated by Charles Wendell. Washington, DC: American Council of Learned Societies, 1953.

ʿAnhuri, Salim. *Siḥr Hārūt*. Damascus: al-Matbaʿa al-Hanafiyya, 1885.

al-Banna, Hasan. *Majmūʿa Rasāʾil al-Imām al-Shahīd Ḥasan al-Bannā*. n.p., n.d.

al-Banna, Hasan. *Mudhakkirāt al-Daʿwa wa-al-Dā ʿiyya*. Kuwait: Maktabat Afaq, 2012.

Baring, Evelyn Earl of Cromer. *Modern Egypt*. 2 vols, London: Macmillan, 1908.

Blunt, Wilfrid S. *Secret History of the English Occupation of Egypt: Being a Personal Narrative of Events*. 2nd edn, London: Fisher Unwin, 1907.

Blunt, Wilfrid S. *The Future of Islam*, edited by Riad Nourallah. London: Routledge Curzon, [1882] 2002.

Broadley, Alexander M. *How We Defended Arabi and His Friends: A Story of Egypt and the Egyptians*. London: Chapman and Hall, 1884.

Browne, Edward G. *A Year amongst the Persians*. Cambridge: Cambridge University Press, [1893] 1927.

Browne, Edward G. *The Press and Poetry of Modern Persia*. Cambridge: Cambridge University Press, 1914.

Dunya, Sulayman (eds). *Al-Shaykh Muḥammad ʿAbduh bayna-l-Falāsifa-wa-l-Kalāmiyīn*, 2 vols. Cairo: ʿIsa al-Babi al-Halabi, 1958.

al-Ghazali. *Freedom and Fulfilment: An Annotated Translation of Al-Ghazali's al-Munqidh min al-dalal and Other Relevant Works of al-Ghazali by Richard Joseph McCarthy*. Boston: Twayne, 1980.

al-Ghazali. *Kīmīyā-yi Saʿādat*. 2 vols, Tehran: Intisharat-i ʿIlmi wa-Farhangi, 1380 SH [2001/2002].

al-Ghazali. *Mizān al-ʿAmal*. Cairo: Dar al-Maʿarif, 1964.

Guizot, François. *The History of Civilization in Europe*. New York: Colonial Press, 1899.

Hamada, ʿAbd al-Munʿim. *Al-Ustādh al-Imām Muḥammad ʿAbduh*. Cairo: al-Maktaba al-Tijariyya, 1945.

Hanotaux, Gabriel. 'L'islam', *Le Journal*, 9(2730) (1900): 1.

Hanotaux, Gabriel. 'L'islam. II', *Le Journal*, 9(2737) (1900): 1.

Husayn, Taha. *Al-Ayyām*. Cairo: Hindawi, [1929] 2014.

Ibn Khaldun. *Muqaddimat ibn Khaldūn*. 3 vols, Damascus: Dar Ya'rib, 2003.

Ibn Khaldun. *The Muqaddimah: An Introduction to History*, translated by Franz Rosenthal, abridged and edited by Nessim Joseph Dawood. Princeton: Princeton University Press, 2015.

Ibn Miskawayh. *Al-Sa'āda li-bn Miskawayh fī Falsafat al-Akhlāq*. Cairo: al-Matba'a al-'Arabiyya, 1928.

Ibn Miskawayh. *Tahdhīb al-Akhlāq*. Cairo: Matba'at al-Taraqqi, 1317H [1900/1901].

Ishaq, Adib. *Al-Durar: wa-Hiya Muntakhabāt al-Ṭayyib al-Dhikr al-Khālid al-Athar al-Marḥūm Adīb Ishaq*. Alexandria: Matba'at Jaridat al-Mahrusa, 1886.

Jawhari, Tantawi. *Al-Jawāhir fī Tafsīr al-Qurʾān al-Karīm al-Mushtamil ʿalā ʿAjāʾib Badāʾiʿ al-Mukawwināt wa-Gharāʾib al-Āyāt al-Bāhirāt*, 13 vols. Beirut: Dar al-Kutub al-'Ilmiyya, 2005.

Kemal, Namık. 'And Seek Their Counsel in the Matter [Qur'an, Sura 3, Verse 159]'. In *Modernist Islam, 1840–1940: A Sourcebook*, edited by Charles Kurzman, 144–8. Oxford: Oxford University Press, 2002.

Makariyus, Shahin. *Kitāb Faḍā'il al-Māsūniyya*, 2nd edn. Cairo: al-Muqattam, 1900.

Maududi, Sayyid Abul A'la. *The Islamic Law and Constitution*, translated and edited by Khurshid Ahmad. Lahore: Islamic Publications, 1960.

Mazandarani, Fazil. *Ta'rīkh-i Ẓuhūr al-Ḥaqq*. vol. 6. Available online: http://www.h-net.org/~bahai/arabic/vol3/tzh6/tzh6.htm (accessed 11 May 2021).

Qutb, Sayyid. *Ma'ālim fī-l-Ṭarīq*. Cairo: Dar al-Shuruq, [1964] 1979.

Rafi'i, 'Abd al-Rahman. *Al-Thawra al-'Urābiyya wa-l-Iḥtilāl al-Injilīzī*. Cairo: Maktabat al-Nahda al-Misriyya, 1949.

Rida, Muhammad Rashid. *Al-Khilāfa* [*aw al-Imāma al-'Uẓmā*]. Cairo: Hindawi, [1922] 2015.

Rida, Muhammad Rashid. *Al-Wahhābiyyūn wa-l-Ḥijāz*. Cairo: al-Manar, 1344H [1925/1926].

Rida, Muhammad Rashid. 'Manāfi' al-Ūrubiyīn wa-Maḍāruhum fī-l-Sharq'. *al-Manār*, 10 (1907), 340–4.

Rida, Muhammad Rashid. 'Mulakhkhaṣ Sīrat al-Ustādh al-Imām'. *al-Manār*, 8 (1905), part 10: 379–400; part 11: 401–16; part 12: 453–65; part 13: 487–95; part 14: 534–52; part 15: 597–9.

Rida, Muhammad Rashid. 'Qawl fī-l-Muftī wa-Taqlīdihī'. *al-Manār*, 6 (1904): 785–6.

Rida, Muhammad Rashid. 'Ta'yīd al-Fatwā wa-Ḥaqīqatuhā wa-mā bihī al-Iftā''. *al-Manār*, 6 (1904): 784–5.

Rida, Muhammad Rashid. *Ta'rīkh al-Ustādh al-Imām al-Shaykh Muḥammad 'Abduh*, 3 vols. Cairo: al-Manar, 1924–31.

Shalash, 'Ali. *Silsilat al-A'māl al-Majhūla Muḥammad 'Abduh*. London: Riad al-Rayyes, 1987.

al-Taftazani, Sa'd al-Din. *Tahdhīb al-Manṭiq wa-l-Kalām*. Cairo: Matba'at al-Sa'ada, 1912.

Tanahi, Tahir (eds). *Mudhakkirāt al-Imām Muḥammad 'Abduh*. Cairo: Dar al-Hilal, n.d.

Taylor, Isaac. *Leaves from an Egyptian Note-Book*. London: Kegan Paul, 1888.
Tusi, Nasir al-Din. *Akhlāq-i Nāṣirī*. Tehran: Khwarizmi, 1356 SH [1977/1978].
Zaydan, Jurji. *Tarājim Mashāhir al-Sharq fī-l-Qarn al-Tāsi' al-'Ashara*, 2 vols. Cairo: al-Hilal, 1902–3.

Secondary sources

Abaza, Mona. 'Southeast Asia and the Middle East: Al-Manār and Islamic Modernity'. In *From the Mediterranean to the China Sea: Miscellaneous Notes*, edited by Claude Guillot, Denys Lombard and Roderick Ptak, 93–111. Wiesbaden: Otto Harrassowitz, 1998.
'Abduh, Ibrahim. *Jarīdat al-Ahrām: Ta'rīkh wa-Fann (1875–1964)*. Cairo: Mu'assasat Sajall al-'Arab, 1964.
Abu Zayd, Nasr Hamid. 'The Dilemma of the Literary Approach to the Qur'an'. *Alif: Journal of Comparative Poetics*, 23 (2003): 8–47.
Abun-Nasr, Jamil M. *The Tijaniyya: A Sufi Order in the Modern World*. Oxford: Oxford University Press, 1965.
Abushouk, Ahmed Ibrahim. 'Al-Manār and the Ḥadhramī Elite in the Malay-Indonesian World: Challenge and Response'. *Journal of the Royal Asiatic Society*, 17 (2007): 301–22.
Adams, Charles C. *Islam and Modernism in Egypt: A Study of the Modern Reform Movement Inaugurated by Muhammad 'Abduh*. London: Oxford University Press, 1933.
Adams, Charles C. 'Muhammad 'Abduh and the Transvaal Fatwa'. In *The MacDonald Presentation Volume*, 13–29. Princeton: Princeton University Press, 1933.
Afshar, Iraj. *Sawād-u Bayāḍ: Majmū'a-yi Maqālāt*. vol. 1, Tehran: Dehkhoda, 1344 SH [1966].
Ahmed, Shahab. *What Is Islam?: The Importance of Being Islamic*. Princeton: Princeton University Press, 2016.
Al-Charif, Maher and Sabrina Mervin (eds). *Modernités islamiques: Actes du colloque organisé à Alep à l'occasion du centenaire de la disparition de l'imam Muḥammad 'Abduh, 9–10 novembre 2005*, Damascus: IFPO, 2006.
Al-Salman, Muhammad b. 'Abdallah. *Rashīd Riḍā wa-Da'wat al-Shaykh Muḥammad b. 'Abd al-Wahhāb*. Kuwait: Maktabat al-Mu'alla, 1988.
Al-Sawi, Ahmad H. 'Muhammad 'Abduh and al-Waqa'i' al-Misriyyah'. MSc diss., Montreal, 1954.
Anjum, Ovamir. *Politics, Law, and Community in Islamic Thought: The Taymiyyan Moment*. Cambridge: Cambridge University Press, 2012.
Ayalon, Ami. *Language and Change in the Arab Middle East: The Evolution of Modern Political Discourse*. New York: Oxford University Press, 1987.

Ayubi, Nazih. *Political Islam: Religion and Politics in the Arab World*. London: Routledge, 1991.

Ayyub, M. 'Islam and Christianity: A Study of Muhammad Abduh's View of the Two Religions'. *Humaniora Islamica*, 2 (1974): 121–37.

Badawi, Zaki. *Three Reformers of Egypt: A Critique of al-Afghani, 'Abduh and Ridha*. Slough: Open Press, 1976.

Barbour, Nevill. 'The Arabic Theatre in Egypt'. *Bulletin of the School of Oriental and African Studies*, 8(1) (1935): 173–87.

Bauer, Thomas. *A Culture of Ambiguity: An Alternative History of Islam*. New York: Columbia University Press, 2021.

Bauer, Thomas. *Die Kultur der Ambiguität: Eine andere Geschichte des Islams*. Berlin: Verlag der Weltreligionen, 2011.

Bayat, Mangol. *Mysticism and Dissent: Socioreligious Thought in Qajar Iran*. Syracuse: Syracuse University Press, 1999.

Bencheneb, Rachid. 'Le séjour du Šayḫ 'Abduh en Algérie (1903)'. *Studia Islamica*, 53 (1981): 121–35.

Berger, Lutz. 'Esprits et microbes: l'interpretation des ǧinn-s dans quelques commentaires coraniques du XXe siècle'. *Arabica* 47(3) (2000): 554–62.

Binder, Leonard *The Ideological Revolution in the Middle East*. New York: Wiley, 1964.

Black, Antony. *The History of Islamic Political Thought: From the Prophet to the Present*, 2nd edn. Edinburgh: Edinburgh University Press, 2011.

Bluhm-Warn, Jutta. 'A Preliminary Statement on the Dialogue Established between the Reform Magazine Al-Manār and the Malay-Indonesian World'. *Indonesia Circle*, 32 (1983): 35–42.

Buessow, Johann. 'Re-imagining Islam in the Period of the First Modern Globalization: Muhammad 'Abduh and His *Theology of Unity*'. In *A Global Middle East: Mobility, Materiality and Culture in the Modern Age, 1880–1940*, edited by Liat Kozma, Cyrus Schayegh and Avner Wishnitzer, 273–320. London: I.B. Tauris, 2015.

Calvert, John. *Sayyid Qutb and the Origins of Radical Islamism*. London: Hurst, 2010.

Carré, Olivier. *L'utopie islamique dans l'Orient arabe*. Paris: Presses de la Fondation Nationale des Sciences Politiques, 1991.

Carré, Olivier. *Mystique et politique: le Coran des islamistes, Commentaire coranique de Sayyid Qutb (1906–1966)*. Paris: Éditions du CERF, 2004.

Caspar, R. 'Le Renouveau mo'tazilite'. *Mélanges d'Institut Dominicain d'Etudes Orientales du Caire*, 4 (1957): 141–201.

Chenoufi, Moncef. 'Les deux séjours de Muhammad 'Abduh en Tunisie'. *Les Cahiers de Tunisie*, 16 (1968): 57–96.

Chodkiewicz, Michel. *Seal of the Saints: Prophethood and Sainthood in the Doctrine of Ibn 'Arabi*. Cambridge: The Islamic Texts Society, 1993.

Chodkiewicz, Michel. *Un océan sans rivage: Ibn Arabî, le Livre et la Loi*. Paris: Éditions du Seuil, 1992.

Cole, Juan R. I. *Colonialism and Revolution in the Middle East: Social and Cultural Origins of Egypt's 'Urabi Revolt*. Princeton: Princeton University Press, 1993.

Cole, Juan R. I. 'Individualism and the Spiritual Path in Shaykh Ahmad al-Ahsa'i'. *Occasional Papers in Shaykhi, Babi and Baha'i Studies*, 1 (1997). http://www.h-net.org/~bahai/bhpapers/ahsaind.htm (accessed 6 May 2021).

Cole, Juan R. I. 'New Perspectives on Sayyid Jamal al-Din al-Afghani in Egypt'. In *Iran and Beyond: Essays in Middle Eastern History in Honor of Nikki R. Keddie*, edited by Rainer Mathee and Beth Baron, 13–34. Costa Mesa: Mazda, 2000.

Cole, Juan R. I. 'Rifa'a al-Tahtawi and the Revival of Practical Philosophy'. *The Muslim World*, 70 (1980): 29–46.

Cole, Juan R. I. 'The World as a Text: Cosmologies of Shaykh Ahmad al-Ahsa'i'. *Studia Islamica*, 80 (1994): 1–23.

Colombe, Marcel (trans). 'Pages choisies de Djamal al-Din al-Afghani'. *Orient*, 21 (1962): 87–115; *Orient*, 22 (1962): 125–59; *Orient*, 23 (1962), 169–90; *Orient*, 24 (1962): 125–51; *Orient*, 25 (1963): 141–52.

Corbin, Henri. *En Islam iranien: Aspects spirituels et philosophiques*. 4 vols, Paris: Gallimard, 1971–3.

Corbin, Henri. *History of Islamic Philosophy*. London: Routledge, 2014.

Cornell, Vincent J. 'Muḥammad 'Abduh: A Sufi-Inspired Modernist?'. In *Tradition and Modernity: Christian and Muslim Perspectives*, edited by David Marshall, 105–14. Washington, DC: Georgetown University Press, 2009.

Dallal, Ahmad S. *Islam without Europe: Traditions of Reform in Eighteenth Century Islamic Thought*. Chapel Hill: University of North Carolina Press, 2018.

Dallal, Ahmad S. 'Review: Ghazali and the Perils of Interpretation'. *Journal of the American Oriental Society*, 122(4) (2002): 773–87.

Daly, Martin W. (eds). *The Cambridge History of Egypt, Volume 2: Modern Egypt, from 1517 to the End of the Twentieth Century*. Cambridge: Cambridge University Press, 1998.

Dawud, 'Ali Al-e. 'Coffeehouse'. *Encyclopaedia Iranica*, 6, fasc. 1 (1992): 1–4.

Delanoue, Gilbert. 'Endoctrinement religieux et idéologie ottmane: l'adresse de Muh'ammad [!] 'Abduh au Cheikh al-Islam, Beyrouth, 1887'. *Revue de l'Occident musulman et de la Méditerranée*, 13–14 (1973): 293–312.

Delanoue, Gilbert. *Moralistes et politiques musulmans dans l'Egypte de XIXe siècle (1798–1882)*. 2 vols, Cairo: Institut Français de l'Achéologie Orientale du Caire, 1982.

De Poli, Barbara. 'Italians, Freemasons and the Dawn of Egyptian Nationalism'. *The Journal of North African Studies* (2021), DOI: 10.1080/13629387.2021.1891533.

Devereux, Robert. *The First Ottoman Constitutional Period: A Study of the Midhat Constitution and Parliament*. Baltimore: John Hopkins University Press, 1963.

Eickelman, Dale F. 'Traditional Islamic Learning and Ideas of the Person in the Twentieth Century'. In *Middle Eastern Lives: The Practice of Biography and Self-Narrative*, edited by Martin Kramer, 35–59. Syracuse: Syracuse University Press, 1991.

Enayat, Hamid. *Modern Islamic Political Thought*. Austin: University of Texas Press, 1982.

Eschraghi, Armin. *Frühe Šaihī- und Bābī Theologie: Die Darlegung des Beweises für Muhammads besonderes Prophetentum* (Ar-Risāla fī Iṯbāt an-Nubūwa al-Ḫāssa). Leiden: Brill, 2004.

Escovitz, Joseph H. '"He was the Muhammad 'Abduh of Syria": A Study of Tahir al-Jaza'iri and His Influence'. *International Journal of Middle East Studies*, 18 (1986): 293–310.

van Ess, Josef. 'Ażod-al-Dīn Ījī'. *Encyclopaedia Iranica*, vol. 3, fasc. 3 (1988): 269–71.

Ezzerelli, Kaïs. 'Muhammad 'Abduh et les réformistes syro-libanais: influence, image, postérité'. In *Modernités islamiques: Actes du colloque organisé à Alep à l'occasion du centenaire de la disparition de l'imam Muḥammad ʿAbduh, 9–10 novembre 2005*, edited by Maher Al-Charif and Sabrina Mervin, 79–105. Damascus: IFPO, 2006.

Fahmy, Khaled. *All the Pasha's Men: Mehmed Ali, His Army and the Making of Modern Egypt*. Cairo: The American University in Cairo Press, 2002.

Fahmy, Khaled. 'The Era of Muhammad 'Ali Pasha, 1805–1848'. In *The Cambridge History of Egypt*, edited by Martin W. Daly, vol. 2, 139–79. Cambridge: Cambridge University Press, 1998.

Fakhry, Majid F. 'Ethics in Islamic Philosophy'. In *Routledge Encyclopedia of Philosophy*, edited by Edward Craig. London: Routledge, 1998.

Fortna, Benjamin C. 'Education and Autobiography at the End of the Ottoman Empire'. *Die Welt des Islams*, 41 (2001): 1–31.

Fortna, Benjamin C. *Imperial Classroom: Islam, the State, and Education in the Late Ottoman Empire*. Oxford: Oxford University Press, 2002.

Fortna, Benjamin C. 'Islamic Morality in Late Ottoman "Secular" Schools'. *International Journal of Middle East Studies*, 32 (2000): 369–93.

Friedmann, Yohanan. *Shaykh Aḥmad Sirhindī: An Outline of His Thought and a Study of His Image in the Eyes of Posterity*, 2nd edn. New Delhi: Oxford University Press, 2001.

Gesinck, Indira Falk. *Islamic Reform and Conservatism: Al-Azhar and the Evolution of Modern Sunni Islam*. London: I.B. Tauris, 2010.

Gilsenan, Michael. *Saint and Sufi in Modern Egypt: An Essay in the Sociology of Religion*. Oxford: Clarendon Press, 1973.

Goldziher Ignaz *Schools of Koranic Commentators*. Wiesbaden: Otto Harrassowitz, 2006.

Gottheil, Richard. 'Mohammad 'Abdu: Late Mufti of Egypt'. *Journal of the American Oriental Society*, 28 (1907): 189–97.

Griffel, Frank. 'Al-Ġazālī's Concept of Prophecy: The Introduction of Avicennan Psychology into Aš'arite Theology'. *Arabic Sciences and Philosophy*, 14 (2004): 101–44.

Griffel, Frank. 'Al-Ghazālī's Use of 'Original Human Disposition' (*Fiṭra*) and Its Background in the Teachings of al-Fārābī and Avicenna'. *The Muslim World*, 102(1) (2012): 1–32.

Griffel, Frank. 'The Harmony of Natural Law and Shari'a in Islamist Theology'. In *Shari'a: Islamic Law in the Contemporary Context*, edited by Abbas Amanat and Frank Griffel, 38–61. Stanford: Stanford University Press, 2007.

Gutas, Dimitri. 'The Empiricism of Avicenna'. *Oriens*, 40(2) (2012): 391–436.

Haddad, Mohamed. "Abduh et ses lecteurs: pour in histoire critique de "lectures" de Muhammad 'Abduh'. *Arabica* 45 (1998): 22–49.

Haddad, Mohamed. 'Les Oeuvres de 'Abduh: histoire d'une manipulation'. *Revue de l'Institut des Belles Lettres Arabes*, 180 (1997): 197–222.

Haddad, Mohamed. *Muḥammad 'Abduh: Qarā'a Jadīda fī Khiṭāb al-Iṣlāḥ al-Dīnī*. Beirut: Dar al-Tali'a li-l-Taba'a wa-l-Nashr, 2003.

Haddad, Mohamed. 'Relire Muhammad Abduh (à propos de l'article "M. Abduh" dans l'Encyclopédie de l'Islam)'. *Revue de l'Institut des Belles Lettres Arabes*, 185 (2000): 61–84.

Haddad, Mahmud O. 'Rashid Rida and the Theory of the Caliphate: Medieval Themes and Modern Concerns'. PhD diss., New York, 1989.

Haddad, Yvonne Y. 'Muhammad Abduh: Pioneer of Islamic Reform'. In *Pioneers of Islamic Revival*, edited by Ali Rahnema 30–63. 2nd edn, London: Zed Books, [1994] 2005.

Haddad, Yvonne Y. 'Muslim Revivalist Thought in the Arab World: An Overview'. *The Muslim World*, 76 (1986): 143–67.

Haj, Samira. *Reconfiguring Islamic Tradition: Reform, Rationality, and Modernity*. Stanford: Stanford University Press, 2009.

Hamza, Dyala. 'Pensée d'Abduh à l'âge utiliaire: l'intérêt general entre *maṣlaḥa* et *manfa'a*'. In *Modernités islamiques: Actes du colloque organisé à Alep à l'occasion du centenaire de la disparition de l'imam Muḥammad 'Abduh, 9–10 novembre 2005*, edited by Maher Al-Charif and Sabrina Mervin. Damascus: IFPO, 2006.

Hanssen, Jens. 'The Birth of an Education Qarter: Zokak el-Blat as the Cradle of Cultural Revival in the Arab World'. In *History, Space and Social Conflict in Beirut: The Quarter of Zokak el-Blat*, edited by Hans Gebhard, 143–74. Würzburg: Ergon, 2005.

Harris, Christina P. *Nationalism and Revolution in Egypt: The Role of the Muslim Brotherhood*. The Hague: Mouton, 1964.

Hartmann, Martin. *The Arabic Press of Egypt*. London: Luzac, 1899.

Hawting, Gerald R. 'The Significance of the Slogan *lā ḥukm^a illā lillāh* and the References to the *ḥudūd* in the Traditions about the *fitna* and the Murder of 'Uthmān'. *Bulletin of the School of Oriental and African Studies*, 61 (1978): 453–63.

Hildebrandt, Thomas. 'Waren Ǧamāl ad-Dīn al-Afghānī und Muḥammad 'Abduh Neo-Mu'taziliten?'. *Die Welt des Islams*, 42(2) (2002): 207–62.

Hockey, Thomas, Virginia Trimble, Thomas R. Williams, Katherine Bracher, Richard A. Jarrell, Jordan D. Maréchall, JoAnn Palmeri and Daniel W. E. Green (eds). *The Biographical Encyclopedia of Astronomers*. New York: Springer, 2007.

Hoffman, Valerie J. 'Annihilation in the Messenger of God: The Development of a Sufi Practice'. *International Journal of Middle East Studies*, 31 (1999): 351–69.

Hoffman, Valerie J. *Sufism, Mystics, and Saints in Modern Egypt*. Columbia: University of South Carolina Press, 1995.

Horten, Max. 'Muhammad 'Abduh: sein Leben und seine theologisch-philosophische Gedankenwelt'. *Beiträge zur Kenntnis des Orients*, 13 (1916): 85–114; 14 (1916): 74–128.

Hourani, Albert. *Arabic Thought in the Liberal Age: 1798–1939*. Cambridge: Cambridge University Press, 1983.

Hourani, Albert. 'Sufism and Modern Islam: Rashid Rida'. In *The Emergence of the Modern Middle East*, edited by Albert Hourani, 90–102. Berkley: University of California Press, 1981.

Hunter, F. Robert. 'Egypt under the Successors of Muhammad 'Ali'. In *The Cambridge History of Egypt*, edited by Martin W. Daly, 180–97. vol. 2, Cambridge: Cambridge University Press, 1998.

Iqtidar, Humeira. 'Theorising Sovereignty in the Colony: Abul A'la Maududi's "Theodemocracy"'. *Review of Politics*, 82(4) (2020): 595–617.

Jansen, J. J. G. *The Interpretation of the Koran in Modern Egypt*. Leiden: Brill, 1974.

Jomier, Jacques. 'La raison et l'histoire dans le commentaire du Manār'. *Mélanges de l'Institut dominicain d'études orientales du Caire*, 19 (1989): 17–45.

Jomier, Jacques. 'La revue al-'Orwa al-Wothqa (13 mars – 16 octobre 1884) et l'autorité du Coran'. *Mélanges d'Institut Dominicain d'Etudes Orientales du Caire*, 17 (1986): 9–36.

Jomier, Jacques. *Le Commentaire Coranique du Manâr: tendances modernes de l'exégèse en Egypte*. Paris: Maisonneuve, 1954.

Jung, Dietrich. 'Islamic Reform and the Global Public Sphere: Muhammad Abduh and Islamic Modernity'. In *The Middle East and Globalization: Encounters and Horizons*, edited by Stephan Stetter, 153–69. New York: Palgrave Macmillan, 2012.

Jung, Dietrich. *Orientalists, Islamists and the Global Public Sphere: A Genealogy of the Modern Essentialist Image of Islam*. Sheffield: Equinox, 2011.

Kalmbach, Hillary. *Islamic Knowledge and the Making of Modern Egypt*. Cambridge: Cambridge University Press, 2020.

Kassab, Elizabeth S. *Contemporary Arab Thought: Cultural Critique in Comparative Perspective*. New York: Columbia University Press, 2010.

Kateman, Ammeke. *Muḥammad 'Abduh and His Interlocutors: Conceptualizing Religion in a Globalizing World*. Leiden: Brill, 2019.

Keddie, Nikki R. *An Islamic Response to Imperialism: Political and Religious Writings of Sayyid Jamāl ad-Dīn 'al-Afghānī'*. Berkeley: University of California Press, 1968.

Keddie, Nikki R. 'Islamic Philosophy and Islamic Modernism: The Case of Jamāl ad-Dīn al-Afghānī'. *Iran*, 6 (1968): 53–6.

Keddie, Nikki R. *Sayyid Jamāl ad-Dīn 'al-Afghānī': A Political Biography.* Berkeley: University of California Press, 1972.

Keddie, Nikki R. 'Symbol and Sincerity in Islam'. *Studia Islamica*, 19 (1963): 27–63.

Keddie, Nikki R. (ed.). *Scholars, Saints, and Sufis: Muslim Religious Institutions in the Middle East since 1500.* Berkeley: University of California Press, 1972.

Kedourie, Elie. *Afghani and 'Abduh: An Essay on Religious Unbelief and Political Activism in Modern Islam.* London: Frank Cass, 1966.

Kemke, Andreas H. E. *Stiftungen im muslimischen Rechtsleben des neuzeitlichen Ägypten: Die shariarechtlichen Gutachten (Fatwas) von Muhammad 'Abduh (st. 1905) zum Wakf.* Frankfurt A.M.: Peter Lang, 1991.

Kenny, L. M. 'Al-Afghānī on the Types of Despotism'. *Journal of the American Oriental Society*, 86(1) (1966): 19–27.

Kerr, Malcolm H. *Islamic Reform: The Legal and Political Theories of Muhammad 'Abduh and Rashid Rida.* Berkeley: University of California Press, 1966.

Khatab, Sayed. 'Hakimiyyah and Jahiliyyah in the Thought of Sayyid Qutb'. *Middle Eastern Studies*, 38 (2002): 145–70.

Knysh, Alexander. '*Irfan* Revisited: Khomeini and the Legacy of Islamic Mystical Philosophy'. *Middle East Journal*, 46(4) (1992): 631–53.

Kohn, Margaret. 'Afghānī on Empire, Islam, and Civilization'. *Political Theory*, 37(3) (2009): 398–422.

Krämer, Gudrun. *Hasan al-Banna.* Oxford: Oneworld, 2009.

Kraiem, Mustapha. 'Au sujet des incidences des deux séjours de Muhammad 'Abduh en Tunisie'. *Revue d'Histoire Maghrébien*, 3 (1975): 91–4.

Kramer, Martin (ed.). *Middle Eastern Lives: The Practice of Biography and Self-Narrative.* Syracuse: Syracuse University Press, 1991.

Kudsi-Zadeh, A. Albert. 'Afghānī and Freemasonry in Egypt'. *Journal of the American Oriental Society*, 92(1) (1972): 25–35.

Kudsi-Zadeh, A. Albert. 'Islamic Reform in Egypt: Some Observations on the Role of Afghānī'. *The Muslim World*, 61(1) (1971): 1–12.

Kudsi-Zadeh, A. Albert. 'The Emergence of Political Journalism in Egypt'. *The Muslim World*, 70(1) (1980): 47–55.

von Kügelgen, Anke. ''Abduh, Muḥammad'. In *Encyclopaedia of Islam, THREE*, edited by Kate Fleet, Gudrun Krämer, Denis Matringe, John Nawas and Everett Rowson. Available online: http://dx.doi.org/10.1163/1573-3912_ei3_COM_0103 (accessed 12 May 2021).

Kundos, Zahiye. 'The Loss of the Mufti: Muhammad 'Abduh in Taha Husayn's Days'. *Europe in the Middle East – The Middle East in Europe (EUME) Berliner Seminar* (2021). Available online: https://www.eume-berlin.de/en/events/calendar/details/the-loss-of-the-mufti-muhammad-abduh-in-taha-husseins-days.html (accessed 12 May 2021).

Landau-Tasseron, Ella. 'The "Cyclical Reform": A Study of the *Mujaddid* Tradition'. *Studia Islamica*, 70 (1989): 79–117.

Langner, Joachim. 'Religion in Motion and the Essence of Islam: Manifestations of the Global in Muhammad 'Abduh's Response to Farah Antūn'. In *A Global Middle East: Mobility, Materiality and Culture in the Modern Age, 1880–1940*, edited by Liat Kozma, Cyrus Schayegh and Avner Wishnitzer, 356–63. London: I.B. Tauris, 2015.

Laoust, Henri (trans.). *Le Califat dans la doctrine de Rašid Rida: Traduction annotée d'al-Hilâfa au al-Imâma al-'Uẓmâ (Le Califat ou l'Imama suprême)*. Beirut: Institute Français de Damas, 1938.

Lassner, Jacob. *The Middle East Remembered: Forged Identities, Competing Narratives, Contested Spaces*. Ann Arbor: University of Michigan Press, 2000.

Lauzière, Henri. *The Making of Salafism: Islamic Reform in the Twentieth Century*. New York: Columbia University Press, 2016.

Lazarus-Yafeh, Hava. 'Tajdīd al-Dīn: A Reconsideration of Its Meaning, Roots, and Influence in Islam'. In *Studies in Islamic and Judaic Traditions: Papers Presented at the Institute for Islamic-Judaic Studies*, edited by William M. Brunner and Stephen David Ricks, 99–108. Atlanta: Scholars Press, 1986.

Lewis, Bernard. 'First-Person Narrative in the Middle East'. In *Middle Eastern Lives: The Practice of Biography and Self-Narrative*, edited by Martin Kramer, 20–34. Syracuse: Syracuse University Press, 1991.

Lia, Brynjar. *The Society of the Muslim Brothers in Egypt: The Rise of an Islamic Mass Movement, 1928–1942*. Reading: Ithaca Press, 1998.

Livingston, John W. 'Muhammad 'Abduh on Science'. *The Muslim World*, 85 (1995): 215–34.

Luizard, Pierre-Jean. 'Muhamamd 'Abduh et la réforme d'Al-Azhar'. In *Modernités islamiques: Actes du colloque organisé à Alep à l'occasion du centenaire de la disparition de l'imam Muḥammad 'Abduh, 9–10 novembre 2005*, edited by Maher Al-Charif and Sabrina Mervin. Damascus: IFPO, 2006.

March, Andrew F. 'Naturalizing *Sharī'a*: Foundationalist Ambiguities in Modern Islamic Apologetics'. *Islamic Law and Society*, 22(1–20) (2015): 45–81.

March, Andrew F. *The Caliphate of Man: Popular Sovereignty in Modern Islamic Thought*. Cambridge, MA: Harvard University Press, 2019.

Mardin, Serif. *The Genesis of Young Ottoman Thought: A Study in the Modernization of Turkish Political Ideas*. Princeton: Princeton University Press, 1962.

Masud, Muhammad Khalid, and Armando Salvatore. 'Western Scholars of Islam on the Issue of Modernity'. In *Islam and Modernity: Key Issues and Debates*, edited by Muhammad Khalid Masud, Armando Salvatore and Martin van Bruinessen, 36–53. Edinburgh: Edinburgh University Press, 2009.

Matthee, Rudi. 'Jamal al-Din al-Afghani and the Egyptian National Debate'. *International Journal of Middle East Studies*, 21(2) (1989): 151–69.

McCants, Will. '"I never understood any of this from 'Abbas Effendi": Muhammad 'Abduh's Knowledge of the Baha'i Teachings and His Friendship with 'Abdu'l-Baha' 'Abbas'. In *Studies in Modern Religions, Religious Movements and the Babi-Baha'i Faiths*, edited by Moshe Sharon, 275–97. Leiden: Brill, 2004.

Merad, Ali. 'L'enseignement politique de Muhammad 'Abduh aux algériens (1903)'. *Confluent*, 42–3 (1964): 643–89.

Mervin, Sabrina. 'The Clerics of Jabal 'Amil and the Reform of Religious Teaching in Najaf since the Beginning of the 20th Century'. In *The Twelver Shia in Modern Times: Religious Culture and Political History*, edited by Rainer Brunner and Werner Ende, 79–86. Leiden: Brill, 2001.

Mitchell, Richard P. *The Society of the Muslim Brothers*. Oxford: Oxford University Press, 1969.

Momen, Moojan. *An Introduction to Shi'i Islam: The History and Doctrines of Twelver Shi'ism*. New Haven: Yale University Press, 1985.

Montada, Josep P. 'Al-Afghânî, a Case of Religious Unbelief?' *Studia Islamica*, 100(101) (2005): 203–20.

Montada, Josep P. 'Muḥammad 'Abduh, la revolución de 'Urâbî: dudas y certezas'. *Cuadernons de Historia Contemporáneo*, 35 (2013): 161–76.

Moreno, Martino M. 'La Mistica di Muhammad 'Abduh'. *Oriente Moderno*, 60 (1980): 403–35.

Musallam, Adnan A. 'Prelude to Islamic Commitment: Sayyid Quṭb's Literary and Spiritual Orientation, 1932–1938'. *The Muslim World*, 80 (1990): 176–89.

Naaman, Erez. 'Nurture over Nature: Habitus from al-Fārābī through Ibn Khaldūn to 'Abduh'. *Journal of the American Oriental Society*, 137(1) (2017): 1–24.

Naguib, Shuruq. 'The Hermeneutics of Miracle: Evolution, Eloquence, and the Critique of Scientific Exegesis in the Literary School of *tafsīr*. Part I: From Muḥammad 'Abduh to Amīn al-Khūlī'. *Journal of Qur'ānic Studies*, 21(3) (2019): 57–88.

Nasr, Sayyid H. *Three Muslim Sages: Avicenna, Suhrawardī, Ibn 'Arabī*. Cambridge, MA: Harvard University Press, 1964.

Nasr, Seyyed Hossein, and Mehdi Aminrazavi (eds). *An Anthology of Philosophy in Persia, Volume 4: From the School of Illumination to Philosophical Mysticism*. London: I.B. Tauris, 2012.

Netton, Ian R. *Allāh Transcendent: Studies in the Structure and Semiotics of Islamic Philosophy, Theology and Cosmology*. Richmond: Curzon, 1989.

Newman, Andrew J. 'Davānī, Jalāl al-Dīn Moḥammad'. *Encyclopaedia Iranica*, vol. 7, fasc. 2 (1994): 132–3.

Newman, Daniel. *Rifa'a Al-Tahtawi: A 19th Century Egyptian Educationalist and Reformer*. Edinburgh: Edinburgh University Press, 2020.

O'Fahey, R. Seán. *Enigmatic Saint: Ahmad Ibn Idris and the Idrisi Tradition*. London: Hurst, 1990.

O'Fahey, R. Seán, and Bernd Radtke. 'Neo-Sufism Reconsidered'. *Der Islam*, 70 (1993): 52–87.

Pakdaman, Homa. *Djamal-El-Din Assad Abadi dit Afghani*. Paris: Maisonneuve, 1969.

Pessagno, J. Meric. 'Irāda, Ikhtiyār, Qudra, Kasb: The View of Abū Manṣur al-Māturīdī'. *Journal of the American Oriental Society*, 104(1) (1984): 177–91.

Pink, Johanna. "Abduh, Muḥammad'. In *Encyclopedia of the Qur'ān*, edited by Jane Dammen McAuliffe. Leiden: Brill, 2001.

Prasch, Thomas 'Which God for Africa: The Islamic-Christian Missionary Debate in Late-Victorian England'. *Victorian Studies*, 33(1) (1989): 51–73.

Quinn, Sholeh A. *Historical Writing during the Reign of Shah 'Abbas: Ideology, Imitation, and Legitimacy in Safavid Chronicles*. Salt Lake City: University of Utah Press, 2000.

Radler, Christopher. *Eine Biographie als politisches Mittel: Muḥammad 'Abduh (1849–1905) und die Rebellion des Aḥmad 'Urābī in der Rezeption Ṭāhir aṭ-Ṭanāḥīs (Mudakkirāt al-Imām Muḥammad 'Abduh)*. Berlin: Klaus Schwarz, 2010.

Radtke, Bernd, and John O'Kane. *The Concept of Sainthood in Early Islamic Mysticism: Two Works by Al-Ḥakīm Al-Tirmidhī*. London: Routledge Curzon, 1996.

Ragep, Sally P. 'Jaghmini'. In *The Biographical Encyclopedia of Astronomers*, edited by Thomas Hockey, Virginia Trimble, Thomas R. Williams, Katherine Bracher, Richard A. Jarrell, Jordan D. Maréchall, JoAnn Palmeri and D. W. E. Green, 584–5. New York, Springer, 2007.

Rahman, Fazlur. 'Dream, Imagination and *'ālam al-mithāl*'. *Islamic Studies*, 3(2) (1964): 167–80.

Rahman, Fazlur. *Islam*, 2nd edn, Chicago: University of Chicago Press, 1979.

Rahman, Fazlur. *Prophecy in Islam: Philosophy and Orthodoxy*. London: George Allen & Unwin, 1958.

Rahman, Fazlur. *The Philosophy of Mulla Sadra*. Albany: State University of New York Press, 1975.

Razavian, Christopher Pooya.'From *fiṭrah* to Perfectionism: The Development of Islamist Political Theory from Rashīd Riḍā to Tabatabai and Motahari'. Paper Presented at the Workshop 'Divine Sovereignty, Morality and the State: Maududi and His Influence', King's College London, 5 September 2019.

Rebhan, Helga. *Geschichte und Funktion einiger politischer Termini im Arabischen des 19. Jahrhunderts (1798–1882)*. Wiesbaden: Otto Harrassowitz, 1986.

Reid, Donald M. *Cairo University and the Making of Modern Egypt*. Cambridge: Cambridge University Press, 1990.

Reid, Donald M. 'Farah Antun: The Life and Times of a Syrian Christian Journalist in Egypt'. PhD diss., Princeton, 1969.

Reid, Donald M. 'The 'Urabi Revolution and the British Conquest, 1879–1882'. In *The Cambridge History of Egypt*, edited by Martin W. Daly, 217–38. vol. 2, Cambridge: Cambridge University Press, 1998.

Reynolds, Dwight F. (ed.). *Interpreting the Self: Autobiography in the Arabic Literary Tradition*. Berkeley: University of California Press, 2001.

Ridgeon, Lloyd. 'Hidden Khomeini: Mysticism and Poetry'. In *A Critical Introduction to Khomeini*, edited by Arshin Adib-Moghaddam, 193–210. Cambridge: Cambridge University Press, 2014.

Ringer, Monica M. *Islamic Modernism and the Re-Enchantment of the Sacred in the Age of History*. Edinburgh: Edinburgh University Press, 2020.

Rosenthal, Franz. *Knowledge Triumphant: The Concept of Knowledge in Medieval Islam*. Leiden: Brill, 2007.

Rudolph, Ulrich. *Al-Māturīdī and die sunnitische Theologie in Samarkand*. Leiden: Brill, 1997.

Safran, Nadav. *Egypt in Search of Political Community*. Cambridge, MA: Harvard University Press, 1961.

Salvatore, Armando. 'Tradition and Modernity within Islamic Civilisation and the West'. In *Islam and Modernity: Key Issues and Debates*, edited by Muhammad Khalid Masud, Armando Salvatore and Martin van Bruinessen, 3–35. Edinburgh: Edinburgh University Press, 2009.

Scharbrodt, Oliver. *Islam and the Baha'i Faith: A Comparative Study of Muhammad 'Abduh and 'Abdul-Baha' 'Abbas*. London: Routledge, 2008.

Scharbrodt, Oliver. 'The Salafiyya and Sufism: Muḥammad 'Abduh and His *Risālat al-Wāridāt* (*Treatise on Mystical Inspiration*)'. *Bulletin of the School Oriental and African Studies*, 70 (2007): 89–115.

Scharbrodt, Oliver, and Mohammad Mesbahi. 'Maḥmūd Ṭāliqānī'. In *The De Gruyter Handbook of Qur'ānic Hermeneutics*, edited by Georges Tamer. Berlin: De Gruyter, forthcoming.

Schulze, Reinhard. *Islamischer Internationalismus im 20. Jahrhundert: Untersuchungen zur Geschichte der islamischen Weltliga*. Leiden: Brill, 1990.

Sedgwick, Mark. *Muhammad Abduh*. Oxford: Oneworld, 2010.

Sedgwick, Mark. *Saints and Sons: The Making and Remaking of the Rashidi Ahmadi Sufi Order, 1799–2000*. Leiden: Brill, 2005.

Sedgwick, Mark. 'Sects in the Islamic World'. *Nova Religio*, 3 (2000): 195–240.

Seferta, Y. 'The Concept of Religious Authority According to Muhammad 'Abduh and Rashid Ridha'. *Islamic Quarterly*, 30 (1986): 159–64.

Sékaly, Achille. 'Le Problème des Wakfs en Egypte'. *Revue des Etudes Islamiques*, 3 (1929): 77–126; 277–337; 395–454; 600–59.

Sharabi, Hisham B. *Arab Intellectuals and the West: The Formative Years, 1815–1914*. Baltimore: Johns Hopkins University Press, 1970

Shalash, 'Ali. *Al-Māsūniyya fī Miṣr*. Cairo: Misr al-Nahda, 1994.

Shepard, William E. 'Islam and Ideology: Towards a Typology'. *International Journal of Middle East Studies*, 19 (1987): 307–36.

Shepard, William E. 'Sayyid Qutb's Doctrine of *Jāhiliyya*'. *International Journal of Middle East Studies*, 35 (2003): 521–45.

Sigalas, Nikos. 'Des histoires des sultans á l'histoire de l'état: Une enquête sur le temps du pouvoir ottoman (XVIe – XVIIIe siècle)'. In *Les Ottomans et le temps*, editd by François Georgeon and Frédéric Hitzel, 99–127. Leiden: Brill, 2012.
Sigalas, Nikos. '*Devlet* et État: Du glissement sémantique d'un ancien concept du pouvoir au début du XVIIIe siècle ottman'. In *Byzantina et Moderna: Mélanges en l'honneur d'Helène Antoniades-Bibicou*, edited by Gilles Grivaud and Sokratis Petmezas, 385–415. Athens: Ekdoseis Alexandreia, 2007.
Sirriyeh, Elizabeth. *Sufis and Anti-Sufis: The Defence, Rethinking and Rejection of Sufism in the Modern World*. Richmond: Curzon, 1999.
Skovgaard-Petersen, Jakob. *Defining Islam for the Egyptian State: Muftis and Fatwas of the Dar al-Ifta*. Leiden: Brill, 1997.
Smith, Charles D. 'The "Crisis of Orientation": The Shift of Egyptian Intellectuals to Islamic Subjects in the 1930's'. *International Journal of Middle East Studies*, 4(4) (1973): 382–410.
Strauss, Johann. 'Nineteenth-Century Ottoman and Iranian Encounters: Ahmed Midhat Effendi and Ebrāhīm Jān Moʿaṭṭar (Moḥammad Bāqer Bawānātī)'. In *The Twelver Shia in Modern Times: Religious Culture and Political History*, edited by Rainer Brunner and Werner Ende, 97–113. Leiden: Brill, 2001.
Tottoli, Roberto. 'Origin and Use of the Term *Isrāʾīliyyāt* in Muslim Literature'. *Arabica*, 46(2) (1999): 193–210.
Trimingham, J. Spencer. *The Sufi Orders in Islam*. New York: Oxford University Press, 1998.
Vatikiotis, P. J. 'Muḥammad ʿAbduh and the Quest for a Muslim Humanism'. *Arabica*, 4(1) (1957): 55–72.
Voll, John O. 'Hadith Scholars and Ṭarīqahs: An Ulama Group in the 18th Century Haramayn and Their Impact on the Islamic World'. *Journal of Asian and African Studies*, 15 (1980), 264–73.
Voll, John O. 'Muhammad Hayya al-Sindi and Muhammad ibn ʿAbd al-Wahhab: An Analysis of an Intellectual Group in Eighteenth-Century Madina'. *Bulletin of the School of Oriental and African Studies*, 38 (1975): 32–9.
Voll, John O. 'Renewal and Reform in Islamic History: *Tajdīd* and *Iṣlāḥ*'. In *Voices of Resurgent Islam*, edited by J. L. Esposito, 32–47. New York: Oxford University Press, 1983.
Walbridge, John. *God and Logic in Islam: The Caliphate of Reason*. Cambridge: Cambridge University Press, 2010.
Waldman, Marilyn R. *Toward a Theory of Historical Narrative: A Case Study in Perso-Islamicate Historiography*. Columbus: Ohio State University Press, 1980.
Weismann, Itzhak. 'Between Sufi Reformism and Modernist Rationalism: A Reappraisal of the Origins of the Salafiyya from a Damascene Angle'. *Die Welt des Islams*, 41 (2001): 206–237.
Weismann, Itzhak. *Taste of Modernity: Sufism, Salafiyya and Arabism in Late Ottoman Damascus*. Leiden: Brill, 2001.

Wielandt, Rotraud. 'Main Trends of Islamic Theological Thought from the Late Nineteenth Century to Present Times'. In *The Oxford Handbook of Islamic Theology*, edited by Sabine Schmidtke, 707–64. Oxford: Oxford University Press, 2016.

Winkel, Eric. 'Ibn 'Arabi's *Fiqh*: Three Cases from the *Futuhat*'. *Journal of the Muhyiddin Ibn 'Arabi Society*, 13 (1993): 54–74.

Zachs, Fruma. *The Making of a Syrian Identity: Intellectuals and Merchants in Nineteenth Century Beirut*. Leiden: Brill, 2006.

Zakariya, Hafiz. 'From Cairo to the Straits Settlements: Modern *Salafiyyah* Reformist Ideas in Malay Peninsula'. *Intellectual Discourse*, 15(2) (2007): 125–46.

Zaman, Muhammad Qasim. 'The Sovereignty of God in Modern Islamic Thought'. *Journal of the Royal Asiatic Society*, 25(3) (2015): 389–418.

Zaman, Muhammad Qasim. *The Ulama in Contemporary Islam: Custodians of Change*. Princeton: Princeton University Press, 2002.

Zeghal, Malika. *Gardiens de l'Islam: Les oulémas d'Al Azhar dans l'Egypte contemporaine*. Paris: Presses de la Fondation Nationale des Sciences Politiques, 1996.

Zemmin, Florian. 'Book Review: Ammeke Kateman: *Muḥammad 'Abduh and His Interlocutors: Conceptualizing Religion in a Globalizing World*'. *Die Welt des Islams*, 61(1) (2021): 127–30.

Zemmin, Florian. 'Modernity without Society? Observations on the Term *mujtama'* in the Islamic Journal "al-Manār" (Cairo, 1898–1940)'. *Die Welt des Islams*, 56(2) (2016): 223–47.

Zemmin, Florian. 'The Janus Face of Kātib Çelebi'. *Turcica*, 50 (2019): 327–54.

Ziadeh, Nicola A. *The Sanusiyah: A Study of a Revivalist Movement in Islam*. Leiden: Brill, 1958.

Index

'Abdallah, Muhammad Ahmad ibn, 'Mahdi of Sudan' 110
'Abd al-Raziq, Mustafa 22–3, 66 n.132, 223–4, 228–9
'Abd al-Baha' 'Abbas Effendi 128–9, 134
Abdel-Nasser, Gamal 69
'Abduh, Muhammad 1, 4. *See also* mystical writings
  about his father 37
  about his mother 37
  apologetics 188–94
  authorship 24
  biography of 2
  birth information 36, 68
  and culture of ambiguity 215–20
  death of 22
  eclecticism 2
  editor of *al-Waqā'i' al-Miṣriyya* (The Egyptian Events) 80–5
  education at 40
  encounter with Sufism 58
  exile 105–35
    eloquence 131–4
    engagement with the religious 'Other' 127–31
    glories and current challenges 111–20
    Ottoman educational politics 123–7
    return to Beirut 120–3
  fatwas 14, 147, 160–2, 167–8, 218
  Freemasonry 78–9, 107, 129, 135
  as grand mufti of Egypt 14, 26, 143–7, 153–4, 159–60, 202
  intellectual legacy 2
  intellectual personality 106
  involvement in politics 16
  letters written to Afghani 45, 47, 145–6
  at the *madrasa* 37
  on modern civilization 70–4
  new cosmopolitan intelligentsia 74–6
  and pious ancestors (*al-salaf al-ṣāliḥ*) 176–80
  praise of his teacher's ability 13
  Qur'an commentaries 194–201
  as reluctant scholar 36–42
  Risālat al-Tawḥīd (Treatise on Divine Unity) 2, 7, 24, 26, 122, 175, 181–3, 185, 187–8, 194–5, 199, 227, 231
  Risālat al-Wāridāt (Treatise on Mystical Inspirations) 23–5, 36, 45, 48, 53, 59–60, 76, 95, 182–4, 215
  Sharḥ al-'Aqā'id al-'Aḍudiyya (Commentary on the Catechism of 'Adud al-Din al-Iji) 23–5, 36, 76, 95, 181, 194, 204, 215
  spiritual and intellectual formation 3
  Tafsīr al-Manār (The Lighthouse Commentary) 3, 175, 194–6, 222, 230
  and the 'Urabi Revolution 86–94
  al-'Urwa al-Wuthqā (The Firmest Bond) 25, 105–7, 110–11, 115–20, 124, 128, 134–5, 144–6, 176, 227
'Abdül-Hamid, Sultan II 77, 146
'Abdül-Mecid, Sultan 225
Abu Bakr 54, 131–2
Abū Naẓẓāra Zarqā' (The Man with Blue Spectacles) 75
activism
  of Afghani 79, 96
  anti-colonial 124, 134, 175
  anti-imperialist 143, 146
  civic 169
  against European imperialism 135
  intellectual 16
  political 16, 59, 76–80, 90–1, 94, 169, 227
  socio-political 67, 156
  socio-religious 155
activist and intellectual, Muslim 67–96
  'Abduh and Egypt's new cosmopolitan intelligentsia 74–6
  'Abduh and the 'Urabi Revolution 86–94
  'Abduh as journal editor 80–5

'Abduh on modern civilization 70–4
constitutionalism and freemasonry 76–80
Egypt under Muhammad 'Ali dynasty 67–70
political debates and activism 76–80
ādāb 83
Adams, Charles C. 3
al-Afghani, Jamal al-Din 66 n.133
'Abduh as student of/relationship with 17, 35, 42, 47, 59, 131
activism 79
alienation from 144–6
al-Radd 'alā al-Dahriyyīn (Refutation of the Materialists) 109
as an orthodox Sunni reformer 17
anti-colonial activism 175
anti-imperialist agitation 106
arrest and expulsion from Egypt 80, 105
biographers of 79
British colonial intrusion 107
in Cairo 43, 50, 121
communicative strategies 13
constitutional reforms 77
early education of 44
encouragement 75
intellectual and spiritual mentorship 58
intellectual formation/ engagement 19, 36
interest in Islam 18
interlocutors 14
Iranian roots of 4
Islamic political philosophy 94
lobbying of French authorities in Egypt 79
Masonic lodges 78
mujaddid 16
mysticism 45, 48, 183
as omniscient 46
opposition towards European imperialism 90
philosophy of 43
reform and politics 16
reformist intellectuals 75
revolutionary activism 78
Shaykhi School 18–9, 215
teaching sessions 24, 55, 59
tutelage 5, 58, 67, 71
Afshar, Iraj 4
Ahmed, Shahab 11, 13–14, 220, 231
What is Islam?: The Importance of Being Islamic 9–10
al-Ahrām (The Pyramids) (newspaper) 75–6, 80, 95, 189–90
al-Ahsa'i, Ahmad 18–19, 215
Aisha (Muhammad's wife) 131–2
'Ali ibn Abi Talib 107, 131–3
'Ali, Isma'il 69
'Ali, Muhammad 36–7, 80, 84, 86, 108, 147, 153
'Ali, Sa'id 69
Al-Munqidh min al-Ḍalāl (The Deliverer from Error) (al-Ghazali) 35
ambiguity(ies) 215–20
discursive 68
intellectual culture of 8, 13, 67, 106, 168, 185, 194, 204
Islam as a culture of 9–14
in legacy 220–4
in Muslim (auto-)biographical writing 20–5
semantic 84, 117, 164
Amin, Qasim 229
al-Mar'a al-Jadīda (The New Woman) 228
Taḥrīr al-Mar'a (The Liberation of Women) 228
Amin, 'Uthman 22
Anas, Malik ibn
Muwaṭṭa' 39
anti-imperialism 168
Antun, Farah 188, 191–3, 195, 208 n.99, 217
'Arabi, Ibn 17, 45, 49
Fuṣūṣ al-Ḥikam (Bezels of Wisdom) 16
mystical philosophy 18
Aristotle 83, 92, 113, 182
Arkoun, Mohammed 4
Arslan, Shakib 123, 128
'aṣabiyya 72, 83, 95, 115, 116–17, 162, 187
al-Ash'ari, Abu al-Hasan 57, 176, 178–9, 217
Ash'ari School 48
al-Awwam, Zubayr ibn 131–2
al-Azhar (institution) 75, 158
Afghani lessons at 43
education of 'Abduh at 40–1

reform/modernization of 22, 26, 143, 153, 158–9
religious education at 71
students 43, 75, 152
al-Azhari, Ahmad 'Abbas 121

Baha' Allah, Husayn 'Ali Nuri 128
al-Banna, Hasan 226–8, 236 n.57
al-Baqillani, Abu Bakr 178
al-Barudi, Mahmud Sami 90
al-Basri, Hasan 178–9, 185
Bauer, Thomas 11–14, 220, 231
Die Kultur der Ambiguität: Eine andere Geschichte des Islams (The Culture of Ambiguity: An Alternative History of Islam) 9–10
Bawanati, Muhammad Baqir 128–9, 134, 140 n.102, 141 n.104
Blunt, Wilfrid Scawen 23, 92, 108, 148
British colonialism 108–9, 111, 221
Broadley, Alexander 93
al-Bustani, Butrus 120

Christian
adultery 12
dignitaries 128
dominance 126
missionary schools in Syria 123–6
notables and merchants 120
Christianity 130
humanity 186
and Islam 128–30, 191, 193, 229
and Judaism 129
moral vision of 74, 113
politico-legal legacy 74
theological features 6
colonialism 147–51
British 108–9, 111
European 107, 114, 117, 134, 146, 151
French 190
Comte, August 186–7
constitutionalism 25, 76–80
Council of Deputies *(majlis al-nawwāb)* 76–9

Dā'ira al-Ma'ārif 120
Dar al-Lisan al-Khadawiyya (Khedivial School of Languages) 71
Dar al-'Ulum 144, 159
Darwish, Shaykh 38, 40, 43
al-Dawani, Jalal al-Din
Risālat al-Zawrā' 43
Dawud, Abu 15

Earl of Cromer 23, 92, 143–4, 147–8, 154
Egypt 143–69
'Abduh's alienation from Afghani 144–6
colonialism 147–51
modernization 147–51
mufti of realms 159–67
under Muhammad 'Ali dynasty 67–70
Muslim intellectual 152–7
new cosmopolitan intelligentsia 74–6
reform of al-Azhar 158–9
Eickelmann, Dale F. 20
eloquence 131–4
erudite scholar *(adīb)* 11
ethnic nationalism *(jinsiyya)* 115–17
European colonialism 107, 114, 117, 134, 146, 151
European imperialism 5, 71, 90, 105–6, 111–12, 115, 117, 135, 168, 190, 222
Europeanization 69, 214, 222
Europeanized Muslims 223

Fahmi, Ridwan 92
al-Farabi 198
Faruq (King of Egypt) 22
first ancestors *(al-salaf al-awwalūn)* 177
fiṭra 51, 87, 197–8, 201, 203
Fortna, Benjamin C. 97 n.8
freemasonry 107
and constitutionalism 76–80
French Revolution 192

Gabrielian Soul 50–1
al-Ghazali, Abu Hamid 1, 8–9, 178–9, 182
Al-Munqidh min al-Ḍalāl (The Deliverer from Error) 35
fiṭra 198
founding Sufi convent 15
inconsistencies and ambiguities in thought of 2
intellectual legacy 215
mystical philosophies 187
philosophy and Sufism 17
spiritual crisis 17

Tahāfut al-Falāsifa (The Incoherence of the Philosophers) 53
thought 2
Gladstone, William 92
Golziher, Ignaz 28 n.16
Greek-Orthodox Christians 126
Guizot, François 50, 74, 113
L'histoire générale de la civilisation en Europe 44

Haddad, Mohamed 4–5
Haj, Samira 5
Reconfiguring Islamic Tradition: Reform, Rationality, and Modernity 29 n.29
Hamada, Muhyi al-Din Bay 121
al-Hamadani, Badiʿ al-Zaman 122
Hanbal, Ahmad ibn 178, 222
Hanim, Zaynab Nazli 144
Hanotaux, Gabriel 188–91, 193
Hartington, Spencer 108
heterodoxy 4, 6, 8, 58
Ḥikmat al-ʿAyn (al-Qazwini) 43
Hilmi, ʿAbbas, II 92, 143, 154, 158–9
Hourani, Albert 2, 220
Husayn, Taha 229, 232

Idris, Ahmad ibn 38–9
al-Iji, ʿAdud al-Din 52
ijtihād 38, 61 n.21, 202–3
ʿIlish, Shaykh 41–2
ʿImara, Muhammad 23
imperialism, European 5, 71, 90, 105–6, 111–12, 115, 117, 135, 168, 222
Iranian Shiism/Shii 19, 44, 131
al-Isfahani, Abu Muslim 178
Ishaq, Adib 75, 77, 80, 117
Islam
authentic ethos of 111, 114, 176
Christianity and 128–9, 192–3
civilizational power 130–1
as culture of ambiguity 9–14
esoteric traditions 107
hermeneutical engagement 10–11
heterodoxy 4
integrity of 71
intellectual heritage of 214, 224
intellectual reform of 5
jurisprudence 12–13
modernism 6
orthodoxy 1, 4
philosophy 3
pre-modern 17
pristine 17
rationalist traditions 203
rationality 39
rationalized interpretation 45
religiosity 38
Shia 186
Sunni 58, 153, 177–8
thought 10
Islamic jurisprudence (*fiqh*) 40, 126
Islamic reform 2–3, 14–20, 151, 175–204
ʿAbduh and pious ancestors (*al-salaf al-ṣāliḥ*) 176–80
ʿAbduh's apologetics 188–94
ʿAbduh's Qur'an commentaries 194–201
theology 180–8
Islamism 12, 231
Islamization of Islam (ʻ*Islamisierung des Islams*') 10
Islamo-Christianity 128
al-Islām wa-Uṣūl al-Ḥukm (Islam and the Foundations of Government) 224
Ismaʿil, Khedive 73, 76–7, 79–80
Ismailism 19

al-Jaghmini, Mahmud ibn Muhammad 43
jāhiliyya 112, 203
Jamal al-Din Effendi 157
al-Jāmiʿa 208 n.99
al-Jarīda (The Magazine) 221
al-Jaza'iri, Tahir 155
Jews 75, 105, 161, 164, 166, 192, 196
Judaism 129, 186

Kedourie, Elie 4
Kemal, Namık 77, 89
al-Khadir, Shaykh Darwish 37
Khalafallah, Muhammad Ahmad 230
Khaldun, Ibn 165–6
anthropocentric view of history 118
badāwa and *ḥaḍāra* 74
Muqaddima 43, 72–3
philosophy of history 106, 112–13, 119–20, 187, 229
political philosophy 87
urban sedentization (*tamaddun*) 95

Khan, Sayyid Ahmad 109, 148
al-Khattab, 'Umar ibn 37
Khedive Tawfiq 81, 84, 86, 88, 90–1, 143, 144, 146
al-Khilāfa aw al-Imāma al-'Uẓmā (The Caliphate or the Supreme Leadership) 225
Khomeini, Sayyid Ruhollah Musavi (Ayatollah) 13
Khosroshahi, Hadi 24
al-Khuli, Amin 229–30, 232
Kitāb al-Ishārāt wa-l-Tanbīhāt (Ibn Sina) 43
Kitāb al-Ishrāq (Suhrawardi) 43
Kurdi, Muhammad 'Ali 123

al-Laqqani, Ibrahim 24
legacy 213–33
  'Abduh and the culture of ambiguity 215–20
  ambiguities in 220–4
  Islamist trajectories 224–31
  liberal trajectories 224–31
legalism and scripturalism 13, 232
Le Journal 189
L'histoire générale de la civilisation en Europe (Guizot) 44
liberalism
  Muslim 222
  and nationalism 221
literary oeuvre 14

al-Madani, Muhammad Zafir 38
al-Madani, Sayyid Muhammad ibn Hamza 37–8
madrasa 11, 37, 52, 158–9
Madrasa Sultaniyya 121–4, 127, 131, 155, 181–2
Mahdavi, Asghar 4
al-Manār (The Lighthouse) 2, 21, 26, 149, 180, 226–7
al-Mar'a al-Jadīda (The New Woman) (Amin) 228
Masonic Lodge 78
Massignon, Louis 27 n.12
al-Maturidi, Abu Mansur 178
Mawdudi, Abu al-A'la 227–8
Middle East 67–8
Midhat Pasha 155
Miskawayh, Ibn 95, 176, 188
  Tahdhīb al-Akhlāq (The Refinement of Manners) 44, 83, 182
Miṣr (Egypt) (newspaper) 75, 77, 117
modern civilization 70–4, 94, 192, 223
modernist Salafism 2, 177, 223
modernization 147–51
  centralization and 159
  development and 71
  institutional 169
  military and bureaucracy 69
  policies 76, 80
  programme 69, 78
muḍāraba 161
mufti of realms 159–67
Muhammad 'Ali dynasty 67–70
Muhamad Sharif Pasha 89
mujaddid 15–16, 223
al-Munqidh min al-Ḍalāl (The Deliverer from Error) (al-Ghazali) 35
Muqaddima (Ibn Khaldun) 43, 72–3
Muslim Benevolent Society (*al-jamiyya al-khayriyya al-islāmiyya*) 155, 169
Muslim intellectual 152–7
Muslimness 12
Mu'tazila 41, 54–6, 178–9, 184–6, 230–1
Muwaṭṭa' (Malik ibn Anas) 39
mystical inspirations (*wāridāt*) 45
mystical writings 35–60
  'Abduh as reluctant scholar 36–42
  sage from the East 42–7
  Sharḥ al-'Aqā'id al-'Aḍudiyya (al-Dawani) 52–7
  treatise on 48–52

Naguib, Shuruq 209 n.117
nahḍa 2, 94
Nahj al-Balāgha (The Peak of Eloquence) 106–7, 122, 131–4
Na'ini, Mohammad 'Ali Pirzadeh 141 n.104
al-Naqqash, Salim 75, 77–8, 80
al-Nasifi, 'Umar 41
Nasir al-Din, Shah 170 n.9
National Archives of Iran 4
nationalism 25, 105
  Egyptian 106
  ethnic 115–17
  European 116
  and liberalism 221
Neo-Sufism 61 n.18

orthodox Islam 1, 4–5
Ottoman educational politics 123–7
Ottoman Empire 107, 130

people of tradition (*ahl al-ḥadīth*) 178
Perfect Man (*al-insān al-kāmil*) 17–18, 44–5, 47, 51
Perfect Shia (*al-shīʿa al-kāmil*) 18–19
Phoenicians 189
pious ancestors. See *al-salaf al-ṣāliḥ*
politics
  debates 76–80
  Egyptian 78, 80, 87, 221
  European 94
  Islamic discourses on 9
  Ottoman educational 123–7
  Platonic ideas of 13
  and religion 190, 218
  religion and 5
  science and 214
Prophet Muhammad 2, 17, 19, 38–9, 131, 224
  biography of 124
  the divine sage (*al-ḥakīm al-ilāhī*)' 50
  sunna (custom/practice) 46

Qajar dynasty 170 n.9
al-Qazwini, al-Katibi
  Ḥikmat al-ʿAyn 43
Qur'an/Qur'anic 8–10, 37, 82, 111, 164
  of bodily resurrection 57
  commentaries 26, 123, 178, 194–201
  exegesis 121, 164, 222
  and modern science 162
  and the *sunna* 15, 39, 53
  sūrat al-ʿaṣr (The Declining Day) 149
  and traditions of Prophet Muhammad 54
al-Qurtubi 178
Qutb, Sayyid 13, 227–8, 231

Rahman, Fazlur 1–2, 8, 61 n.18
Rashti, Sayyid Kazim 19
Razi, Qutb al-Din
  Sharḥ al-Shamsiyya 43
al-Razi, Fakhr al-Din 179
religious 'Other' 127–31
revelations (*tajalliyyāt*) 45
Rida, Muhammad Rashid 4, 16–17, 32 n.98, 33 n.99, 33 n.116, 43, 58
  'Abduh's influential disciple 2, 91–2, 123
  biography 222
  in Egypt 196
  Salafi portrayal of his teacher 3
  sceptical of Sufism 14
  Ta'rīkh al-Ustādh al-Imām al-Shaykh Muḥammad ʿAbduh (The History of Muhammad ʿAbduh) 21–3, 141 n.109
Ringer, Monica M. 29 n.36, 138 n.62
Risālat al-Tawḥīd (Treatise on Divine Unity) (ʿAbduh) 2, 7, 24, 26, 122, 175, 181–3, 185, 187–8, 194–5, 199, 227, 231
Risālat al-Wāridāt (Treatise on Mystical Inspirations) (ʿAbduh) 23–5, 36, 45, 48, 53, 59–60, 76, 95, 182–4, 215
Risālat al-Zawrā' (al-Dawani) 43
Riyad Pasha 43, 75, 78, 80, 94, 144
Roman Empire 113
Russo-Turkish War of 1877–78 75, 77

Sadra, Mulla 18–19
Safavid Sufi 21
al-salaf al-ṣāliḥ ('the pious ancestors') 2–3, 165, 176–80, 222
Salafis/Salafism 2–3, 5, 13, 27 n.12, 58, 177, 223
Sanuʿ, Yaʿqub 75, 78
Sanusiyya 38
al-Sayyid, Ahmad Lutfi 221
scripturalism and legalism 232
seal of saints (*khātim al-awliyā'*) 17
Sedgwick, Mark 28 n.15
Shadhili Sufi order (*ṭarīqa*) 38–9
Shalash, ʿAli 66 n.132
Sharḥ al-ʿAqā'id al-ʿAḍudiyya (Commentary on the Catechism of ʿAdud al-Din al-Iji) (ʿAbduh) 23–5, 36, 76, 95, 181, 194, 204, 215
Sharḥ al-ʿAqā'id al-Nasfiyya (Commentary on the Catechism of al-Nasafi) (Taftazani) 41
Sharḥ al-Shamsiyya (Razi) 43
shariʿa (Islamic law) 83, 88–9, 120, 219, 225–6
  courts 153, 163, 230

marginalization of 153
not being oppressive 133
socio-political order 118
shaykh al-azhar 158, 163
Shaykhi School 18–19, 44
Shii Islam 18, 106, 134
Shii learning (*ḥawza*) 17
Shii Muslims 19
Sina, Ibn (Avicenna) 1, 48, 51, 122, 176, 183, 216
al-Hidāya 43
Kitāb al-Ishārāt wa-l-Tanbīhāt 43
Sirhindi, Ahmad 31 n.76
Sirriyeh, Elizabeth
Sufis and Anti-Sufis: The Defence, Rethinking and Rejection of Sufism in the Modern World 60 n.1
Society of the Muslim Brothers (*jamā ʿat al-ikhwān al-muslimīn*) 226
spiritual genealogy (*silsila*) 39
spiritual world (*ʿālam-i maʿnawī*) 18
state law *(qānūn)* 12, 74, 83, 89, 96, 119, 219, 226
substantial movement (*ḥaraka jawhariyya*) 50
successors (*khalaf*) 179
Sufi litanies *(dhikr)* 40
Sufis and Anti-Sufis: The Defence, Rethinking and Rejection of Sufism in the Modern World (Sirriyeh) 60 n.1
Sufis/Sufism 4, 38, 236 n.57
anti-modern 12
conservative representative of 39
divine revelation 10
Iranian 52
mystical poetry of 9
philosophy and 9, 24, 135, 215
quasi-prophetic status 44
religious traditionalism 38
rituals 11
sainthood 17
Suhrawardi, Shihab al-Din 49
Kitāb al-Ishrāq 43
sulṭān (ruler) 18, 118, 224
sunan allāh 138 n.62
Sunni 120, 131, 225
caliphate 107, 190
catechism 33 n.116
notions of orthodoxy 7, 14, 23, 47, 180, 222
religious scholarship 22
Sunni Islam 58
Sunnism 4
theology 1, 9, 48, 96, 119, 122, 178, 216
al-Suyuti, Jalal al-Din 16
Syrian Christians 75

al-Tabari 178
Tafsīr al-Manār (The Lighthouse Commentary) (ʿAbduh) 3, 175, 180, 194–6, 222, 230
Tafsīr Juzʾ ʿAmma 26, 194, 196, 198
al-Taftazani, Saʿd al-Din
al-Talwīḥ ilā Kashf Ḥaqāʾiq al-Tanqīḥ 43
Sharḥ al-ʿAqāʾid al-Nasfiyya (Commentary on the Catechism of al-Nasafi) 41
Tahdhīb al-Manṭiq wa-l-Kalām (The Refinement of Logic and Theology) 122
Tahāfut al-Falāsifa (The Incoherence of the Philosophers) (al-Ghazali) 53
Tahdhīb al-Akhlāq (The Refinement of Manners) (Ibn Miskawayh) 44, 83, 182
Tahdhīb al-Manṭiq wa-l-Kalām (The Refinement of Logic and Theology) (al-Taftazani) 122, 182
Taḥrīr al-Marʾa (The Liberation of Women) (Amin) 228
al-Tahtawi, Rifaʿa 68
Talha ibn ʿUbayd Allah 131–2
al-Talwīḥ ilā Kashf Ḥaqāʾiq al-Tanqīḥ (al-Taftazani) 43
taqiyya (pious dissimulation) 19–20, 53
taqlīd 38, 175
ṭarīqa muḥammadiyya (Path of Muhammad) 39–40
Tawfiq (crown prince of Egypt) 78–80
Tawil, Shaykh Hasan 40
Taylor, Isaac 129–31
Taymiyya, Ibn 178, 203, 222
Thamarāt al-Funūn (The Fruits of the Arts) 122–3, 130
theology 180–8
Tijaniyya 38
al-Tirmidhi, Hakim 17

Transvaal Fatwa 166–8
Tusi, Nasir al-Din 43, 73–4, 87
Twelver Shia Islam 4, 13

'ulamā' (scholars) 109–10, 148–9, 156, 225
  conservative 43, 147–8, 155, 158, 167, 220
  reformist 148–9
  setting laws 85
Umayyad dynasty 132
'Urabi, Ahmad 86
'Urabi Revolution 21, 80–1, 97 n.6
  'Abduh and 85–94, 146
  European powers 25
al-'Urwa al-Wuthqā (The Firmest Bond) 25, 105–10, 115, 124, 128, 134–5, 144–6, 176, 227
  colonial context of 110–11

waḥdat al-wujūd (unity of being) 48, 49
al-Waqā'i' al-Miṣriyya (The Egyptian Events) 80, 84, 87, 92, 111, 124
Westernization 226

Zaghlul, Sa'd 78, 91, 221
Zayd, Nasr Hamid Abu 213, 230–1
Zoroastrians 192

CPSIA information can be obtained
at www.ICGtesting.com
Printed in the USA
LVHW080159160822
726066LV00004B/18

9 781838 607302